Clay MacCauley

An introductory course in Japanese

Clay MacCauley

An introductory course in Japanese

ISBN/EAN: 9783742876386

Manufactured in Europe, USA, Canada, Australia, Japa

Cover: Foto ©Andreas Hilbeck / pixelio.de

Manufactured and distributed by brebook publishing software
(www.brebook.com)

Clay MacCauley

An introductory course in Japanese

AN
INTRODUCTORY COURSE
IN
JAPANESE

BY

CLAY MacCAULEY, A. M.

PRESIDENT OF SENSHIN GAKUIN (SCHOOL FOR ADVANCED LEARNING)

TŌKYŌ, JAPAN.

———————

YOKOHAMA, SHANGHAI, HONGKONG, SINGAPORE.

KELLY AND WALSH, LTD.

1896.

TO

CHARLES CARROLL EVERETT, D. D.

DEAN OF THE DIVINITY FACULTY OF HARVARD UNIVERSITY,

THIS MANUAL,—

AN ATTEMPT TO OPEN A WAY

INTO KNOWLEDGE AND USE OF THE JAPANESE LANGUAGE,—

IS GRATEFULLY INSCRIBED.

There is, perhaps, nothing more marvellous in the world than the identity of language through all generations. Words become obsolete. New words spring into being; languages and dialects share the fate of the nations and tribes that speak them. All changes affect the fundamental principles and identity of language no more than the falling and budding leaves affect the structure and identity of the oak.

CHARLES CARROLL EVERETT.

PREFACE.

The work here made public, although from its size seemingly pretending much, will I hope be judged by students as being exactly what its title professes for it, "An Introductory Course" in the Japanese language. It is a manual for beginners, not a treatise for advanced scholars. Yet, it is not a mere primer. As far as it goes, it is an attempt at a thorough exposition of its subject. It is intended for adult minds, and demands patient study. Above all, the aim held constantly in view in its preparation has been the practical mastery of the beginnings of a correct reading, writing and speaking of the language common in polite social intercourse in Japan. This aim makes necessary an apparently slow advance for the student; but I believe that the way here opened, if faithfully followed, will leave but little for the learner to unlearn, and will in the end secure for him the most rapid real progress.

In the composition of the book, I have not hesitated to appropriate to its use whatever fit materials have been made available by the work of competent expositors of the Japanese language; but I have acknowledged direct quotation, and, for the rest, have presumed to shape in my own way the products of others' studies. In one important relation, however, I have allowed myself to offer an independent contribution to the grammatical study of Japanese. I have attempted to introduce some symmetry into, and therewith to avoid a certain existing confusion in, the naming of the four primary verbal variations that have been accepted by Western grammarians as the forms with which an ordinary study of the Japanese verb should begin. I have felt at liberty to do this since the names for these forms are still under discussion, and, especially, since the changes I have made are not radically subversive of approved usage.

The second section,—" The Elements of Grammar," —has been given a place in the manual not as a grammar with the ordinary pretence of the name, but as a preliminary explication of some of the most noticeable embarrassing differences that separate Japanese from English speech. A thorough grammatical study of the Japanese language, for reasons set forth in the chapter " On Method in Acquiring Japanese," does not come within the range covered by the book. A like qualification should also be applied to the " Notes on the Conversations." These notes are few and are quite elementary. They accompany only the first five conversations, and are intended merely to clear out of the student's path the most prominent and crippling obstacles to his use of the method commended in the chapter devoted to Method.

The third section,—" Practice in the Colloquial,"— may attract the attention of some scholars of Japanese on account of the comparativaly free use in it of personal pronouns,—that is to say, a use of them much more frequent than was characteristic of social speech in Japan in former years. But a change in this direction is noticeably taking place in the intercourse of the younger generation of the Japanese people, along with their increasing familiarity with, and use of, the languages of the West.

Among the works used in the preparation of the manual, I make public acknowledgment of indebtedness to Dr. J. J. Hoffmann's, "Japanese Grammar;" to Mr. W. G. Aston's, "Grammar of the Japanese Written Language," and to his grammar of the "Spoken Language;" to Rev. William Imbrie's "English-Japanese Etymology;" to Professor Rudolf Lange's "Lehrbuch der Japanischen Umgangssprache;" and to Dr. J. H. Hepburn's "Japanese-English Dictionary;" also to the English grammatical writings of Professor W. D. Whitney. Besides, I wish to make particular mention of Professor Basil Hall Chamberlain's, "Handbook of Colloquial Japanese," which I have freely used. I commend Prof. Chamberlain's book to students of this manual as a rich storehouse for them of practical grammatical exposition and illustration.

Personally, I am under obligation to several friends and helpers. To Professor Chamberlain, and to Dr. Karl Florenz, I owe profitable suggestions; to Rev. Arthur Lloyd, M. A. and to Mr. W. B. Mason, I am indebted for generous assistance in the reading of proofs of the English text. The Japanese text has been carefully read in proof by Mr. Iwao Hasunuma, Mr. Saichiro Kanda, and Mr. Hisato Kikuchi. The Japanese text of section third,—"Practice in the Colloquial,"—is a rendering into a polite yet familiar colloquial of the English given on the pages opposite. This rendering was made by Mr. Saichiro Kanda and Mr. Iwao Hasunuma; but chiefly by Mr. Hasunuma, under whose work and supervision the whole rendering received its final

form.   To all these gentlemen my grateful acknowledgment is due.   My thanks are also owing to the Shūeisha,
for the excellent typography of the book, in which,
when the great difficulties attendant upon type-com-
position in the English language in Japan, and upon
an unusual arrangement of Japanese syllabics and words
are considered, comparatively few errors appear.

With the hope that this manual, however imperfectly
its aim has been followed, may be helpful to those who
shall accept the course of study it opens, I submit it to
the indulgent judgment of its students, and of the
friends of the Japanese language.

C. MacC.

Senshin Gakuin,
        Tōkyō, Japan.
    May, 1896.

TABLE OF CONTENTS.

The numerals refer to paragraphs, unless otherwise specified.

GENERAL INTRODUCTION, (pp. 1–19).

SECTION FIRST.

THE SYLLABARY: WRITING AND PRONUNCIATION.

CHAPTER I.

THE KATAKANA, 1.

CHAPTER II.

THE SEPARATE KANA SYLLABLES, 2–22.

CHAPTER III.

THE SYLLABLES AS AFFECTED BY JUXTAPOSITION.

I.

VARIATIONS OF VOWEL SOUNDS, 23–34.

II.

CHANGES IN VOWEL SYLLABLES, 35 41.

III.

CHANGES IN JUXTAPOSED VOWEL AND CONSONANT SYLLABLES, 42–48.

SECTION SECOND.

ELEMENTS OF GRAMMAR.

CHAPTER I.

CLASSES OF WORDS, 94–95.

CHAPTER II.

ARRANGEMENT OF WORDS IN SPEECH, 96–102.

SECTION THIRD.

PRACTICE IN THE COLLOQUIAL.

CHAPTER I.

ON METHOD IN ACQUIRING JAPANESE, 301-316.

The best method is in membership in a Japanese family, 301. Best substitute for this method is life in Japan under faithful teachers, 302. What is attempted in this manual,—to supply in part a substitute for the method of nature, 304. Attempt in first section, 305 ; in second section, 306. The third section composed of " Conversations " given in a polite familiar colloquial, 307. How to use these " Conversations," 308-316. Japanese sentences must be understood as their speakers understand them, 309-310. Japanese sentences not subject to literal translation, 310-311. Use of the "Elements of Grammar," 312-314. What a real acquirement of a language means, 315. What a student of this book may expect to accomplish, 316.

CHAPTER II.

THE *I-RO-HA*. 317-325.

To complete the transcription of the forty-eight illustrative proverbs from *Katakana* into *Hiragana*, 317. *Go-jū-on*, 318. *I-ro-ha*, or Kōbō Daishi's arrangement of the syllabary, 320-322. The initial syllabics of the illustrative proverbs, used here to show the *I-ro-ha* arrangement of the syllabary, 322. Kōbō Daishi's mnemonic verse, in tabular form, 324. The illustrative proverbs arranged so as to illustrate the *I-ro-ha* syllabary, 325.

CHAPTER III.

FRIENDS IN CONVERSATION, (pp. 208-531).

Forty-eight Conversations given in the Japanese language, in the order of the *I-ro-ha* syllabics, with equivalent English sentences placed on opposite pages, pp. 208-523.

An *I-ro-ha* hymn, named *Nori no Hatsu-Ne*, or the " First Note of the Law," with an English paraphrase, line for line, of the hymn on opposite pages, pp. 524-531.

AN INTRODUCTORY COURSE

IN

JAPANESE.

~~~~~~~~

GENERAL INTRODUCTION.

Every existing form of human speech is a body of arbitrary and conventional signs for thought, handed down by tradition from one generation to another, no individual in any generation receiving or transmitting the whole body, but the sum of the separate givings and takings being effective to keep it in existence without essential loss. Yet the process of traditional transmission always has been, is now, and will ever continue to be, in all parts of the world, an imperfect one: no language remains or can remain, the same during a long period of time. Growth and change make the life of language, as they are everywhere else the inseparable accompaniment and sign of life.

WILLIAM DWIGHT WHITNEY,

AN INTRODUCTORY COURSE

IN

JAPANESE.

GENERAL INTRODUCTION.

This manual is named, "An Introductory Course in Japanese." The title really descriptive of the book would be,—A Progressive Course in Reading, Writing and Speaking the Polite Dialect of Tōkyō in Japan, conducted by means of the two Japanese Syllabaries, the *Katakana* and the *Hiragana*.

I. *The Tōkyō Colloquial as Source of the prospective Japanese Language.*—But the shorter title is, after all, not very far a misnomer. The signs of the times, as the present writer sees them, indicate the rise of colloquial Japanese to the dignity of being distinctively the language of Japan. The signs of the times also point to the polite form of the dialect of Tōkyō, as the instrument of chief effect in shaping the development of the colloquial towards its culmination as the literary, scientific, official as well as popular, language of the whole people. Indeed, the Tōkyō dialect is already so much the standard of the Japanese spoken language, that, in using it, a speaker can be understood by ordinarily educated persons in any part of the empire ; a fact not true of the user of any other

of the many dialects of the people. Besides, the Tōkyō
dialect is now the standard language for instruction in
the thousands of the public schools, the medium for the
debates in Parliament, the means of communication
from the lecture platform and in the columns of the
popular newspapers, magazines and books with which
daily the printing press teems. Within one generation,
that is since the Imperial Restoration of 1868, this
greater revolution, this change in the expression of the
Japanese intellectual life, has been begun and has been
directed into the course it will in all probability take.

II. *Parallel between Tudor English and
Meiji Japanese.*—The Japanese language at the present time seems to be passing through a period very
like that through which the English language passed
in the Fifteenth Century, soon after the " Wars of the
Roses " and the strengthening of the power of England's
king by the establishment of the royal House of Tudor.

In the fall of the Shōgunate and the accompanying
arousing of the people from their feudal lethargy ; in the
breaking down of the barriers erected about the empire ;
in the restoration of the Emperor to a real sovereignty ;
and in the removal of the Imperial throne to Tōkyō,—a
general national transformation was initiated. In the
course of this change language has been radically
affected. As, before the wars of Lancaster and York,
among the numerous dialects of England, that of Kent
and Surrey had a slight lead, and, over them all, Latin
reigned as the language of the clergy and the learned,
so, in Japan, before the Restoration, the dialect of Kyōto
had a little precedence over the other dialects of the
people, and the Chinese language controlled whatever

literature the priests and scholars put forth. The parallel seems to have followed the further progress of events in both countries. By the victory of the Tudor House in England the power of the nobles decreased. The barons were deprived of their armed retainers. Commerce began to be of great importance. The artisans' guilds were weakened. Trade and traders grew in popular esteem and increased in wealth. The Caxton printing press, the first in England, was then set up. Its publications were distributed throughout the kingdom, becoming thereby the main channels for Modern English, of which the Midland, or London, colloquial was the fountain-head. The full parallel has not yet been drawn, but, in large part, England's Fifteenth Century history has been repeated in Japan, in the present age of Meiji. Events look prophetic of a substantial re-petition in Japan of the remaining events of the English Renaissance. As Latin fell into disuse in England, except as a treasury of words for service in the maturing colloquial there, so has Chinese fallen in Japan. As the dialect of Kent gave way to that of London, so has the dialect of Kyōto yielded to the colloquial of Tōkyō. The rest will probably come to pass in good time. The matured Tōkyō colloquial seems destined to become the dominant force directing the language,—literary, scientific, official and social,—of Great Japan, in a not very distant future.

III. *Beginnings of the History of Writing in Japan.*—A glance at linguistic history in Japan, especially the history of written speech, will interest, and will probably be of some use to, the student of this manual. As far as is known, the Japanese people of prehistoric times were not a writing people. They used a language of course, but they had no means of communication with one another other than that of spoken speech. Certainly, there are no remains of written Japanese dating earlier than at some time late in the first seven Christian centuries. Tradition reports, that at about the opening of the Christian era, under the Emperor Sūjin's reign, a regular intercourse between Japan and Korea began; that, as Chinese literature had already become widely known in Korea, many Korean immigrants into Japan and Japanese travellers returning from Korea, brought with them a knowledge of Chinese writing. Japanese tradition affirms positively, that towards the close of the Third Century, the Emperor Ōjin's son was placed under the care of a Chinese tutor and was taught the Chinese Classics. About a hundred years afterwards, at the opening of the Fifth Century, it is claimed that national records were made by a body of historiographers, adepts in Chinese writing. As the Sixth Century opened, large numbers of scholars,—men of science, teachers of literature, physicians and the like, —came into Japan from Korea and took important positions under the Government. So far as there was any literature in Japan then, they were its creators and guides. No attempt was made to express in writing the language of the country.

IV. *Effect of the Incoming of Buddhism upon Literature in Japan.*—It was at the middle of the Sixth Century that Buddhism gained a permanent position in Japan. With its priests, came in full energy the varied influences of Chinese civilization.

The life of the Japanese people rapidly changed under the working of the new forces. Chinese literature and the Buddhistic creed set in motion a radical national transformation. In art and in industry, the people were advanced to a position never before reached by them. Before long there were Imperial officers, appointed especially to care for education. Public schools were opened. At Kyōto, a university was organized. The topics of the course of education, however, were in the main those of China, taught in the language of China. Education did not have for its object much beyond the training of candidates for public office. Culture meant, chiefly, knowledge of the Chinese Classics. But, through the extended education, a large number of the Japanese people became skilled writers of Chinese.

V.   *Use of Chinese Ideographs in the Japanese Sentence.*—Then it was that a new movement in writing was made, which, in time, became an influence of very great importance in the development of the Japanese language. In the Seventh and Eighth Centuries, numbers of writers attempted to express the meanings of Japanese words by the use of synonymous Chinese characters, arranged sometimes in the Chinese, sometimes in the Japanese, order of speech. With Chinese ideographs so manipulated, the two great repositories of ancient Japanese historical tradition, the *Kojiki*, 712 A. D., and the *Nihongi*, 720 A. D., were composed. But, the task of giving Chinese equivalents for Japanese words was a labor of immense difficulty. So then, as the needs of literary expression rapidly became greater, Japanese writers gradually began to use the Chinese ideographs, without much reference to their Chinese meanings. They used them chiefly for their phonetic values. The *Man-yóshū*, a collection of poems appearing about the middle of the Eighth Century, shows the way over which the transition that was made from the old Chinese writing to writing by means of what are now known as the *Kana* syllabaries, passed. In the *Man-yóshū* the Chinese characters were written in full, but, in the main, their phonetic values for rendering the Japanese words were considered.

VI. *Origins of the Kana Syllabaries.*—But this device for expressing the Japanese language did not last long. The work of writing down the selected Chinese ideographs was too difficult for common use. Gradually, consequently, only the main strokes of the ideographs were copied. At length only simple remnants of the original Chinese characters were left, to be written as representatives of Japanese syllables. In this way, at last, the first Japanese syllabary came into being, the *Katakana*, the remnants of forty-seven Chinese square characters, which had been chosen as the signs with which to represent Japanese sounds and words. The *Katakana* is said to have been perfected in 757 A. D., by a scholar and statesman of the Nara Era, Kibi no Makibi. The other syllabary, the *Hiragana*, is said to have been perfected by the marvellous priest Kōbō Daishi, 834 A. D., soon after the opening of the new age for Japan which followed the transfer of the Imperial throne from Nara to Kyōto, in 794 A. D. The *Hiragana* consists of abbreviations of quite a large number of cursive forms of Chinese characters. The *Hiragana* syllabics are not so simple to read and not so easy to write as the syllabics of the *Katakana*, but, as the cursive

Chinese ideographs had become the scholarly script of the Japanese in the Seventh and Eighth Centuries, the prestige of these ideographs was transmitted to the *Kana* formed from them. That prestige has remained to the present day, making the *Hiragana* much more popular than the simpler *Katakana*, when *Kana* syllabics are needed in writing the Japanese language.

VII. *The Kana Classics of the Tenth and Eleventh Centuries.*—When the Tenth Century opened, the Japanese people thus had, at last, been provided in the two syllabaries with fairly adequate instruments for writing their own language. But, strangely, even then the homage yet paid to Chinese learning prevented the adoption of the syllabaries as the national means for literary expression. Many writers, like whom are some men even of the present day, ambitious to be esteemed scholars in eminence, continued to use Chinese ideographs and Chinese words. The *Kana* were accepted chiefly by women, and were relegated by men to a secondary place in literature. As it turned out, however, through the Tenth, and during the first part of the Eleventh Centuries, while the Kyōto Court was becoming degenerate through luxury and effeminacy, a succession of female writers, writing with the *Kana*, appeared, whose works, for example, the *Genji Monogatari* of Murasaki Shikibu and the *Makura no Sōshi* of Sei Shōnagon, were of such excellence that they are now valued as standards for the study of pure Japanese. These works embody the native language spoken by the refined and Court circles of the time in which they were written. ·Especially is the *Genji Monogatari* a classic of the Japanese cultured colloquial used at the close of the Tenth Century.

VIII. *Literary Degeneracy following the Political Revolution of the Twelfth Century.*— But the promise then made for the *Kana* and for the spoken language of Japan did not reach fulfilment.   A great political revolution occured in the Twelfth Century, which, for hundreds of years afterwards, almost wholly put a stop to the development of literature; which, certainly, effectually checked the growth of any literature in the language and writing of the people. Japan became a battle field for great clans struggling for supremacy under the Emperor. With the military ascendency everywhere, letters, as a popular accomplishment, decayed. What literature came into being was created and directed almost exclusively by priests who were then, and for a long time afterwards, the only guardians of learning and letters in the empire. Whatever of general or popular interest had been aroused in letters during the preceding three centuries died away. The people were burdened with the overhard tasks of war. Literature remained in the care of the priests. But the studies of the priests were chiefly in Chinese. They added Chinese words and phrases, in large numbers, to the language as written. They neglected the colloquial of the country more and more. In fact, they made of Japanese literature, what has been styled an "almost unreadable chaos of mixed Chinese and Japanese."

IX. *Separation between the Colloquial and the Written Language.*—It was in this way, and during this period of civil wars, that the gulf, which in after centuries lay, and down to the present day has lain, between the so called "Written Language" and the popular speech, or "Colloquial," was opened. This

separation between the two forms of expression grew
wider as the centuries passed. The Colloquial, for
literary use, became increasingly neglected and degrad-
ed. The language as written, grew more and more an
alien thing to the warriors and to the peasants who con-
stituted an enormous majority of the population of the
war-stricken empire.

X. *Literary Revival under the Tokugawa
Shōgunate. Age of Genroku.*—No change for
the better for Japanese literature took place until
towards the close of the Seventeenth Century. A
hundred years previously the whole empire had lapsed
into a state almost anarchic. Feudal Germany was not
more completely disintegrated. But, with the close of
the Sixteenth Century, arose the mighty Tokugawa
Shōgunate, under which political recovery speedily took
place. Then, following the political prosperity under
the fifth of the Tokugawa Shōguns, a period of literary
revival and achievement was started, so vigorous and rich
in its way that it is now called the golden age of
Japanese literature,—the age of Genroku, (1688–1703.)
However, the Genroku period would better be named,
as it has been named, the "golden era of Chinese
literature." That revival was not so much a revival of
Japanese literature and the furtherance in literature of
the popular language, as the study of the profound and
admirable Chinese literature of the Confucian school
of the *Sung* dynasty; a dynasty which had fallen before
the Mongol Kublai, in the Thirteenth Century. The
great Ieyasu, the founder of the Tokugawa dynasty, had
been a munificent patron of literature. He did much to
save valuable ancient books from destruction during the

wars he waged. When the power of Ieyasu was fully established, many of the subdued daimyōs became patrons of literature. "Clan" schools were established in many places. Learning was rapidly rehabilitated outside the priest classes. The successors of Ieyasu in the Shōgunate, followed the example set by their leader. A sort of university at Yedo (now Tōkyō) received graduates from the clan schools. Private schools also were organized for the education of the children of the artisan and peasant classes. History, the Chinese Classics, poetry and the art of composition, were the topics of study in the higher schools. The *Kana* and some Chinese writing, reading and primary mathematics, occupied the children of the common classes.

XI. *The Mito School of Historians. The Genroku Novelists.*—The two events of the Seventeenth and Eighteenth Centuries, however, which most bore upon the course of affairs leading up to the present political and social condition of the Japanese people, and have mainly opened the way for the writing of such a book as this, were the achievements of the school of historians gathered under the patronage of the Prince of Mito, grandson of Ieyasu, and the complete amalgamation, at last, of Chinese words and Japanese linguistic forms into a standard literary language. The influence of the historical school of Mito, though a revival and popularization of the ancient records, of Japanese imperialism, of the Shintō religion and of the old Japanese literature, was to prepare the way for the complete breaking up of the Shōgunate in the present century. The further effect of the work of the writers coming forward in the literary revival,—especially the novelists—

was to do away wholly with foreign forms of expression in literature, and to make a really representative, or standard, Japanese literary language. In the Fourteenth Century, Urabe Kenkō, author of *Tsure-zure-gusa*, " Weeds of Idleness," had produced for literature, in the form first spoken of, a work which yet remains a classic of almost pure old Japanese. It was a work in which Chinese words were, in fact, set into Japanese forms of speech, without violence to the Japanese modes of expression. At the close of the Eighteenth Century, the novelist Bakin, chief among many writers whose works were widely read and exercised a powerful popular influence, perfected this endeavor to make a wholly successful incorporation of Chinese words into the Japanese sentence. At about the same time the old Japanese Classics underwent a radical critical investigation and comment, under the study of such men as Kamo Mabuchi, Motoori Nobunaga, Hida Harumitsu and others. These scholars did great service in helping onward the elaboration of what has long been known as the standard Written Language of Japan.

XII. *The Standard Written Language.*—Thus it came about, that at the opening of the Modern Era in Japan there was in existence, recognized at last, a standard Written Language. It was a language which in form was purely Japanese. The Chinese elements in it did not affect its idioms or construction. Its Chinese constituents had become, just what the Greek and Latin elements are in English, merely parts of the vocabulary. Its Chinese words were presented, it is true, in their Chinese forms, that is, as ideographs, but they were regarded only as imported words; they took position and underwent inflection by the use of Japanese particles, like any Japanese words. They contributed only their meanings to the Japanese sentence. There was still, at the opening of the present era, some literature for the Japanese people written in the Chinese language. Official documents, especially, were modelled after Chinese documents and were largely charged with Chinese idioms. But, this notwithstanding, Japanese literature at the opening of the present era, was almost as a whole embodied in a language distinguished by the dominance in it of Japanese forms over all the materials of which the sentences were composed.

XIII. *Language during the Meiji Age. The Written Language.*—But during the past thirty and more years, the whole language of the country has been undergoing notable changes.

The Written Language, whose career we have just glanced at, has, so far, not been much changed except by enlargement of vocabulary. Many new Chinese terms have been added to it to meet some needs arising from the incoming civilization of the West; many European words also have been incorporated into the written speech. The Chinese words have been appropriated in their Chinese forms; the European words have been put into writing, as far as their sounds can be reproduced, by means of the syllabaries, the *Katakana* syllabics being as a rule used for this purpose. A farther important recent change in the Written Language has been a steady increase of the use of the *Kana* syllabics, placed alongside the Chinese ideographs, to give to the less educated readers either the proper pronunciation or the Japanese meanings of the ideographs.

XIV. *Influences operating to dignify Colloquial Japanese.*—But the linguistic change of greatest moment in the new era of Japan is, as noted before, not so much one that is taking place in the Written Language, so named, as one operating on the language of common speech. The Written Language and the Colloquial, as we know, were separated centuries ago. The latter was excluded from service in honored literature, and gradually lost its earlier grace and excellence. The former became more and more the luxury of the Court writers and of the learned classes. It gradually became refined almost wholly beyond the use or comprehension of any but a very small number of the people. The present era however is, above all else, the era of the whole people. It is a portion of the growing democracy of the new age which is advancing around the world. Feudal aristocracy is gone now in Japan, as in the West. A new era with new needs has come to the East as well as to Europe and America. The people have become the heirs of all that once was the privilege of only king and noble. Law making and its administration, science, art, commerce, general industry and the like, have been taken in charge by the people. Education and literature are conducted for every one now, not for the privileged few. These being the facts characteristic of the new age, a necessity has for years been increasingly felt in Japan for the simplification and the popularization of language embodied in written form. The Japanese language written in its present form is an aristocratic appurtenance. Existing side by side with the language spoken by a people but lately released from serfdom, and now inspired by the free individualism of the present age, it is glaringly out of place, unless it may be so modified as to be adapted to the wants of the new times.

XV. *Probable Merging of the Written Language into the Colloquial.*—It is the judgment of the writer that this necessary modification has already been begun, and is to be carried far forward in a future not very distant. The Japanese Colloquial has already made its rising power felt in literary expression. For more than the decade past, all newspapers, whose object has been to gain circulation among the former lower millions of the empire, have been compelled to put their reading matter, in large measure, into Colloquial phrasing; to print the Colloquial extensively in the *Kana*; and to interpret their appropriated Chinese ideographs by means of *Kana* as side syllabics. With the use of moveable type and printing presses, many books in fiction, science, biography, travel, etc., have, for some time now, been printed in the Spoken Language. Moreover, the numerous varieties of the *Hiragana* syllabics,—once over four hundred,—have been reduced as metal type to comparatively few standard characters. In the common schools of the country, now more than twenty five thousand in number, attended by more than three million children, also in the thousands of private schools as well as in the Middle and Higher Middle institutions, the students are studying numerous branches of modern science. These students are yearly becoming too much busied with their studies to pay proper attention to the forms and ideographs of the standard Written Language. Besides, they receive whatever instruction they get in the cultivated, expanding Colloquial.

The commercial and industrial growth of the nation has associated with it many societies, in all which business discussions are carried on in the Colloquial. In many of these societies, reports of business and other papers are rendered in the language of common speech. The lecture platform is the place whence, daily, thousands of address to the people, in a refined Colloquial, are made. The number of the lecturers who change their addresses from the original colloquial into the written style before publication, is steadily decreasing. And of the highest importance is the fact, that the speeches and debates taking place in the Houses of Parliament, also reports of the proceedings of the courts of the country, now appear in print and are put upon record, practically as they were spoken. The Government's official notices, although still put forth in the Written Language, have in the country districts *Kana* translations laid along their margins. In yet other ways the fact is made clear, that the contemned and neglected Colloquial has, by the necessities of the times, become a decided force in Japanese literature.

No insurmountable obstacle to a yet farther advance of the Colloquial to the dignity of being the language of Japan, seems to be in the way. Rather is it likely that democratic Japan will, as time goes by, put aside most that is distinctive of its medieval Written Language, along with other of its aristocratic, feudal legacies, and elaborate, for both literature and for oral intercourse, one language,—the Tōkyō Colloquial, refined, adorned and dignified with much that is worth saving from the discarded Written Speech of the past, and enriched with new verbal creations and appropriations from other

languages fit to express the growing needs of the new
life of the people.

XVI. *The Kana as Basis for the Future
Medium of Literary Expression.*—Further, a simplification of the writing of the language seems to be
a necessary consequence of the development of the
Modern Era. The great majority of the people, even
now, have not time for a mastery of the large number
of Chinese ideographs that have been incorporated into
the Written Language along with the adopted Chinese
words. Much less, will the great majority of the people
have leisure sufficient for this work in the near future.
Many Chinese ideographs will, of course, for a long time
remain in all writing and print, but the present prospect is, that for the Japanese people, as such, the *Kana*
will more and more become the main body of their
language as written. Compared with a generation ago,
the books, magazines, newspapers, pamphlets, etc., to-
day printed wholly in the *Kana*, or in *Kana* mixed with
Chinese ideographs having *Kana* side translations and
transliterations, are enormously great in number and
excellent in literary worth. Many educationists are
beginning to recognize the fact that school pupils can
not become proficient writers of a really serviceable list
of Chinese ideographs and at the same time master
the curriculum of studies necessary for them to gain
more than an elementary acquaintance with the
modern sciences and industries. One or the other
effort must at length give way. It is hardly probable
that the learning of ideographs will push aside the
modern educational curriculum. Especially is this
not probable, since a simple syllabary is at hand which

can easily be so modified as to express all that is necessary or desirable in the literature of modern science, art, industry, politics religion, and philosophy.

To some persons, this opinion may seem far from predicting the course events will take, but those who are familiar with the facts, know that the domain of the *Kana* is daily widening, and that no insuperable difficulty lies in the way to making the *Kana* the instrument for embodying in writing the whole intellectual life of the people. Conservative impulse; fancy for a greater show of learning; the love of artistic grace which has long made the writing of Chinese ideographs one of the fine arts in Japan; and the ability to write the ideographs which scholars of mature years now possess,—chiefly these are especially strong reasons for resistance to the prospective acceptance of the *Kana* as the instrument for writing Japanese. But even these reasons will scarcely be able to withstand long the necessities accompanying the maturing of modern civilization in the country. Economy of time for the student, and for the man of business ; economy of capital and labor in the printing office which now must carry thousands of fonts of type for unnecessary Chinese ideographs ; the demands of the lower classes for information and literary diversion which they can not gain from books offered to them made up of ideographs they can not understand ; these, and other reasons, will in all probability secure as time goes on, a recognition of the excellence of the *Kana*,—will go a long way towards making the *Kana* at last the one vehicle for Japan's written and printed thought.

XVII. *The Service this Manual may render to a Student of the Japanese Language.*— This manual having been prepared as an exposition of the polite Tokyo dialect, by means of the two Japanese syllabaries, the *Katakana* and the *Hiragana*, may therefore be properly named "An Introductory Course in Japanese."

But, however much the writer may be at fault in his speculations upon the future of the *Kana* and the Colloquial, just given, at least this is true of the book,—the student who faithfully studies and masters what is here offered him, may feel confident that he can travel throughout Japan and make himself understood wherever he may go ; and that he can express his thoughts in writing so that his words can be read by every ordinarily educated man, woman, and child with whom he may communicate. Moreover, he will have opened up to him a growing realm of literature, consisting of newspapers, magazines and books ; a domain not dominant yet, to be sure, but large enough to occupy his researches for a long time, and valuable enough to inform him of the regular current of events in the country, and to acquaint him with the people's simpler poetry, fiction, history, biography, and even with some of the deeper thought of the Japanese in matters of science, ethics and religion.

XVIII. *Special Suggestions for using this Manual.*

Let the student remember that this book offers "A Progressive Course" of study. It is not to be passed over by "leaps and bounds," but by slowly taken steps. Each step should be made carefully. Nothing connected with it should be ignored or neglected, if one would reach the desired goal.

1. Read the "Exercises" set forth,—over and over again and aloud,—according to the rules of pronunciation given with them.

2. Write the syllabics in each "Exercise" until they become perfectly familiar to the eye, and are reproduced in imagination when pronounced.

3. Do not be impatient at not receiving English equivalents for Japanese words, at the outset. Accept the "Exercises" as though they were so many vocalizations for elocution, or five finger movements in piano study.

4. In the Second Section do not study only the Romaji renderings of the Hiragana syllables. The Romaji is given there only for the purpose of enabling the student to master the Hiragana. In the Third and most important Section of the Manual, no Romaji appears in the "Conversations." Mastery of the Kana in both forms is a prerequisite for successful use of the Third Section.

5. Read all the "Exercises" after the manner of the Japanese. That is, read commencing at the right hand side of the page, following the columns downwards and continuing, column by column, towards the left.

6. "Examples," "Illustrations," and "Illustrative Words" and "Phrases," of the Japanese syllabics and words, —all Japanese writing incorporated into the English text of the book, is to be read after the manner of the reading of English, that is, from left to right, across the page.

SECTION FIRST.

THE SYLLABARY:

WRITING AND PRONUNCIATION.

It was unfortunate for an inflected tongue like the Japanese to be obliged to resort to China for an alphabet; and although a thoroughly practical and convenient set of characters, of syllabic value, easy to write and to read, was at one time devised, being made out of parts of Chinese ideographs, it is of very restricted use; and the mode of writing generally employed for literary texts is the greatest existing obstacle to the acquirement of the language.

WILLIAM DWIGHT WHITNEY.

CHAPTER I.

THE KATAKANA.

1. The *Katakana* is the simplest and most easily remembered group of the signs by which the Japanese express the sounds of their language. Although it is not so much in popular use as the other form of the syllabary, the more elaborate and difficult *Hiragana*, it opens the way, better than the *Hiragana*, for students beginning a study of the unique orthography and pronunciation of Japanese speech. Japanese words, as written and as pronounced, like English written and spoken words, are in large measure—though not in so large a measure as in English,—divergent. Once, in Japan as in England, writing was practically a real representation of speech. That relationship, however, disappeared in both countries with the movement of each growing colloquial away from the conservative writing. He, therefore, who would study Japanese that he may know it, as the Japanese people know their language, should do just what a successful student of English must do,—see and speak words as they are written and spoken at home. The *Kana* syllabary is the instrument used for showing how Japanese is written, and how, through laws of syllabic combinations, it is sounded. Children in Japan are taught first the *Katakana*. Students from the West can not do better than take the same comparatively easy path into the Japanese language. Having learned, by means of the *Katakana*, the peculiarities of the word formations and of the mutual relations of the sounds of the language, the student will find his way onwards, with the *Hiragana* as chief means of help, made comparatively smooth and successful.

	A	I	U	E	O	
	ア a	イ i	ウ u	エ e	オ o	
K	カ ka	キ ki	ク ku	ケ ke	コ ko	
G	ガ ga	ギ gi	グ gu	ゲ ge	ゴ go	
S	サ sa	シ shi	ス su	セ se	ソ so	
Z	ザ za	ヂ ジ ji	ッ ズ zu	ゼ ze	ゾ zo	
T	タ ta	チ chi	ツ tsu	テ te	ト to	
D	ダ da	ヂ dji	ヅ dzu	デ de	ド do	
N	ナ na	ニ ni	ヌ nu	子 ne	ノ no	ン n
H	ハ ha	ヒ hi	フ fu	ヘ he	ホ ho	
B	バ ba	ビ bi	ブ bu	ベ be	ボ bo	
P	パ pa	ピ pi	プ pu	ペ pe	ポ po	
M	マ ma	ミ mi	ム mu	メ me	モ mo	
Y	ヤ ya	イ $(y)i$	ユ yu	エ $(y)e$	ヨ yo	
R	ラ ra	リ ri	ル ru	レ re	ロ ro	
W	ワ wa	井 $(w)i$	ウ $(w)u$	ヱ $(w)e$	ヲ wo	

CHAPTER II.

THE SEPARATE SYLLABLES.

At the outset the student should familiarize himself with the syllabary characters separately, that is, as distinct wholes in form and in sound.

In accordance with the sounds they represent, the syllabics may be classified as, I. VOWEL SYLLABLES, and as, II. CONSONANT SYLLABLES.

I. VOWEL SYLLABLES.

ア　　イ　　ウ　　エ　　ヲオ

A　　I　　U　　E　　O

2. These syllable are pronounced as pure vowels, having much the qualities of the vowels *a, i, u, e, o,* of the European "Continental" alphabets. In the English alphabet, approximate equivalents for their sounds may be rendered by the vowels *a, i, u, e, o,* as pronounced in the following words :—

a in *part,* which is very like the ordinary sound of ア

i „ *pique,* „ „ „ „ „ „ „ „ イ

u „ *pull,* „ „ „ „ „ „ „ „ ウ

e „ *prey,* „ „ „ „ „ „ „ „ エ

o „ *port,* „ „ „ „ „ „ „ „ オ

In the Japanese syllabary these five characters,— the vowel syllables,—do not represent vowels in the same sense as the letters *a, e, i, o, u,* of the English and the "Continental" alphabets represent vowels. The vowel letters of the European alphabets are, as a rule, mere signs of vowel sounds, and, as such, take part in the formation of every syllable and word. In the Japanese syllabary, however, these vowel characters are all independent words, whose sounds happen to be the sounds of pure vowels. They are not necessary either to the writing, or to the pronunciation, of any of the other characters of the syllabary. Their existence in any word is a matter of contingency. In fact,—*each character of the Japanese syllabary is an independent whole.* The consonant syllables, of course, contain vowel elements, but these elements are integral parts of the syllables. They are in no way derived from the five above named characters, whose sounds are those of pure vowels.

EXERCISE FIRST.

エ ウ オ エ ア イ オ ウ イ ア
オ オ エ イ ウ オ ウ エ ア エ
ウ ア イ ウ エ ア エ イ オ イ
ア イ ウ ア オ エ イ ア ウ オ
イ エ ア オ イ ウ ア オ エ ウ

II.   CONSONANT SYLLABLES.

The combination of consonantal and vowel elements for the purpose of linguistic expression, tends to modify, more or less, both these vocal elements. In the Japanese language this tendency becomes noticeable for consonantal elements, in the formation of several of the consonant syllables. The changes which the vowel elements undergo, become audible chiefly as the effect of the interaction of the sounds of associated syllables. In the present chapter, which is given to the study of the separate syllables, some of the changes affecting consonantal elements are noticed.

The vowel elements of the syllables here illustrated, should be read for the present, as given above, that is, with the sounds of *a, i, u, e, o,* in the words *part, pique, pull, prey* and *port.*

1. K SERIES.

カ	キ	ク	ケ	コ
KA	KI	KU	KE	KO

3. These syllables are pronounced by combining the consonantal element of the English letter *k* with the pure vowel sounds as just illustrated.

EXERCISE SECOND.

	2.						**1.**		
オ	エ	ウ	イ	ア	コ	ケ	ク	キ	カ
カ	カ	カ	カ	カ	カ	カ	カ	カ	カ
オ	エ	ウ	イ	ア	コ	ケ	ク	キ	カ
キ	キ	キ	キ	キ	キ	キ	キ	キ	キ
オ	エ	ウ	イ	ア	コ	ケ	ク	キ	カ
ク	ク	ク	ク	ク	ク	ク	ク	ク	ク
オ	エ	ウ	イ	ア	コ	ケ	ク	キ	カ
ケ	ケ	ケ	ケ	ケ	ケ	ケ	ケ	ケ	ケ
オ	エ	ウ	イ	ア	コ	ケ	ク	キ	カ
コ	コ	コ	コ	コ	コ	コ	コ	コ	コ

2. G SERIES.

ガ ギ グ ゲ ゴ

GA   GI   GU   GE   GO

4. The sound heard in the English *g* hard, spoken in such words as *garb, gig, good, gate* and *go,* is rendered in Japanese by the K series of syllables, written with the addition to the right of the syllables of the mark (ᵥ) called the *nigori,* or sign of impurity in sound.

Examples :—

カ ガ is read *ka ga*   カ ゴ is read *ka go*

ケ ゴ „ „ *ke go*   ケ ギ „ „ *ke gi*

ク ギ „ „ *ku gi*   ク ゲ „ „ *ku ge*

ガ ク „ „ *ga ku*   ゴ ク „ „ *go ku*

ガ ケ „ „ *ga ke*   ギ ギ „ „ *gi gi*

ゲ ゲ „ „ *ge ge*   グ ゴ „ „ *gu go.*

5. This rule is without exception when these syllables *begin* words. Also, in some parts of Japan, these syllables represent the hard *g* sound wherever placed.

It should be noticed here, however, that in Central Japan, especially in Tokyo, when these syllables *do not stand at the beginnings* of words, their consonantal element becomes like *ng* in the word *singer.*

a. Thus カ ゴ is read in Tokyo not *ka-go* but *kang-o :*— observe, the reading is not *kan-go* but *kang-o,* or *ka-ngo.*

Examples :—

クギ is read *kung-i,* or *ku-ngi.*

カガ „ „ *kang-a,* „ *ka-nga.*

ケギ „ „ *keng-i,* „ *ke-ngi.*

ギギ „ „ *ging-i,* „ *gi-ngi.*

グゴ „ „ *gung-o,* „ *gu-ngo.*

ゴゲ „ „ *gong-e,* „ *go-nge.*

b. The syllable ガ *ga,* when used as a particle, is usually pronounced as though it were written *nga.*

Examples :—

ガク	ガ	カケタ	カ	is read
ga-ku	*nga*	*ka-ke-ta*	*ka.*	

ケイキ	ガ	ゴク	キイ	„ „
ke-i-ki	*nga*	*go-ku*	*ki-i*	

クギノ	キキ	ガ	イカガシイ	„ „
ku-ngi	*no*	*kiki*	*nga*	*i-ka-nga-shi-i.*

3. S SERIES.

サ	シ	ス	セ	ソ
SA	SHI	SU	SE	SO

6. These syllables, with one exception, are pronounced by combining the consonantal element of the English letter *s* sharp with the pure vowel sounds.

The Japanese of Central Japan are unable to combine the consonantal element of *s* with the vowel sound *i*. They can more easily, in this relation, sound the *sh* of such a word as *shield*. They therefore read シ *shi*, not *si*.

For example:—

ア シ *a shi*, イ シ *i shi*, ウ シ *u shi*, エ シ *e shi*, and オ シ *o shi*.

EXERCISE THIRD.

	2.						1.		
レ	ソ	ス	セ	サ	ソ	セ	ス	シ	サ
ガ	ガ	ア	キ	カ	ガ	キ	サ	ゲ	カ
ク	イ	シ	ソ	サ	ソ	セ	ス	シ	サ
					シ	コ	シ	カ	ケ
シ	ソ	ス	セ	サ	ソ	ア	ア	ウ	ク
ゲ	ク	グ	イ	カ	コ	セ	ス	シ	サ
キ	イ	キ	ゴ	セ					
					ソ	エ	イ	イ	ア
					ゲ	セ	ス	シ	サ
シ	ソ	ス	セ	サ	ソ	ゴ	ス	シ	サ
ゴ	ゲ	コ	ガ	ク	グ	セ	ソ	コ	キ
ク	キ	シ	イ	イ					

4. Z SERIES.

ザ　　ジ　　ズ　　ゼ　　ゾ

ZA　　JI (DJI)　　ZU (DZU)　　ZE　　ZO

7. The S series of consonant syllables, by the addition of the *nigori* (ヽヽ), is changed into a series representing **Z** sounds. Most of these syllables are pronounced by combining the consonantal element of the soft *s* in such words as *rose*, or that of the *z* in *maze*, with the vowels.

8. The syllable ジ, however represents practically the sound *dji*, and the syllable ズ has much of the sound *dzu*. These are the changes that the consonantal element of soft *s* receives in Japanese speech before the *i* and *u* vowel sounds.

For example :—

カザ　is read *ka za*, but

カジ　becomes *ka ji (dji)*, and

カズ　　„　　*ka zu (dzu)*.

a. The negative ending ズ, of a verbal form, is pronounced distinctly *dzu* not *zu*.

Examples :—

カカズ　　is read *ka ka dzu.*

カクサズ　„　„　*ka ku sa dzu.*

EXERCISE FOURTH.

1.

ゾ	ゼ	ズ	ジ	サ
ク	イ	キ	ギ	ザ
コ	カ	ズ	ジ	サ
ゾ	ゼ	サ	ゴ	ジ
カ	セ	キ	ジ	ザ
ゾ	キ	ズ	カ	カ
エ	ケ	ク	ジ	サ
ゾ	セ	ズ	キ	グ
ゾ	サ	ウ	ジ	ザ
コ	セ	ズ	ク	キ

2.

ゾ	ソ	ス	キ	サ
ク	ク	ズ	レ	ガ
ゴ	レ	キ	ク	ス
サ	ソ	ス	コ	ア
ク	コ	ク	ゴ	カ
イ	イ	セ	レ	シ
セ	ク	コ	ジ	ザ
キ	サ	ク	ケ	グ
ソ	レ	ジ	イ	サ

5. T SERIES.

タ	チ	ツ	テ	ト
TA	CHI	TSU	TE	TO

9. Most of these syllables are pronounced by combining the consonantal element of the English letter *t* with the pure vowel sounds.

The combined sounds *ti* and *tu*, however, do not exist in the Japanese language. The nearest approaches to them are made in the syllables チ, *chi* (*tchi*) and ツ, *tsu*. These syllables have therefore found place in the T series.

EXERCISE FIFTH.

1.

ト	タ	チ	ゴ	ア
ザ	テ	チ	ゴ	カ
イ	コ	ク	ツ	ツ

ト	カ	ツ	サ	サ
ヅ	ス	シ	ガ	タ
キ	タ	カ	テ	テ

ツ	ク	ウ	ト	ク
ギ	サ	ス	ケ	セテ
キ	ス	イ	イ	テ

2.

ト	テ	ツ	チ	タ
イ	タ	チ	タ	タ
ト	テ	カ	チ	タ
ク	キ	ツ	チ	チ

ト	テ	ツ	チ	タ
ス	コ	キ	カ	ツ
ト	テ	ツ	チ	タ
コ	ス	イ	ソ	テ

ト	テ	ツ	イ	タ
カ	サ	タ	チ	ト

6. D SERIES.

ダ	ヂ	ヅ	デ	ド
DA	DJI (JI)	DZU (ZU)	DE	DO

10. Most of these syllables are pronounced by a combination of the consonantal element of the English letter *d* with the pure vowels. For *di* and *du* the Japanese organs of speech enunciate *dji* and *dzu*.

EXERCISE SIXTH.

1.   **2.**

セグツ	クダケ	キドク	タダシ	トドキ	ドク	デゲ	ヅタ	ヂク	ダダ
					ドキ	デイ	クヅ	ヂキ	ダイ
クジク	ジダイ	トギレ	テダイ	トガキ	ドセイ	デカカタ	カヅキ	ヂセイ	ダイガ
クドイ	キダテ	ドカタ	カドタ	ツダシ	ドダイ	デキレ	ケツキ	ヂカタ	ダイギ

7. N SERIES.

ナ　ニ　ヌ　子　ノ　ン
NA　NI　NU　NE　NO　N

11. These syllables are pronounced by combining the consonantal element of the English letter *n* with the pure vowels.

In this series the character ン, used as a final *n* sound for syllables and words, properly has place, although its quality is often more like that of the *ng* sound of the word *song*, than that of the pure *n* in *man*.

12. This ン *n* syllabic has another peculiarity, to which attention may be called here, namely, that of being pronounced *m* before the labials, or syllables of the B, M and P series.

For example :—

カンムリ is read *kam mu ri*, not *kan mu ri*, ヂンブツ is read *nem bu tsu*, not *nen bu tsu*; and エンピツ is read *em pi tsu*, not *en pi tsu*.

EXERCISE SEVENTH.

2.	1.
ツ 子 ヌ ニ ナ ナ ツ キ ジ ガ	ズ ノ 子 ヌ ニ ナ ン ニ ナ ヌ ナ ニ
ト ニ キ ヌ ナ ノ チ ノ ク ク	セ ノ 子 ヌ ニ ナ ン ナ ニ ニ ニ ヌ
チ ス エ ノ ニ ン ナ ダ ト シ	ケ ナ 子 ヌ ニ ナ レ 子 ヌ 子 ヌ 子
ス レ テ ア ニ ノ ノ ツ ナ ク コ ギ ド タ キ	ク ノ 子 ヌ ニ ナ レ ノ 子 ナ 子 ノ
	タ ノ 子 ヌ ニ ナ ン ヌ ノ ノ ノ ナ

8. H or SPIRANT SERIES.

ハ　　ヒ　　フ　　ヘ　　ホ

HA　　HI　　FU (FWU)　　HE　　HO

13. These syllables, with the exception of フ, are pronounced—approximately only—by combining the consonantal element of the English letter *h* with the pure vowels. *These syllabics, however, are spirant rather than aspirate in quality.*

The character フ is pronounced by means of an impure, or labial, English *f* sound, in combination with the vowel *u*. The enunciation, gently breathed, of such a word as *fwu*, would most nearly express フ, in English speech.

EXERCISE EIGHTH.

1.

ハイ　ハダ　ヒキ　ビガ　フデ　フチ　ヘイ　ヘス　ホネ　ホス

ハチ　ハフ　ヒト　ヒサ　フナ　フソ　ヘタ　ヘソ　ホテ　ホド

ハフ　ヒク　フジ　ヘド　ホイ

2.

ハナレ　ホガイ　ヘンコ　ハタゴ　フヌケ

ホグス　ヒソク　ヒノコ　ナホス　ヘダテ

ヒガン　ヒドコ　ハダギ　ヘイジ　カクス

9. B SERIES.

バ　　ビ　　ブ　　ベ　　ボ

BA　　BI　　BU　　BE　　BO

14. The H series, modified by the *nigori* (ヽ), stands for the combination of the consonantal element of the English letter *b* with the pure vowels.

EXERCISE NINTH.

2.					1.				
ニブ子	ソバイ	タバ子	シビト	キブイ	ボギ	ベイ	ブビ	ビク	ババ
					ホキ	ベイ	ブブ	ビン	バ
					キ	ベ	ブ	ン	バヂ
ナンブ	ソビク	タバコ	シボツ	キボ子	ボク	ベキ	ブツ	ビソ	バグ
					キ	ベン	ブ	ビ	バカ
ニバン	ソブツ	タブン	シブイツ	キブイツ	ボン	ベツ	ブコ	ビジ	バケ

10. P SERIES.

パ　　ピ　　プ　　ペ　　ポ

PA　　PI　　PU　　PE　　PO

15. A small circle (o) called the *han nigori*, placed at the right of the H series of syllables, represents, in Japanese

speech, a combination of the consonantal element of the English letter *p* with the pure vowels.

EXERCISE TENTH.

2.					1.			
ニンヂン	ゴトレ	カヘス	アツサ	ノゾク	ポク ポク	ポン ポン	プン ブン	ピン ピン	パンガ子
ヌスビト	キイテ	オヂズ	フイテ	ウツレ	リツパ	シツポ	パシヤ	ペンキ	ポカン
シンピ	ガンギ	アカク	コトバ	ナスビ	ポカ ポカ	パタ パタ	ポツ ポツ	ピカ ピカ	パチ パチ

11. M SERIES.

マ	ミ	ム	メ	モ
MA	MI	MU	ME	MO

16. The consonantal element of the English letter *m* combined with the pure vowels sounds best represents these syllables.

EXERCISE ELEVENTH.

1.

ママ　ミミ　ムガ　メゲ　モム

マミ　ミメ　ムダ　ノイ　モミ

マメ　ミコ　ムゴ　メク　モジ

マク　ミキ　ムチ　メヅ　モノ

マゴ　ミヌ　ム子　メシ　モト

2.

子マキ　マケテ　サノミ　カミン　ハンム

子ミズ　ニモツ　サムシ　カノイ　アタマ

メイケン　モエクヒ　スミカキ　タヅ子テ　タカサズ

12. Y SERIES.

ヤ	ユ	ヨ
YA	YU	YO

17. These syllables are pronounced by combining the consonantal element of the English letter *y* with the pure vowels.

18. NOTE. It will be observed that a syllable for *yi* or *ye* does not appear. No special characters having these sounds exist in the Japanese language. The character イ *i* is often spoken as though it were *yi*, so also is the character 井 (w)i which is given in the W series. The character ヱ (w)e, given in the W series is also often spoken ye. It is almost a matter of indifference whether ヱ is pronounced ye or e.

EXERCISE TWELFTH.

2.

タ	子	ミ	マ	ヨ
ヤ	ヤ	ザ	ユ	ウ
レ	ス	メ	ゲ	チ
ヤ	ニ	マ	メ	ユ
イ	ヤ	ヤ	ヤ	バ
バ	キ	ク	ス	ナ
ツ	ヤ	ユ	ミ	ユ
ヨ	イ	ダ	ヨ	ダ
ミ	バ	ン	レ	キ

1.

ハ	フ	マ	ヨ	ヤ
ヤ	エ	ヤ	ド	バ
ツ	ヘ	マ	ヤ	ヤ
ユ	ヤ	ユ	ヨ	ニ
ツ	ヒ	ミ	ヨ	ヤ
ヤ	ヤ	ヤ	ビ	ス
ヨ	ユ	モ	ヨ	ヤ
メ	ズ	ズ	リ	キ
ヤ	ユ	フ	ヨ	ヤ
子	メ	ヨ	カ	マ

13. R SERIES.

ラ リ ル レ ロ

RA   RI   RU   RE   RO

19. These syllables can not be represented by means of English vocables, just as they are pronounced in Japanese speech. But, the consonantal element of the English letter *r* combined with the pure vowel sounds most nearly reproduces this series. Especially is it to be noticed, that the character, リ *ri* is often spoken more as if it were a softly enunciated *dr i* than a distinct *ri*. Moreover, no one of the R syllabics ever receives the sound of the European rolling *r*.

The characters ル *ru* and ロ *ro*, like リ *ri*, often seem to involve the consonantal element of *d* in pronunciation.

EXERCISE THIRTEENTH.

	2.						1.			
ト	チ	カ	ユ	ヤ		ロ	レ	ル	リ	ラ
ン	ヨ	シ	ル	ライ		バ	イ	リ	ヒ	チ
デ	ギ	ラ	イ	イ		ロ	レ	ル	リ	ラ
						ビ	キ	フ	ジ	イ
モ	ヒ	オ	ユ	ソ						
ト	カ	ツ	ル	シ		ロ	レ	ル	ハ	ラ
ム	リ	ル	リ	リ		ヒ	ン	ス	リ	ク
						ロ	レ	ル	リ	ラ
ア	ル	ソ	ナ	ホ		シ	ツ	ル	キ	レ
ヤ	井	ヨ	カ	マ		ロ	ヤ	ア	リ	ラ
ウ	ラ	グ	レ	レ		ク	ル	ル	ン	ン
シ	ン									

SPECIAL NOTE:—

THE CONSONANTAL ELEMENT OF L.

20. In the Japanese language there is no equivalent for the English consonant *l*. Recently, that is, since the Japanese people have come into intimate relations with

Occidental languages and literature, the need of some
equivalent for the Western *l* has been felt by some native
linguists, especially that they may better represent foreign
words in Japanese newspapers and books. It has therefore been proposed by some scholars to introduce into
the syllabary an L series, by a *han-nigori* marking of the R
syllabics, as,—

ラ°	リ°	ル°	レ°	ロ°
LA	LI	LU	LE	LO

Attention is called here to this proposition, that students of the language may understand the meaning of the
R syllabics *nigoried*, should they happen to come across
them in their readings.

14. W SERIES.

ワ	ヰ	ウ	ヱ	ヲ
WA	(W)I	(W)U	(W)E	WO

21. These syllables are most nearly pronounced by a
combination of the consonantal element of the English
letter *w* and the pure vowels.

22. The W syllables undergo important changes in
combination with other syllables :—

a. At the beginning of a word ヲ *wo*, invariably drops its
w sound.

b. The pronunciation of ヰ (*w*)*i*, varies as *i*, *wi*, and *yi*,
according to association.

c. The pronunciation of ヱ (*w*)*e*, is almost indifferently
e, *we*, or *ye*.

d. As a particle ヲ *wo* retains its *w* sound.

e. The syllable ウ *u*, sometimes pronounced *wu*, has
been adapted by many Japanese, by the use of the *nigori*
(ゝゝ) ヴ, to represent the sound of the English *v*.

In the following exercise read the syllables as given above. Do not forget to drop the *w* sound from ヲ *wo* when it begins a word.

EXERCISE FOURTEENTH.

1.

ワビ	アワ	ヲチ	井ル	クエ
ワガ	フワ	ヲカ	井ド	エバ
ワケ	シワ	ヲケ	井ギ	ウエ
ワキ	セワ	ヲル	井ゴ	エン
ワル	ウチ	ヲリ	井ン	ヤク

2.

ヲトメ	アチダメ	ヲリハ	ワヅカ	ミガカザ
アヲバ	ヲリメ	ヲカメ	ワスル	レバ
アヲニ	ヲリク	オリ井	ワタル	スグレバ

CHAPTER III.

THE SYLLABLES AS AFFECTED BY JUXTAPOSITION.

23. When the vocal elements of the Japanese language are brought together by the pronunciation of juxtaposed syllabics, many modifications of their original values become audible. Both consonantal and vowel sounds undergo changes, some of which are of radical importance to a learner of the language. These modifications are noted and illustrated at considerable length in the present chapter. Many of the "Examples," and "Illustrative Words" given, however, are but seldom,—some of them never,—met with in common speech. They are put forward here, not that place need ever be found for them in the student's vocabulary, but simply that they may furnish the student with ample exercise in learning the phonetic changes which take place through the various associations of the Japanese vocal elements. These changes should be carefully studied.

I. VARIATIONS OF VOWEL SOUNDS.

24. The vowel syllables, better than the consonant syllables, retain their full values under juxtaposition. These syllables seldom appear except at the beginnings of words; consequently they are not often prevented from free utterance by antecedent consonants. They receive almost invariably the sounds already given, of *a* in *part*, of *i* in *pique*, of *u* in *pull* and of *o* in *port*. Their quantity in utterance may be long or short, but their true quality does not perceptibly change.

25. This fact, however, does not hold good of the vowel elements which are incorporated in the consonant syllables. The consonant syllables occur under all kinds of relations in speech ; at the beginnings, in the middles, and at the ends of words. Their vowel sounds are lengthened and shortened, rounded and flattened, long drawn and almost silenced, by the changing vocalization of their associated consonants. These changes very rarely, if ever, happen to the vowel syllables. Specifically :—

26. *a.* The *a* element of ㅏ *ka* and of the rest of the consonant syllables containing *a*, is often so flattened that it sounds much like *a* in *past* or in *mash*.

27. *b.* The *i* element of ㅣ *ki* and of all the other consonant syllables containing *i*, often becomes hastened and shortened into the sound of *i* in *pick*. Under some circumstances this sound is so lightly touched that it is almost inaudible.

28. *c.* The *u* element of ㅜ *ku* and of all the consonant syllables containing *u*, frequently becomes so much shortened that it is much like the *u* in *put*. This sound, like that of *i*, is also often so lightly enunciated that it is practically silenced.

29. *d.* The *e* element of ㅔ *ke* and of all the consonant syllables containing *e*, is often so rounded and shortened that it is much like the *e* of *pen*.

30. *e.* The *o* element of ㅗ *ko* and of all the consonant syllables containing *o*, is often so slowed and lengthened that it is sounded much like the *o* in *pore*.

31. The interaction of the consonant syllables occasions, consequently, such modifications of their vowel elements in speech, that these elements are sounded, according to circumstances, much as,—

a	either in	*part*	or in	*past*
i	„ „	*pique*	„ „	*pick*

u	,,	,,	*pull*	,,	,,	*put*
e	,,	,,	*prey*	,,	,,	*pen*
o	,,	,,	*pore*	,,	.,	*port.*

32. These changes can not be well indicated by written examples. But, a good working direction for the student who may not have opportunity for intimate intercourse with the Japanese people, may be found in his remembering that, as a rule, these changes are the results of the positions naturally taken by the vocal organs in an ordinary enunciation of the various combinations which the Japanese language makes of the consonantal and pure vowel sounds.

33. *α.* The following words, however, can be regarded as illustrations of the changes just referred to :—

アマレ	contains both round and flat *a,*	*amashi*
キリン	,, ,, long and short *i,*	*kirin*
クブン	,, ,, ,, ,, ,, *u,*	*kubun*
ケゲン	,, ,, ,, ,, ,, *e,*	*kegen*
ボンゴ	,, ,, short and long *o,*	*bongo.*

34. *β.* The quickening or silencing of the *i* and *u* sounds is exemplified in the pronunciation of such words as,

レタ *shi ta,* which, with one of its meanings, is generally sounded like . . . . *sh'ta*

ツキ *tsu ki,* which, with one of its meanings, is generally sounded like . . . . *ts'ki*

and マツ *ma tsu,* which, with one of its meanings, is generally sounded like . . . *mats'.*

This peculiarity will receive further attention on another page.

II. CHANGES IN THE VOWEL SYLLABLES.

The vowel syllables, when in juxtaposition, are generally affected as follows :—

35. *a.* The pronunciation of a doubled vowel syllable is practically that of a double long, or slow, sound of the vowel ; *e.g.* ア ア *a a*＝*ā,* イ イ *i i*＝*ī,* ウ ウ *u u*＝*ū.*

オ オ ヂis *ōji,* イ イ エ is *īyē,* エ エ is *ē.*

This combination, however, very rarely occurs.

36. *b.* The pronunciation of unlike vowel syllables generally exhibits their separate sounds as true diphthongs, —but with certain modifications, as here noted :—

37. *α.* ア *a* tends to change a following エ *e* into *ye,* and オ *o* into *wo.*

38. *β.* イ *i* tends to give an initial *y* sound to other vowels following.

39. *γ.* ウ *u* and オ *o* tend to give an initial *w* sound to other vowels following.

Examples :—

ア エ ル	sounds	much	like	*ayeru*
ア オ リ	,,	,,	,,	*awori*
イ ア テ ル	,,	,,	,,	*iyateru*
イ エ ツ	,,	,,	,,	*iyetsu*
ウ エ ル	,,	,,	,,	*uweru*
オ イ ル	,,	,,	,,	*owiru*
ウ イ ウ	,,	,,	,,	*uwiyu.*

40. *δ.* When ア *a* and ウ *u* are written together as ア ウ *au,* they very seldom receive a diphthongal pronunciation. They ordinarily coalesce into a double long, or slow, *ō* sound. The same change takes place in the juxtaposition オ ウ *ou.* Their sound is also that of *ō.*

Examples :—

ア ウ ギ	................................*ōgi*
ア ウ ア ウ	...........................*ō-ō*

アウト ....ōto

アウヅクコク .... ōzokkoku (54)

オウブン ....ōbun

オウブサ ....ōbusa

オウホウ ....ōhō (43)

オウケン ....ōken

オウメウ ....ōmyō (44)

オウナ ....ōna

オウセツ ....ōsetsu

オウエン ....ōyen

41. ε. When エ e and ウ u are written, エウ e u, they
are pronounced almost without exception as yō.   In
Aston's "Grammar of the Written Language," this
peculiarity is explained thus ; " In Japanese etymology e
is equal to i+a. E u therefore equals i a u." As we
have above noted, ア ウ a u are pronounced ō. The elements i a u, therefore easily coalesce in speech into iō or yō.
Examples :—

エウ .... yō

エウチ ....yōchi

エウチエン ....yōchiyen

エウテウ ....yōchō (44)

エウドウ ....yōdō

エウフン ....yōfun (47)

エウガク ....yōgaku

エウヂョ ....yōjo (50)

エウラク ....yōraku

ドエウビ ....doyōbi

III.   CHANGES IN JUXTAPOSED VOWEL AND
CONSONANT SYLLABLES.

1.   Vowel preceding Consonant Syllables.

When the vowel and the consonant syllables are written in juxtaposition, *the vowels preceding the consonants*, several peculiarities in pronunciation are produced.

42.   *a.*   The consonant syllables most affected by this association are those of the **H** or Spirant series, ハ *ha* ヒ *hi* フ *fu* ヘ *he* ホ *ho*. When these syllables follow the vowel syllables, or, indeed, what amounts to the same thing, when they follow the vowel sounds of any syllables, they lose, with but few exceptions, whatever spirant quality they have.   ハ *ha*, then, is pronounced much like *wa*. The other syllables of the series, practically as pure vowels, *i*, *u*, *e*, *o*, combine with the preceding vowels into true diphthongs. The few exceptions to this rule need not be noticed here.

Examples :—

ア	ハ	*a ha*	is pronounced		*awa*
イ	ハ	*i ha*	„	„	*iwa*
ウ	ハ	*u ha*	„	„	*uwa*
ア	ヒ	*a hi*	„	„	*ai*
イ	ヒ	*i hi*	„	„	*ii*
オ	ヒ	*o hi*	„	„	*oi*
ア	フ	*a fu*	„	„	*au* or *ō*
イ	フ	*i fu*	„	„	*iu*
オ	フ	*o fu*	„	„	*ou* or *ō*
イ	ヘ	*i he*	„	„	*ie*

ウヘ　　　*u he*　　„　　　„　　　*ue.*

オホ　　　*o ho*　　„　　　„　　　*oo* or *ō.*

NOTE.   It will be well to remember the following general
rule.   When the syllables of the H series do not commence a word, drop their spirant sound, read ヘ *ha* as *wa,*
and leave to the remaining syllables their pure vowel
qualities.

ILLUSTRATIVE WORDS :—

アハヒ ....*awahi*.................*awai*(**45**)

アハビ ....*awabi*

アハセ ....*awase*

イハバ ....*iwaba*

イハヒ ....*iwahi*..................*iwai*

イハフ ....*iwafu* ....*iwau* (**46**)

イハホ ....*iwaho* ....*iwao*(**45**)

イハシ ....*iwashi*

イハウ ....*iwau* ....*iwō*

ウハエ ....*uwaye*

ウハベ ....*uwabe*

オホワ ....*ōwa*

オハセル ....*owaseru*

オホウヲ ....*ōuwo*

オホフ ....*ōu*

イフイフ ....*iuiu*

アヒダ ....*aida*

アヒハン ....*aihan*

イヒアワセル ....*iiawaseru*

イヒガヒ .... *iigai*

イイアフ .... *iiau* (46)

イヘデ .... *iede*

ウヘナキ .... *uenaki &c.*

2. *Consonant preceding Vowel Syllables.*

43. *a.* The peculiarities of pronunciation arising from the juxtaposition of the vowel and consonant syllables, *the consonants preceding the vowels*, are practically the same as those arising from the juxtaposition of the vowel syllables only, as shown above, (**40**).

Examples :—

	カ ウ	*ka u*	is pronounced		*kō*
	ガ ウ	*ga u*	,,	,,	*gō*
	ロ ウ	*ro u*	,,	,,	*rō*
	ホ ウ	*ho u*	,,	,,	*hō &c.*
and	ニ ウ	*ni u*	,,	,,	*nyŭ*
	リ ウ	*ri u*	,,	,,	*ryŭ*
	キ ウ	*ki u*	,,	,,	*kyŭ &c.*

ILLUSTRATIVE WORDS:—

カウヤク .... *kōyaku*

ハウバウ · .... *hōbō*

ゴウゴウ .... *gōgō*

サウマイ .... *sōmai*

ラウボ .... *rōbo*

タウメ .... *tōme*

ヤウカ .... *yōka*

ノ ウ カ ウ .... *nōkō*

マ ウ ヨ ウ .... *mōyō*

Among many other illustrations a few typical words are
the following :—

ニ ウ ボ .... *nyūbo.*

ニ ウ バ ウ .... *nyūbō*

ニ ウ ボ ウ .... *nyūbō*

リ ウ ト ウ .... *ryūtō*

リ ウ エ イ .... *ryūyei*

リ ウ カ ウ .... *ryūkō*

リ ウ キ ウ .... *ryūkyū*

キ ウ ゲ ン .... *kyūgen*

キ ウ ギ ウ .... *kyūgyū*

キ ウ ラ フ .... *kyūrō* (**45**) *&c.*

44. *b.* The peculiarity noted before (**41**), namely, that
of the pronunciation of エ ウ *e u* as *yō*, follows the vowel
sound *e* when it appears in consonant syllables having
the same associations as the vowel エ *e.*, *e.g.* テ ウ *te u* is
pronounced as though written *chō*. That is, *e u* becomes
yō and *t* before the sound *i* or *yi*, has its equivalent, as we
have seen, in *chi* (**9**). From these changes comes *chi yo*, and
that is transformed into *chō*. Thus, also, for like associations of other syllabics in *e* and *u*.

Examples :—

テ ウ	*te u*	=	*chi yo*	=	*chō*
デ ウ	*de u*	=	*ji yo*	=	*jō*
セ ウ	*se u*	=	*shi yo*	=	*shō*
ベ ウ	*be u*	=	*bi yo*	=	*byō*

ケ ウ	ke u	=	ki yo	=	kyō
レ ウ	re u	=	ri yo	=	ryō
メ ウ	me u	=	mi yo	=	myō
ヘ ウ	he u	=	hi yo	=	hyō
子 ウ	ne u	=	ni yo	=	nyō
グ ウ	ge u	=	gi yo	=	gyō &c.

ILLUSTRATIVE WORDS:—

テ ウ バ ウ	*chōbō*
テ ウ チ ン	*chōchin*
ニ フ テ ウ	*nyūchō*
デ ウ テ ツ	*jōtetsu*
セ ウ バ ウ	*shōbō*
ベ ウ ダ ン	*byōdan*
ケ ウ ガ フ	*kyōgö* (**45**)
レ ウ シ	*ryōshi*
メ ウ ク ワ	*myōkwa* (**56**)
ヘ ウ リ ウ	*hyōryū*
子 ウ ケ ツ	*nyōketsu*
グ ウ タ イ	*gyōtai*
セ ウ ジ ウ	*shōjū*
レ ウ リ	*ryōri*
ヘ ウ セ イ	*hyōsei*
ケ ウ ハ フ	*kyōhō* (**45**)
セ ウ ダ イ	*shōdai.*

45. *c.* As the syllables of the H series, when not placed at the beginning of words, are practically vowels, the changes occurring in their pronunciation, when follow-

ing consonant syllables, should be studied. They undergo
in this relation practically the same changes as those to
which they are subjected when they follow the vowel
syllables :—

Examples :—

ハ フ	*ha fu*	....	*hau*	....	*hō*
ハ ヘ	*ha he*	....		..	*hae*
ホ フ	*ho fu*	....	*ho u*	......	*hō*
ホ ホ	*ho ho*	....	*ho o*	......	*hō*
ニ ヒ	*ni hi*	....			*nii*
リ フ	*ri fu*	....			*ryū*
ヌ フ	*nu fu*	....			*nuū*
タ ヘ	*ta he*	....			*tae*
タ ヒ	*ta hi*	....			*tai*
ス ヒ	*su hi*	....			*sui*
ス フ	*su fu*	....			*suū*
ナ ハ	*na ha*	....			*nawa*
ジ フ	*ji fu*	....			*jū*
ゴ フ	*go fu*	....	*yo u*	......	*gō*
キ ハ	*ki ha*	....			*kiwa*
ユ フ	*yu fu*	....			*yuu*
ユ ヒ	*yu hi*	....			*yui*
コ ヒ	*ko hi*	....			*koi*
ナ ホ	*na ho*	....			*nao*
ヲ ヒ	*wo hi*	....	*o hi*	......	*oi.*

ILLUSTRATIVE WORDS:—

バ ヒ ア フ .... *baiau* (46)

ハ	ヘ	ル		*haeru*
ハ	ヒ	コ	ム	*haikomu*
ヒ	ハ	リ		*hiwari*
ホ	ホ	ダ	テ	*hōdate*
ハ	フ	フ	ク	*hōfuku* (**47**)
フ	ハ	フ		*fuhō*
ニ	ヒ	ム	ロ	*niimuro*
リ	フ	ロ	ン	*ryūron*
ナ	ホ	ス		*naosu*
ニ	ホ	フ		*niou* (**46**)
ニ	ホ	ヒ		*nioi*
ヌ	ヒ	メ		*nuime*
タ	ヘ	ル		*taeru*
タ	ヒ	ラ		*taira*
ス	ヒ	モ	ノ	*suimono*
ス	ハ	ゥ		*suō*
ジ	フ	キ		*jūki*
コ	ハ	イ		*kowai*
ソ	フ			*sou* (**46**)
キ	ハ	ミ		*kiwami*
ユ	ヒ	ナ	フ	*yuinō*
ヲ	ヒ	ヨ	メ	*oiyome &c.*

46. *α.* When the syllable フ *fu* terminates a verb, following syllables whose vowel element is *a* or *o*, フ *fu* loses its spirant quality only. The resulting sound is the diphthong *au* or *ou*.

ILLUSTRATIVE WORDS: --

ナフ	is not	*nō*	but	*nau*
モラフ	,, ,,	*morō*	,,	*morau*
オモフ	,, ,,	*omō*	,,	*omou*
シマフ	,, ,,	*shimō*	,,	*shimau* &c.

47. β. There are some purely Japanese words in which フ *fu* does not loss its spirant quality when following other syllables.

ILLUSTRATIVE WORDS :—

オフダ	is not	*ōda*	but	*ofuda*
アフレル	,, ,,	*ōreru*	,,	*afureru*
ハフリ	,, ,,	*hōri*	,,	*hafuri*
子フス	,, ,,	*nyōsu*	,,	*nefusu* &c.

48. SPECIAL NOTE. To these examples may be added from the H series a few more illustrative words to show how *e u* is changed in pronunciation into *yō* or *ō*.

ILLUSTRATIVE WORDS :—

セフ	*se fu* = *se u* = *shiyō* = *shō*
セフフク	.......................*shōfuku*
セフサツ	...................*shōsatsu*
テフテフ	......................*chōchō*
テフテフシイ	................*chōchōshii*
テフツガヒ	....................*chōtsugai.*

IV. CHANGES IN CONSONANT SYLLABLES.

49. The influence, in its general character, of the consonant syllables upon one another, may be easily learned from what has already been said of the vowel and consonant syllables in their mutual relations. There remains

for notice but little of an exceptional character. The chief
exception lies in the fact, that often there is such a blend-
ing of the sounds of two or more syllables, that the result-
ant pronunciation is more or less unlike that of any of the
constituent syllables when pronounced separately. This
peculiarity has, to some extent, been already noticed in the
blendings of vowel and consonantal sounds. Something
of what has already been said may be repeated below.

50. 1. *Coalescent Sounds.*—When the conson-
ant syllables シ *shi*, ジ *ji*, and チ *chi*, precede the syllables ヤ *ya*, ウ *u*, ユ *yu*, ヨ *yo*, or the diphthongal syllables ヤウ *yō*, ヨウ *yō* and the like, the first and the
last sounds only of the juxtaposed syllables are audible.

Examples :—

レ ヤ	*shi ya*	is pronounced	*sha*
レ ヨ	*shi yo*	„ „	*sho*
レ ヤ ウ	*shi ya u*	= *shi yō* =	*shō*
レ ウ	*shi u*	is pronounced	*shu*
レ ユ ウ	*shi yu u*	= *shi yŭ* =	*shŭ*
ジ ヤ	*ji ya*	is pronounced	*ja*
ジ ヤ ウ	*ji ya u*	= *ji yō* =	*jō*
ジ フ	*ji fu*	= *ji yŭ* =	*jŭ*
ジ ユ	*ji yu*	is pronounced	*ju*
ジ ユ ウ	*ju yu u*	„ - „	*jŭ*
ヂ ヨ	*ji yo*	is pronounced	*jo*
ヂ ヤ ウ	*ji ya u*	= *ji yō* =	*jō*
チ ヤ	*chi ya*	is pronounced	*cha*
チ ヨ	*chi yo*	„ „	*cho*
チ ヤ ウ	*chi ya u*	= *chi yō* =	*chō*

チ ョ ウ	chi yo u	=	chi yō	=	chō
チ エ	chi ye	is pronounced			chie

ILLUSTRATIVE WORDS:—

チ ャ ボ ン .... *shabon*

レ ヤ ク .... *shaku*

レ ョ ブ ン .... *shobun*

レ ヤ ウ バ イ .... *shōbai*

レ ユ ウ ヤ .... *shūya*

レ ウ ト メ .... *shūtome*

レ フ イ .... *shūi*

シ フ ジ .... *shūji*

ジ ヤ ク .... *jaku*

ジ ヤ ハ フ .... *jahō*

ジ ヤ ウ ダ ン .... *jōdan*

ジ ヤ ウ ダ ウ .... *jōdō*

ジ フ ア ク .... *juaku*

ジ フ ブ ン .... *jubun*

ジ ユ バ ン .... *juban*

ジ ユ ウ ビ ン .... *jūbin*

ヂ ョ チ ゥ .... *jochū*

ヂ ヤ ウ バ ン .... *jōban*

ヂ ユ ウ ビ ヤ ゥ .... *jūbyō*

チ ヤ ダ イ .... *chadai*

チ ョ ボ .... *chobo*

チ ョ ウ ボ .... *chōbo*

チ ヤ ウ ボ .... *chōbo*

チヤウチヤウ ....chōchō

チョウアイ ....chōai

チエヅク ....chiezuku.

51. **2. *Rapid, or Suppressed, Sounds.*** It often happens that sounds associated with syllables as written, are almost, and sometimes wholly, suppressed when the syllables are spoken. We have already referred to this peculiarity, but more special attention to it should be given. In the illustrations shown in this book of this change, the sign ⌣ is used ; *e.g.* ŭ or ĭ.

52. *a.* The sound *u*, whether appearing in a vowel syllable or as part of a consonant syblable, should it happen to end a word, is usually so lightly spoken that it may be said to be suppressed, or practically silenced.

Examples :—

アリマス   *a ri ma su*   =   *arimasŭ.*

タテダレヌ   *ta te ra re nu*   =   *tolerarenŭ.*

53. *b.* When the syllable ツ *tsu*, not at the beginning of a word, precedes a *ch* sound, the sound *u* disappears.

Examples :—

イツチ   *i tsu chi*   =   *itschi*   =   *itchi*

イツテウ   *i tsu te u* = *itsteu* = *itchiyō* = *itchō.*

54. *c.* When the syllables ク *ku*, not at the beginning of a word, is followed by another syllable of the K series, カ *ka*, キ *ki*, ケ *ke* or コ *ko*, it loses its vowel sound,—the resulting sound being that of double *k*.

Examples :—

ガクカウ   *ga kŭ kō*   =   *gakkō*

ビ ク コ	bi kŭ ko	=	bikko
カ ク キ	ka kŭ ki	=	kakki
ラ ク ク ワ	ra kŭ kŭ wa	=	rakkwa (56)

55. *d.* When the syllable ッ *tsu*, not at the beginning of a word, precedes the syllables of the K, S, T or P series, its sound is silenced, and the consonantal sound following is doubled.

ILLUSTRATIVE WORDS:

カ ツ カ ウ	ka tsŭ kō	=	kakkō
マ ツ ス グ	ma tsŭ su gu	=	massugu
テ ツ バ ウ	te tsŭ pō	=	teppō
マ ツ タ ク	ma tsŭ ta ku	=	mattaku
ヒ ツ コ ム	hi tsŭ ko mu	=	hikkomu.
ツ モ ツ テ	tsumotsŭte	=	tsumotte
バ ツ キ ン	batsŭkin	=	bakkin
ア ツ タ	atsŭta	=	atta
チ ツ ト	chitsŭto	=	chitto
カ ツ テ	katsŭte	=	katte.

NOTE. This peculiarity has given rise to the custom, with some writers, of using the ッ *tsu* as the phonetic sign of the doubling of a sound in a word. It is often, when used in this way, marked with a small circle, the *han nigori* so called ; *e.g.* ッ°.

56. *e.* Before ワ *wa*, the *u* sound of ク *ku*, and of グ *gu*, is usually lost in speech.

Examples :—

ク ワ イ シ ヤ	= kŭ wa i shi ya	=	kwaisha or kaisha
ク ワ ジ	kŭ wa ji	=	kaji or kwaji
グ ワ イ コ ク	gŭ wa i ko ku	=	gwaikoku or gaikoku
ラ ク ク ワ	ra ku ku wa	=	rakkwa.

57. *f.* The sounds *u* and *i*, as elements of the consonant syllables of the K, H, S and T series, tend to become silent in polysyllabic combinations.

ILLUSTRATIVE WORDS :—

ク サ リ	.....................kŭsari
ヒ カ ル	.....................hikaru
シ カ シ	.....................shĭkashi
ス コ シ	.....................sŭkoshi
ス ク ナ シ	.....................sŭkunashi
ツ ケ ル	.....................tsŭkeru
ツ ケ ギ	.....................tsŭkegi
チ ク シ ヤ ウ	.....................chikŭshō
ニ シ キ	.....................nishĭki
カ ク ベ ツ	.....................kakŭbetsu
カ ク シ テ	.....................kakŭshite
ア タ ラ シ キ	.....................atarashĭki
フ ク ム	.....................fŭkumu
フ ス マ	.....................fŭsuma.

EXERCISE FIFTEENTH.

1. アシタ ミマヒ ニ マヰリマセウ。アマシ。アエル。
2. アサハン マヘ ウンドウ スル。オウブン。ヨウヂ。
3. トウキヤウ ガ ヒロイ。アハビ。カウヤク。
4. サウ ナサリマス カ。ニウバウ。テウバウ。
5. アチ ヘ ヨリマセウ。ハヘル。モラフ。
6. ハオリ ヲ カフ。オフダ。テフテフ。
7. ワタクシ ノ キヤウダイ。シヤボン。シウトメ。
8. ヒト ニ ハラッタ。イッテウ。ガクカウ。

1. *Ashita mimai ni mairimashō. Amashi. Ayeru.*
2. *Asa-han mae undō suru. Ōbun. Yōji.*
3. *Tōkyō ga hiroi. Awabi. Kōyaku.*
4. *Sō nasarimasu ka? Nyūbō. Chōbō.*
5. *Achi ye yorimashō. Haeru. Morau.*
6. *Haori wo kau. Ofuda. Chōchō.*
7. *Watakushi no kyōdai. Shabon. Shūtome.*
8. *Hito ni haratta. Itchō. Gakkō.*

EXERCISE FIFTEENTH.

16.	15.	14.	13.	12.	11.	10.	9.

カンジヤウ チヤウ ヲ ハヤク ドウカ。シカタ ガ ナイ。サヤウナラ。

コンバン ハ メンボク ガ ナイ。モウ ヨロシイ。オハヤウ。

ケフ ハ ヨイ テンキ デス。ハオリ。フスマ。

コノ チヤウ ノ キンジヨ デ ゴザイマス カ。グワイコク。ラククワ。

ジフ ジ ニ チヤ ヲ イッパイ モッテ キテ オクレ。クワジ。ヒッコム。

モウシタ コトバ ヲ オッシヤッテ ドウゾ。オモフ。ナフ。

レウリニン ニ サウ イッテ クダサイ。セフサツ。ケッカウ。

ホンチヤウ ドホリ デ アイマセウ。シヤウバイ。オホヲ。

---

9. *Honchō dōri de aimashō. Shōbai. Ōuwo.*
10. *Ryōri nin ni sō itte kudasai. Shōsatsu. Kekkō.*
11. *Mōshita kotoba wo osshatte dōzo. Omou. Nau.*
12. *Jū ji ni cha wo ippai motte kite o kure. Kwaji. Hikkomu.*
13. *Kono chō no kinjō de gozaimasŭ ka? Gwaikoku. Rakkwa.*
14. *Kyō wa yoi tenki desŭ. Haori. Fusuma.*
15. *Komban wa memboku ga nai. Mō yoroshii. O hayō.*
16. *Kanjō chō wo hayaku dōka. Shikata ga nai. Sayōnara.*

NOTE. There are other modifications of pronunciation peculiar to the Japanese language, but those which have been exhibited so far, are most worth the attention of student in beginning his study. Should one faithfully apply the rules here given, he can be confident, that, although he may never read or speak Japanese like one native born, he will not make many serious failures in his attempts at enunciating Japanese words.

CHAPTER IV.

PUNCTUATION, GRAPHIC SIGNS, AND ACCENT.

I. PUNCTUATION.

58. Properly speaking, Japanese ·writing is without PUNCTUATION MARKS, or equivalents of the periods, colons, semicolons, commas etc., which abound in the books and manuscripts of the West. Japanese writing does not even show separately the words which compose it. It is practically a continuous succession of syllabic characters, which the intelligence of the reader, it is supposed, will enable him to group into the words and phrases intended to be understood. Sentences, however, or completed expressions of thought, and certain rhythmical phrases in sentences, are indicated in most manuscripts and printing by a few well understood marks. Recently, under the stress of " modern " needs, attempts at systematic punctuation have appeared in many periodical publications. But, as yet it may be said, that with the few exceptions spoken of, there is no general agreement among the Japanese as to the marks to be used, to designate, in writing, the divisions of their thought and its expression.

59. The marks commonly in use are these: open, and solid, circles o •, and open, and solid, pendants ゝ ゝ. These marks have different significations when placed in different positions.

60. A large open, or solid, circle is used to show a *headline*, or beginning of chapter or section ; ◯ or ●.

61. A small open, or closed, circle placed at the lower right hand corner of a word, serves as a *period ;* o or •.

62. Small open, or closed, circles placed along the right side of a word, or sentence, indicate *emphasis* ;—o or ●.

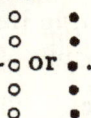

63. A *pendant* ◗ may indicate either a *full stop*, or a *comma*-like pause, when placed at the lower right hand corner of a syllable or word. At the present time it generally does a comma's work.

64. Along the right side of a word, or succession of words, the pendants, open and closed, indicate a *secondary emphasis* ; ◗ or ◗. The emphasis intended by large sized type, or by circles, is of more importance than that of the pendants.

The succession of degrees of emphasis is made by big type, or large writing, solid and open circles, solid and open pendants ; *e.g.* ⊘, ●, o, ◗, ◗. The best writers and publishers, however, are not disposed now to favor the growing use of these marks.

65. An *exclamation* mark (!), has lately been added to the type fonts of the newspaper offices.

66. *Interrogation* is embodied in a sentence by the use of the syllable ヵ *ka*, or the mark (?).

II. GRAPHIC SIGNS.

67. In addition to the punctuation marks above described, which, as we have seen, serve also in a measure as GRAPHIC SIGNS, there are other marks now in use, which the learner of the Japanese language should be prepared to understand when he meets with them.

68. The line, single ———, and doubled ═══, is used

as a *coupler of syllables* into names of persons, and places. A single line placed at the right of the characters indicates the name of a person ; two lines designates the name of a place. Thus, ロ ヒ ゾ ゾ ゾ ; or thus, ゾ カ コ.

69. A short line —, is often used in print to show *subsections and paragraphs* subordinated to the main divisions, which are marked by the large open, or closed, circle ; ○ or ●.

70. *Chief subdivisions* are sometimes headed by solid diamonds ◆, or pyramids ▲, according to the publisher's fancy.

71. *Quotation* is shown by the brackets ⌈ . . . . ⌋. Sometimes two lines = before, and two lines = after, a phrase, mark quotation ; *e.g.* = ... =.

72. *Abbreviation* is generally indicated by a line of small dots . . . . in the body of a sentence ; or by two long lines ========= between groups of characters.

73. *Parenthesis* is shown, as it is in Western writing, by arcs (   ), or brackets [   ].

74. *Repetition* of a syllable in a word is indicated by placing under the syllable a closed pendant ; *e.g.* ゛. When *two or three syllables* are repeated the repetition sign is usually a long obtuse angle,— ⟨ ; *e.g.* ⟨.

NOTE. It might be well to notice also a few special marks, often appearing in writing and printing ; as

7 and ろ = *koto.*

朴 stands for *toki* = " when "

疋 „ „ *tomo* = " although "

乙 „ „ *gozaru* = " to be " (formal)

ノ   „   „   *shite*   =   "having done"

升   „   „   *masu*   =   "to be" (polite

termination of verbal forms).

There are other graphic signs in use in Japanese writing,
but they need not be described here. They are mostly
to be found in ancient classical literature. Familiarity
with the marks here shown will make plain the punctuation and signs used in the newspapers, periodicals and
books which compose the current literature of the people.

III.   ACCENT.

In reference to this feature of speech very little serviceable information can be conveyed by description. Only
personal intercourse with the people, and extended acquaintance with the vocabulary, can give, if ever, satisfactory accent, rhythm and cadence to a foreigner's
attempts at reading or speaking Japanese. But there
are some rules which, if observed, will prevent really gross
errors in enunciation.

75. Accent in the Japanese language is not nearly so
prominent as in the speech of the peoples of the West.
Quickened, or silenced, vowel sounds often cause the other
parts of a spoken word to stand out with exceptional
prominence, but, as a rule, the values of all the syllables
appear pretty well equalized when sounded. The sound
of the word *arimasu*, for instance, is an almost evenly toned
a-ri-mas, the final *u* being almost mute, and the syllable
masu being but *very slightly* emphasized ; the emphasis
over the stress given the other two syllables being hardly
noticeable.

76. 1. In words of two syllables, as a rule, the accent
is on the first syllable.

Examples:—   ツ ル = *tsúru*,   サ ト = *sáto*,

コ ト = *kóto,* ヒ ロ = *híro,*

ム リ = *múri,* タ キ = *táki.*

Exceptions. When a short *u* or *i* is the vowel sound of the first syllable, or when a double long vowel sound appears in the second syllable, the accent falls on the second syllable.

Examples :—

ツ キ = *tsŭki,* シ カ = *shĭka,*

サ ト ウ = *satō,* ヒ ロ ウ = *hirō,*

ム ス ウ = *musŭ,* タ カ ウ = *takō.*

77. 2. In words of three syllables, as a rule, the accent falls upon the second syllable.

Exception. If the second syllable is short, as *i* or *ŭ*, the first syllable receives the accent, unless the last syllable has a double long vowel sound, when, of course, the primary accent goes to the last syllable, and a secondary accent to the first syllable.

Examples :—

ア ラ レ   *aráshi,* illustrates the general rule.

Then

ア ツ ク   *átsŭku,* shows an exception with short *u*

ア リ ソ   *áriso,*   „   „   „   „   „   *i*

カ シ ラ   *káshira,*   „   „   „   „   „   *i*

タ ヒ ラ   *táira*   „   „   „   „   „   *i.*

78. 3. In words of more than three syllables the accent, as a rule, falls upon the syllable before the last, unless sent elsewhere by short, or double long, syllables, whose values must be respected.

Examples :—

アサガラ	*asagára,*	so, also,
アサマダキ	*asamadáki* ; but	
アサギタ	*aságita,*	and
アルヘイタウ	*aruheitó*	and
カクシテ	*kákŭshite.*	

79. 4. In all words, let it be remembered, accent always goes to the double long, or slow, syllables. When two such long syllables are juxtaposed they are pronounced with even tones, like a spondee in English verse.

80. 5. In some,—not very many,—words which are written exactly alike, there are differences of pronunciation which can not be illustrated in any way by rule. Each set of these words must be learned for itself, as, for example,

the four	ハシ	*hashi,*
the half dozen	カシ	*kashi,*
the several	カキ	*kaki*

and the numerous

$\left\{\begin{array}{l} コ \\ コ ウ \\ コ フ \\ ク ワ ウ \end{array}\right.$

ko and *kō.*

These last difficulties, however, need not trouble a beginner in·the study of Japanese speech. The rules above given will be sufficient for all ordinary needs of the student.

IV. MARKS FOR TRANSLITERATION.

81. In seeking to ·reproduce Japanese sounds in this book, by the use of English equivalents, it has not been thought necessary to burden the text with many arbitrary signs.

The pure sounds of the vowels such as

a	in	*part*	and	*past*
i	„	*pique*	„	*pick*
u	„	*pull*	„	*put*
e	„	*prey*	„	*pen*
o	„	*pore*	„	*port*

are all represented by the unmarked vowels *a, i, u, e, o.* Taking the sounds in *part pique, pull, prey* and *port* as basal sounds, the student will naturally modify them practically aright, as in *past, pick, put, pen* and *pore* in pronouncing them in connection with the consonantal elements of Japanese words.

a. The double long, or slow, sound of a vowel is indicated by a letter having a short, straight line over it ; as, *ā, ō.*

b. The quick, short, or suppressed, sound of a vowel is indicated by a letter having a short breve over it ; as, *ĭ, ŭ.*

c. The sound of *u* like *ng* in *singer*, when marked, is shown by the letter *n* with a small dot over it as *ṅ.*

d. Accent, where marked, is shown by a letter having over it a short inclined line ; as, *kà, mè, mì.*

CHAPTER V.

NUMERALS.

82. In the Japanese language the treatment of NUMBERS is a work of considerable length and complexity. But, every beginner in the study of the language should know enough of the numbers, to enable him to read them, should he meet with them in writing, and to recognize them should he hear them spoken.

83. The characters which show cardinal enumeration from *one* to *ten*, and which stand for *one hundred*, *one thousand* and *ten thousand*, are the elements of the numerals. These should be learned by every student of the *Japanese syllabary*.

84. From *one* to *ten*, in present Japanese speech, is represented by two groups of sounds. These sounds are applied to one series of characters. One of these groups of sounds is purely Japanese in its origin. The Japanese sounds for the numerals above *ten* are for the most part obsolete. They remain only in a few compound words, and in ancient literature. The other of these groups of sounds is of Chinese origin. This group furnishes the sounds for a great deal of enumeration from *one* to *ten*, and for almost all numbers from *ten* upwards.

The elements of counting in Japanese speech are therefore as follows :—

CHARACTERS.	JAPANESE SOUNDS.	CHINESE SOUNDS.	VALUES.
一	*Hitotsu*	*Ichi*	1
二	*Futátsu*	*Ni*	2

三	*Mítsu*	*San*	3
四	*Yótsu*	*Shi*	4
五	*Itsútsu*	*Go*	5
六	*Mútsu*	*Róku*	6
七	*Nanátsu*	*Shĭchi*	7
八	*Yátsu*	*Háchi*	8
九	*Kokonótsu*	*Ku*	9
十	*Tō*	*Jŭ*	10
百		*Hyákŭ*	100
千		*Sen*	1000
萬		*Man*	10,000

85. In counting between *ten* and *one hundred*, combinations from the Chinese group, such as *ten one, ten two, ten three* are used. Twenty is *two ten*, twenty-one is *two ten one*, thirty is *three ten*, etc.

Examples :—

CHARACTERS.	KANA WRITING.	PRONUNCIATION.	VALUES.
十 一	ジフ イチ	*jŭ ichi*	11
十 二	ジフ ニ	*jŭ ni*	12
十 三	ジフ サン	*jŭ san*	13
二 十	ニ ジフ	*ni jŭ*	20

二 十 一 .. ニ ジフ イチ ....*ni jŭ ichi* ..21

三 十 ...... サン ジフ .... *san jŭ* 30

四 十 ...... シ ジフ .... *shi jŭ* 40

六 十 ...... ロク ジフ .... *róku jŭ* ...60

八 十 ...... ハチ ジフ .... *háchi jŭ* ..80

. ... *&c.*

86. Higher numbers are produced by combining, in like manner, the lower numerals.

Examples:—

CHARACTERS.	KANA WRITING.	PRONUNCIATION.	VALUES.
一百	イツピヤク	*ippyáku*	100
二百	ニヒヤク	*nihyáku*	200
三百	サンビヤク	*sambyáku*	300
六百	ロツピヤク	*roppyáku*	600
一千	イツセン	*issén*	1,000
二千	ニセン	*nisén*	2,000
一萬	イチマン	*ichĭmán*	10,000
十萬	ジフマン	*jŭman*	100,000
百萬	ヒヤクマン	*hyákuman*	1,000,000

87. A year number is represented by a combination of the numerals, somewhat as in English. To illustrate,—

一千八百九十五 = *issén happyáku ku jŭ go* = 1895.

Recently, just such combinations of numerals as are found in English have become quite frequent in Japanese. *Examples :—*

七二 = *shichi jŭ ni* = 72

一五〇 = *hyáku go jŭ* = 150

一一二八 = *sen hyáku nijŭ háchi* = 1128

88. In connection with the numeral characters certain other characters are in constant use. A few of these should be learned by the student, even though his work should be confined to the *kana*. Such, for example, are the characters for *day, month* and *year :—*

CHARACTERS.		KANA WRITING.		PRONUNCIATION.		TRANSLATION.
日	=	ニチ	=	*nichi*	=	" day "
月	=	グツ / ツキ	=	*getsŭ / tsŭki*	=	" month "
年	=	チン	=	*nen*	=	" year."

Examples :—

一日	=	イチニチ	=	*ichi nichi*
一年	=	イチチン	=	*ichi nen.*

According to circumstances, the character for month is read by the use of either the Chinese, or the Japanese, group of numeral sounds.

Example :—

一月　　=　　　either *ichi getsu* or *hitotsŭki*.

89. The Japanese group of sounds, when used for purposes of enumeration, is abbreviated throughout, as follows :—

CHARACTERS.	NUMERALS.		ABBREVIATIONS.	
一	ヒ ト ツ	=	ヒ ト *hito* or	ヒ ....*hi*
二	フ タ ツ	=	フ タ *fŭta* or	フ ...*fu*
三	ミ ツ	=	....	ミ ....*mi*
四	ヨ ツ	=	....	ヨ ....*yo*
五	イ ツ ツ	=	....	イ ツ ....*itsu*
六	ム ツ	=	....	ム ....*mu*
七	ナ ナ ツ	=	....	ナ 丶 ....*nana*
八	ヤ ツ	=	....	ヤ ...*ya*
九	コ コ ノ ツ	=	....	コ ノ ....*kono*
十	ト フ	=	....	ト フ ....*tō*.

90. The student will find, as he progresses with his reading of Japanese, that the Japanese numeral sounds are used chiefly in combination with Japanese words, and that Chinese numeral sounds *below ten* are, as a rule, used with Chinese words. *Above ten*, Chinese numeral sounds, with a very few exceptions, are used for the expression of all numeral combinations.

CHAPTER VI.

THE HIRAGANA.

91. The *Hiragana* form of the syllabary is the popular medium in use for the representation of Japanese speech. Its chief excellence, and probably a reason to be added to the main reason given in the General Introduction for the preference over the *Katakana* shown it by the people, lies in its easy adaptability for the purposes of writing. The characters composing the *Hiragana* are easily joined to one another.

In former times each syllabic of the syllabary was rendered in the *Hiragana* by a large number of differing characters. At the present time most of these characters have become obsolete. They remain enshrined in ancient literature, and are honored to-day chiefly in ornamental script. The tendency at present is steadily towards reducing the variety yet remaining, to the simplicity of the *Katakana*, in which there is but one sign for each syllable.

In the *Hiragana* syllabary next given, those characters are reproduced which are becoming standard. They are learned by the children in the schools of the empire, and are, with but few exceptions, the characters now in use in the printing of the newspapers and the books which are prepared for the reading of the common people, and in the publications in which the *Kana*, as side letters, serve to interpret Chinese ideographs. The less used, and some of the obsolete, *Hiragana* characters will be given in another table of the syllabary printed at the beginning of the Third Section.

I. TRANSITION FROM KATAKANA TO HIRAGANA.

For the purpose of preparing the student for a mastery
of the *Hiragana*, we shall now transcribe from the *Katakana*
into the *Hiragana*, the Illustrative Proverbs which are to
serve as texts to the reading and conversation composing
the Third Section of this manual.   Let the student be
content for the present with learning only to read, and to
pronounce correctly, the Japanese text of these proverbs.

ILLUSTRATIVE PROVERBS IN KATAKANA.

1. イチ ヲ キイテ, ジフ ヲ シル。

2. ロン ニ マケテ モ, リニ カツ。

3. ハリ ノ アナ カラ, テン ヲ
    ノゾク。

4. ニンゲン ワズカ, ゴジフ ヂン。

5. ホマレ アラン ヨリ, ソシリ
    ナカレ。

6. ヘタ ノ ナガ ダンギ。

7. トンデ ヒ ニ イル ナツ ノ ムシ。

8. チリ ツモツテ ヤマ ト ナル。

9. リカ ニ カンムリ ヲ タバサズ。

10. ヌスビト ヲ ミテ ナワ ヲ ナフ。

11. ルイラン ヨリ モ アヤウシ。

12. ヲカメ ハチ モク。

13. ワザハヒ モ サイハヒ ノ ハシ
    ト ナル。

14. カシラ カクシテ ヲヲ カクサズ。

15. ヨメ ガ シウトメニ ナル。

16. タマ ミガヽザレバ ヒカリ ナシ。

17. レイ スグレバ シツレイ ト
    ナル。

18. ソデ ウツシ ニ モノ ヲ ヤル。

19. ツノヲ ナホス トテ ウシ ヲ
    コロス。

20. 子ヅミ トル 子コ ハ ツメ ヲ
    カクス。

21. ナキヅラ ヲ ハチ ガ サス。

22. ラツクワ エダ ニ カヘラズ。

23. ムリ ガ トホレバ, ダウリ
    ヒツコム。

24. ウリ ノ 夕子 ニ ナスビ ハ
    ハヘヌ。

25. 井ド ノ ナカ ノ カハズ ダイカイ
    ヲ シラズ。

26. ノドモト スグレバ アツサ ヲ
    ワスル。

27. オニ ノ チンブツ。

28. クチ ニ ト ハ タテラレヌ。

29. ヤスモノ カイノ ゼニ ウシナイ。

30. マガラ子バ ヨ ニ タ丶レズ。

31. ケヲ フイテ, キヅ ヲ モトム。

32. フルキ ヲ タズ子テ アタラシキ
     ヲ シル。

33. コトバ オホケレバ, シナ
     スクナシ。

34. エミ ノ ウチ ニ, ヤイバ ヲ
     フクム。

35. テノ ウラ ヲ カヘス。

36. アタマ ソラン ヨリ コ丶ロ ヲ
     ソレ。

37. サル モ キ カラ オチル。

38. キングン ミ丶 ニ サカフ。

39. ユダン, タイテキ。

40. メクラ ヘビ ニ オヂズ。

41. ミメ ヨリ コヽロ。

42. シユ ニ マジハレバ. アカク ナル。

43. エバ ハ ニクキ モノ ニ アタヘ ヨ。

44. ヒト ノ ヨ ヲ ワタル ハ マルキバレ ノ ゴトレ。

45. モヘクヒ ニ ハ ヒ ガ ツキ ヤスイ。

46. センドウ オホク シテ フ子 ヤマ ヘ ノボル。

47. スミカキ ノ ナカ カラ メイケン ガ デル。

48. イチ ジ セン キン。

II. THE HIRAGANA SYLLABARY.

92. Ordinarily the *Hiragana* syllabary has a different arrangement from that here given, but as a mnemonic aid it may be well to write it first in the same order as that of the *Katakana* syllabary already shown.

	A	I	U	E	O	
	あ ア	い イ	う ウ	え エ	れ オ	
K	か カ	き キ	く ク	け ケ	こ コ	
G	が ガ	ぎ ギ	ぐ グ	げ ゲ	ご ゴ	
S	さ サ	し シ	す ス	せ セ	そ ソ	
Z	ざ ザ	じ ジ	ず ズ	ぜ ゼ	ぞ ゾ	
T	た タ	ち チ	つ ッ	て テ	と ト	
D	だ ダ	ぢ ヂ	づ ヅ	で デ	ど ド	
N	な ナ	に ニ	ぬ ヌ	ね 子	の ノ んン	
H	は ハ	ひ ヒ	ふ フ	へ ヘ	ほ ホ	
B	ば バ	び ビ	ぶ ブ	べ ベ	ぼ ボ	
P	ぱ バ	ぴ ピ	ぷ プ	ぺ ぺ	ぽ ポ	
M	ま マ	み ミ	む ム	め メ	も モ	
Y	や ヤ	い イ	ゆ ユ	え エ	よ ヨ	
R	ら ラ	り リ	る ル	れ レ	ろ ロ	
W	わ ワ	ゐ ヰ	う ウ	ゑ エ	を ヲ	

III. TRANSCRIPTION OF THE ILLUSTRATIVE
PROVERBS.

93. As a further aid to memorizing the *Hiragana*, the student is advised to transcribe the Illustrative Proverbs above given, from the *Katakana* into the *Hiragana*, by a gradual substitution of the syllabics of the latter for the syllabics of the former. To this end, comparative groupings of the *Hiragana* syllables are here shown. The syllables are given, arranged in ten groups. The syllables most resembling one another are written side by side. Their distinguishing marks may thus be more easily discovered among their confusing resemblances. The arrangement, especially among the later groupings, is somewhat arbitrary and unequal, but it may serve its purpose. The characters having the most familiar, and the simplest, lines are presented first.

NOTE. The numbers which precede the proverbs, as here given, refer to the proverbs as numbered in the *Katakana* series, appearing on page 78. The purpose of the first numbering of the proverbs will be seen later.

The numbers which appear in the " *Notes on Pronunciation*," which follow each group of the *Hiragana* syllabics, refer to the paragraphs of the manual, bearing the same numbers.

a. **First Group :—**

か　く　へ　て　つ

KA　　KU　　HE　　TE　　TSU

ILLUSTRATIVE PROVERBS :—

14. かシラ かくシて ヲ ヲ かくサズ。
Kashira　　kakūshite,　　o　wo　　kakūsazu.

28. くチ ニ ト ハ タてラレヌ。
Kuchi　ni　to　wa　　taterarenū.

6. ヘタ ノ ナガ ダンギ。
Heta　　no　　naga　　dangi.

35. て ノ ウラ ヲ かヘス。
Te　　no　　ura　　wo　　kaésŭ.

19. つノ ヲ ナホス トて ウシ ヲ
Tsuno　　wo　　naosŭ　　tote,　　ushi　　wo

コロス。
korosŭ.

Notes on Pronunciation.

14. In the words *kakushite* and *kakusazu*, the sounds *u* and *i* are almost silent (**57** *f.*), excepting the *u* sound of the final *zu* in *kakusazu* (**8** *a.*). The particle ヲ *wo* retains its *w* sound (**22** *d.*). *Kashira* receives accent upon the first syllable, (**77** *Ex.*) The accent of *kakushite* is thrown forward to the first syllable (**78**).

28. For the pronunciation of the word *taterarenu* see **75** and **52.**

6. *Naga* (**5** *a.*) *Dangi* is pronounced distinctly as two syllables, *dan-gi*, the *n* being here the final tone for ダ (**11**).

35. The word pronounced *kaesu* is written *kahesu*. Its pronunciation is governed by the rule given in **42.**

b. **Second Group:—**

し す り い ん
SHI　　　SU　　　RI　　　I　　　N

42. しユ ニ マじハレバ アかく。
Shu　　ni　　majiwárebá　　akaku

ナル。
naru.

47. すミかキ ノ ナかかラ メいケん
Sumikaki　　no　　naka-kara　　meiken

が でル。
ga　　deru.

9. りか ニ かんムり を(ヲ) タダサズ。
  Rika   ni   kámmuri   wo   tadasázu.

1. いチ を キいて ジフ を しル。
  Ichi   wo   kiite   jŭ   wo   shiru.

48. いチ じ せん きん。
  Ichi   ji,   sen   kin.

Notes on Pronunciation.

42. For *shi-yu* coalesent as *shŭ*, see **50**. *Majiwareba* is pronounced with even tones, emphasizing slightly the distinguishing verbal termination *ba*.

47. *Meiken*, (**77** Ex). *Ga*, see **5** *b*.

9. *Kanmuri* pronounced *kammuri*, see **12**.

1. *Jifu* pronounced *jŭ*, see **50**.

c. **Third Group:—**

こ と ひ れ に
KO TO HI O NI

33. こ と バ れ ホ ケ レ バ し ナ
  Kótoba   *ōkerebá*   *shina*
すくナし。
  sŭkunáshi.

7. とんで ひ に いル ナつ ノ ムし。
  Tonde   hi   ni   iru   natsu   no   mushi.

44. ひと ノ ヨ を ワタル ハ マルキ
  Hito   no   yo   wo   watáru   wa   máruki
バ し ノ ご と し。
  hashi   no   gotóshi.

27. れ に ノ 子んブつ。
  Oni   no   nembutsŭ.

4. にんゲん　ワづか　ごジフ　ヂん。
Ningen　　*wazŭka*　　*gojŭ*　　*nen.*

Notes on Pronunciation.

33. *Kotoba*, in having the three full vowel sounds o, o, a is pronounced with scarcely any perceptible accent. The word written *ohokereba* is pronounced *ōkereba* according to rule **42.** For *sŭkunashi* see **57** *f.*

27. *Nembutzu* for nenbutzu, see **12.**

4. *Go ji fu = gojŭ* see **50.**

d. Fourth Group:—

さ　　き　　ち　　も　　む
SA　　KI　　CHI　　MO　　MU

37. さル　も　き　かラ　おつル。
Saru　*mo,*　*ki*　*kara*　*otsŭru.*

38. きんゲん　ミミ　に　さかフ。
Kingen　　*mimi*　*ni*　*sakáu.*

8. ちり　つもッて　ヤマ　と　ナル。
Chiri　*tsumótte*　*yama*　*to*　*naru.*

45. もエくひ　に　ハ　ひ　が　つき
Moyékui　　*ni*　*wa,*　*hi*　*ga*　*tsŭki*

ヤすい。
yásui.

23. むり　　が　　とホレバ　　だウり
Muri　　*ga*　　*tōreba,*　　*dōri*

ひッこむ。
hikkomu.

Notes on Pronunciation.

8. *Tsumotte* for *tsumotsute* see **55.**

45. *Moyekui* for *moyekuhi* see **42.** See **42** also for *ha ハ* read as *wa.*

23. *Tōreba* for *tohoreba,* see **45.** *Dōri* for *dauri* see **43**, and **40.** *Hikkomu* for *hitzukomu,* see **55.**

e. **Fifth Group :—**

う そ ら ろ る
U   SO   RA   RO   RU

24. うり ノ タ子 に ナすび ハ
Uri   no   tane   ni,   nasubi   wa

ハヘヌ 。
haénu.

18. そで うつし に もノ を ヤる 。
Sode   utsushi   ni,   mono   wo   yaru.

22. らくく ワ エダ に かヘラず 。
Rákkwa,   eda   ni   kawrázu.

2. ろん に マケて も り に かつ 。
Ron   ni   mákete   mo,   ri   ni   katsu.

11. る井ラん ヨり も アヤうし 。
Rúirán   yori   mo,   ayaúshi.

Notes on Pronunciation.

24. *Haeru* for *haheru* see **45**.

22. *Rakkwa* for *rakukuwa*, see **54** for the doubling of the *k* ; see **56** for the elision of the *u* sound from the second *ku*.

11. *Ayaushi* is an example of an exception under the rule referred to in **43**. In this word the syllabics ヤ ウ remain separate in sound.

よ ま け は ほ
YO   MA   KE   HA   HO

15. よメ が しウとメ に ナる 。
Yome   ga   shutome   ni   naru.

30. まがら子バ よに タタレず 。
Magáranebá,   yo   ni   tatarézu.

31. け を フ い て きず を もとむ。
　　Ke wo fúite, kizu wo motómŭ.

3. はり ノ アナ から てん を
　　Hari no ana kara, ten wo
　　ノ ぞく。
　　nozókŭ.

5. ほまレ アらん より ろ しり
　　Homáre arán yori, sóshiri
　　ナ かレ。
　　nakáre.

Notes on Pronunciation.

15. *Shūtome* written *shiutome* see **43**, *a.*

g.　**Seventh Group:—**

の　め　ぬ　ゆ　あ
NO　ME　NU　YU　A

26. のど もと すぐレバ あつさ を
　　Nodo moto súgurebá, atsŭsa wo
　　ワ する。
　　wasuru.

40. めくら へび に おぢず。
　　Mékura hebi ni ojizŭ.

10. ぬすびと を ミ て ナワ を ナフ。
　　Nusubito wo mite, nawa wo nau.

39. ゆ ダん タい てき。
　　Yudan, tai teki.

36. あタま そらん より こころ を
Atama   során   yori   kokoro   wo

そレ。
sore.

Note on Pronunciation.

10. *Nau* instead of *nŏ*, see **46.** As verb ending in *a u*, rather *a fu*, the separate vowel sounds are retained.

h. **Eighth Group:—**

ね	れ	わ	ゐ	に
NE	RE	WA	YI	E

20. ねずミ とる ねこ は つめ を
Nézumi   toru   neko   wa,   tsume   wo

かくす。
kakúsu.

17. れい すぐれば しつれい と ナる。
Réi   sugurebá,   shitsuréi   to   naru.

13. わざはひ も さいはひ の はし
Wazawái   mo   sáiwái   no   hashi

と ナる。
to   naru.

25. ゐご の ナか の かはづ ダいかい
Ido   no   naka   no   kawázu,   daikai

を しらず
wo   shirázu.

34. にミ の うち に ヤいば を
Emi   no   uchi   ni,   yaiba   wo

フくむ
fúkumu.

i. Ninth Group:—

な	を	た	ふ	ゑ
NA	WO	TA	FU	E(YE)

21. なきづら を はち が さす。
    Naki-zura   wo   hachi   ga   sasu.

12. をかめ はち もく。
    Okame,   hachi   mokŭ.

16. たま ゝがかざれば ひかり なし。
    Tama   migakazárebá,   hikári   nashi.

32. ふるき を たづねて あたらしき
    Furuki   wo   tázunete,   a'aráshĭki

    を しる。
    wo   shiru.

43. ゑば は にくき もの に あたへ
    Eba   wa   nikuki   mono   ni,   atáe

    よ。
    yo.

Notes on Pronunciation.

12. *Okame* for *wokame*, see **22** a.
43. *Atae* for *atahe* see **42**, note.

k. Tenth Group:—

み	や	せ
MI	YA	SE

41. みめ より こころ。
    Mime   yori,   kokoro.

29. やす　もの　かい　の　ぜに
　　Yasu　*mono*　*kai*　*no*　*zeni*

うしない。
ushinái.

26. せんごう　れほく　して　ふね
　　Sendō　*ōku*　*shite*　*fune*

やま　へ　のぼる。
yama　*ye*　*nobóru.*

Notes on Pronunciation.

　41.　For pronunciation of such words as *kokoro*, see **79**.
　46.　*Sendō* for *sendou* as written, see **43**.　*Ōku* for *ohoku* see
42.　For *he* pronounced *ye*, see **18**, and **42**.

SECTION SECOND.

ELEMENTS OF GRAMMAR.

It is still doubtful under what family of languages Japanese should be classed. There is no relationship between it and Aino, the speech of the hairy aborigines whom the Japanese conquerors have gradually pushed eastwards and northwards. In structure, though not to any appreciable extent in vocabulary, Japanese closely resembles Korean; and both it and Korean may possibly be related to Mongol and to Manchu, and therefore claim to be included in the Altaïc group. Be this as it may, Japanese is what is generally termed an agglutinative language, that is to say that it builds up its words and grammatical forms by means of suffixes loosely soldered to the root or stem.

BASIL HALL CHAMBERLAIN.

ELEMENTS OF GRAMMAR.

It is not proposed to attempt in this manual any thing like a complete presentation of the grammar of the Japanese language. But the progress of the student will be made much easier as he enters the next section, if, previously, he shall have become familiar with some of the most prominent facts peculiar to the usages of speech among the Japanese. The student should at least know in general how the Japanese classify and dispose of their words ; how ordinarily they modify them and relate them to one another ; and how they combine them into common phrases and sentences.

The Japanese language is quite different in structure and character from the languages of the West. Being the expression of the thinking of human beings it is, of course, essentially the same in its parts, composition and operation as all expression of human thought. It must name things, and tell somewhat about the things named ; in fact it must contain, in some form, practically all the "PARTS OF SPEECH" that are known in any language. But the Japanese language is, after all, a very different thing from any tongue known as Occidental. The Western student can not, consequently, make satisfactory progress in using its forms of expression, without first acquainting himself with its chief distinguishing characteristics, and without, also in a measure, investigating its peculiarities by the aid of acknowledged grammatical principles. In a primary way we shall now seek to do this work.

CHAPTER I.

CLASSES OF WORDS.

94. 1. Like all human beings the Japanese have words which are names of things, events, and persons, and are also names of certain relations among things, events and persons. These words are not divided by the native grammarians, as Western peoples divide such words. They are however equivalent to what we know as nouns, pronouns, numerals, adverbs, prepositions, conjunctions and interjections. These words are nearly all uninflected. The Japanese separate them into two classes according to their importance, namely, as *a.* な NA, and *b.* てにをは TENIWOHA.

a. NA are NAME-WORDS proper.

b. The TENIWOHA are the suffixed words, or PARTICLES, which in Japanese speech are equivalent to Western prepositions, conjunctions and, we may also say, interjections. They are also like the signs of case in declension. These particles further serve as terminal inflections for verbs and adjectives.

95. 2. Also, like other human beings the Japanese have words which express qualities of things; and words also which tell of how things, events and persons exist, act, and endure. These words are equivalent to what we of the West know as adjectives and as verbs. The Japanese grammarians call them ことば KOTOBA, "words," or はたらき ことば HATARAKI-KOTOBA, i.e. "working words," so naming them not because they are in largest part the words of action, the vital force in speech; but because they are active words; words undergoing constant change. They are inflected in many ways to show time, mood and other states and changes of being and action.

NOTE. Dr. J. J. Hoffmann, in the introduction to his " Japanese Grammar," says of the *kotoba*, it is " the word (*verbum*) by eminence and is considered as the living element (*Hataraki-kotoba*, working word) of the sentence." But Mr W. G. Aston in Chapter II. of his " Grammar of the Written Language " has this pertinent foot note. " In the ことば の ちかみち *Kotoba no Chikamichi*, *na* are called (な ことば) *i-kotoba*, or words which remain at rest as opposed to (はたらき ことば) *hataraki-kotoba*, or words of action, the term which in that treatise has been applied to the *kotoba* of older writers. By 'rest' and 'action' are here meant 'want of inflection' and 'inflection,' and *hataraki*, 'working' or ' action,' has no reference to the usual meaning of verbs as expressing action."

In the Japanese language therefore there are properly but two classes of words :—1. Uninflected words, including NA and TENIWOHA; and 2. Inflected words *i.e.* the working words, HATARAKI-KOTOBA. Any distinctions which foreign students may make among Japanese words other than those here given, are not made in accordance with the Japanese way of dealing with language, but simply that they may meet their own convenience in study.

CHAPTER II.

ARRANGEMENT OF WORDS IN SPEECH.

The Japanese have ways, peculiar to themselves, of putting the NAMES and the WORKING-WORDS together.

96. 1. Mr. W. G. Aston in his "Grammar of the Japanese Spoken Language," thus describes the order of words in a sentence ; "The first place in a Japanese sentence is occupied by the nominative case, the next by the indirect object of the verb or by a noun followed by a postposition, the third by a direct object of the verb (accusative case), and the last by the verb or the adjective in the verbal form."

Among the illustrative proverbs **(91.)** used for these lessons, Proverb 18 shows the order here described. (あの ひと は *Ano hito wa*) そで うつし に *sode-utsushi ni* もの を *mono wo* やる *yaru*. Literally,—(" *That person as for*," subject understood),—" *sleeve transferring in* " or " *by*," indirect object,—" *thing* " followed by accusative sign *wo*, direct object,—" *gives*," verb. Or, " *He, by transferring through his sleeve, thing gives.*" More freely rendered the proverb means, " He gives a thing secretly by passing it through his sleeve " *i.e.* the long sleeve of the Japanese dress.

Exception :—An exception to this order of words arises in making comparisons, when the object with which the comparison is made is usually put first.

Proverb 41, is みめ より こゝろ " *Mime yori, kokoro.*" Literally,—" *Face than, heart.*" Freely rendered, " The heart is better than the face," *i.e.*, " Goodness of heart is to be preferred to beauty of face."

97. 2. The fundamental law governing the combinations and relations of Japanese speech is that the words, clauses &c. qualified, follow the words, clauses &c. which qualify them. Prof. B. H. Chamberlain in his "Handbook of Colloquial Japanese," thus summarizes this rule :— "The adjective or genitive precedes the noun which it defines, the adverb precedes the verb, and explanatory or dependent clauses precede the principal clause. The object likewise precedes the verb. The predicative verb or adjective of each clause is placed at the end of that clause, the predicative verb or adjective of the main clause rounding off the entire sentence."

Examples :—

In Proverb 21, なきづらをはちがさす *Naki zura wo, hachi ga sasu,* "Weeping face (ᵃᶜᶜ.ₛᵢgₙ) bees sting," or, "Bees sting a weeping face," なき *naki,* "weeping," precedes づら *zura (tsura),* "face."

In Proverb 24, うりのたねになすびははえぬ *Uri no tane ni, nasubi wa hayenu,* "Melon of seed from, egg plant (ⁿᵒᵐ.ₛᵢgₙ) does not grow ;" or, "An egg-plant does not grow from a melon's seed," the genitive うりの *Uri no,* "melon's," precedes たね *tane,* "seed."

In Proverb 42, しゆにまじはればあかくなる *Shu ni majiwareba, akaku naru,* "Vermillion with if you are intimate, red becomes ;" or "If you handle vermillion you will become red." Here the adverbial adjective form, あかく *akaku,* "red," precedes the verb なる *naru,* "becomes."

Then, in Proverb 34, えみのうちにやいばをふくむ *Emi no uchi ni, yaiba wo fukumu,* "Smile of interior in, sword (ᵃᶜᶜ.ₛᵢgₙ) conceals ;" or, "Conceals a sword, within a smile," the explanatory and subordinate clause, *Emi no uchi ni,* "within a smile," precedes *yaiba wo fukumu,* "conceals a sword."

In Proverb 3, はりのあなからてんをのぞく *Hari*

no ana kara, ten wo nozoku, " *Needle of hole from, heaven* (acc. sign) *peep at* ; " or " To peep at the heavens through a needle's eye," the object てん *ten*, "heaven," precedes のぞく *nozoku*, " to peep at."

In Proverb 1, いちをきいてじふをしる *Ichi wo kiite, jū wo shiru*, " *One* (acc. sign) *hearing, ten* (acc. sign) *knows* ; " or " Having heard one thing, he knows ten," the predicative verbs きいて *kiite*, and しる *shiru*, end the clause, and the sentence.

98. 3. *a.* It is customary in Japanese speech, when two or more nouns are coordinated in a sentence, for the last noun of the series to take the particle belonging to each.

Example :—

Here are linked together a series of nouns, in which only the last receives the declension sign of the accusative:—だれ が あめ つち ひ つき みづ かげ ひ を おつくり なされました か *Dare ga ame, tsuchi, hi, tsuki, mizu, kaze, hi wo otsukuri, nasaremashita ka*, " *Who* (nom. sign) *heaven, earth, sun, moon, water, air, fire* (acc. sign *wo*) *august-author has become?* " Or, " Who has made heaven, earth, sun, moon, water, air and fire ?"

b. It is the rule also when several verbs or adjectives succeed one another in a sentence, that the last verb or adjective only takes the inflection or particle belonging to each, and that the verbs or adjectives preceding take the gerund, or indefinite Main Stem form.

Illustrative of *b.* is Proverb 8:—ちり つもつて やま と なる *Chiri tsumotte, yama to naru*, " *Dust heaping, mountain becomes ;* " or, " Dust heaped up becomes a mountain."

99. 4. In Japanese speech quotation is usually made without any change in the form of the words quoted (71). The added particle と (*to*), " that," with some verb meaning "said," points out the quotation. A quoted sentence thus is repeated as orignally spoken and is closed by the words, " that he said."

Example :—

みやうにち まゐる と いゝ ました *Myonichi mairu, to iimashita.* " 'To-morrow I come,' that he said "; or, " He said, ' I will come to-morrow.' "

100. 5. Interrogation is indicated by the particle か *ka?* at the end of a clause or sentence. (**66.**)

Example :—

きました か *Kimashita ka.* " Has he come ? " きました *Kimashita.* " He has come."

101. 6. Expressions concerning time ordinarily precede expressions concerning place.

Examples :—

いちじ から がくかう に いく *Ichi ji kara, gakkō ni iku.* " From one o'clock I go to school ;" or, " I go to school at one o'clock."

102. 7. Final verbs and adjectives are often omitted and understood in many colloquial phrases. The meaning is clear without them.

For example :—

It is not necessary to say おはやう ございます *O hayō gozaimasŭ,* in friendly morning greeting ; おはやう *O hayō,* is sufficient. The verb ございます *gozaimasŭ,* though used among comparative strangers for the sake of formal politeness, is generally dropped among intimate friends. ちよいと *Choito!* " A little ! " is a call to a friend, meaning ちよいと (こちらへ おいで なさい) *Choito (kochira ye o ide nasai).* " *A little here to, honorably come, deign ;*" or, " Please come here for a moment." Many other like forms of speech are in use.

CHAPTER III.

WESTERN GRAMMAR IN JAPANESE SPEECH.

I. THE ARTICLE.

103. There is no ARTICLE among Japanese words.

When a speaker of the Japanese language wishes to single out, or to make definite, any thing named, he does so by the use of pronouns, verbs, adjectives and various distinguishing phrases. So far as its ordinary construction is concerned, the Japanese language is both indefinite and impersonal.

For example :—

In English "the book," invariably points out a particular book which has in some way been previously brought to one's attention. To reach the same end in Japanese one must say something like "book just named," "bought book," "book this man wrote," "that book servant just brought," and like periphrases.

II. THE NOUN.

In the Japanese language the NOUN, *i.e.* the name proper, is not inflected in any way to distinguish for it number, gender or case. In other words, the Japanese noun has no declension.

1. NUMBER.

104. *a.* SINGULAR. If, however, it is necessary to specify only one thing of a kind, the numeral for "one," ひとつ *hitotsu*, ひと *hito*, or いち *ichi*, is added to the noun either as prefix or suffix.

For example :—

ほん ひとつ *hon-hitotsu,* "one book" = "a book;" いち じ *ichi ji,* "one syllable" = "a syllable"; ひと はこ *hito-hako,* "one box" = "a box."

b. PLURAL. When more than one thing is referred to, the Japanese add such words as ども *domo,* がた *gata,* ら *ra,* しう *shū,* and たち *tachi* to the noun.

For example :—

わたくし ども *watakushi-domo* = "we;" あなた がた *anata gata* = "you;" こども ら *kodomo ra* = "children"; ひやくせう しう *hyakushō shū* = "farmers"; やくにん たち *yakunin-tachi* = "officers." Among these plural suffixes, がた *gata* and たち *tachi* are used for polite speech; among the others ら *ra* is least courteous.

c. Plurality is also shown in many instances by doubling the noun.

For example :—

われ われ *ware ware* = "we"; いろ いろ *iro iro* = "all kinds"; くすり ぐすり *kusuri-gusuri,* = "medicines"; ところ どころ *tokoro-dokoro* = "places"; くに ぐに *kuni-guni* "countries," and so on.

2. GENDER.

105. Difference in gender is indicated in a very few cases by the use of different words.

For example :—

をとこ *otoko,* "man ;" をんな *onna* "woman ;" むすこ *musuko,* "boy" ("son"); むすめ *musume,* "girl" ("daughter").

Sometimes sex is distinguished by a prefix, を *o* or をん *on,* as masculine ; め *me* or めん *men,* as feminine.

Example :—

を うし *o ushi,* "a bull ;" or めん どり *men dori,* "a hen."

But these distinctions are exceptional. Japanese words, as a rule, ignore number or sex. Such qualifications must usually be inferred from the rest of the sentence.

3. CASE.

106. By the use of particles, as suffixes, equivalents for the case forms common to the Western languages may be expressed.

ILLUSTRATIVE WORD.

やま *Yama*, "mountain."

Nom.	やまが (or は)	*Yama ga* (or *wa*) = "a mountain."
Gen.	やまの	*Yama no* = "of a mountain."
Dat.	やまに (or へ)	*Yama ni* (or *ye*) = "to a mountain."
Acc.	やまを	*Yama wo* = "a mountain."
Voc.	やまよ	*Yama yo!* = "O mountain!"
Abl.	やまより (or から)	*Yama yori*, (or *kara* &c.)
		= "from a mountain." &c.

4. CLASSES OF NOUNS.

107. As in all other languages, so in Japanese, nouns are of various kinds ;—SIMPLE, DERIVATIVE and COMPOUND.

108. *a.* SIMPLE NOUNS. These are original, undecomposable nouns, or, at least, names whose components are no longer separable without destroying the words : such as て *te* "hand"; と *to* "door"; いぬ *inu* "dog"; やま *yama* "mountain"; くに *kuni* "country."

109. *b.* DERIVATIVE NOUNS. These nouns are formed in Japanese by adding either prefixes or suffixes to nouns and to other words. There are for example :—

110. *α. Abstract Nouns.* These nouns are derived chiefly from the stems of adjectives by adding to them the syllable さ *sa*, which is equivalent to the English "ness."

For example :—

あつさ *atsusa* = "hotness," or "heat,"; たかさ *takasa* = "highness," or "height"; おもさ *omosa*, "heaviness," or "weight," and so on.

III. The word こと *koto* "fact," added to true adjectives forms also equivalents of abstract nouns, as :—しろい こと *shiroi koto* "white fact," or "whiteness ;" ふかい こと *fukai koto* "deep fact," or "depth," and the like.

112. The same word こと *koto*, added to some verbal forms, also produces equivalents of abstract nouns: as こまること *komaru koto* = "trouble fact," or "anxiety;" できない こと *dekinai koto* = "can not fact," or "impossibility;" しらない こと *shiranai koto* = "know not fact," or "ignorance."

113. *β. Concrete Nouns.* By the addition of the word もの *mono* "thing," to adjectives and certain verbal forms equivalents of concrete nouns are produced. *For example* :—あを もの *ao mono* made up from " green," and " thing," = " vegetables ;" うまい もの *umai mono* from " delicious," and " thing," = " delicacy ;" ぬひ もの *nui mono* from " sew," and " thing," = " embroidery," or " needlework," いれ もの *ire mono*, from " put into, " and " thing," = " receptacle."

114. *γ. Diminutive Nouns.* These nouns are formed by prefixing こ *ko* " little," to nouns, as :—こ いぬ *ko inu* " little dog," or " puppy ;" こ やま *ko yama* "little mountain," or " hill," and so on.

115. *δ. Augmentative Nouns.* The prefix おほ *ō* = " great," forms with nouns a class of magnifying nouns, such as :—おほ やま *ō yama*, " great mountain ;" おほ あらし *ō arashi* = " great storm," or " tempest ;" おほ ぶね *ō bune* = " great boat," or "ship ;" おほ ぐらい *ō gurai* = " a great eater," or " glutton."

116. *Verbal Nouns.* The Main Stems of verbs are often used as nouns. *For example:—* そしる *soshiru* means "to speak evil," そしり *soshiri* the Main Stem of *soshiru* is used in Proverb 5, as equivalent to "evil speaking;" よろこぶ *yorokobu* means "to be happy," and よろこび *yorokobi* = joy; わらふ *warau* = "to laugh," わらい *warai* = "laughter;" ひかる *hikaru* = "to shine," ひかり *hikari* = "lustre," or "brightness." つき *tsuki* in Proverb 45, is the Main Stem of つく *tsuku* "cleaves to," or "fastens on," used substantively in the sense of "the act of applying fire."

117. COMPOUND NOUNS. This class of nouns is numerous, and may be indefinitely enlarged. The compound nouns are for the most part composed as follows :—

118. *α.* A noun with a preceding qualifying noun. *For example:—* くすりや *kusuri ya*, made up of "medicine," and "house," = "drug-store ;" がくもん *gakumon*, from "learning," and "gate," = "science;" かまくら *Kamakura* from "sickle," and "ware-house," = name of a celebrated city.

119. *β.* A noun combined with an adjective preceding. *For example:—* わるくち *warukuchi*, made up of "bad," and "mouth," = "evil speaking ;" たかごゑ *takagoe* from "high," and "voice," (こゑ *koe*) = "loud voice ;" やすもの *yasu mono* from "cheap," and "thing," = "cheap article;" めいけん *mei ken* from "famous" and "two-edged sword," = "famous sword."

120. *γ.* A noun combined with a verbal form preceding. *For example:—* なきづら *naki zura*, made up of "weeping," and "cheek," (つら *tsura*) = "crying face ;" ぬすびと *nusubito*, from "steal," and "person," = "thief ;" もえくひ *moyekui* from "burn," and "stake," = "brand," or "charred stick."

121. *δ.* A noun combined with a verbal form following. *For example:*—すみ かき *sumi kaki*, made up from "charcoal," and "to scrape," = "fire-scraper;" ひと ごろし *hito goroshi*, from "person," and "killing," = murder or murderer; なつ まけ *natsu make* from "summer," and "lose in contest," = "summer-languor."

122. ε. Two verbal forms combined are often used substantively. *For example:*—かち まけ *kachi make*, made up of "win," and "lose," = "the question of victory or defeat;" ひきかへ *hikikaʾ*, from "draw," and "return," = "exchange"; ぬきがき *nukigaki*, from "draw out," and "write down," = "an epitome," or "abstract."

SPECIAL NOTE. *a.* In compound nouns the consonantal element of the first syllabic of the second word of the compound, as a rule, receives the にごり *nigori* (4), and is correspondingly changed in pronunciation. *For example:*— たかごゑ *taka-goe* has ごゑ *goe* for こゑ *koe*; なきづら *naki-zura* has づら *zura* for つら *tsura*; ぬすびと *nusu-bito* has びと *bito* for ひと *hito*: ひとごろし *hito-goroshi* has ごろし *goroshi* for ころし *koroshi*: ぬき がき *nuki-gaki* has がき *gaki* for かき *kaki*.

Prof. B. H. Chamberlain thus formulates the law concerning these changes;—"The broad law governing the use of the にご *nigori*, is that the initial surd, (*ch, sh, f, h, k, s, ts* or *t*,) of an independent word,—especially of a noun,—changes into the corresponding sonant (*j, b, g, z* or *d*) when the word is used as the second member of a compound."

b. In compounds the vowel element of the terminal syllabic of the first word of the compound often changes. Especially does the *e* element change into the *a* sound, as :—

たかはら *taka-hara*, "bamboo-grove," a compound of たけ *take*, and はら *hara*; さかをけ *saka oke* "a sake vat," compounded of さけ *sake*, and をけ *oke*; しらは *shira ha*, "white teeth," compounded of しろ *shiro*, and は *ha*; かざ でつぼう *kaza-deppō*, "air-gun," compounded of かぜ *kaze*, and てつぼう *teppō*; うは ぐつ *uwa-gutsu* "overshoes," or "slippers," compounded of うへ *ue*, and くつ *kutsu*.

III. THE PRONOUN.

The SUBSTITUTES FOR NOUNS used by the Japanese are nouns which, by long service, have become purely pronominal. They are gathered into several groups expressing the different degrees of politeness or respect peculiar to Japanese speech.

123.   1. PERSONAL PRONOUNS.

SINGULAR.

First Person.	I.	わたくし *watakushi* (polite); わたし *watashi* (familiar, and used by women).
		ぼく *boku* (used by students and soldiers).
		てまへ *temae* (humble); それ *ore* (rude).
Second Person.	You.	あなた *anata* (polite); おまへ さん *omae san* (familiar).
		きみ *kimi* (used by students &c.).
		おまへ *omae* (used by superiors); きさま *kisama* (rude).
Third Person.	He.	あの おかた *ano o kata* (polite); あの ひと *ano hito* (familiar).
	She.	*ano o kata* (polite); あの をんな *ano onna* (familiar).
		あれ *are* (rude, for "he" or "she").
	It.	それ *sore*.

PLURAL.

Plurals for these pronouns are formed as for nouns, by adding ど も *domo,* がた *gata,* ら *ra,* しう *shū* and たち *tachi.*

There are other substitutes for personal pronouns, but the names just given will serve for the present. It is to be noted especially that Japanese speakers make but very little use of personal pronouns.

124. 2. POSSESSIVE PRONOUNS. The particle *no* added to the personal pronoun forms makes them *possessive :*—

わたくし の *watakushi no,* "my," or "mine ;" あなた の *anata no,* "your," or "yours ;" わたくし ども の *watakushi domo no,* "our," or "ours."

125. 3. DEMONSTRATIVE PRONOUNS. The chief words for pointing out, directing attention, are the pronominal nouns :—

126. *a.* これ *kore,* "this one," when the object is near, or possessed by, the speaker ; それ *sore,* "that one," when the object is near, or in possession of the person spoken to, and あれ *are,* "that one," when the object is far away, or not in possession of the person spoken to. Also :—

127. *b.* この *kono* "this," その *sono* "that," and あの *ano* "that," are words used as pronominal adjectives. They are used in the same relations respectively, as,—これ *kore,* それ *sore* and あれ *are.*

128. *c.* Besides these words, there are such derivatives as,—こんな *konna,* "this kind of," そんな *sonna,* "that kind of," and あんな *anna,* "that kind of," and their equivalents かう いふ *kō iu,* "this called," さう いふ *sō iu,* "that called," and あゝ いふ *ā iu,* "that called."

ILLUSTRATIVE PHRASES :—

これ は いくら です か *Kore wa ikura desu ka?* "As for this one, how much is it ?"

それ は てうど よい *Sore wa chōdo yoi.* "As for that one, (it is) just right."

あれ は なん です *Are wa nan desu?* "As for that, what is (it)?"

この みち *Kono michi.* "This road."

その はこ *Sono hako.* "That box."

かう いふ らふそく *Kō iu rōsoku.* "This kind of a candle."

129. 4. INTERROGATIVE PRONOUNS. The chief words used for inquiring, or asking questions, are the pronominal nouns だれ *dare,* "who," どれ *dore,* "which," and なに *nani,* "what." Among other words used in the same way the adjective どなた *donata,* "which side," (a polite substitute for どれ *dore*), is of especial importance.

ILLUSTRATIVE PHRASES :—

だれ が さう いつた *Dare ga sō itta?* "Who said so?" (familiar.)

どなた です *Donata desu?* "Who is it?" (polite.)

どれ が いちばん いゝか *Dore ga ichiban ii ka?* "Which is the best?" (familiar.)

なに ご よう で ございます か *Nani go yō de gozaimasu ka?* "What honorable business is there?" *i.e.* what can I do for you?" (polite.)

130. 5. RELATIVE PRONOUNS. In the Japanese language reference, or relation, to another noun, or pronoun, in a sentence is secured by using the verb of the relative clause as an adjective. There are no relative pronouns proper.

ILLUSTRATIVE PHRASES :—

にげた どろぼう *Nigeta dorobō.* "The ran away robber," *i.e.* "the robber who ran away."

かれた まつ *Kareta matsu.* "The withered pine," *i.e.* "the pine which withered."

さいちらう と いふ ひと *Saichirō to iu hito.* "Saichirō

that called person," *i.e.* "the person who is named Saichirō."

131. 6. INDEFINITE PRONOUNS. There are certain words which, used pronominally to express distribution, number, quantity, comparison &c., may be called indefinite pronouns. These words are formed by adding か *ka*, も *mo*, でも *demo*, and ぞ *zo* to the interrogatives, as:—

だれ か *dare ka*, "somebody."

だれ も *dare mo*, "anybody," or "somebody."

だれ で も *dare de mo*, "anybody."

なに か *nani ka*, "anything."

なん で も *nan de mo*, "anything whatever."

どれ か *dore ka*, "some one thing."

どれ も *dore mo*, "any one thing," or "nothing."

どれ で も *dore de mo*, "anything whatever."

なに も *nani mo*, "anything," or "nothing."

なん ぞ *nan zo*, "anything."

Polite form for だれ *dare*,—

どなた か *donata ka*, "somebody."

どなた も *donata mo*, "everybody."

どなた で も *donata de mo*, "anybody."

だれ も *dare mo*, どれ も *dore mo*, and なに も *nani mo*, are, as a general rule, used with negative verbs, and are equivalent to the English words "nobody," and "nothing."

ILLUSTRATIVE PHRASES:—

だれ か さう いつた *Dare ka sō itta.* "Somebody said so."

だれ も しつて いません *Dare mo shitte imasen.* "Nobody knows it."

だれ で も しつて います *Dare de mo shitte imasu.* "Everybody knows it."

どなた も いかれません *Donata mo ikaremasen.* "Nobody can go."

どなたでもいかれる *Donata de mo ikareru.* "Anybody can go."

どれか ひとつ ちやうだい *Dore ka hitotsu chōdai.* "Please give me one or the other."

どれも いけませんか *Dore mo ikemasen ka.* "Wont one of these suit you?"

どれでも ちやうだい *Dore de mo chōdai.* "Please give me any one of them.

なにか ちやうだい *Nani ka chōdai.* "Please give me something."

なにも ありません *Nani mo arimasen.* "I have nothing at all."

なんでも よろしい *Nan de mo yoroshii.* "Anything whatever will do."

IV. THE VERB.

VERBS, or the words which assert, or declare, something about the things named by nouns, are peculiarly treated in the Japanese language.

1. CLASSES OF VERBS.

132. As in other languages, so in the Japanese language, the verbs, in accordance with their use, separate into two main classes, TRANSITIVE and INTRANSITIVE. That is, some verbs have objects which receive the action expressed by them, and others of the verbs express the action fully in themselves.

For example:— なほす *naosu* "I mend," or "cure," is a transitive verb. On hearing it spoken one wishes to know what is mended, or who is cured. But なほる *naoru* "I get well," describes in itself fully the action it expresses. なほる *naoru* is an intransitive verb.

133. The transitive or intransitive character of Japanese verbs, however, does not show itself in any peculiarity of structure. Many verbs having roots or stems in common, as transitive or as intransitive, have reciprocally different terminations.

For example,—カヘす *kaesu* "give back," or "return," is transitive, and カヘる *kaeru* "return," is intransitive. But this peculiarity does not definitely distinguish these verbs as transitive, and as not transitive. There are verbs which have just the contrary formation and character, as,—たつ *tatsu* "stand," which is intransitive, and たてる *tateru* "set up," which is transitive. But やく *yaku* "burn," is transitive, and やける *yakeru* "burn," is intransitive ; while あく *aku* "be open," is intransitive, and あける *akeru* "open," is transitive. Only by familiarity with its use can a student know whether a Japanese verb is transitive or not.

2. NUMBER AND PERSON.

134. Japanese verbs have no forms which show either number or person.

For example,—the word なほす *naosu* whose meaning is "mend," or "cure," remains the same in a sentence whether one intends to say "I, you, we, or they, mend," or "he, she, or it, mends ; " so also まける *makeru* "lose," or "lower a price," stands for "I, you, we, or they, lower a price," or "he, she, or it, loses." This fact holds good for every verb.

135. *a.* Distinction of PERSON is generally understood through the use of pronouns. Especially by the use of humble or honorific verbs does a speaker make it known whether he is referring to himself, or to others.

b. Distinction of NUMBER, when necessary, is made by the use of associated pronouns, numerals, and by other auxiliary words.

3. TENSE.

136. Inflection of verbs for the purpose of specifying the TIME of the action, or the state, told of by the verbs, is almost wholly confined to forms which indicate present, or past time, and this time as either certain, or probable. In Japanese speech therefore there are properly only four tenses:—*1. The Certain Present; 2. The Probable Present; 3. The Certain Past, and 4. The Probable Past.*

a.   *Future time* is expressed by words associated with the present tenses, and often by the Probable Present tense alone.

1.   The verb, *e.g.,* なほす *naosu,* or まける *makeru,* has thus really by inflection only four tenses, as follows :—

TENSE.	ヂ台すなほす NAOSU.直す	まける MAKERU.	負け
Certain Present.	なほす *naosu,* mend, or mends.	まける *makeru,* lose, or loses.	
Probable Present (or Future.)	なほさう *naosō (naosa-u),* probably mends, or will mend.	まけやう *makeyō,* probably loses, or will lose.	
Certain Past.	なほした *naoshita,* mended.	まけた *maketa,* lost.	
Probable Past.	なほしたらう *naoshitarō,* probably mended.	まけたらう *maketarō,* probably lost.	

137.   2.   There is a further time inflection of Japanese verbs, an indefinite tense form. It is named *The Alternative,* or *Frequentative Form.* It seldom is used without a companion word having the same inflection. Its function is to show occasional action, or alternation of action. *E.g.* :—

Alternative Form.	なほしたり *naoshitari,* sometimes mends.	まけたり *maketari,* sometimes loses.

4. MODE.

138. Inflection for the purpose of showing the MODE or MANNER of the assertion made by the verbs consists of forms expressing simple declaration, contingency or doubt, and command. That is, there are (1) Indicative, (2) Subjunctive, and (3) Imperative Mode forms among Japanese verbs.

The Subjunctive Mode consists practically of two forms, *a.* The Conditional, and *b.* The Concessive, according as the action of the verb shows dependence, or involves concession.

TENSE.	1. INDICATIVE MODE.	
Present.	なほす *naosu,* (I) mend.	まける *makeru,* (he) loses.
Past.	なほした *naoshita,* (he) mended.	まけた *maketa,* (I) lose.

TENSE.	2. SUBJUNCTIVE MODE. *a.* CONDITIONAL.	
Present.	なほせば *naoseba,* if (he) mend.	まければ *makereba,* if (she) lose.
Past.	なほしたら *naoshitara,* if (I) had mended.	まけたら *maketara,* if (he) had lost.

TENSE.	2. SUBJUNCTIVE MODE. b. CONCESSIVE.	
Present.	なほせど *naosedo*, though (he) mend.	まけれど *makeredo*, though (I) lose.
Past.	なほしたれど *naoshita-redo*, though (I) have mended.	まけたれど *maketaredo*, though (she) lost.

	3. IMPERATIVE MODE.	
	なほせ *naose*, mend!	まけろ *makero*, lose!

5.   ADJECTIVAL VERB FORMS.

139. There are some other forms of the verb whose uses give them a larger than verbal character: they are closely allied with adjectives. These forms are generally classed under the names, *a. Gerund, Participle, or Subordinative Form,* and *b. Desiderative Form,* or *Desiderative Adjective.*

GERUND.

なほして *naoshite*, mending, having mended.	まけて *makete*, losing, having lost.

DISIDERATIVE FORM.

なほしたい *naoshitai*, wishes to mend.	まけたい *maketai*, wishes to lose.

6.   PROCESS OF INFLECTION.

140. The ultimate element of the verb, or its simplest form, is named THE ROOT. From the root all inflection proceeds. In the Japanese verb the root is often hidden, or its immediate growth is difficult to trace. We need not attempt a study of this perplexing subject.

141. VERBAL INFLECTION, so far as the student of this manual need study it, may commence with certain developed forms of the verb which can be accepted as PRIMARY STEMS, or BASES, to which all further inflections have been joined. These forms are four ; and they are at but a small remove from the root. They give practical starting places for verbal study.

142. Western grammarians have named these primary verbal variations, not in accordance with their full functions, but after some especially prominent service they perform in speech. They have been designated by different writers, as :—1. "The Root," or "The Stem," or "The Indefinite Form"; 2. "The Negative Base"; 3. "The Indicative," or "The Certain Present," and 4. "The Conditional Base."

In exhibiting the inflection of the verb, some of the writers who have named one of the variations "The Root," or "The Stem," have treated the three other variations as though they were derived from this "root," or "stem," by a series of terminal changes. It is not probable that these forms were in fact so derived. The several stems apparently have only a root in common. In this manual these four primary inflection forms shall therefore be figured under the name STEMS OF INFLECTION.

143. The STEMS OF INFLECTION shall be treated as though related to one another like so many different stems separating from the same root. We do not propose, however, to make any essential change in the names which foreign grammarians, generally, have agreed to give to these four primary verbal variations. We shall adopt the names most commonly held, only modifying them so as to sustain the

metaphor *stem* here proposed, and substituting among them for the term "The Root," or "The Stem," or "The Indefinite Form," the term *The Main Stem.*

The four primary Japanese verbal variations as studied in this manual appear, therefore, as the STEMS OF INFLECTION, named severally,—

1. The Main Stem,
2. The Negative Stem.
3. The Certain Present Stem, and
5. The Conditional Stem.

144. *1. The Main Stem.* This primary variation supports a larger number of verbal inflections than any of the others. It terminates with a syllabic in either ɪ or ᴇ, as *for example:*—with し *shi* in なほし *naoshi* of the verb meaning "mend;" with け *ke* in まけ *make* of the verb meaning "lose;" and with ぢ *ji* in をぢ *oji* of the verb meaning "fear."

145. *a.* By the addition of various words and particles, the Main Stem supports the positive past tenses in all modes, also the positive alternative form, the positive gerund, and the desiderative form of all verbs. Moreover, it supports all the inflections of the large number of verbs which are grouped together as the Second Conjugation, and also all modes and tenses of the polite forms of inflection.

146. *b.* In sentences where several verbs occur in different clauses, each, however, characterized by the same time and mode, all the verbs, except the last, take the Main Stem form, leaving for the final verb the function of giving time and mode to the action of the whole sentence by means of proper inflection.

147. *c.* The Main Stem also appears at times as a noun ; also, it forms compounds with other parts of speech.

148. 2. *The Negative Stem.* This stem stands next

to the Main Stem in importance in the process of inflection. It terminates in a syllabic in A for all the verbs which are grouped together as the First Conjugation. In the Second Conjugation its terminal is either an E syllabic, or an I syllabic.

For example :—なほさ *naosa* is the Negative Stem for the verb meaning "mend;" まけ *make* for the verb "lose;" and をぢ *oji* for the verb "fear."

149. *a.* In the group of verbs making the First Conjugation, the Negative Stem supports nearly all negative inflections. It supports the probable present tense, and the passive, or potential, and causative inflections also.

150. *b.* In the Second Conjugation the Main Stem and the Negative Stem, as said before, are the same ; that is, the Negative Stem in the Second Conjugation is but a name given to the Main Stem, for the sake of convenience in exhibiting the verbal paradigms.

151. 3. *The Certain Present Stem.* This stem does not take any extended part in the process of inflection. It supports only the negative probable present, and the negative imperative inflections. It assists, also, in the formation of some *quasi* forms of inflection. Standing alone, it indicates the certain present tense.

152. *a.* In form, the Certain Present Stem terminates in a syllabic in U ; that is, in the First Conjugation its terminal is any one of the syllabics in U, but in the Second Conjugation its terminal is the syllabic RU suffixed to the Main Stem.

For example :—す *su* forming なほす *naosu* for the verb "mend;" and る *ru* forming まける *makeru* and をちる *ojiru* for the verbs "lose" and "fear," produce the Certain Present Stems of these verbs.

☞ **153.** *b.* *The Certain Present Stem has been selected as the name by which each verb is known.*

For example:—the verb meaning "mend" is なほす *naosu*; "lose" is まける *makeru*; "fear" is をぢる *ojiru*; "hear" is きく *kiku*; "know" is しる *shiru*; "wear" is きる *kiru*; "grow" is はねる *haeru*; "see" is みる *miru*; "eat" is たべる *taberu*; "go out" is でる *deru*, &c.

☞ **154.** *c. By means of the Certain Present Stem in connection with the Main Stem, the special groupings of Japanese verbs in Conjugation are determined.*

155. *d.* The Certain Present Stem does duty in speech not only as a verb, but often as a noun, and also as an adjective.

156. 4. *The Conditional Stem.* This stem serves to support inflection in the two forms of the subjunctive mode, *i.e.* the present conditional and the present concessive. It is also identical with the imperative mode of the verbs grouped in what is called the First Conjugation. In form it terminates in a syllabic in E; that is, in the First Conjugation its terminal is any one of the syllabics in E, but in the Second Conjugation its terminal is the syllabic RE suffixed to the Main Stem.

For example:—se forming なほせ *naose* for the verb "mend"; れ *re* forming まけれ *makere* and をぢれ *ojire* for the verbs "lose" and "fear," produce the Conditional Stems of these verbs.

157. SUMMARY

For the Verbs	なほす Nao su	まける Make ru	をぢる Oji ru
The Main Stem is	なほし nao shi	まけ make	をぢ oji.
The Negative Stem is	なほさ nao sa	まけ make	をぢ oji.

THE CERTAIN PRESENT STEM IS	なほ す *nao su*	まけ る *make ru*	おぢ る *oji ru.*
THE CONDITIONAL STEM IS	なほ せ *nao se*	まけ れ *make re*	おぢ れ *oji re.*

158. The PROCESS OF INFLECTION for Japanese verbs therefore takes its start, so far as it is examined in this manual, from these four Stems of Inflection: the Main Stem; and its associates,—the so-called Negative; the Certain Present; and the Conditional Stems. All verbal inflection will here be considered as proceeding from, or as being supported by, one or the other of these primary variations.

7. GROUPINGS IN INFLECTION: CONJUGATION.

159. As the PROCESS OF INFLECTION goes on from these primary variations,—the Stems of Inflection,—the verbal forms differentiate into two distinctly marked groups, which are named CONJUGATIONS. The two Conjugations may be distinguished as follows :—

160. 1. THE FIRST CONJUGATION. This conjugation consists of all verbs whose Main Stems end in a syllabic in I, and whose Certain Present Stems end in the U syllabic of the same series as that of the Main Stem terminal. (**154.**)

Illustrations:—If the Main Stem of a verb ends in キ *ki* and the Certain Present in ク *ku;* or, if further, the former ends in ギ *gi* and the other in グ *gu;* or in シ *shi* and in ス *su;* ジ *ji* and ズ *zu;* チ *chi* and ツ *tsu;* ヒ *hi* (*i*) and フ *fu* (*u*); ミ *mi* and ム *mu;* リ *ri* and ル *ru*, and so on throughout the several series of syllables as shown in the syllabary of the *Katakana* on page 24, that verb may be classed in the First Conjugation.

161. All the forms of inflection of verbs whose Main

Stems and Certain Present Stems are so marked follow one model,—euphonic changes in the stems excepted.

ILLUSTRATIVE VERBS :—

		MAIN STEM	CERTAIN PRESENT
	"mend"	なほし *naoshi*	なほす *naosu*
	"hear"	きゝ *kiki*	きく *kiku*
	"smell"	かぎ *kagi*	かぐ *kagu*
	"know"	しり *shiri*	しる *shiru*
	"look at"	のぞき *nozoki*	のぞく *nozoku*
勝フ	"win"	かち *kachi*	かつ *katsu*
	"enter"	いり *iri*	いる *iru*
綯ふ	"twist"	なひ *nai*	なふ *nau*
	"return"	かへり *kaeri*	かへる *kaeru*
	"draw back"	ひつこみ *hikkomi* ...	ひつこむ *hikkomu*
	"shine"	てり *teri*	てる *teru*
	"go" or "come"	まゐり *mairi*	まゐる *mairu*
	"row"	こぎ *kogi*	こぐ *kogu*
	"blow"	ふき *fuki*	ふく *fuku*
	"fly"	とび *tobi*	とぶ *tobu*
	"hold in the mouth"	ふくみ *fukumi*	ふくむ *fukumu*
	"pile up"	つもり *tsumori*	つもる *tsumoru*
探ル	"take" 把ル	とり *tori* 執ル	とる *toru* 捕ル
	"become" grow	なり *nari*	なる *naru*
	"climb"	のぼり *nobori*	のぼる *noboru*
遣ル	"give"	やり *yari*	やる *yaru*
	"buy"	かひ *kai*	かふ *kau*
在ル	"be"	あり *ari*	ある *aru*
	"go"	いき *iki*	いく *iku.* ?

162. *Euphonic Changes :*—In all verbs of the First Conjugation certain changes, chiefly euphonic, take place within the Main Stem during the process of inflection. These changes appear particularly in the gerund, in the past tenses, and in the alternative form.

To ILLUSTRATE :—

163. *a.* If the Main Stem ends in the KI syllabic, the consonantal element K is dropped.

Examples :—

VERB.	MAIN STEM.	GERUND.	CERTAIN PAST.	CONDITIONAL PAST, ETC.	ALTERNATIVE FORM.
やく *Yaku* burn.	やき *yaki*	やいて *yaite*	やいた *yaita*	やいたら *yaitara*	やいたり *yaitari*
きく *Kiku* hear.	きゝ *kiki*	きいて *kiite*	きいた *kiita*	きいたら *kiitara*	きいたり *kiitari*
とく *Toku* melt.	とき *toki*	といて *toite*	といた *toita*	といたら *toitara*	といたり *toitari*
せく *Seku* hurry.	せき *seki*	せいて *seite*	せいた *seita*	せいたら *seitara*	せいたり *seitari*
ふく *Fuku* blow.	ふき *fuki*	ふいて *fuite*	ふいた *fuita*	ふいたら *fuitara*	ふいたり *fuitari*
のぞく *Nozoku* peer.	のぞき *nozoki*	のぞいて *nozoite*	のぞいた *nozoita*	のぞいたら *nozoitara*	のぞいたり *nozoitari*

Exception:—ᴠᴧ〈 *iku* "go," Main Stem ᴠᴧ ᵻ *iki*, forms its gerund as 〉ᴄᴧᴧ *illi*, its past tenses and alternative form as ᴠᴧᴧᴛ *illa* etc., ᴠᴧᴧᴛ ᴑ *illari*.

164. *b.* If the Main Stem ends in the ᵻ *gi* syllabic, the consonantal element G is dropped and the T sound of the suffixes is changed into D.

Examples:—

VERB.	MAIN STEM.	GERUND.	CERTAIN PAST.	CONDITIONAL PAST &c.	ALTERNATIVE FORM.
Kagu smell.	*kagi*	*kaide*	*kaida*	*kaidara*	*kaidari*
Kogu row.	*kogi*	*koide*	*koida*	*koidara*	*koidari*
Hegu peel off.	*hegi*	*heide*	*heida*	*heidara*	*heidari*

165. *c.* If the Main Stem ends in the ぶ *bi* or む *mi* syllabic, the vowel element ɪ is dropped. The ʙ or ᴍ element is changed into an ɴ sound, and the ᴛ sound of the suffixes becomes the sound of ᴅ.

Examples :—

VERB.	MAIN STEM.	GERUND.	CERTAIN PAST.	CONDITIONAL PAST, ETC.	ALTERNATIVE FORM.
とぶ *Tobu* fly.	とぶ *tobi*	とんで *tonde*	とんだ *tonda*	とんだら *tondara*	とんだり *tondari*
あむ *Amu* weave.	あみ *ami*	あんで *ande*	あんだ *anda*	あんだら *andara*	あんだり *andari*
ひっこむ *Hikkomu* draw back.	ひっこみ *hikkomi*	ひっこんで *hikkonde*	ひっこんだ *hikkonda*	ひっこんだら *hikkondara*	ひっこんだり *hikkondari*
ふくむ *Fukumu* hold in the mouth.	ふくみ *fukumi*	ふくんで *fukunde*	ふくんだ *fukunda*	ふくんだら *fukundara*	ふくんだり *fukundari*

166. *d.* If the Main Stem ends in a ち *chi* syllabic, the vowel element ɪ is dropped, and the consonantal element CH, or rather TCH, is sounded with the suffixes as a doubled T.

Examples:—

VERB.	MAIN STEM.	GERUND.	CERTAIN PAST.	COND. PAST.	ALT. FORM.
Katsu win.	かち *kachi*	かって *katte*	かった *katta*	かったら *kattara*	かったり *kattari*
Motsu hold.	もち *mochi*	もって *motte*	もった *motta*	もったら *mottara*	もったり *mottari*
Butsu beat.	ぶち *buchi*	ぶって *butte*	ぶった *butta*	ぶったら *buttara*	ぶったり *buttari*

167. *e.* If the Main Stem ends in a り *ri* syllabic, the vowel element ɪ is dropped, and the consonantal element R is sounded with the suffixes as a doubled T.

Examples :—

Verb.	Main Stem.	Gerund.	Cert. Past.	Cond. Past, Etc.	Alt. Form.
つもる Tsumoru accumulate.	つもり tsumori	つもって tsumolle	つもった tsumolla	つもったら tsumollara	つもったり tsumollari
とる Toru take.	とり tori	とって tolle	とった tolla	とったら tollara	とったり tollari
なる Naru become.	なり nari	なって natte	なった natta	なったら nattara	なったり nattari
ある Aru be.	あり ari	あって atte	あった alla	あったら attara	あったり allari
しる Shiru know.	しり shiri	しって shitte	しった shilla	しったら shittara	しったり shillari
のぼる Noboru climb.	のぼり nobori	のぼって nobotte	のぼった nobotta	のぼったら nobottara	のぼったり nobottari
やる Yaru give	やり yari	やって yalle	やった yalla	やったら yattara	やったり yallari

168. *f.* If the Main Stem ends in the syllable い *i* or ひ *hi*, the vowel syllable is dropped, and the initial consonantal element of the suffixes, T, is doubled.

Examples :—

VERB.	MAIN STEM.	GERUND.	CERTAIN PAST.	COND. PAST, ETC.	ALTERNATIVE FORM.
なう *Nau* twist.	ない *nai*	なって *natte* / のうて *nōte*	なった *natta* / のうた *nōta*	なったら *nattara* / のうたら *nōtara*	なったり *nattari* / のうたり *nōtari*
かう *Kau* buy.	かい *kai*	かって *katte* / こうて *kōte*	かった *katta* / こうた *kōla*	かったら *kattara* / こうたら *kōtara*	かったり *kattari* / こうたり *kōtari*
いう *Iu* say.	いい *ii*	いって *itte* / いうて *iute*	いった *itta* / いうた *iuta*	いったら *ittara* / いうたら *iutara*	いったり *ittari* / いうたり *iutari*
わらう *Warau* laugh.	わらい *warai*	わらって *waratte*	わらった *waratta*	わらったら *warattara*	わらったり *warattari*

169. Note. In verbs of this class, properly speaking, the terminal syllabics belong to the H or Spirant series of syllables, and their euphonic changes follow the changes peculiar to the syllabics は *ha*, ひ *hi*, ふ *fwu*, へ *he*, ほ *ho*.

Especially to be noted is the fact that the Negative Stem appears as WA, and not as A or HA. For example, the Negative Stem of なふ *nau* (*nafu*) is なは *nawa* (*naha*) not *naa*. So, of かふ *kau* (*kafu*), かは *kawa* is the Negative Stem. Of いふ *iu* (*ifu*) いは *iwa*, and of わらふ *warau* (*warafu*) わらは *warawa*, are the Negative Stems. Thus with other verbs also.

170. 2. The Second Conjugation. The Second Conjugation consists of all verbs whose Main Stems end in a syllabic in either E, or in I, and whose Certain Present Stems are formed by the addition of the syllabic る *ru* to the Main Stems.

For example :—If the Main Stem of a verb ends in け *ke* and the Certain Present in ける *keru;* or further, the former in き *ki* and the other in きる *kiru;* or further, in せ *se* and in せる *seru;* ぢ *ji* and ぢる *jiru;* or ね *ne* and ねる *neru;* に *ni* and にる *niru;* or め *me* and める *meru;* or み *mi* and みる *miru*, and so on throughout the several series of the E and I series of syllabics, that verb is classed in the Second Conjugation.

Illustrative Verbs :—

	MAIN STEM	CERTAIN PRESENT
" lose "	まけ *make*	まける *makeru*
" fear "	れぢ *oji*	れぢる *ojiru*
" wear "	き *ki*	きる *kiru*
" sleep "	ね *ne*	ねる *neru*
" grow "	はえ *hae*	はえる *haeru*
" be "	ゐ *i*	ゐる *iru*
" get "	え *e*	える *eru*

	MAIN STEM	CERTAIN PRESENT
" go out "	で *de*	でる *deru*
" cool"	さめ *same*	さめる *sameru*
" see "	み *mi*	みる *miru*
" eat "	たべ *tabe*	たべる *taberu*
" bathe "	あび *abi*	あびる *abiru*
" break "	をれ *ore*	をれる *oreru*
" borrow "	かり *kari* . . . . :	かりる *kariru*.

171. In the Second Conjugation the process of inflection divides the inflected forms into TWO SERIES. These series are distinguished from one another, however, only by the syllabic in E, or in I, with which the Main Stem terminates. In all other respects the forms of inflection conform to one model. For this reason we group these two series of inflections in one Conjugation, and distinguish them as the. FIRST, and the SECOND, FORMS of the SECOND CONJUGATION.

8. PARADIGMS OF THE VERBS.

172. Japanese verbs may therefore be grouped into two Conjugations, and their process of inflection may be considered as being supported by FOUR STEMS.

TABLE OF STEM SIGNS.

FIRST CONJUGATION.		SECOND CONJUGATION.	
		FORM I.	FORM II.
Main Stem, ending with a syll. in I,		in E,	in I.
Negative Stem, ,, ,, ,, ,, ,, A,		,, E,	,, I.
Cert. Pres. Stem, ,, ,, ,, ,, ,, U,		,, ERU,	,, IRU.
Cond. Stem, ,, ,, ,, ,, ,, E,		,, ERE,	,, IRE.

Beginning with the form of the verb declaring direct, simple action, that is, with the primary variation here named the Main Stem, let us follow the process of inflection.

We shall take as illustrative verbs, the three which have been named なほす *naosu*, まける *makeru*, and をちる *ojiru*. The Main Stems of these verbs are なほし *naoshi*, まけ *make*, and をぢ *oji*.

173. 1. *The Main Stem,* as said before, bears a larger number of inflections than any of the other primary variations. In some verbs it is apparently the root of the word: in the Second Conjugation this stem in reality supports all inflection.

174. *a.* In the FIRST CONJUGATION for the verb なほす *naosu* we have the Main Stem—

なほし naoshi.

By the use of suffixes to the Main Stem the following forms are produced for this verb :—

Gerund	なほし－て	*naoshi-te,*	having mended, mending
Cert. Past	„	－た	„ -*ta,*	mended, have mended
Cond. „	„	－たら	„ -*tara,*	if (I) had mended
Prob. „	„	－たらう	„ -*tarō,*	probably (he) mended
Conc. „	, „	－たれど	„ -*taredo,*	though (he) mended
Alt. Form	„	－たり	„ -*tari,*	at times mending
Des. „	„	－たい	„ -*tai,*	(he) wishes to mend

175. NOTE. Polite inflection for the First Conjugation, and for the Second Conjugation also, is made by adding most of the inflected forms of the verb ます *masu* to the Main Stem of a verb. *For example:*—なほす *naosu* is made to serve polite speech under the form なほします *naoshimasu*. In the inflections of the verb compounded as なほします *naoshimasu*, only the suffix ます *masu* undergoes change.

176. *b.* In the SECOND CONJUGATION there are for the verbs まける *makeru* and をぢる *ojiru*, the Main Stems—

まけ *make* and をぢ *oji*

from which are produced the

Gerund	まけて *make te*	and	をぢて *oji te*
Certain Past „	„ た „ *ta* „	„	„ た „ *ta*
Cond. „ „	„ たら „ *tara* „	„	たら „ *tara*
Probable „	„ たらう „ *tarō* „	„	たらう „ *tarō*
Conces. „ „	„ たれど „ *taredo* „	„	たれど „ *taredo*
Alt. Form „	たり „ *tari* „	„	„ たり „ *tari*
Desid. Form „	たい „ *tai* „	„	„ たい „ *tai*

177. NOTE. But, besides these inflections which are here given simply for the purpose of running a parallel with the inflections of the First Conjugation just shown, the Main Stem really supports all the forms of inflection of the Second Conjugation, as appears in the process of inflection continued below.

178. 2. *The Negative Stem* is second in importance to the Main Stem in supporting inflection. It exists as an independent stem only in the First Conjugation. In the Second Conjugation, what is called the Negative Stem is only the Main Stem as it appears in the forms of inflection which correspond to the inflection forms supported by the First Conjugation Negative Stem.

179. *a.* In the FIRST CONJUGATION for the verb なほす *naosu* the Negative Stem is

なほさ *naosa.*

By the use of suffixes the following forms are produced from なほさ *naosa :—*

	Japanese	Romanized	English
Probable Present, (Pos.)	なほさう	naosa-u (naosō)	probably mend or shall mend
Certain (Neg.)	な "" ない	"" nu "" nai	do not, shall not, mend
Conditional ""	なば "" なければ	"" neba "" nakereba	if (I) do not mend
Concessive ""	など(も) "" なけれど	"" nedo (mo) "" nakeredo	though (he) does not mend
Certain Past ""	なかった "" なんだ	"" nakatta "" nanda	(he) did not mend
Probable ""	なかったらう "" なんだらう	"" nakattarō "" nandarō	probably he did not mend

Conditional Past (Neg.)	ナほゑナかつたら (ば)	*nawsanakattara (ba)*	if he does not mend
" "	ナんだら (ば)	" *nandara (ba)*	
Concessive "	ナんだれど (ゑ)	" *nandaredo (mo)*	though I do not mend
Alternative Form "	ナかつた り	" *nakattari*	at times not mending
	ナんだ り	" *nandari*	
Gerund "	ず	" *zu*	not mending, not having mended
	ナくて	" *nakutte*	

180. *b.* In the SECOND CONJUGATION as Negative Stems for the verbs まける *makeru* and おぢる *ojiru* there are まけ *make* and おぢ *oji* from which are produced :—

Form	まけう5 makeryō		and おどう5	おじう5 ojiyō
Probable Present (Pos.)				
" " (Neg.)	" まい mai	"	" まい	" mai
Certain "	{ " ぬ " nĕ	" ぬ	" ぬ	" nĕ
" "	{ " ぬく " mai	" ぬく mai	" ぬく	" mai
Conditional "	" なければ " nakerĕba	" なければ	" なければ nakerĕba
Concessive "	" なけれど (も) " nakeredo (mo)	" なけれど (も)	" nakeredo (mo)
Certain Past	" なかった " nakatta	" なかった	" nakatta
Probable "	" なかったら5 " nakattarō	" なかったら5 nakattarō
Conditional "	" なかったら (ば) " nakattara (ba)	" なかったら (ば)	" nakattara (ba)
Concessive "	" なかれど (も) " nakeredo (mo)	" なかれど (も)	" nakeredo (mo)
Alternative Form	" なかったり " nakattari	" なかったり	" nakattari
Gerund "	{ " ず " zu	" ず	" zu
"	{ " ぬく " nakute	" ぬく	" nakute
Positive Imperative	" ろ " ro!	" ろ	" ro.

181. 3. *The Certain Present Stem* supports but few inflections. It is a primary verbal variation in the First Conjugation. In the Second Conjugation it is an inflection of the Main Stem by the use of the suffix る *ru*.

182. *a.* In the FIRST CONJUGATION for the verb なほす *naosu*, the Certain Present Stem is

なほす naosu.

This stem is inflected as follows :—

Cert. Pres.	なほす	*naosu*	(he) mends, (they) mend.
Improbable „	„ まい „ *mai*		probably (I) do not, will not mend.
Neg. Imperative „	な „ *na*		do not mend

183. *b.* In the SECOND CONJUGATION the Certain Present Stems of まける *makeru* and おぢる *ojiru* are the verbs as named ;—

まける makeru,   おぢる ojiru.

Certain Present	まける *makeru* (I) lose, shall lose	おぢる *ojiru* (I) fear, shall fear
Neg. Imperative	まけるな *makeruna!* do not lose !	おぢるな *ojiruna!* do not fear !

184. 4. The *Conditional Stem,* like the Certain Present Stem, supports but a small inflection. In the First Conjugation this stem is a primary variation of the verb. In the Second Conjugation it is an inflection of the Main Stem by the use of the suffix れ *re*.

185. *a.* In the FIRST CONJUGATION for the verb なほす *Naosu* the Conditional Stem is

なほせ *naose.*

This stem is inflected as follows :—

Conditional Present	なほせば *naoseba*	if (I) mend
Concessive „	„ と „	*do* though (he) mend.
The Positive Imperative takes the form of this stem	なほせ *naose !*	mend !

186. *b.* In the SECOND CONJUGATION the Conditional Stems of the verbs まける *makeru* and をぢる *ojiru* are

まけれ *makere,*   をぢれ *ojire.*

Cond. Present まければ *makere ba* and をぢれば *ojire ba*	
Conc. „ „ と „ *do* „ „ と „ *do*	

SUMMARY OF FORMS OF INFLECTION.

Exhibiting all these forms together, and classifying them in accordance with the arrangement generally made by Western grammarians we get the accompanying verbal paradigms.

187. FIRST CONJUGATION.

ナヲス Naosu, "mend."

Tense.	Voice.	Indicative Mode.
Certain Present.....	Positive.	ナヲス Naosu,—(I) mend, will mend.
	Negative.	ナヲサヌ Naosa-nu, ナヲサヌイ Naosa-nui—(I) do not mend.
Probable Present....	Positive.	ナヲサウ Naos-ô,—(sa-u), probably mend, or shall mend.
	Negative.	ナヲサヌイ Naosa-nui,—(I) probably do, or shall not, mend.
Certain Past.........	Positive.	ナヲシタ Naoshi-ta,—(I) mended, (he) has mended.
	Negative.	ナヲサナカツタ Naosa-nakatta, ナヲサナンダ Naosa-nanda, } (ho) did not mend.
Probable Past	Positive.	ナヲシタラウ Naoshi-tarô,—(they) probably mended.
	Negative.	ナヲサナカツタラウ Naosa-nakattarô, ナヲサナンダラウ Naosa-nandarô, } (he) probably did not mend.
Alternative Form....	Positive.	ナヲシタリ Naoshi-tari,—at times, or at one time, mending.
	Negative.	ナヲサナカツタリ Naosa-nakattari, ナヲサナンダリ Naosa-nandari, } at times, or at one time, not mending.
Desiderative Form ..	Positive.	ナヲシタイ Naoshi-tai,—(I, wo, they) wish to mend.
	Negative.	ナヲシタクナイ Naoshi-takunai,—(I, or they) do not wish to mend.
Gerund	Positive.	ナヲシテ Naoshi-te,—mending, having mended.
	Negative.	ナヲサズ Naosa-zu, ナヲサナクテ Naosa-nakute, } not having mended, not mending.

187. FIRST CONJUGATION.

(Continued.)

TENSE.	VOICE.	SUBJUNCTIVE MODE.		IMPERATIVE MODE.
		CONDITIONAL.	CONCESSIVE.	
Certain Present......	Pos.	なほせ ば Naose-ba, —if (I) mend. なほ-すければ Naosu-nakereba, } if (he) does not なほ-さ-ねば Naosa-neba, } mend.	なほせ-ど Naose-do, } though (I) なほ-すけれど Naosu-keredo, } mend. なほ-さ-ねけれど Naosa-inkeredo, } though do not なほ-さ-ねど Na sa-nedo, } mend.	なほせ Naose! } mend! なほす-な Naosu-na! } do not mend!
	Neg.			
Probable Present......	Pos. Neg.			
Certain Past.	Pos.	なほし-たら (ば) Naoshi-tara (ba), —if (he) had mended. なほ-さかつたら Naosa-nakattara, } if (he) had not なほ-さんだら Naosa-nandara, } mended.	なほし-たれど Naoshi-taredo, } though (he) has なほし-たけれど Naoshi-ta-keredo, } mended. なほ-さ-なかつたけれど Naosa-nakattakeredo, } though (I) なほ-さ-なんだけれど Naosa-nandakeredo, } have not } mended.	
	Neg.			
Probable Past	Pos. Neg.			

188. SECOND CONJUGATION.

First Form. まける MAKERU, "lose."　　*Second Form.* おぢる OJIRU, "fear."

TENSE.	VOICE.	INDICATIVE MODE.	
		Form I.	*Form II.*
Certain Present	Positive.	まける Make-ru.	おぢる Oji-ru.
	Negative.	まけぬ Make-nu.	おぢぬ Oji-nu.
		まけない Make-nai.	おぢない Oji-nai.
Probable Present	Positive.	まけよ Make-yo	おぢよ Oji-yo.
	Negative.	まけまい Make-mai.	おぢまい Oji-mai.
Certain Past	Positive.	まけた Make-ta.	おぢた Oji-ta,
	Negative.	まけなかった Make-nakatta.	おぢなかった Oji-nakatta.
		まけなんだ Make-nanda.	おぢなんだ Oji-nanda.
Probable Past	Positive.	まけたろう Make-tarō.	おぢたろう Oji-tarō.
	Negative.	まけなかったろう Make-nakattarō.	おぢなかったろう Oji-nakattarō.
		まけなんだろう Make-nandarō.	おぢなんだろう Oji-nandarō.
Alternative Form	Positive.	まけたり Make-tari.	おぢたり Oji-tari.
	Negative.	まけなかったり Make-nakattari.	おぢなかったり Oji-nakattari.
		まけなんだり Make-nandari.	おぢなんだり Oji-nandari.
Desiderative Form	Positive.	まけたい Make-tai.	おぢたい Oji-tai.
	Negative.	まけたくない Make-takunai.	おぢたくない Oji-takunai.
Gerund	Positive.	まけて Make-te.	おぢて Oji-te.
	Negative.	まけず Make-zu.	おぢず Oji-zu.
		まけなくて Make-nakute.	おぢなくて Oji-nakute.

188. SECOND CONJUGATION.

(*Continued.*)

| TENSE | VOICE | SUBJUNCTIVE MODE. | | | | IMPERATIVE MODE. | |
| | | CONDITIONAL. | | CONCESSIVE. | | | |
		Form I.	Form II.	Form I.	Form II.	Form I.	Form II.
Certain Present	Pos.	まけ-れば Make-reba.	おぢ-れば Oji-reba.	まけ-れど Make-redo.	おぢ-れど Oji-redo.	まけ-ろ Make ro.	おぢ-ろ Oji ro.
	Neg.	まけ-なければ Make-nakereba. / まけ-ねば Make-neba.	おぢ-なければ Oji-nakereba. / おぢ-ねば Oji-neba.	まけ-なけれど Make-nakeredo. / まけ-ねど Make-nedo.	おぢ-なけれど Oji-nakeredo. / おぢ-ねど Oji-nedo.	まけ-るな Make-runa.	おぢ-るな Oji-runa.
Probable Present	Pos. Neg.						
Certain Past	Pos.	まけ-たら Make-tara.	おぢ-たら Oji-tara.	まけ-たれど Make-taredo.	おぢ-たれど Oji-taredo.		
	Neg.	まけ-なかつたら Make-nakattara. / まけ-なんだら Make-nandara.	おぢ-なかつたら Oji-nakattara. / おぢ-なんだら Oji-nandara.	まけ-なかつたけれど Make-nakattakeredo. / まけ-なんだれど Make-nandaredo.	おぢ-なかつたけれど Oji-nakattakeredo. / おぢ-なんだれど Oji-nandaredo.		
Probable Past	Pos. Neg.						

189. *5. Verbal Inflection in Polite Form.* In
social intercourse in Japan, language has been given a special
character for the purposes of courtesy. Except among
relatives and with one's own servants, verbal forms in the
main parts of sentences almost always differ somewhat
from the simple inflections just given, in order to express
politeness, respect or reverence. The subject of honorific
language can not be dealt with at any length here.

We may not, however, pass by the use of the verb ます
masŭ, meaning " be," which, as a suffix to the Main Stems of
verbs, relieves the verbs from the familiarity and curtness of
the simple inflections. The inflections of this verb are constantly in use, and are universally applicable to other verbs.
In fact, ます *masŭ* has now no independent function. It
appears always as a suffix.

190. *a.* The inflection of the verb ます *masŭ* is somewhat unlike that of either of the verbs whose paradigms
have already been given. The Main Stem of the verb is
まし *mashi ;* its Negative Stem is ませ *mase ;* its Certain
Present is ます *masŭ*, and its Conditional Stem is ますれ
masure. It has no desiderative form. Knowing these
peculiarities the student can easily complete its paradigm.

191. *b.* All the inflections of ます *masŭ*, however, are
not in common use. The forms most frequently met with
are the following :—

Cert. Pres.	Pos. Neg.	ます *masŭ* ませ－ぬ *mase-nŭ*
Prob. „	Pos. Neg.	ま－せう *ma-shō (seu)* ます－まい *masŭ-mai*
Cert. Past	Pos.	まし－た *mashi-ta*

Prob. Past	Pos.	まし－たらう *mashi-tarō*	
Cond. Pres.	Pos.	まし－たれば *mashi-tareba*	
	Neg.	ませ－なかつたれば *mase-nakattareba*	
Cond. Past	Pos.	まし－たら（ば） *mashi-tara (ba)*	
Alt. Form	Pos.	まし－たり *mashi-tari*	
	Neg.	ませ－なかつたり *mase-nakattari*	
Gerund	Pos.	まし－て *mashi-te*	
	Neg.	ませ－なくつて *mase-nakute*	

192. *c.* Several of the forms for the Negative Voice of ます *masŭ* are by preference in popular speech rendered by combining with the negative certain present, ません *masen*, such auxiliary forms as でせう *deshō*, でした *deshita*, でしたら *deshitara*, which are remote abbreviations of the particle で *de*, and inflection forms of the verb ござる *gozaru*.

Examples :—

Cert. Past,	Neg.	is ません でした *masen deshita*
Prob. „	„	„ ません でしたらう *masen deshitarō*
Cond. „	„	„ ません でしたら（ば） *masen deshitara(ba)*

193. *d.* In polite usage a Desiderative Form for verbs has been devised by changing the final syllabic of the ordinary desiderative form from たい *tai* to たう *tō* for the Positive Voice, and to たく *taku* for the Negative Voice, and suffixing the polite verb ござります *gozarimasŭ*, or ございます *gozaimasŭ*, Positive or Negative.

Examples :—

Polite Desiderative Form なほす *naosu.*	Pos.	なほしたう－ござります *naoshitō-gozarimasu*
	Neg.	なほしたく－ござりません *naoshitaku-gozarimasen*
Polite Desiderative Form まける *makeru.*	Pos.	まけたう－ございます *maketō-gozaimasu*
	Neg.	まけたく－ございません *maketaku-gozaimasen*
Polite Desiderative Form おちる *ojiru.*	Pos.	おちたう－ございます *ojitō-gozaimasu*
	Neg.	おちたく－ございません *ojitaku-gozaimasen.*

c. The Imperative Mode in polite form is commonly formed by the help of certain auxiliaries, with or without the verb ます *masu.* For the present, the auxiliary なさる *nasaru*, "please do," associated with ます *masu*, may illustrate this form of inflection, as ;—

Imperative Mode.	Pos.	なさいませ *nasaimase !* or なさいまし *nasaimashi !*
	Neg.	なさいますな *nasaimasu na !* or なさいまするな *nasaimasuru na !*

In polite inflection the verb to which なさいます *nasaimasu* is auxiliary is accompanied by the honorific お *o.*

SUMMARY OF POLITE INFLECTION FORMS.

Exhibiting these forms together, and classifying them in accordance with the arrangement generally made by Western grammarians, we have the following paradigm.

194. e. ILLUSTRATIVE POLITE INFLECTION:—

なほす Naosu, "mend."

Mode and Tense.	Positive Voice.	Negative Voice.
Indicative Mode. Certain Present	なほし‐ます Naoshi-masŭ	なほし‐ません Naoshi-masen
Probable „	なほし‐ませう Naoshi-mashō	なほし‐ますまい Naoshi-masumai
Certain Past	なほし‐ました Naoshi-mashita	なほし‐ません でした Naoshi-masen deshita
Probable „	なほし‐ましたらう Naoshi-mashitarō	なほし‐ません でしたらう Naoshi-masen deshitarō
Subjunctive Mode. Conditional Present	なほし‐ますれば Naoshi-masureba	なほし‐ませなければ Naoshi-masenakereba
Conditional Past	なほし‐ましたら Naoshi-mashitara	なほし‐ません でしたら Naoshi-masen deshitara

Mode and Tense.	Positive Voice.	Negative Voice.
Alternative Form	なほし—ました り Naoshi-mashitari	なほし—ませなかった り Naoshi-masenakattari
Gerund	なほし—まして Naoshi-mashite	なほし—ませなくて Naoshi-masenakute
Desiderative Form	なほし—たう ございます Naoshi-tō gozaimasu	なほし—たく ございません Naoshi-taku gozaimasen
Imperative Mode.	お なほし—なさいませ or (し) O naoshi-nasaimase or (shi)	お なほし—なさいますな O naoshi-nasaimasuruna

195. NOTE. Polite inflection for almost every other Japanese verb can be made by substituting in the above paradigm for the Main Stem なほし naoshi, the Main Stem of the verb to be inflected.

196. 6. *Two Verbs of Irregular Inflection.* There are a few verbs of somewhat irregular inflection constantly met with in ordinary speech. Two of these are of so great importance that their paradigms are here given. The verbs are くる kuru, and する suru, whose nearest equivalent meanings in English are "come," and "do." They are of especial use as auxiliaries in expanding and explaining the actions of other verbs, and in giving verbal meanings to substantives, etc.

197. PARADIGMS OF "KURU," AND "SURU."

Verbs.	くル Kuru, "come."	すル Suru, "do."
Main Stem	き KI	し SHI
Negative ,,	こ KO	せ SE
Cer. Pres. ,,	くル KURU	すル SURU
Cond. ,,	くレ KURE	すレ SURE

Mode and Tense.	Positive Voice.	Negative Voice.	Positive Voice.	Negative Voice.
Indicative Mode. Certain Present	く-ル ku-ru come, (I) shall come	こ-ぬ ko-nŭ こ-ナイ ko-nai not come, (I) shall not come	す-ル su-ru do, (I) shall do	せ-ぬ se-nŭ し-ナイ shi-nai not do, (I) shall not do
Probable ,,	こ-ヨう ko-yō き-ヨう ki-yō probably come, or (I) shall come	こ-マイ ko-mai き-マイ ki-mai probably not come, or shall not come	し-ヨう shi-yō せう shō probably do or (I) shall do	し-マイ shi-mai せ-ナイ se-nai probably not do, or shall not do

Mode and Tense	Positive Voice.	Negative Voice.	Positive Voice.	Negative Voice.
Certain Past	*ki-la* came, has come	*ko-nakatta* *se-nanda* came not, has not come	*shi-la* did, has done	*shi-nakatta* *se-nanda* did not, has not done
Probable „	*ki-larō* probably came or has come	*ko-nakattarō* *ko-nandarō* probably did not come	*shi-larō* probably did, or has done	*shi-nakattarō* *se-nandarō* probably did not do
SUBJUNCTIVE MODE. —— Conditional Present	*kure-ba* if (he) come	*ko-nakereba* *ko-neba* if (he) does not come	*sure-ba* if (he) do	*shi-nakereba* *se-neba* if (he) does not do
Conditional Past	*ki-lara (ba)* if (he) came	*ko-nakatta* *ko-nandara* if (he) do not come	*shi-lara (ba)* if he did	*shi-nakatta* *se-nandara* if (he) did not do

SUBJUNCTIVE MODE.				
Concessive Present	kure-*do* though (I) come	ko-*nakeredo* ko-*nedo* though (I) do not come	sure-*do* though (he) does	shi-*nakeredo* se-*nedo* though (I) do not
Concessive Past	ki-*taredo* though (I) came	ko-*nakattaredo* ko-*nandaredo* though (I) had not come	shi-*taredo* though (he) did	shi-*nakattaredo* se-*nandaredo* though (I) did not
Alternative Form	ki-*tari* at times coming	ko-*nakattari* ko-*nandari* sometimes not coming	shi-*tari* at time doing	shi-*nakattari* se-*nandari* sometimes not doing
Desiderative Form	ki-*tai* (I) want to come	ki-*takunai* (I) do not want to come	shi-*tai* (I) wish to do	shi-*takunai* (I) do not wish to do

Mode and Tense.	Positive Voice.	Negative Voice.	Positive Voice.	Negative Voice.
Gerund	き-て ki-te coming, having come	こ-ず ko-zu こ-なくて ko-nakute not coming, not having come	し-て shi-te doing, having done	せ-ず se-zu し-なくて shi-nakute not doing, not having done.
Imperative Mode.	こ-い! ko-i! come!	く-るな! kuru-na! do not come!	し-ろ! shi ro! do!	する-な! suru-na! do not!

3. PHRASE VERBS.

198. The Japanese language abounds in combinations of words which have the function of single parts of speech. Such combinations are especially noticeable among verbs. They may be called PHRASE-VERBS, or VERB PHRASES, because they consist of some primary verbal variation combined with one or more auxiliary verbs, all together forming phrases which pass through various inflections as though they were simple verbs. By means of phrase-verbs the Japanese construct verbal forms which express voice in other than a directly active relation. There are, thus, equivalents of (1) PASSIVE, (2) POTENTIAL, and (3) CAUSATIVE VOICES among Japanese verbal forms.

The full treatment of these phrase-verbs lies outside the scope of this manual. But some acquaintance with them is desirable for any student of the language. A few facts concerning their formation and use are therefore appended.

199. 1. THE PASSIVE VOICE. When that which is the object of a verb in ordinary form is represented as having become a subject, affected by the action expressed in the verb, the verb is said to have taken on the PASSIVE VOICE. For example, the active verb-phrase " he knows me," is made passive when it becomes "I am known by him." Likewise " I see," becomes passive when phrased "I am seen," &c.

220. The change from the active to the passive voice in Japanese is made by adding to the Negative Stem of the First Conjugation the syllables れる RERU, and to the same stem of the Second Conjugation the syllables られる RARERU.

For example ;—the verbs しる *shiru* "know," える *eru* " obtain," and みる *miru* "see," are made Passive as follows ;—

CONJUGATION.	NEGATIVE STEM.	PASSIVE VOICE.
First Conj.	しら *shira*	しられる *shira reru* "to be known"
Second Conj. {	I. え *e*	えられる *e rareru* "to be obtained"
	II. み *mi*	みられる *mi rareru* " to be seen."

201. *a.* Strictly speaking, however, there is no passive voice in Japanese speech. Etymologists teach that the so called passive termination is a condensed compound made up of the verbs, あり *ari* " being," and える *eru* " get " which means " get being." The verb しられる *shirareru*, therefore, is a verb-phrase meaning "to get being knowing." This phrase by an easy transition comes to mean " " to be known." This change applies to all passives. They are, as Prof B. H. Chamberlain describes them, "actives in disguise."

202. *b.* The paradigms of all the so called passives are shaped in accordance with the **First Form** of the **Second Conjugation.**

ILLUSTRATIVE PHRASES :—

わたくし に よく しられる
Watakushi ni yoku shirareru "He is well known by me."

どこ を みられましたか
Doko wo miraremashita ka "Where were you seen ?"

203. 2. THE POTENTIAL VOICE. Having power to do anything, *i.e.* POTENTIALITY, is expressed by the same phrase-verbs as those used to convey passive meanings.

ILLUSTRATIVE PHRASES :—

Prov. 28. くち に と は たてられぬ
Kuchi ni to wa taterarenu "One can not set up a door for a man's mouth."

こられる か きいて みませう
Korareru ka kiite mimashō "I will ask him if he can come."

まいられません と いゝました
Mairaremasen to iimashita "He said, he can not come. (*Can not come, that he said.*)"

204. *a.* In the First Conjugation most of the verbs have a SECOND potential form, which, in almost every instance, is formed by adding the syllabic る RU to the Conditional Stem.

For example;—for the verb しる *shiru* "know," there are the two forms しられる *shirareru*, and しれる *shireru*, both phrase-verbs meaning "may," or "can, know." By preference, however, the idea of permission, or "may," is associated with しられる *shirareru*, and with all verbs in RERU; and of positive ability, or "can," with しれる *shireru* and all such verbs in る RU. There are some variations in the formation of the second potential form, such as きこゑる

kikoeru instead of きける *kikeru*, which should be learned.

205. *b.* In the Second Conjugation the two potential forms for みる *miru* "see";—that is, みられる *mirareru* "may see," and みえる *mieru*, "can see," should be noticed as the exceptional two potentials in the Second Conjugation.

206. 3. The Causative Voice. There are many phrase-verbs whose meanings express CAUSING OF ACTION, *e.g.* "causing to know," or "to get," or "to see." Such causation is expressed by the addition to the Negative Stem of a verb, in the First Conjugation of the syllablis SERU, and in the Second Conjugation of the syllablis SASERU.

For example ;—the verbs しる *shiru*, える *eru*, and みる *miru*, become Causative as follows ;—

CONJUGATION.	NEGATIVE STEM.	CAUSATIVE VOICE.	
First Conj.	しら *shira*	しらせる *shira seru*	"to cause to know."
Second Conj. {	I. え *e* II. み *mi*	えさせる *e saseru* みさせる *mi saseru*	"to cause to obtain" "to cause to see."

All causative verbs are conjugated according to the paradigm for the First Form, Second Conjugation.

207. Note. The irregular verbs くる *kuru*, and する *suru*, form causatives in the forms こさせる *kosaseru* "cause to come," and させる *saseru* "cause to do."

ILLUSTRATIVE PHRASES :—

すぐにきかしてください "Please let me know at once."
Sugu ni kikashite kudasai

みな うれる なら はやく きて しらせて ください
Mina ureru nara hayaku kite shirasete kudasai
" If you can sell all, please come quickly and let me know."

しづか に させなければ いけない "You must make them
Shizuka ni sasenakereba ikenai   keep still."

V. THE ADJECTIVE.

208. In the Japanese language, words and phrases added to nouns for the purpose of describing, defining, limiting the meanings of the nouns, differ much in construction, and in ways of use, from their equivalents in English speech, THE ADJECTIVES. For instance, Japanese adjectives have neither number, gender, nor a true succession of degrees, such as positive, comparative, and superlative. But they have an inflection which, as far as it goes, is almost exactly like the inflection of verbs.

209. True verbs, too, and adverbial words, are in constant use as adjectives.

1. COMPARISON.

210. The Japanese do not express degrees of comparison among things by such terminals as " er," and " est," or by a succession of auxiliaries of relation, such as " more," and " most." They use a simple adjective like ながい *nagai* " long," or やすい *yasui* " easy," " cheap," and make comparison as follows :—

211. *a.* FOR THE COMPARATIVE DEGREE. They use ordinarily the particle より *yori* " than," with the adjective ; saying, for example,—" *This than, that long is,*" or " *cheap is.*" That is to say, " *Than this, that is long* " or " *cheap,*" which means what is understood in English by the words " That is longer " or " cheaper, than this." For example, among the illustrative proverbs take numbers 11, and 41.

Proverb 11.   るいらん より も あやうし
Ruiran yori mo ayaushi.

"*Pile of eggs than even, dangerous*," that is, "*Even than a pile of eggs, dangerous*," or "More dangerous than even a pile of eggs."

Proverb 41.   みめ より こゝろ
Mime yori kokoro.

"*Face than heart*," that is, "*Heart than, face (is better)*," or, "The heart is more to be desired than the face."

211. NOTE. Excess in quality of one thing over another is sometimes expressed by such words as もっと *motto*, "more," なほ *nao* "yet," or "still," &c.

For example :— もっと ながい *motto nagai*, "more long," なほ やすい *nao yasui*, "yet cheap," that is, "longer," "cheaper."

213. *b.* FOR THE SUPERLATIVE DEGREE. The extreme degree of quality is expressed by the use of such words as いち ばん *ichi ban*, "number one," だい いち の *dai ichi no* "first," "chief," &c.

For example :— いち ばん ながい なは *Ichi ban nagai nawa*, "Number one long rope," is equivalent to the English words, "The longest rope."

2. INFLECTION.

214. The simplest form of the adjective is what may be called THE STEM. By the addition of certain syllabics to the Stem, various adjective words and phrase words, are formed. These are simple adjectives, adverbial adjectives, and verbal adjectives, all having special mood and tense forms. By INFLECTION these adjectival words receive both affirmative and negative expression.

215. *a.* The syllabic い *i* added to the Stem of an adjective, forms the simple adjective, which is usable either as an attribute or as a predicate.

For example ;—from the Stems なが *naga,* and やす *yasu,* the simple adjectives ながい *nagai* "long" and やすい *yasui* "easy," or "cheap," are formed. One can say ながい なは *nagai nawa,* "long rope," or なは が ながい *nawa ga nagai* "the rope is long"; and やすい はり *yasui hari,* "a cheap needle," or はり が やすい *hari ga yasui,* "the needle is cheap."

216. Note. In Proverb 32;—ふるき を たづねて あたらしき を しる *Furuki wo tazunete, atarashiki wo shiru,* "Inquiring after old (things) he learns new (things)," the adjectives "old," and "new," terminate in the syllabic き KI. This syllabic is the Classical termination of all adjectives. In common speech the K sound has been dropped, leaving the I vowel element as the ordinary, simple adjective terminal.

217. *b.* The syllabic く KU, added to the Stem of an adjective, forms an adverbial adjective, or an adjectival adverb. In ordinary speech this form has predicative force. When adverbial it is followed by the verb which it qualifies.

Examples :—

From the Stems なが *naga,* and やす *yasu,* are thus formed ながく *nagaku,* and やすく *yasuku,* which may be used as follows ;—

この なは が ながく ございます *Kono nawa ga nagaku gozaimasu.* "*This rope* (*nom. sign.*) *long is,*" that is, "This rope is long."

やすく できました *Yasuku dekimashita,* "cheap made," that is, "It is made cheaply."

218. Note. In common speech the K sound is often dropped from the adverbial form of the adjective, and the U sound is combined with the vowel element of the preceding syllabic. *To illustrate ;*—ながく *nagaku* often passes into the form ナガウ *nagō* by dropping the к sound, leaving the word ナガウ *nagau*, which is sounded as *nagō*. (43.) So, also, やすく *yasuku* becomes やす *yasū*, does this change take place. Especially before the polite verb ござる *gozaru* "to be," Such a sentence as この ナハ が ナガウ ございます *Kono nawa ga nagaku gozaimasu*, is, therefore, in ordinary speech rendered この ナハ が ナガウ ございます *Kono nawa ga nagō gozamasu.*

219. *c.* In addition to these simple inflections forming true adjectival and adverbial forms, the adjective has also inflections, like true verbs, for mood and tense. These verbal inflections are made by adding various forms of the verb ある *aru* "be," positive and negative, to a modified adverbial form of the adjective, as follows :—

INFLECTION OF THE ADJECTIVE.

ADJECTIVE STEMS.	あたらし ATARASHI.	ふる FURU.
Simple Adjective	あたらしき or あたらしい *atarashiki or atarashii* new	ふるき or ふるい *furuki or furui* old
Adverbial Adjective	あたらしく *atarashiku* new-ly	ふるく *furuku* old-ly

ADJECTIVE STEMS.	あたらし ATARASHI.		ふる FURU.	
Polite Predicate Form	あたらしう ございます or ございません &c. *alarashiu gozaimasu or gozaimasen &c.* is new is not new		ふるう ございます or ございません *furu gozaimasu or gozaimasen* is old is not old	
VERBAL FORMS.	POSITIVE.	NEGATIVE.	POSITIVE.	NEGATIVE.
INDICATIVE MODE. Certain Present	あたらしい *alarashii* is new	あたらしく ない *alarashiku nai* is not new	ふるい *furui* is old	ふるく ない *furuku nai* is not old
Probable Present	あたらしかろう *alarashikaro* probably is, or will be new	あたらしく なかろう *alarashiku nakaro* probably is not new, or will not be new	ふるかろう *furukaro* probably is, or will be old	ふるく なかろう *furuku nakaro* probably is not, or will not be old
Certain Past	あたらしかった *alarashikatta* was new	あたらしく なかった *alarashiku nakatta* was not new	ふるかった *furukatta* was old	ふるく なかった *furuku nakatta* was not old

Probable Past	あたらしかつたらう *atarashikattarō* was probably new	あたらしくなかつたらう *atarashiku nakattarō* was probably not new	ふるかつたらう *furukattarō* was probably old	ふるくなかつたらう *furuku nakattarō* was probably not old
SUBJUNCTIVE. ——— **Conditional Present**	あたらしければ *atarashikereba* if it is new	あたらしくなければ *atarashiku nakereba* if it is not new	ふるければ *furukereba* if it is old	ふるくなければ *furuku nakereba* if it is not old
Conditional Past	あたらしかつたら (ば) *atarashikattara (ba)* if it should be new	あたらしくなかつたら(ば) *atarashiku nakattaru(ba)* if it should not be new	ふるかつたら(ば) *furukattara(ba)* if it were old	ふるくなかつたら(ば) *furuku nakattara(ba)* if it were not old
Concessive	あたらしけれど *atarashikeredo* though new	あたらしくなけれど *atarashiku nakeredo* though not new	ふるけれど *furukeredo* though old	ふるくなけれど *furuku nakeredo* though not old
Alternative Form	あたらしかつたり *atarashikattari* being at times new	あたらしくなかつたり *atarashiku nakattari* being sometimes not new	ふるかつたり *furukattari* being at times old	ふるくなかつたり *furuku nakattari* being at times not old
Gerund	あたらしくて *atarashikute* being new	あたらしくなくて *atarashiku nakute* not being new	ふるくて *furukute* being old	ふるくなくて *furuku nakute* not being old

3. ADJECTIVAL WORDS AND PHRASES.

220. Many words, not originally adjectives, take on an ADJECTIVAL CHARACTER by combination, or association, with other words.

221. *a. Nouns* followed by the particle の NO, and the abbreviated syllable な NA, (なる *naru* " be "), serve as adjectives.

Examples :— きん の *kin no* "of gold "=" golden ";まこと の *makoto no* " of truth " = " truthful;" and あきらか な *akiraka na*, "bright being " = " bright ;" ばか な *baka na* " fool being " = " foolish," and so on.

222. *b. Nouns* followed by らしい RASHII, meaning " like " or "appearance," become adjectival.

Examples :— ばか らしい *baka rashii* "like a fool" = " foolish;" こども らしい *kodomo rashii* " like a child " = "childish;" ほんとう らしい *hontō rashii* " like the truth " = " truthseeming," and the like.

223. *c. Verbs,* in present and past forms, often become adjectives in use.

Examples :— できる *dekiru* and できない *dekinai* meaning " able to do," and " not able to do," are equivalents of " possible," and "impossible," when used as adjectives. あいた *aita* meaning " has become open " = " open," is used as an adjective, and the like.

224. *d.* There are many phrases in use by the Japanese which are practically units, and may be called *phrase-adjectives,* such as あし の はやい *ashi no hayai*, " quick of foot," = " swift ;" いし の おほい *ishi no ōi*, "abounding of stone," = " stony;" いぢ の わるい *iji no warui* "bad of spirit," = " ill-tempered," and so on.

When these and like phrases are used predicatively, の *no* is replaced by が *ga*, as あし が はやい *ashi ga hayai*, for あし の はやい *ashi no hayai;* みゝ が とほい *mimi ga tōi* "distant of ear," = "deaf," め が ちかい *me ga chikai* "near of eye," = "short sighted."

225. *e.* The ***Desiderative Form*** of the verb, that is, the Main Stem having the syllabics たい *tai* suffixed, is in common use as an adjective.

Examples :— なほしたい *naoshitai,* "desirous of mending," "curing" = "helpful," "kind ;" おぢたい *ojitai,* "desirous of fearing" = "anxious," "timid."

VI. THE ADVERB.

226. Words and phrases whose functions are equivalent to those of ADVERBS in the English language, are numerous in Japanese speech. In origin and chief use most of the adverbial forms are adjectives, verbs, and nouns, which, by means of particles and combinatives, are made descriptive of the action expressed in the verbs.

227. 1. There are a few ***true adverbs ;***—such as あまり *amari,* "too much ;" ばかり *bakari* "only ;" ちつと *chitto* "slightly ;" どう *dō* "how? ;" ごく *goku* "very ;" はなはだ *hanahada* "very ;" いかゞ *ikaga* "how ;" いつ *itsu* "when? ;" きつと *kitto* "positively ;" まだ *mada* "yet;" なぜ *naze* "why? ;" さつぱり *sappari* "wholly ;" たゞいま *tadaima* "presently ;" やはり *yahari* "also ;" and some others.

228. 2. The ***adjectival form*** ending in く KU is practically a true adverb ;—as ながく *nagaku* "long;" やすく *yasuku* "cheaply," "easily ;" あたらしく *atarashiku* "newly;" ふるく "old ;" はやく *hayaku* "quickly ;" よく *yoku* "well," etc.

229. 3. *Nouns* which are made to serve as adjectives by the addition of の *no,* or な *na,* become adverbial

by the use of the suffix に NI in the place of NO, or
NA ;—as まこと に *makoto ni* "truthfully," "really;" しづか
に *shizuka ni* "gently," "quietly ;" しまい に *shimai ni*
"finally ;" しんせつ に *shinsetsu ni* "kindly ;" ていねい
に *teinei ni* "politely ;" やう に *yō ni* "in the manner of ;"
ほか に *hoka ni* "in another way ;" おほき に *ōki ni*
"greatly ;" すで に *sude ni* "already ;" だいじ に *daiji
ni* " carefully," and the like.

230. 4. *Words reduplicated* often take on an adverbial character ;—as だんく *dan-dan* "gradually," (だん
dan "a step);" いろく *iro-iro* "various kinds," (いろ *iro*
"sort) ;" にちく *nichi-nichi* "daily," (にち *nichi* "day");
ときく *tokidoki* "sometimes," (とき *toki* "time"), and so on.
Many such reduplicatives are followed by the particle
と *to*.

231. 5. The *gerunds* of many verb have in practice
become adverbs;—as はじめて *hajimete* "for the first time,"
(はじめる *hajimeru* "begin"); かへつて *kaette* " on the contrary " (かへる *kaeru* "return"); けつして *kesshite* "never,"
used with a negative verb, (けつする *kesshiru*, "determine");
さだめて *sadamete* "probably " (さだめる *sadameru* "con-
firm"); だまつて *damatte* "silently" (だまる *damaru*
"silent "); まちがつて *machigatte* "wrong" (まちがふ
machigau "err"); よろこんで *yorokonde* "gladly"
(よろこぶ *yorokobu* "glad "). Also negative gerunds, such
as かならづ *kanarazu* "necessarily;" しらづ *shirazu* "un-
consciously."

232. 6. *Onomatopoetic words* in large number have
been produced by the Japanese, and do service as adverbs ;
as ばらく *para-para* "sound of rain ;" ぴかく *pika-pika*
"flashing of lightning ;" ごろく *goro-goro* "rolling of thun-

der;" そろ〱 *soro-soro* "slowly moving;" ぱち り *patchiri* "sudden breaking;" ぴつしや り *pisshari* "slamming of a door;" ぽん〱 *pon-pon* "sound of guns;" ぷん〱 *pun-pun* "spreading of perfume," and many more.

233. 7. *Responsives.* The Japanese have not yet reduced their responses to questions to the simple "Yes!" or "No!" of English. As a rule their replies are repetitions of the verb of the question, either affirmatively or negatively. Their negative answer イーエ *iiye*, is almost an equivalent for "No!" Their response ヘイ *hei!* or ハイ *hai!* may mean "Yes!" but generally it shows only that the person spoken to has heard, or is paying attention to, the speaker.

ILLUSTRATIVE PHRASES:—

この てほん は あまり すくない "These examples are
Kono tehon wa amari sukunai too few."

Prov. 42. しゆ に まじはれば あかく なる
Shū ni majiwareba akaku naru
"If intimate with vermillion (you) will become red."

さくばん は まこと に こまつた "Really last night (I)
Sakuban wa makoto ni komatta was troubled."

ときぐ おめ に かゝ ります
Tokidoki o me ni kakarimasu "(I) see you now and then."

はじめて おめ に かゝ りました "(I) have met you for
Hajimete o me ni kakarimashita the first time."

てつぼう が ぽん〱 と いふ
Teppō ga pon-pon to iu "The gun says, 'pon-pon.'"

てがみ を やれませう か
Tegami wo yaremashō ka "Can (I) send a letter?"

やれませう
Yaremashō "Yes! (you) can probably send it."

ロビンソン さん は をります か "Is Mr. Robinson in?"
Robinson san wa orimasu ka

イーエ, まだ まゐりません "No! (he) has not yet come."
Iiye mada mairimasen

VII. THE PARTICLES. (TENIWOHA.)

234. There are many words used in the Japanese language, named by the Japanese,—from four of the most important ones among them, て に を は *te, ni, wo, ha,*— TENIWOHA.   In English their equivalents are named PARTICLES.   They hold the same offices in sentences as those which are held in English by PREPOSITIONS, CONJUNCTIONS and INTERJECTIONS.

235. *a.* The PARTICLES in Japanese speech are generally suffixes.   Especially is this fact true of the Japanese equivalents of prepositions.   These particles are postposed, not preposed, to the words with which they are directly connected.   In consequence of this peculiarity, they have received from Western grammarians the distinctive name "POSTPOSITIONS," not prepositions.

236. *b.* Considering the meaning and uses of the particles, we divide them into four groups :—

1. Case Signs,
2. Postpositions,
3. Conjunctions, and
4. Interjections.

These words constitute a highly important part of the structure of the Japanese language.   But we can not here give more than glances at some of the facts concerning them, which are of most practical value.

1. CASE SIGNS.

237. Among the particles are several which, as we have seen, are attached to nouns and pronouns to indicate their CASE, or state with respect to the other words of a sentence.   They are が *ga* and は *wa,* の *no,* に *ni* and へ *ye,* and を *wo.*

238. Properly speaking, が *ga* for the nominative case, and を *wo* for the accusative case, are the only particles which may be regarded distinctively as case signs. But, since the other particles, の *no*, に *ni* and へ *ye*, excepting は *wa*, render the same service to the words with which they are associated, as that rendered by the case terminations in Latin or Greek declension, we shall name them, also, CASE SIGNS. The particle は *wa* has a unique function. The particle の *no*, also, has uses special to itself.

239. 1. が *Ga* and は *Wa*. The particle が *ga*, though originally a genitive sign, may now be regarded as the generic NOMINATIVE SIGN for Japanese words. As a rule, it now simply denotes the name of the thing of which something is affirmed, as ;—

なつがきました *Natsu ga kimashita* "Summer has come."

フヂ サン が みえます *Fuji san ga miemasu* "Mount Fuji is visible."

240. *a.* The presence of が *ga* in a sentence has no meaning beyond this. But, were a speaker desirous of calling especial attention to the relation existing between subject and predicate ; for instance, did he wish to EMPHASIZE the fact of the advent of summer, or the visibility of Mount Fuji, he would in all probability substitute は *wa* for が *ga*, and say なつ は きました *Natsu wa kimashita*, and フヂ サン は みえます *Fuji san wa miemasu*. The particle は *wa*, as associated with the subject of a sentence, is apparently an index pointing from subject to predicate.

241. *b.* But the function of は *wa* is more than that of an index to predication. It serves also as a sign of ANTITHESIS, or CONTRAST, very much,—so some writers think—like the Greek μέν—δε, which are equivalent to "indeed—but."

Example:—カルヰザワ と ニツクワウ と は どちら が すいしい でせう *Karuizawa to Nikkō to wa dochira ga suzushii deshō.* "Which is cooler, Karuizawa or Nikkō?"

カルヰザワ は すゞしい が ニックワウ は きれい で
ございます *Karuizawa wa suzushii ga Nikkō wa kirei de
gozaimasu.* "Karuizawa, indeed, is cool, but Nikkō is
beautiful."

Here, は *wa* with は *wa* is the sign of contrast.

242. In the sentence これ は うまい あれ は まづい
Kore wa umai, are wa mazui. "This is delicious but that is
disagreable," an antithesis is expressed by は *wa* with
は *wa*.

243. *c.* As an ISOLATING, or separative, sign は *wa* takes a
prominent place in such sentences as the one given above;—

カルヰザワ と ニックワウ と は どちら が すゞしい
でせう *Karuizawa to Nikkō to wa dochira ga suzushii deshō.*
The words preceding は *wa* are isolated by this particle
from the rest of the sentence, which remainder thereby
becomes a simple sentence, in which が *ga* is the nominative
sign.

あの くるまや は あし が はやい *Ano kurumaya wa
ashi ga hayai.* "That kurumaya, as for, foot swift" *i.e.*
"As for that kurumaya, he is swift of foot."

In Proverb 45,—もえくひ に は ひ が つき やすい
Moyekui ni wa, hi ga tsuki yasui, は *wa* is also separative, and
が *ga* is the nominative sign for the remainder of the
sentence.

244. *d.* The particle は *wa* has other functions than
those here noted; but what has been said of it will suffice
for present purposes.

α. As a PREDICATIVE INDEX it has no equivalent in English.
β. It stands as a MARK OF EMPHASIS. *γ.* As a SIGN OF AN-
TITHESIS, or contrast, it is best rendered by the word "but,"
at the beginning of the second clause, or sentence, of the
parts in the antithesis. *δ.* As an isolating, or SEPARATIVE

SIGN, it is equivalent to the words "as for," "so far as concerns, &c."

245. 2. *No, as Genitive sign.* の *No* means "of," and, after a noun, signifies possession.

Examples :—

はり の あな *Hari no ana.*

"*Needle of hole*" = "*hole of needle*" = "needle's eye."

ゐど の なか *Ido no naka.*

"*Well of interior*" = "*interior of well*" = "well's interior."

をに の ねんぶつ *Oni no nembutsu.*

"*Demon of prayer*" = "*prayer of demon*" = "demon's prayer.'

246. 3. *Ni, and ye, as Dative signs.* に *Ni* means "to," or "into." へ *Ye* means "to," "towards," "at." Both words represent the thing named as being added to, or as having something done to, or for, it.

Examples :—

トウキヤウ に まゐります
Tokyo ni mairimasu.

"*Tokyo to go*" = "I go to Tokyo."

Proverb 7. とんで ひ に いる なつ の むし
Tonde hi ni iru natsu no mushi.

"*Flying fire into enters summer of insect*"
= "Summer's insect flies into the fire."

いつ アメリカ へ かへります か
Itsu America ye kaerimasu ka.

"*When America to return?*"
= "When do you return to America?"

247. 4. *Wo, as Accusative sign.* Like が *ga*, を *wo* is a true case sign. It signifies that its associated word is the object in the sentence.

Examples :—

Proverb 1. いち を きいて じふ を しる
Ichi wo kiite jū wo shiru.

"*One (acc.) hearing ten (acc.) knows*"
= "Hearing one thing, he knows ten."

Proverb 9.　りか に かんむり を たいさず
Rika ni kammuri wo tadasazu.

"Under a plum tree, do not adjust your cap."

Proverb 10.　ぬすびと を みて なは を なふ
Nusubito wo mite nawa wo nau.

" *Thief* (acc.) *seeing rope twists* "

= " Making a rope, having seen the thief."

The accusative case may be signified by the use of other words than と *wo*, and by the form of the sentence, but the particle と *wo* (which like が *ga* is untranslateable into English,) is properly named the ACCUSATIVE SIGN in Japanese speech.

248. NOTE. Equivalents for a VOCATIVE, and an ABLATIVE case can be made for Japanese nouns, by using the exclamation よ *yo* "O!", and the postpositions から *kara*, and より *yori*, "from," and "since."

Examples :—

Vocative.　おとつさん よ　*Ototsan yo!*　"O father !"

Ablative.　ヨーロツパ から かいます　"I buy from
　　　　　Yoroppa kara kaimasu.　　Europe."

2. POSTPOSITIONS. (PREPOSITIONS).

249. POSTPOSITIONS proper do not form a large group among Japanese words. They are で *de*, から *kara*, まで *made*, に *ni*, の *no*, と *to*, へ *ye*, より *yori*. It is very difficult for a foreign student to understand the real meanings, and to make correct use, of these words. Only long familiarity with the language will enable him to express himself with them satisfactorily to himself, or to his Japanese hearers. But, in the main, these words may be understood as follows :—

250. 1. で ***De.*** This particle primarily expresses the meanings conveyed by the English prepositions "by," "with," and "by means of." *De* also stands for "at," "in," "of," and "for."

Examples :—

くるまでいきました
Kuruma de ikimashita.   " (I) went by kuruma."

しやぼんであらひました
Shabon de araimashita.   "Washed (it) with soap."

ヨコハマでとけいをかひませう
Yokohama de tokei wo kaimashō.   " (I) shall buy a watch at Yokohama."

トウキヤウでさうばはいくら
Tokyo de soba wa ikura ?   "What is the price in Tokyo."

けやきでこしらへました
Keyaki de koshiraemashita.   " (It) is made of *keyaki* wood."

いちゑんでかひます
Ichi yen de kaimasu.   " (I) will buy (it) for one yen."

251. 2. から *Kara.* When used after nouns, this particle primarily means "from." から *Kara* also means "since."

Examples :—

シナガハから オホモリ まで
Shinagawa kara Ōmori made.   "From Shinagawa to Omori."

さくじつから *Sakujitsu kara.*   "Since yesterday—— "

252. 3. まで *Made.* This particle can be rendered into English by such words as "to," "as far as," "until" &c.

Examples :—

ヨコハマまではちり
Yokohama made hachi ri.   "Eight ri to Yokohama."

イカホまであるいていきます
Ikao made aruite ikimasu.   " (I) shall walk as far as Ikao."

こんばんまでまちます
Komban made machimasu.   " (I) will wait until this evening."

253. 4. に *Ni.* This particle stands for quite a number of English prepositions. By original usage it expresses the meanings "in," and "into." に *Ni* may be rendered also by such words as "at," "on," to, "by," and "for."

254. に *Ni* is also part of several phrase-postpositions meaning "upon," "without," "beyond," "among," "around," "before," "behind," "between," "except," "instead of," "under," "according to," and so on.

ILLUSTRATIVE PHRASES :—

トウキヤウ に すんで をります
Tokyo ni sunde orimasu.
"(He) lives in Tokyo."

てら に はいりました
Tera ni hairimashita.
"(He) has gone into the temple."

いち じ はん に はじまります
Ichi ji han ni hajimarimasu.
"(It) commences at half-past one."

よつか に ちやくします
Yokka ni chakushimasu.
"(It) is due on the fourth."

だい に をいて ください
Dai ni oite kudasai.
"Please put (it) on the table."

はな を み に ゆきます
Hana wo mi ni ikimasu
"(I) go to see the flowers."

ねこ は いぬ に かまれた
Neko wa inu ni kamareta.
"The cat was bitten by the dog."

とし に は じやうず な こ
Toshi ni wa jōzu na ko.
"A clever child for (his) years."

255. *a.* Among phrase-postpositions including に *ni* are these :—の うへ に *no ue ni* "upon;" なし に *nashi ni* "without;" の そば に *no soba ni* "beside;" の なか に *no naka ni,* "inside;" と いつしよ に *to issho ni* "together with;" の ため に *no tame ni* "for the sake of;" の かはり に *no kawari ni* "instead of," の むかふ に *no mukō ni* "across;" の さき に *no saki ni* "beyond;" の うち に *no uchi ni* "among," "within;" の まはり に *no mawari ni* "around;" の まへ に *no mae ni* "before;" の うしろ に *no ushiro ni* "behind;" の あと に *no ato ni* "after;" の あひだ に *no* *aida ni* "between;" の ほか に *no hoka ni* "except;" の した に *no shita ni* "under."

256. *b.* Preceding, that is, being a real preposition to gerundial verbal forms, に *ni* produces certain equivalents of English prepositions, such as に ついて *ni tsuite* "belonging to;" に して は *ni shite wa* "considering that," or "for;" に よつて *ni yotte* "according to;" に あたつて *ni atatte* "just at;" に したがつて *ni shitagatte* "in accordance with."

257. *c.* For the use of に *ni* as an adverbial ending, see **229.**

258. For the use of に *ni* as a conjunctive particle, see **273.**

259. 5. の *No.* This particle, as noted before, means "of," and shows possession.

a. Together with its use as the sign of the genitive case, の *no* combines with many other words, as we have just seen, to make phrase-postpositions.

ILLUSTRATIVE PHRASE :—

の うち に *no uchi ni :—*

Prov. 34. えみ の うち に やいば を ふくむ

Emi no uchi ni, yaiba wo fukumu.

"Within a smile to conceal a sword."

260. *b.* の *No* is also used to show two nouns as being in apposition.

Examples :—

タイワン のくに	"The province of Taiwan
Taiwan no kuni.	(Formosa)."
くるまや の ツナキチ	"The kurumaya Tsunakichi."
Kurumaya no Tsunakichi.	

261. *c.* の *No* is often used attributively, after adjectives, having the sense of the word "one."

Examples :—

ながい の を もつて おいで   "Bring a long one."
Nagai no wo motte o ide.

きれい な の を みたい   " (I) wish to see a pretty one."
Kirei na no wo mitai

262. *d.* When the cardinal numbers precede the nouns
they qualify, the numbers are usually followed by the
particle の *no,* (**284.**)

Examples :—

みつ の いし   "Three stones," *instead of*
Mitsu no ishi, ——   *the rendering*——

いし みつ   "Three stones."
Ishi mitsu, ——

263. 6. と **To.** The meaning of the English preposition "with," is at times rendered by と *to.*

Examples :—

あの ひと と しばゐ に いきました   " (I) went with him
Ano shito to shibai ni ikimashita.   to the theatre."

264. 7. ヘ **Ye.** This particle signifies "to," "into,"
and is an equivalent, when suffixed to nouns, of the dative
case sign. ヘ *Ye* sometimes has the force of "at."

Examples :—

ステーション ヘ はやく   " Quick ! to the
Station ye hayaku !   station."

がくかう ヘ いつて お まち なさい   "Please go and wait
Gakkō ye itte o machi nasai.   at the school."

265. 8. より **Yori.** Like から *kara,* より *yori* means
"from," or "since."

ミヤノシタ より   " From Miyanoshita."
Miyanoshita yori ——

さくねん より   " Since last year."
Sakunen yori ——

いま より   " Henceforth."
Ima yori ——

3. CONJUNCTIONS.

266. The particles which in Japanese speech render a like service with that rendered by CONJUNCTIONS in English are が *ga*, か *ka*, から *kara*, も *mo*, に *ni*, し *shi*, と *to* and や *ya*, and several conjunction-phrases such as だが *da ga*, だの *dano*, けれ ども *keredomo*, も やはり *mo yahari*, しかし ながら *shikashi nagara*, さう して *sō shite*, そんなら *sonnara*, それ で は *sore de wa*, それ で も *sore de mo*, ところ へ (or が) *tokoro ye* or *ga*, ゆへ に *yue ni*, やう に *yō ni*, より いっそ *yori isso*, and several others.

267. 1. が *Ga*. This particle is an equivalent for the adversative conjunction "but," when placed at the end of a clause.

Examples :—

> ありがたう ございます が いかねば なりません
> *Arigatō gozaimasu ga ikaneba narimasen*
> "I thank you, but I must go."

> いつ か ニホン ご が できる やう に なれば いゝ が
> *Itsu ka Nihon go ga dekiru yō ni nareba ii ga*
> "If I am able to speak Japanese sometime it will be well, but ——."

268. 2. か *Ka*. か *Ka* repeated in a sentence has the force of the alternative "or," or the correlatives "whether —— or" in English.

Examples :—

> くま か いぬ か しりません
> *Kuma ka inu ka shirimasen.*
> "I do not know whether it is a bear or a dog."

> これ は あたらしい か ふるい か
> *Kore wa atarashii ka furui ka.*
> "Is this new or old?"

269. 3. から *Kara*. Placed after verbs, から *kara* is best rendered as the subordinating conjunction "because."

Examples :—

> あつく なりました から トウキャウ の はう が たまらない
> *Atsuku narimashita kara Tōkyo no hō ga tamaranai.*
> "Because it has become hot, Tokyo is intolerable."

るす だつた から しらない   "I do not know because I
Rusu datta kara, shiranai.   was absent."

270. 4. ₰ *Mo.* *a.* This particle alone is best rendered
by the English copulative conjunction "also," or "too."

271. *b.* When repeated in an affirmative sentence, it
stands for "both —— and."

272. *c.* When repeated in a negative sentence, it is best
rendered by the correlatives "neither —— nor."

Examples :—

a.   あなた ₰ いらつしやい
        Anata mo irasshai

    "You come too."

b.   さじ ₰ さら ₰ ₰つて きて ₰くれ
        Saji mo sara mo motte kite o kure.

    "Bring both spoon and plate."

c.   さじ ₰ さら ₰ うち に ありません
        Saji mo sara mo uchi ni arimasen.

    "There is neither spoon nor plate in the houses."

273. 5. に *Ni.* The particle に *ni* serves often as the
conjunction "and," in the enumeration of several things.

Examples :—

さけ に ぶどう に みかん に その ほか いろ〱 あります
Sake ni budō ni mikan ni sono hoka iro iro arimasu.

    "There are wine, grapes, and oranges, besides several
other things."

274. 6. し *Shi.* This particle often serves as the
copulative "and."

Examples :—

やすい しな ₰ ある し たかい の ₰ ある
Yasui shina mo aru shi takai no mo aru.

"There are cheap things, and also dear ones."

275. 7. ₤ *To.* *a.* When placed between nouns, ₤ *to*
may be understood as the the copulative conjunction
"and."

b. と *To* also has the meaning of the English subordinating conjunction "that," introducing an assertion.

Examples :—

a. こほりと みずと を もつて おいで
Kōri to mizu to wo motte o ide.

"Bring some ice and water."

b. こほりと みずと いひました
" *Kōri to mizu*," *to iimashita.*

"Ice and water," that he said."

276. 8. や *Ya.* や *Ya*, used with conjunctive meaning, is equivalent to the copulative "and," especially when the addition intended is rather indefinite. It expresses also hesitation and reflection.

Examples :—

ほん や すみ や ふで が あります
Hon ya sumi ya fude ga arimasu.

"There are books, ink and pens, and such."

はな や てふ や
Hana ya chō ya.

"The flowers and the butterflies."

277. 9. There are *various phrases* in common use in Japanese, which as above noted, are best rendered in English by conjunctions. More particularly these are ;—

だ が *da ga,* or ところ が *tokoro ga,* which, in beginning a sentence has the meaning "still," or "well then," and "that being so";—だ の *dano* occurring in a sentence has the meaning "and,"—it serves to give distinctness to the things counted ;—も やはり *mo ya-hari* means "like-wise";—しかし ながら *shikashi nagara* is equivalent to "but";—さう して *sō shite* (so doing) means "and ";—そんなら *sonnara,* and それ で は *sore de wa,* should be rendered by "then ";—それ で も *sore de mo* is equivalent to "though";—ゆへ に *yue ni* is "because";—やう に *yō ni* means "that," "so that";—and よ り い つ そ *yori isso* signifies "than," "rather than."

278. Many other words and phrases perform the the service of conjunctions in Japanese speech.

4. INTERJECTIONS.

279. The Japanese language is plentifully supplied with EXPRESSIONS OF FEELING, which make frequent appearance in ordinary social intercourse. The most common among these exclamations are ア *A!* ア 丶 *Aa!* ア ラ *Ara!* ア イ *Ai!* ア イ タ *Aita!* ド ツ コ イ シ ヨ *Dokkoishō!* ド ー モ *Dōmo!* エ 丶 *Eh!* ヘ イ *Hei!* ハ イ *Hai!* ハ ア *Hā!* マ ア *Mā!* ナ ル ホ ド *Naruhodo!* ネ *Ne!* オ イ *Oi!* オ ヤ *Oya!* サ *Sa!* ヤ ア *Yaa!* ヤ *Ya!* ゾ *Zo!* and many onomatopoetic words.

280. A brief explanation of these words will be sufficient. ア *A!* shows attention, and often assent, on the part of a listener. ア 丶 *Aa!* may express either admiration or grief, —— and, when long drawn out, usually tells of weariness. エ 丶 *Eh!* may tell of dislike. It is also an equivalent for wonderment, and often of sympathy, on the part of one listening. ア ラ *Ara!* tells of either joy or fear. Spoken quickly, chiefly by women, ア ラ *Ara!* shows surprise. ア イ *Ai!* often answers a call. ア イ タ *Aita!* tells of sudden pain, like the English "Ouch!" イ タ イ *Itai!* tells of continued pain. ド ツ コ イ *Dokkoi!* or ド ツ コ イ シ ヨ *Dokkoisho!* is a signal for encouragement, like the English "Now altogether!" spoken when several persons make a united, laborious effort; or, it is like the English "Up she goes!" exclaimed when a person lifts a heavy burden. ド ウ モ *Dōmo!* shows the speaker to be puzzled, not knowing just what to do, or as telling how difficult was the situation he is describing. ヘ イ *Hei!* and ハ イ *Hai!* are exclamatory acknowledgments that the speaker has heard what was said to him. ㅅ *Ha!* is an expression of attention, often of assent. マ ア *Mā!* means surprise, and wonder, like "Oh!" and also entreaty like "Do! do please!" ナ ル ホ ド *Naruhodo!* stands for attention, surprise, sympathetic wonderment in conversation. Generally, to foreign ears the interjection *Naruhodo!* seems repeated with embarrassing frequency. It is like "Really!" "You dont say so!" "Indeed!" and like interjections in English conversation. ネ *Ne!* is in more common use in ordinary conversation than even ナ ル ホ ド *Naruhodo!* ナ ル ホ ド *Naruhodo* is a listener's word; ネ *Ne!* is a speaker's word. It calls attention to a preceding word or clause, and often has the force of the interrogations, "Isn't it?" "Don't you think so?" &c. オ イ *Oi!* is a call, summoning a servant or an intimate friend. オ ヤ *Oya!* is an expression of astonishment; it is ordinarily a woman's exclamation. サ ア *Sā!* is an exclamation to arouse one to action. ヤ ア *Yā!* an expletive accompanying expressions of profound contempt. ヤ *Ya!* shows pleasurable excitement over what is being witnessed. It is often heard in theatres as an expression of applause. ヨ *Yo!* indicates address to some one. ヨ *Yo!* generally means emphasis, and often warning. ゾ *Zo!* added to a word gives it strong emphasis.

CHAPTER IV.

SOME PECULIARITIES IN ENUMERATION.

In addition to what has already been said, (82—90) concerning the numerals used by the Japanese, a few notes showing certain SPECIAL CHARACTERISTICS OF ENUMERATION should be noted.

281. 1. NUMERAL AUXILIARIES.—In counting objects, the Japanese usually enumerate them as so many things of a certain kind, or class. They seldom associate numbers and nouns as these are associated in English. Ordinarily the noun is spoken first, the numeral and class following.

For example :—

ふで ご ほん *Fude go hon,* "*pencil five stick,*" = "five pencils ; " さら じう まい *sara jiu mai,* "*plate ten flat,*" = " ten plates," and so on. This peculiarity is very like the English colloquial descriptive enumerations,—" five set of harness," " three pair of hose," " two yoke of oxen," " six ton of hay," " four gross of matches," and the like.

These auxiliaries to the numerals are numerous. Those most commonly heard are the following :—

てふ *Chō ;*—for things with " handles," such as *kuruma,* guus, cannon ; also for candles, sticks of ink, tools, and utensils, *e.g.* くるま に てふ *kuruma ni chō,* " two *kuruma ;*" らふそく いつてふ *rōsoku itchō* "one candle," etc.

ふく *Fuku ;*—for things like "doses" of medicine, "cups" of tea, " smokes " of tobacco, *e.g.* くすり に ふく *kusuri ni fuku,* "two doses of medicine ;" たばこ いつぷく *tabako ippuku,* " a smoke;" おちや さんぷく *o cha sam buku,* 'three times taking tea," etc. There is another ふ く *fuku*, used as a numeral auxiliary for pictures and maps.

はい *Hai ;*—used for so many "fills" of a cup, of a bowl, etc., *e.g.* こつぷ いつぱい の みず *koppu ippai no mizu,* "a cup full of water."

ひき *Hiki ;*—used in connection with "animals," a "draught" of a net, and "pieces" of silk, etc. *e.g.* うし なんびき *ushi nambiki?* "how many head of cattle?" きぬ いつびき *kinu ippiki,* "one piece of silk.

ほん *Hon ;*—used for "stick," or "cylinder," like things, as masts, posts, bottles, etc.

でふ *Jō ;*—used for mats which cover the floors of Japanese houses, and designate the areas of rooms.

まい *Mai ;*—is applied to "flat," broad things like coin, sheets of paper, plates, etc.

にん *Nin ;*—is used to enumerate human beings.

さつ *Satsu ;*—is used for "volumes" of books. For copies of books, the auxiliary ぶ *bu* is used.

そく *Soku ;*—helps to count shoes, socks, sandals, etc.

さう *Sō ;*—is applied to boats, ships, and to all kinds of "navigating vessels."

わ *Wa ;*—is used in counting "birds" and "bundles," *e.g.* つる いち わ *tsuru ichi wa,* "one stork;" まき さんば *maki sam ba,* "three bundles of wood."

282. There are other numeral auxiliaries in use:—like だい *dai* for things supported on a base; like けん *ken* for houses ; つう *tsū* for documents, letters; つゝみ *tsutsu-mi* for packages; めん *men* for mirrors; くみ *kumi* for sets of things like suits of clothes, and sets of toys ; すじ *suji* for line-like things, such as roads, rivers ; むね *mune* for ridge-things, or houses, and many more. The auxiliaries given above, however, will meet nearly all ordinary needs.

283. 2. ORDINAL NUMERALS. *a.* The order of things in series is shown often by the addition of the word め *me,* as a suffix to the cardinal numbers. **(84.)** *b.* But chiefly is ordinal enumeration shown by suffixing the word ばん *ban,* or ばんめ *bamme,* or by prefixing the word だい *dai* to the cardinal numbers. **(84.)**

284. *a.* As with the cardinal numbers, so with the ordinals, when they precede a noun, the particle の *no* is interposed between the numeral and the noun.

ILLUSTRATIONS :—

ひとつ め *Hitotsu me,* or ⎫
いち ばん *Ichi ban,* or ⎬ " First."
だい いち *Dai ichi.* ⎭

ミタ にちやう め に ばん ち   " Second lot, second ward,
Mita ni chō me ni ban chi   Mita."

さん ばん の きしや   " The third train."
Sam ban no kisha

だい いち の やくにん   " The chief officer."
Dai ichi no yakunin

285. *b.* When there is a specification in time, place, quantity, or kind, in enumeration, the name of the thing specified is generally interposed between the cardinal numeral and the word め *me,* to form ordinal enumeration.

Examples :—

に ちやう め *Ni chō me* " second ward;" さん ど め *san do me* " the third time;" よ にん め *yo nin me* " the fourth man;" ご まい め *go mai me* " the fifth page;" ろつぼん め *roppon me* " the sixth bottle," etc.

286. 3. QUESTIONS CONCERNING NUMBER AND QUANTITY. *a.* When questions are asked as to the *number* of persons, or things? the interrogation いくつ *ikutsu* " how many?" is often used. But more frequently the numeral auxiliary, representing the object of inquiry, in

connection with the adverbial いく *iku* "what number?"
that is, "how many?" is heard.

Examples :—

いく にん *Iku nin*, also いく たり *iku tari*, in asking
"how many human beings?" ふね は いく さう *fune wa iku
sō* "how many ships?" ふで は いく ほん *fude wa iku hon*
"how many pencils?" べつさう は いく けん *bessō wa iku
ken* "how many country houses?"—("one country house"
is いく けん *ikken*). いくつ ございます *Ikutsu gozaimasu*
"how many" (of anything) "are there?"

287. *b.* Questions concerning *quantity* are asked by the
adverbial いか *ika*, or どれ *dore*, or なに *nani*, "which?" or
"what?" followed by ほど *hodo*, meaning "degree of quantity." Also, どの くらい *dono kurai*, meaning "which
grade?" These phrases are each equivalent to "how
much?"

288. The interrogative いくら *ikura* "about how
much?" is used in inquiring as to amount of price.

Examples :—

いか ほど あります か *Ika hodo arimasu ka*	"How much is there?"
どれ ほど はいり ます か *Dore hodo hairi masu ka*	"How much will it hold?"
どの くらい いります か *Dono kurai irimasu ka*	"How much do you want?"
これ は いくら *Kore wa ikura*	"How much does this cost."

289. Note. Frequently one hears よ *yo* as a substitute for し *shi*; なな *nana* instead of しち *shichi*; and
きう *kyu* instead of く *ku*; spoken for the numbers "four,"
"seven" and "nine." This usage avoids certain ambiguities
of sound, and an unpleasant association of the numeral
phrase し にん *shi nin* "four persons," with the word
しにん *shinin* "dead person."

CHAPTER V.

HONORIFIC FORMS OF SPEECH.

290. One of the great difficulties in acquiring a proper use of the Japanese language, arises from the fact that the social relations of the Japanese people have been characterized almost as much by different forms of speech, as by legislation and customary ordinance. Between subject and lord, servant and master, host and guest, children and parents, women and men, words, as well as manner, have been shaped to an exceptionally marked degree so as to show the relations of inferior and superior, real or formal.

A few remarks about the honorific forms of Japanese speech must suffice for us in this manual.

291. 1. A foreign student, in beginning the study of spoken Japanese, should remember that, IN SPEAKING TO EQUALS, or to any persons, except intimate friends or his own servants, he should always make use of what are called the polite and honorific forms of speech, especially such forms occurring among verbs.

292. 2. The student should never apply an honorific form of speech to HIMSELF, or to HIS OWN POSSESSIONS.

293. 3. In speaking ABOUT OTHER PEOPLE, custom varies. If the person spoken of is decidedly superior in position to the speaker, honorific expressions are to be adopted; otherwise, the speaker is left largely to his own pleasure in choosing an ordinary or an honorific word or phrase.

294. 4. The foreign student would do well not to try to use THE SPECIAL FORMS OF ADDRESS WHICH MARK THE SPEECH OF SUPERIORS TO INFERIORS. Even with his own servants he would better be liberal in expressing himself by means of at least polite verbal forms, that is, of those forms which are inflected with the verb ます *masu*. Of course, he should not use honorifics in speaking to his servants; but polite verbal forms are in place for all relationships except those of the family, or of the most intimate friendship.

295. 5. NOUNS ARE MADE HONORIFIC by using either お *o* or ご *go* as a prefix.

For example :— お たく *o taku* "honorable house," meaning "your" or "his house;" ご しようち *go shōchi*, "honorable assent," meaning "your" or "his assent."

The suffix さん *san*, or さま *sama*, exalts the name of a person addressed,— さま *sama* being more honorific than さん *san*. だんな さま *Danna sama* is a very respectful address from a servant to a master; カンダ さん *Kanda san*, is the equivalent for "Mr. Kanda;" お ハナ さん *O Hana san* is "Miss Flower." おくさま *Okusama*, is the title given to "the lady of a house" in polite society. The word さま *sama* refines such phrases as お きのどく さま *o kinodoku sama*, "I am sorry for you;" ご くらう さま *go kurō sama*, "Thank you for your trouble;" お まちどほ さま *o machidō sama*, "I have kept you waiting;" ご たいくつ さま *go taikutsu sama*, "It must be tedious for you."

296. 6. FAMILY RELATIONSHIPS receive an honorific or humble character, not so much by the use of prefixes and suffixes with one class of names, as by choosing for the relationships appropriate DIFFERING NAMES, and by adding to them the honorifics お *o* and ご *go*, and さん *san* and さま *sama*.

For example :—The ordinary name for mother is はゝ *haha* "my mother," but "your" or "his mother" is called おつかさん *okkasan;* "my father" is ちゝ *chichi*, or おやぢ

oyaji, "your or his father" is をとつさん *otottsan*, or ご しんぷ *go shimpu*; "my husband" is だんな *danna*, or ていしゆ *teishu*, "your" or "her husband" is だんな さま *danna sama*, or ご ていしゆ *go teishu*; "my wife" is かない *kanai*, "your or his wife" is さいくん *saikun*, or おくさん *okusan*, or おくさま *okusama*; "my son" is むすこ *musŭko*, "your son" is generally ご しそく *go shisoku*; "my daughter" is むすめ *musŭme*, "your daughter" is お じやう さん *ojō san*; "my brother" is あに *ani* (elder), or おとゝ *ototo* (younger), "your brother" is お あに さん *o ani san*, or おとゝ ご *ototo go*; "my sister" is あね *ane* (elder), or いもうと *imōto* (younger), "your sister" is お あね さん *o ane san*, or お いもと ご *o imōto go*. There is quite a long list of these relationship names.

297. 7. DIFFERENT VERBS are used by the Japanese to HONOR, or to HUMBLE, THE SAME ACTIONS. A speaker almost always humbles his own acts, and dignifies the same acts when performed by another. Sometimes, a speaker will use the ordinary form of a verb in speaking of the actions of servants, and their like; sometimes, but not often, he will apply to a servant's actions the humble verb forms.

For example:—The verb いく *iku* is the ordinary expression for the "act of going." But if I tell an acquaintance that "I am going," I should humble myself, and honor him, by saying まゐる *mairu*. Should I request him to go, I should honor him by using some form of いらつしやる *irassharu*. Ordinarily, "I say," is いふ *iu*. To another I should in politeness express the same act by まうしあげる *mōshi ageru*. I should request another to "say" by using some form of をつしやる *ossharu*. "I see," is みる *miru*. To another, I, asking permission to look, should use はいけん する *haiken suru*; requesting him to look I should use some form of ごらん なさる *goran nasaru.* やる *Yaru* is "to offer," or "give." "I give to another," using the verb あげる *ageru*; "I ask another to give," with some form of くださる *kudasaru*, or くれる *kureru.* もらふ *Morau* is "to receive;" but "I receive from another," using some form of いただく *itadaku.* たべる *Taberu* is "I eat;" but I request another to eat, with めしあがる *meshi agaru.*

298. NOTE. The POTENTIAL FORMS of ordinary verbs are in a measure honorific ; and in common polite intercourse they are often heard, especially when persons are spoken of.

299. 8. From what has just been said, it is evident that FORMS FOR ADDRESS TO OTHERS BECOME OF SPECIAL IMPORTANCE. In this act the imperative mode would naturally be used, but the Japanese use the common imperative mode comparatively seldom. In honorific speech an honorific imperative is usually accepted. But various substitute imperatives are as a rule heard in ordinary intercourse. The verbs なさる *nasaru* "please do," or "deign," and くださる *kudasaru* "condescend," are constantly in demand to transform common verbs into polite imperative phrase. (193).

For example :—The common verb なほす *naosu* "mend," if used in a request would not be なほせ *naose!* "mend!", but probably would be なほして ください *naoshite kudasai* "mending condescend," = "Please mend this!" or it would be おなほしなさいませ *o naoshi nasai mase* "honorably mend deign," = "Please mend this!" So, みせて ください *misete kudasai*, or おみせなさい *o mise nasai*, not みせ *mise!* would stand for "Please show me." Seldom would one say まて *mate!* "Wait!" except perhaps to a coolie ; he would get around the blunt word with おまちなさい *o machi nasai* "Please wait!" Less often would he say こい *koi!* "Come." Hardly would he say this at the present day, even to a coolie. The least

polite phrase one would commonly use for " Come ! " would
be おいで *o ide*, the honorific *o* with " Come ! " To equals he
would say, おいでなさい *o ide nasai !* But to unfamiliar
friends, to guests, and to superiors he would at least say
いらっしゃい *irasshai !* the honorific imperative, requesting one to come.

300. As a general rule, there need be no hesitation on
the part of the student in using polite and honorific forms
of speech, when holding social intercourse with the
Japanese people of all classes. Politeness, in word and
in act, is part of the general popular culture in Japan. The
extravagant dignity and humiliation expressed in word,
and by ceremonial act, in formal, and even in ordinary,
social relations are, at the present day at least, but the
pleasant forms with which Japanese society is graced.

SECTION THIRD.

PRACTICE IN THE COLLOQUIAL.

He that travelleth into a country before he hath some entrance into the language, goeth to school, and not to travel.

FRANCIS BACON.

A child does not waste his mental activity on vain theories; he goes straight to the phraseology; he listens and understands, he imitates and speaks. He owes his progress to example *not to* precept; *to* practice, *not to* theory.

It is under the impulse of these instincts that we acquire the language of our parents. The same process applied to any other language must produce the same result; and success will be the more certain, as we follow more closely in the steps of nature. IMPRESSION *of language which is effected through* hearing *and* reading, *must therefore precede* EXPRESSION, *which is effected by* speaking *and* writing.

C. MARCEL.

CHAPTER I.

ON METHOD IN ACQUIRING JAPANESE.

301. The best method by which to learn Japanese is this:—let the student go to Japan; enter, there, an intelligent and sociable Japanese household, and become, in language at least, like a child. As an interested member of the family, sharing with it the home life and its relations with society also, he would be master of a goodly domain of the desired speech before a year would pass. But among the many who may wish to know Japanese, those who can take this best way are exceedingly few : so few are they that nothing further need be said here about this method: nothing except this,—that it is the natural way for a real, practical acquirement of the language; and that, in any method adopted for learning Japanese, it should, as far as possible, be followed.

302. The best substitute for this best method is life in Japan, in intimate contact with the Japanese people, under the faithful guidance of a competent native teacher. The student adopting this method would thereby be subjected to often repeated impressions of the true sounds of words and the rhythm and cadence characteristic of the native tongue. If attentive and inquisitive, his vocabulary would enlarge daily; and, by bold attempts in reading and in conversation under his teacher's correction, he would make steady progress in fluent and idiomatic expression of what he might wish to say. Such student could hope to have the language under easy command, within a comparatively short time. But even this way is fully opened to comparatively few.

303. Most learners of Japanese,—even most students

resident in Japan,—do not have the advantages of intimate intercourse with the Japanese people, and, except rarely, do not find satisfying native instructors. For this large majority, the method for acquiring the language most available is, therefore, whatever intercourse with Japanese speaking people and teachers may be secured, and, beyond that, whatever may be wrought out through books, that will most nearly make good the want of intimate intercourse with native household, people and teacher.

304. This Manual embodies an attempt,—at least so far as the beginnings of acquiring Japanese are concerned,—to do what may be done by a book to supply to those who seek a practical knowledge of the language, the aid which would be found in the method of nature. In the preparation of the book it has been assumed that the student who can make proper use of the lessons is intellectually mature. However childish much of the work he is asked to do may be, he is not to be instructed here as one would instruct a child. In a purely natural method imitation and memory are the most powerful agencies in operation. Here these agencies are to a great degree to be supplemented by reflection and the judgment.

305. In the First Section of the manual an attempt has been made to set forth by means of comparisons drawn from the student's own language, sound by sound, the tones and the tone-combinations common to Japanese speech. At the same time the signs by which the Japanese express in writing the sounds of their language were represented. It is supposed now that the student has learned how to write and to read both forms of the *Kana;* and that, so far as the sounds of English can teach him, he is able to pronounce, and he knows how to write, Japanese words.

306. In the Second Section a systematized, though

brief, summary, copiously illustrated, of the distinctive usages regulating Japanese speech was given. It is not supposed as yet that the student has mastered this summary; but it is expected that in general he has become so well acquainted with the summary that he can use it intelligently in his study of the remaining, and most important, part of the book.

307. With this preparation we now propose to open the way for the student to become familiar with a large measure of the Japanese language as it is really current in polite social intercourse. The Conversations which make up this Third Section are to be regarded as being among the best substitutes,—as far as a book can furnish a substitute,—for the companionship of living beings. They are attempts at faithful reproductions of the intercourse of persons imagined to be members of the middle and refined social circles of Japan. They embody just such language as would most become the intercourse of a cultured foreigner with the Japanese people.

308. Through a proper use of these Conversations the student may hope to go a good way towards his goal. As much as possible let him forget that the Conversations are part of a book. Let him look upon them as reports from life. Let him think of " Mr. Robinson " and " Mr. Mikata " as friends with whom he may associate daily,—to whom he can listen until their words are common place and are fixed in memory. He will find at length that these talks cover a large part of ordinary, every-day experience, and that familiarity with them has introduced him into a wide knowledge of, and given him considerable use of, the language he is seeking to master.

309. In order to secure best the result aimed at in the Conversations, it will be necessary for the student, as soon as possible, to understand them just as their speakers understand them. The English sentences standing opposite them are not their literal translations. Literally, it is not possible to carry over a Japanese sentence into English, or into any other Western language, and along with such translation to convey the true Japanese meaning. Translation from Japanese into English is a very different thing from the turning of,—let us say,—German into English. The English sentences here given are to be considered almost wholly as .but the equivalents in usage and in meaning, of the Japanese sentences with which they are associated. To illustrate :—take the first phrase of the Conversations,—Mr. Robinson's greeting to his friend ;—" *O hayō gozaimasu !*" In literal translation, Mr. Robinson in this phrase declares, with an honorific prefix, that, "Early is," or rather," " It is early." In such literal translation these words are to an English speaking person only a common-place assertion about the time of day. But to a Japanese the assertion is a friendly morning greeting. Its real equivalent in English is " Good Morning!" a phrase which in turn is to a Japanese, in literal translation, no greeting at all, but only an awkward declaration about the quality of the morning. A German and an Englishman meeting early in the day might say the words " *Guten Morgen !*" and "Good Morning!" to each other, each using a literal translation of the other's words and each conveying to the other exactly the same meaning. But Mr. Robinson may not translate his English greeting to his friend; he must use its Japanese equivalent. Still farther removed from use in literal translation is Mr. Mikata's answer to his friend Robinson's apologetic inquiry, " Do I interrupt you?" His reply is,—" *Sŭkoshi mo !*," literally " *A little even !*" Literally, to Mr. Robinson this answer is nonsense, but Mr. Mikata means to say, and Mr. Robinson so understands him, exactly what an Englishman would intend to say in the words, "Not at all!", "Not in the least!" or in any other complimentary phrase, waiving the apology.

310. So then, in a study of these Conversations, indeed in the learning of all Japanese phrasing, the student should first seek to understand the Japanese sentences as their speakers understand them. In all languages, words necessarily are used,—sometimes many, sometimes few,—which are only different signs for the same things. *Separate words* are almost always translateable. But very often a Japanese speaker, as we have just seen, uses even translateable words, applying them to relations designated by an Englishman through entirely different words. Much more often, *phrases* in Japanese and in English, having the same intentions, differ from one another interms and in composition. Yet further, there is never any real likeness in construction and in verbal content between extended *sentences* of the two languages. The Japanese language must, in fact, be studied as a development of speech almost wholly independent of any tongue of the West. The most that the English language can do towards helping a student towards a knowledge of Japanese arises from the fact that English like Japanese is a human language. Consequently, to an English vocabulary almost throughout, Japanese words denoting the same ideas and things may be attached ; further, the laws of universal grammar, the distinctions of parts of speech, and their fundamental modes of relationship, may be illustrated for Japanese speech through their manifestation in English; and, as is done in these Conversations, English *equivalents* for what is expressed in Japanese sentences may be constructed, thereby making the Japanese forms of expression somewhat the more easy of comprehension and of appropriation. But, beyond these limits, the student must depend for his

progress in the language almost wholly upon the help he can find in the language itself.   In this connection some counsel given by Prof. Chamberlain in his "Handbook" is worth remembering.   He writes;—

"The student should endeavour to place himself from the outset at the Japanese point of view.   This he can do only by dint of much learning by heart.—The necessity for memorising can not be too strongly insisted upon.   It is the sole means of escape from the pernicious habit of thinking in English, translating every sentence literally from a whispered English original, and therefore beginning and ending by speaking English Japanese instead of Japanese Japanese.   It is not only that the words and idioms of Japanese differ from our English words and idioms, but that the same set of circumstances does not always draw from Japanese speakers remarks similar to those which it would draw from European speakers."

311.   Let the student then, as far as possible, familiarize himself through both eye and ear with the Japanese text of this section, informing the text with the meanings embodied in the English with which it is associated, but aiming to make the text his own so completely that he might as readily use its forms in addressing a Japanese, as he would use the English forms in addressing an English speaker, when he had the thought common to both texts in mind.   This task may seem very tedious in prospect and to promise but little in achievement, but really, in time, its slowness will result in the best possible speed attainable when the purely natural method is not available.

312.   In carrying on the work of comprehending and appropriating these Conversations the student will find the section on the "Elements of Grammar" especially helpful. Grammar, is not correctly apprehended when it is looked upon as the art of speaking and writing a language. Grammar, imparts no power of speech to him who has not already the materials and ability for expression. It is specifically but a record and generalization of the usages which prevail in the speech and writing of those who are considered good writers and speakers. It is a systematized presentation and explanation of standard linguistic forms.

313. As such systematization of linguistic forms and usages, however, the Elements of Grammar here presented will be found to have a large value for the student. Constant reference to it will make clear why the Japanese give the distinctive forms to the expression of their thought, shown in the Conversations, and, in general, will explain unique linguistic usages which to the Western understanding must otherwise remain obscure.

314. But beyond this service, a thorough study of the Conversations in intimate association with the Elements of Grammar will do much to hasten the progress of the student toward the culminating gain which every one must make in order actually to acquire a language,— namely independence of a literal repetition of the forms set for him in the models he studies, and power to express his own thought in phrases characteristically his own.

315. The real acquirement of a language means in the end, freedom from a literal imitation of models, and an ability of one's self to originate speech. The best aid given by this manual, or by any other help to the learning of a language, is, at last therefore, just how much it may hasten such independence and self reliance. Indeed, all books, teachers, companions, even the largest and most intimate fellowship with others are to be regarded in the main as only guides and helpers towards the time when the student, emancipated from his pupilage, shall be able to go forward dependent upon his own strength

and inventiveness.   The natural and accomplished speaker
is he who has gained so large a mastery of the teach-
ings of others, that they all serve him in the development
of a language which is characteristically his own.   So
far as this manual is concerned, therefore, the aim in its
preparation will have been reached, when it shall have
become to those who may use it, no longer a collection of
models to be exactly copied, but chiefly a store of words
and of sentences, and of laws of speech, from which the
users shall take what they will, combining the words and
phrases into new relationships, creating new sentences and
distinctive modes of expression,—in a word, making the
book secondary to self-direction in linguistic progress.

316.   There is no more a royal road into the learning
of Japanese than into any other learning.   He who seeks
such path would better never begin the search.   But among
the ways over which one may enter this domain, some
are less difficult to traverse than others.   The way which
we have here attempted to open;—the way of long endur-
ing submission to often recurring impressions of sounds
and signs of speech ; of continuously repeated contact
with syllables, words, phrases, sentences and paragraphs,
read, memorized, and imitated until the mind has become
thoroughly familiar with them as speech or writing ; of
study of numerous conversations from real life, illustrated
and explained by the general usages of Japanese speech
and by their equivalents rendered in the student's own
language; this way though seemingly very slow and, it may
be, difficult, we nevertheless believe to be comparatively
the easy way, and the way really the most rapid in ad-
vancement towards the longed-for goal,—a practical
mastery of Japanese speech.

CHAPTER II.

THE I-RO-HA.

317. At the close of the First Section of this book the student was recommended to make himself familiar with the *Katakana* writing of forty-eight proverbs, and then to transcribe the proverbs with the *Hiragana* syllabics. The transcription was proceeded with there only in part. The complete transcription was left for the opening of the present section, that it might serve to illustrate the arrangement of the *Hiragana* syllabics in the order by which the Japanese ordinarily know them.

318. The arrangement of the syllabary with which the student has become familiar is called the "*Go-jū-on*," or "Fifty Sounds." There are in fact but forty-seven basal sounds in the syllabary ; the syllabics イ, ヰ and ヱ being repeated in the "Y" and "W series," chiefly for the sake of a symmetrical filling out of the table ; and the syllabic ending ン being in fact but a variation of ム. The *Go-jū-on* is easily memorized ; the five pure vowel sounds *a, i, u, e, o* constituting a series of sounds to which the nine consonants *k, s, t, n, h, m, y, r* and *w*, with the five consonantal softenings *g, z, d, b* and *p*, are prefixed, as,—

ka, ki, ku, ke, ko,
ga, gi, gu, ge, go, etc.

This arrangement, as we have seen, is very helpful to the student, especially in the study of verbal inflection and of the phonetic changes in words.

319. But, symmetrical, simple and helpful as the *Go-jū-on* order of the syllabary is, it is not the order most widely known, and generally in use, among the Japanese people. The *Go-jū-on* and the *Katakana* are usually put together. Yet this combination, though effecting the simplest and easiest treatment of the group of sounds by which the Japanese language is expressed is, as said, less known and less in popular favor than the *Hiragana*, and the syllabic order devised for the latter.

320. The customary arrangement of the *Hiragana* is known as the *I-ro-ha*, a name formed from the first three syllabics of the series, just as the name *Al-pha-bet* was formed from the first three of the letters with which the sounds of the Greek and kindred languages are uttered. *Kōbō Daishi*, as before noted (page 6), not only was the deviser of the *Hiragana* syllabary; tradition affirms also, that it was he who gave the syllabary its *I-ro-ha* form. He, Buddhist priest and teacher of souls, it is said, turned the syllabics, prosaic in the *Go-jū-on*, into a poem on the vanity of existence, as proclaimed in the Buddhist scriptures; thus by mnemonic verse teaching those who studied it not only new characters by which to write their language, but at the same time impressing upon them what he held to be one of the great truths necessary to their best welfare. He, so it is said, wrote :—

> " *Iro wa nioedo,*
> *Chirinuru wo—*
>   *Waga yo tare zo*
> *Tsune naran ?*
>
>   *Ui no oku-yama*
> *Kyō koete,*
>   *Asaki yume mishi,*
> *Ei mo sezu :* "—

which means, according to Prof. Chamberlain's liberal paraphrase ;—"Though their hues are gay, the blossoms flutter down, and so in this world of ours who may continue forever? Having to-day crossed the mountain-fastness of existence, I have seen but a fleeting dream, with which I am not intoxicated."

321. But whatever may true of the origin of the *Hiragana* and its *I-ro-ha* form and meaning, and whatever may be the real reason for its favored place in popular usage, the student who wishes to know the Japanese language as the Japanese write it ; to consult native *Kana* lexicons ; to understand catalogues, read newspapers or any unmodernized literature, must memorize *I-ro-ha* as he once committed his own *A, B, C,* to memory, and must read and write the *Hiragana* as he once conquered the letters of English script.

322. In recognition of the prominent place occupied by the *I-ro-ha* in the literary expression of Japanese, we selected the forty-eight proverbs (which the student is now transcribing from *Katakana* into *Hiragana*,) so that the initial syllabic of each proverb should be one of the forty-seven basal sounds of the Japanese language, adding one proverb more containing the terminal sound N. These proverbs, as first written in *Katakana*, (91), were arranged and numbered so as to illustrate the syllabary in its *I-ro-ha* form. The forty-eight Conversations which occupy the present section as "Practice in the Colloquial," have received as "texts" or "motives," these illustrative proverbs, in their *I-ro-ha* order of succession.

32 . The student is recommended to complete now the transcription of the Illustrative Proverbs. As a preparation for that work the *Hiragana* syllabary is repeated here, but we give the *Hiragana* in its usual order as *I-ro-ha,* and incorporate in the table some of the less used characters, which still appear in manuscript, and sometimes find way even into print. With the full transcription of the proverbs we have associated literal translations and their equivalent renderings in English. We recommend to the student, before he proceeds with the Conversations, a thorough study of these wise sayings, in their Japanese forms.

324. I-RO-HA SYLLABARY.

KŌBŌ DAISHI'S VERSE.

イ I	ロ Ro	ハ Ha	ニ Ni	ホ Ho	ヘ He	ト To
チ Chi	リ Ri	ヌ Nu	ル Ru	ヲ Wo	ソ So	
ワ Wa	カ Ka	ヨ Yo	タ Ta	レ Re		
ツ Tsu	ネ Ne	ナ Na	ラ Ra	ム Mu		

マ MA		ン SHI	
ヤ YA		ミ MI	ン N
ク KU	テ TE	メ ME	ス SU
オ O	エ E (y)e	ユ YU	セ SE
ノ NO	コ KO	キ KI	モ MO
ヰ I (wo)i	フ FU	サ SA	ヒ HI
ウ U	ケ KE	ア A	エ E (w)e

325. ILLUSTRATIVE PROVERBS IN
HIRAGANA.

1. いち を きいて じふ を しる。
One *(acc. sign)* *hearing* *ten* *(acc. sign)* *knows.*
Hearing one thing, he knows ten.

2. ろん に まけて も り に かつ。
Argument in *losing* *even principle in* *wins.*
Though beaten in argument, victorious in principle.

3. はり の あな から てん を のぞく。
Needle of *hole* *from* *heaven* *(acc. sign)* *peeps at.*
Peeps at the sky through a needle's eye.

4. にんげん わづか ごじふ ねん。
Man *short space* *fifty* *years.*
Man's life is but fifty years.

5. ほまれ あらん より そしり なかれ。
Praise *shall be* *than* *defame* *be not.*
No-blame is better than praise.

6. へた の なが だんぎ。
Unskillful of *long* *sermons.*
An awkward priest for long sermons.

7. とんで ひ に いる なつ の むし。
Flying *fire into* *enters summer* *of* *insect.*
Summer insects fly into the fire.

8. ちり つもつて やま と なる。
Dust *heaping* *mountain that becomes.*
Piled up dust becomes a mountain.

9. りか に かんむり を だゞさず。
Plum-tree under   cap   (acc. sign)   not adjust.
Adjust not your cap under a plum tree.

10. ぬすびと を みて なは を なう。
Thief   (acc. sign)   seeing,   rope   (acc. sign)   twist.
He makes a rope, having seen the thief.

11. るいらん より も あやうし。
Piled eggs   than   even   perilous.
More hazardous even than a pile of eggs.

12. をかめ はち もく。
Land eyes   eight   checker-board squares.
A bystander sees eight moves in the game.

13. わざはひ も さいはひ の はし と なる。
Adversity   also   prosperity   of bridge that becomes.
Even adversity becomes a bridge to prosperity.

14. かしら かくして を を かくさず。
Head   hiding   tail (acc. sign)   not hiding.
Though the head be hidden the tail is seen.

15. よめ が しうとめ に なる。
Bride (nom. sign)   mother-in-law   to becomes.
A bride becomes a mother-in-law.

16. たま みがかざれば ひかり なし。
Jewel   if not polished   shines   not.
A jewel unpolished will not glitter.

17. れい すぐれば しつれい と なる。
Politeness if exceed   rudeness   that becomes.
Too much politeness becomes rudeness.

18. そで うつし に もの を やる。
Sleeve transferring in thing (acc. sign) *gives.*
Gives, by passing it through the sleeve.

19. つの を なほす とて うし を ころす。
Horn (acc. sign) *mending that saying ox* (acc. sign) *kills.*
Intending to mend the horn, he kills the ox.

20. ねずみ とる ねこ は つめ を かくす。
Rat catching cat as for claws (acc. sign) *hides.*
The rat catching cat hides her claws.

21. なきづら を はち が さす。
Weeping face (acc. sign) *bee* (nom. sign) *stings.*
Bees sting a weeping face.

22. らつくわ ゐだ に かへらず。
Fallen flower branch to not returning.
A fallen flower returns not to its branch.

23. むり が とほれば だうり ひつこむ。
Unreason (nom. sign) *if pass by reason draws back.*
Reason shrinks back when passion goes by.

24. うり の たね に なすび は はえね。
Melon of seed in egg-plant as for not produces.
An egg plant does not grow from a melon seed.

25. ゐど の なか の かはず だいかい を
Well of middle of frog great sea (acc. sign)
しらず。
knows not.
The frog in a well does not know the ocean.

26. のど-もと　　すぐれば　　あつさ　　を
Throat-base　　*having passed*　　*hotness*　　(acc. sign)

わする。
forget.

If a thing be swallowed its heat is forgotten.

27. おに　の　ねんぶつ。
Demon　of　prayer.

A devil's prayer.

38. くち　に　と　は　たて　られぬ。
Mouth　to　door　as for　set up　cannot be.

A door cannot be made for a man's mouth.

29. やすもの　かひ　の　ぜに　うしなひ。
Cheap thing　buyer　of　money　losing.

He who buys cheap loses his money.

30. まがらね　ば　よ　に　たゝれず。
Not bending　if　world　in　keep up cannot.

No keeping up in the world without bending.

31. け　を　ふいて　きづ　を　もとむ。
Hair (acc. sign) *blowing　wound* (acc. sign) *obtains.*

He blows away the hair, only to find a wound.

32. ふるき　を　たづねて　あたらしき　を
Old　(acc. sign)　*studying*　　*new*　　(acc. sign)

しる。
knows.

New things are learned by studying the old.

33. ことば　おほけれ　ば　しな　すくなし。
Words　abundant　if　materials　few.

Many words, small matter.

34. えみ の うち に やいば を ふくむ。
Smile of the middle in blade (acc. sign) contains.
He conceals a sword within a smile.

35. て の うら を かへす。
Hand of palm (acc. sign) turns over.
Reversing the palm of the hand.

36. あたま そらん より こゝろ を それ。
Head shave than mind (acc. sign) shave.
Cleanse the heart rather than shave the head.

37. さる も き から おつる。
Monkey even tree from falls.
Even monkeys fall from trees.

38. きん-げん みゝ に さかふ。
Golden-saying ears to oppose.
Wise sayings are disagreeable.

39. ゆだん たい てき。
Negligence great enemy.
Negligence is a great enemy.

40. めくら へび に おぢず。
A blind man snake at fearing not.
A blind man is not afraid of a snake.

41. みめ より こゝろ。
Face than heart.
Goodness of heart is better than beauty of face.

42. しゆ に まじはれば あかく なる。
Vermillion with mixed if red becomes.
He who handles vermillion is stained red.

43. ゑば は にくき もの に あたへ よ。
Bait   as for   the detestable thing   to   give!

Give food even to detestable things!

44. ひと の よ を わたる は まるきばし
Man   of world (acc. sign) passing   as for   log-bridge

の ごとし。
for   is like.

Man's journey through this world is like crossing a round bridge.

45. もゆくひ に は ひ が つき やす い。
A fire-brand   to   as for fire (nom. sign) catch   is easy.

A brand easily takes fire.

46. せん どう おほくして ふね やま へ
Sailors   numerous being   ship   mountain   to

のぼる。
go up.

Too many sailors run the ship ashore.

47. すみかき の なか から めい けん が
Pokers   of the middle   from   famous sword (nom. sign)

でる。
comes out.

Famous swords sometimes are made from fire-scrapers.

48. いちじ せん きん。
One letter   a thousand pieces of gold.

One letter is worth a thousand dollars.

だい さん しやう

ともだち どし の はなし

だい いち

い す

いち を きいて じふ を しる。

こ は <u>トウキヤウ</u> の <u>ミカター</u>し の いへ なり。<u>ミカター</u>し はなその を まへ に せる みなみ-むき の へや にて かきもの を なし たれり。

1. <u>ロビンソン</u>-し この ところ へ いりきたり, あいさつ を して <u>ミカター</u>し に むかひ:—
お-はやう ございます。お-じやま では ありますー まい か。

2. <u>ミカター</u>し:—イーエ すこし も。どうぞ お-かけ なさいまし。よく お-いで なさいました。お-まち まうして ゐた ところ です。

3.—ありがたう ございます。はなはだ しつれい で ございます が, この やう に すはります。

4.—どうぞ ご ず-ゐい に。いす は いかゝ です。いす の はう が ざぶとん より お-らく で ございます。

CHAPTER III.

FRIENDS IN CONVERSATION.

I. PROVERB FOR (ん) *I.*

Hearing one thing, he knows ten.

PLACE :—*Mr. Mikata's house, Tōkyō. South room, opening upon the garden. Mr. Mikata, writing :—*

1.—*Mr. Robinson entering, bows, and says :*—Good morning. Do I interrupt you ?

2.—*Mr. Mikata :*—Not at all ! Please, take a seat. I am glad to see you. I have been expecting you.

3.—Thank you. Be kind enough to excuse me for sitting down in this way.

4.—Do make yourself comfortable ! Won't you have a chair ? A chair will be easier for you than a cushion.

5.—イーエ この やうに あし を なげ-だして も
よろし-ければ この はう が かへつて かつて で
ございます。

6.—さ　ふ　る　おーらく　に。あなた と わたくし
の なか に ゑんりよ は いりません。 コレ
ヨ子 おーちや を もつて おーいで。 そまつ
な たばこ です が めしあがり なさいまし。

7.—いかにも けつこう な おーには で ございます
ね。 こなた は まつたく さむい かぜ を よけて
ゐます から, けさ は そと で は じつに さむい
かぜ が ふいて をります が, この おーざしき で
は じうぶん あつたか で ございます。

8.—かんちう で も ひ の さします とき
には しやうじ を みな あけはなつて をられます。
につちう に は ひばち も いりません。 ほと-
んど ひ に てり-つけられる くらゐ です。 おーちや
いつ-ぷく おーあがり なさいまし。

9.—ありがたう。 とき に この あひだ おーはなし
いたして をきました くわいわ を けふ は はじめ
たう ございます が, あなた は それ に ついて なに
か まだ よい おーかんがへ が ございません でした
か。 ごーしようち の とほり ことば は もう
かなり ぞんじて をりますし, きく こと も
たいてい は わかります が, はなす こと に なる
と じつに こまります。 それ ゆゑ どうか あなた

5.—No, indeed! If you won't mind my rudeness in shoving out my feet, I would rather sit as I am.

6.—Make yourself at home. You and I need not stand upon ceremony.—Say, *O Yone!* bring some tea.—Here are some good cigarettes. Try them.

7.—How much you must enjoy your garden! You seem so entirely protected here from the cold winds. It is delightfully warm in this room. Really, there is quite a cold breeze from the north, this morning.

8.—Even in mid-winter, when the sun shines, I can sit here with all the *shōji* open. During mid-day I do not even use a *hibachi.* I can almost bake myself in the sun's heat. Will you have a sip of tea?

9.—Thank you. .... Well, —— I should like to begin to-day the conversations we spoke of a short time ago. Have you thought out any good plan for them yet? You know that I have a pretty good vocabulary already. I understand much that I hear. Speaking is my difficulty. I need practice with a guide like you.

の やう な お-かた と れんしう いたしたう
ございます。

10.―しかし はなし を する ため のみ に
はなし を する と いふ の は ずゐぶん
たいくつ な こと で ございます。わたくし は
どうか あなた が わが くに の ことば を じ-
いう に お-つかひ なさる やう に なれば
よい と おもひます。もし それ が でき たら
あなた が ニホン に お-すまひ なさる こと
も いま より よほど おもしろく なる で
ございませう。どう いふ はうばふ に よれば
よい か と いろく かんがへて みました が。
あなた が ひらがな を よんだり かいたり
する こと を お-ならひ なさつた とき の
ことわざ に ついて はなし を して は いかゝ
でせう。

11.―あなた は わたくし を せわ して くださる
お-いしや-さま と おなじ です から なん でも
あなた の お-さしず どほり に いたしませう。
あなた の お-かんがへ と いふ の は
どう-いふ の で ございます か。

12.―さう です ね。これら の ことわざ の
うち に どう-いふ いみ が ある か, さがして
み-やう じや ありません か。ことわざ は ちゑ
を まるめて ドル に した やう な もの で

10.—But talk for talk's sake only, is very tiresome. I am anxious that you should be able to use our language freely. If you could do so, your life in Japan would be so much more interesting than it is now. I have been thinking a good deal about some plan for us to follow. How would you like to talk over the proverbs which you used in learning to read and to write the *Hiragana?*

11.—You are the doctor for this patient, you know. Just as you decide. What is your plan?

12.—Why, —— let us try to find out what meaning is shut up in these wise words. A proverb is wisdom turned into coin. It circulates among the people, and makes them rich. These proverbs are some of Japan's oldest treasures. See! here they are. I have arranged them in the order of

ありまして, せかい に つうよう して ひとく
の とみ と なる の です。 これら の こと
わざ は ニホン の ふるき たから-もの の
いちぶ-ぶん で ございます。 これ が その
ことわざ で ございます。 わたくし は いろは
じゅん に ならべて おきました。 これ を
はなし の だい に して は いかゞ で
ございませう。

13.—よう ございませう。 しかし あなた は
つうべん を して くださら なければ
なりません。

14.—あなた の ぶん は あなた で じうぶん
できませう。 さて こゝ に 「い」 の ことわざ
が ございます。 わたくし は ときゞ この
ことわざ は まこと に よく あなた の こと に
あたつて をる と おもひます。 もちろん
それ が じふ を きいて いち を しる と
できて をれば すこし も あなた に くわんけい
は ありません。

15.—ご-あいさつ ありがたう ございます。 この
のち ほめて いたゞきたい とき に は ご-
ちそう に あがりませう。 です が アメリカ で
まうします アイルランド-じん の なぞ と
いふ やう な もの なら ほしく ありません。

16.—それ は どう いふ もの です か。

our "*I-ro-ha.*" What do you say to making them the texts for our talks?

13.—All right! But you must be the interpreter.

14.—I think you can do your full share. Now, there is the "*I*" proverb. I sometimes think that it really applies to you. Certainly, if it were shaped so as to read, "*Hearing ten things, he knows one,*" you would have no part in it at all.

15.—Much obliged to you for the compliment. When I am hungry for praise, I shall come to you for a feast. But I know that I do not need, what we call in America, an "Irish hint."

16.—What is that?

17.—あし で もつて わたくし を いへ の そと へ けり-だして, その や の しゆじん が わたくし を きやく に する の を このまぬ と いふ こと を しらせ やう と いふ の です。

18.—あなた の おつしやる の は この ことわざ を へん な ぐあひ に つかふ の です。 ダが あなた が それ と ちがつた こと を おつしやつた ため に この ことわざ の いみ が あきらか に なりました。 しろい もの も くろい もの の そば に おく と なほ しろく みゆる だうり です から。

19.—この ことわざ は <u>ニホン</u>-じん に あて-はまりませう か いかが でせう。

20.—こくみん と して みれば われ〱 は ばか で は ありません。 いち-ぶ を きいた ばかり で ぜんたい を さつする に は すばやい はう です。 わが くに で どくりうかう する うた は たいてい なぞ で で-きて ゐます。 それ に また われ〱 は ぎろん の はじめ を きく と たいち に その けつろん に とんで ゆく と いふ ひなん を たび〱 かうむります。

21—わたくし は あなた の お-くに の ひと は よほど さかしい と おもひます。 たとへば わたくし の うち の めしつかひ の もの-ら

17.—To be kicked out of a house in order that one may understand that its master does not wish one to be his guest.

18.—That is an odd way for using this proverb. You give its meaning by showing what it is not. Of course, white is plainly white when it stands beside black.

19.—Is this proverb true of the Japanese people? What do you think?

20.—As a nation we are not stupid. We are rather quick to guess at the whole, when we know only a part. Our most popular poetry consists largely of suggestive fancies. Also, we are often blamed for jumping at a conclusion, as soon as we hear the beginning of an argument.

21.—I fancy that your people are very clever. My servants, for example, hear my awkward attempts to give them orders. I am often astonished at the ten things they

でも　わたくし　が　そまつなる　ことば　にて　めいずる　こと　を　しようち　いたします。　わたくし　は　しば〴〵　おどろく　こと　が　ございます。　それこそ　わたくし　が　いはう　と　おもつて−ある　こと　を　ひと　こと　を　も　きかぬ　うち　に，わたくし　が　ほしい　と　おもつてる　こと　を　とを　まで　も　しようち　して　をります。

22.—その−とほり　です。　わたくし　も　われ〳〵　<u>ニホン</u>−じん　は　あまり　はや−がてん　し−すぎる　と　おもひます。　われ〳〵　の　こゝろ　は　びん−せふ　で　あります　が，びんせふ　で　ある　ため　に　まゝ　しらぬ　こと　を　も　しつて　ゐる　と　おもふ　こと　が　ございます。　もつとも　ある　とき　は　よつつ　を　きいて　むつつ　を　しれば　つがふ　の，よい　こと　が　ございませう。　また　なゝつ　を　きいて　みつつ　を　しる　も　しば〴〵　けつこう　な　こと　で　あります　が，いち　を　きいて　じふ　を　しる　と　おもつて　ゐた　とき　に　その　わづか　に　きいた　ひとつ　を　も　しらなかつた　なら　まこと　に　ふつがふ　な　こと　で　こざいませう。　さうして　みれば　この　ことわざ　は　さかしい　ひと　を　ほめる　に　は　もつとも　よい　こと　です　が，たれ　でも　すぐ　に　これ　を　じぶん　の　こと　だ　と　おもうて　は　よく　ありますまい。

23.—こんにち　は　いろ〳〵　ありがたう　ございま−

know of what I want, before they have in fact heard the one thing I try to say.

22.—Indeed, I think we are often too much in a hurry in such matters.   Our people are mentally quick.   But that quickness, possibly, at times makes us think we know when we don't know.   Occasionally it would be better for us to hear four things, and know six.   Even to hear seven things and know three, would often be best.   To hear one thing and think we know ten, when we do not know even the one thing we have heard, is not wisdom.   This proverb is excellent praise for clever men.   But every body should be very slow to think it true of himself.

23.—You have been very kind to-day.   I am sorry to

した。ちやうざ を いたしまして まうしわけ
が ありません。しつれい な こと を まうす
やう です が, あなた の ちしき に ついて
の ご-しなん が わたくし のみ の ため に
なる こと は, ことば に ついて の ご-しなん
に おとる こと は ありません。それ では
お-いとま まうします。

24.—いま まだ たくさん の じかん が
ございます が, それ とも お-かへり ならば また
みやうにち お-まち まうします。ゆふかた ろくじ
じふん に お-いで なさる こと は できま-
せん か。ご-いつしよ に ばんめし を たべませう。

25.—ありがたう ございます。お-こゝろざし は
ふかく しやうくわん いたします。さやうなら。

26.—さやうなら。コレ お-ヨ子, お-きやく
さま が お-かへり だ。ぼうし と ぐわい-たう
を もつて お-いで。お-き を お-つけ なさいまし。

———

だい に
ろ 語
ろん に まけて も り に かつ。

1. ロビンソン-し:—こん-ばん は。くるまや
が ひじやう に ぐづく して ゐました の
で, つひ おそく なりました。

have taken so much of your time. Pardon me, if I say that your lesson in wisdom is fully as helpful as your lesson in words. I must go now.

24.—There is yet plenty of time. But if you must go, I shall expect you again to-morrow. Can you not come in the evening, about six o'clock? Come, and take supper with me.

25.—Thank you. I should enjoy your hospitality exceedingly. Good bye!

26.—Good bye! Say, *O Yone!* our guest is about to leave. Bring his coat and hat. Take care of yourself.

———

II. PROVERB FOR (ろ) *RO*.

Though beaten in argument, victorious in principle.

1. *Mr. R.* :—Good evening. I am afraid I am late. My *kurumaya* was very slow.

2. ミカタ—し：—まだ そんな に おそく ございません。やうく ろくじ じつ—ぷん です。くるまや は わるい の です か。

3.—イーエ ほんたう の びやうき で は ありません が, さくばん さけ を のみ—すぎ ました の で, けふ は やく に たいん の です。めしつかひ に は よい もの です が, ときぐ のんだくれて こまります。

4.—それ は くるまひき の うち に は ありうち の こと で ございます。あれら の しごと は なかく ほね が をれます から, つひ のみ—すぎる くせ が つく の です。わたくし の うち の くるまや も ある とき は どうも しかた が ない こと だ と いつて をります。どうぞ こちら へ お—なほり なさいまし。ごらん うけ の とほり, ほんの かない の ひと どうやう に いたします。ニホン れうり の ほか なに も ございません。

5.—わたくし の ため に ゆふ—ごぜん の お—したく を かへて くださらぬ はう が かへつて ありがたう ございます。ニホン れうり は けつこう で ございます。

6.—どうぞ ご—じいう に。ビール か さけ を めしあがります か。

7.—ありがたう ございます が, どちら も

2. *Mr. M.* :—You are not late.   It is only ten minutes past six.   Is your man ill ?

3.—He is not really ill, but last night he drank too much *saké.*   To-day he is not to be depended upon.   He is a good servant, but every now and then he will get drunk.

4.—That is a common fault with *jinrikisha*-men.   But, as you know, they become very tired at their work.   Then, they easily fall into the habit of drinking too much.   My own *kurumaya* says, that it is sometimes a case of " Can't be helped ! " with himself.   Please sit there.   You see I have treated you just like one of my own family.   I have only Japanese food for you.

5.—I feel honored that you make no difference in your supper on my account.   I like good Japanese food.

6.—Please help yourself.   Will you have some beer, or *sake ?*

7.—Thank you, I will not take either.   I prefer tea.

いたゞきません。 それ より は をーちや を
いたゞきませう。

*　　　*　　　*　　　*　　　*

8.—もう なに も をーめしあがり なさいません か。
それ では をーヨ子, こゝ に ある もの を
さげて, たばこ の はこ を もつて をーいで。
さて, あなた は 「ろ」 の ことわざ に ついて
いか に をーかんがへ です か。

9.—わたくし は それ は まいにち せかい
ぢう に をこる こと の てきーひやう で ある
と をもひます。 ごーしようち の とほり ぎろん
の たくみなる こと は しんり の ある
しやうこ に なりません。 アメリカ で がつかう
の こども が をそはる ごく よい をしへ の
いちぶ は まつたく この ことわざ の うち に
あります。 アメリカ の こども は コロンバス
や ガリレオ や また は ルーサー の れきし を
しつて をります が, これら の ひとゞ は いづれ
も ぎろん に は まけました が, じつさい の
うへ で は みな かち を とりました。

10.—そのーとほり です。 この ことわざ は
かり に よの かいかくしや の ふどう と いたし
ませう。 これ から 「は」 の ことわざ に
なります が, 「は」 の ことわざ は あつせいか
の ふどう だ と いつて よからう と をもひ
ます。 (にの さき げぢよ いり きたる)。 だんな さま, を一

*   *   *   *   *

8.—Won't you have something more?   *O Yone!* take away these things and bring a tobacco box.   Well, what do you think of our " *Ro* " proverb?

9.—It is a good comment on what happens every day all over the world.   Everybody knows that skill in argument is no proof of truth.   Some of the best lessons which American school children learn are, in fact, about this proverb.   They all know of the lives of such men as Columbus, Galileo and Luther.   Every one of these men was defeated in argument.   But, really, all were victorious.

10.—Yes! Let us set the motto down as true reformers. Now we come to the " *Ha* " proverb.   Shall we name it the motto for bigots?

(Servant enters) :—Master, a gentleman has just called. Here is his card.

Ask the gentleman to come in.   I am very sorry that our talk must stop now.   A friend has just arrived from Kyōto.

きやく さま が いらつしやいました。 これ が
その お-かた の めいし で ございます。

こちら へ ご-あんない まうし な。 はなはだ
お-きのどくさま で ございます が, お-はなし
を こい まで に いたして おかなければ
なりません。 じつ は いま <u>キヤウト</u> から
ともだち が ひとり まゐりまして, わたくし に
たいせつ な ようじ が ある の です。 みやうにち
は わたくし は たく に をりますまい から
みやうごにち お-いで を ねがわれませう か。

11.—わたくし は いつ でも よう ございます。
わたくし の なぐさみ で お-じやま を
いたして は なりません。 いつ も ご-しんせつ
を うけて ありがたう ございます。 たいてい
なん じ ころ に お-ひま で ござります か。

12.—あさはん の すぐ のち なら いちばん
よう ございます。 く じ ごろ に お-いで に
なれば じうぶん お-はなし が いたされませう。

13.—おくさま へ よろしく。 どうぞ これ
にて。 げんくわん まで は きようしゆく で
ござります。

14.—いや すこし も ご-しんぱい に お-
よびません。 それ に ともだち を むかへ に
でます から。 あなた は てうちん を ご-
ぢさん です か。 こんや は たいへん くらう
ござります。

He has important business with me.   To-morrow I shall
not be at home.   Can you come the day after to-morrow?

11.—Any time will suit me.   My pleasure must not inconvenience you.   You are always very kind.   What hour
shall you be at leisure?

12.—Just after breakfast will be the best time.   Come
about nine o'clock.   Then we can have a long talk.

13.—Present my compliments to Mrs. Mikata.   Do not
trouble yourself to go to the door with me.

14.—It is no trouble at all.   And I shall welcome my
friend.   Have you a lantern?   The night is very dark.

15.—みち を よく ぞんじて をります。お-やすみ
なさい。

16.—お-やすみ なさい。

———

だい さん

は い ま

はり の あな から てん のぞく。

1. ロビンソン-し:―しばらく で-ぶさた いたし
ました。わたくし の てがみ は で-らん に
なりました か。

2. ミカター-し:―ハイ。 もう で-ぜんくわい
だらう と おもひます が, いつたい どう
なさつた の です か。

3.―ッヒ かぜ を ひきました の で, ひどい
め に あひました。 せんだつて こなた へ
まゐりました よくじつ の こと です が,
わたくし は タカヲ-さん へ まゐりました。
そして やま を あるいて あがりました の
で ひじやう に あつたかく なつてきまして
たいさう あせ を かきました。ところ が お-
てら へ まゐりました とき に つめたい かぜ が
ふいて ゐまして そこ に しばらく の あひだ
きうそく いたして をります と, つひ ぞくく
と さむく なつて まゐりました。

15.—I know the path very well. Good night.

16.—The same to you.

————-

III. PROVERB FOR (は) *HA.*

Peeps at the sky, through a needle's eye.

1. *Mr. R. :*—It is some time since we have seen each other. Did you receive my letter?

2. *Mr. M. :*—Yes! I hope you are feeling quite well, now. What was the matter?

3.—I caught a bad cold. The day after I was here last, I went out to Takao-san. The walk up the mountain made me very warm. I perspired freely. When I reached the temple, a cold wind was blowing. I sat down for a few moments to rest and was chilled through and through.

4.—それ は はなはだ ぶようじん で ございました ね。あなた は ぐわいたう を おーもち で なかつた の です か。

5.—もつて は をりました が, ふもと の はう で は なかく あつたか で ありました から, そこ の ちやーや で くるま の うへ に おいて-きた の です。

6.—この ごろ の あき の ひより は けんのん で ございます。につちう たにーま で は あつたかい こと も あります・が, やま の いたゞき で は さむい かぜ が ふいて をりーます。

7.—その ひ は おそく なつて から くるま が ハチワウジ まで かへりました が ひのくれ-がた に は かぜ が おひく さむく なつて きました。その ばん は だいぶん ねつ も ありまして たうとう いつしう かん ばかり たく に ひつこんで をりました。

8.—いま で は もう すつかり おーよろしい の で ございませう ね。(にのさき ミカタ ふじん ざしき へ いり きたれり)。

9. ロビンソン-し:—こんにち は。しばらく ごーぶさた いたしました。ひとーつき あまり も おーめ に かゝりません でした が けふ は おーひさしぶり で ございます。

4.—That was not very prudent.   Did you take an over-coat with you?

5.—Yes! but I left it in my *kuruma* at the tea-house at the foot of the mountain.   The sun was quite warm there.

6.—These fall days are dangerous.   Mid-day is often warm in the valleys.   But on the hill tops the winds are cold.

7.—I had a late ride back to Hachiōji.   The air grew very cold towards sunset.   I was quite feverish that night. I have been in the house for almost a week.

8.—You are all right now, I am pleased to see?—(*Mrs. Mikala comes into the room*).

9. *Mr. R:*—Good day.   It is sometime since we have met.   This is the first time I have had the pleasure of seeing you for a month or more.

10.—(ミカタ ふとん は お‐とぎ を なして。) たく で も たびた お‐うはさ を いたして をりました。こゝ は あなた に お‐さむく は ござりません か。ひばち へ もつと すみ を つぎませう。お‐ちや で も めしあがり なさいまし。この お‐くわし は いかゝ で ございます。あなた は だんた ニホン‐で を お‐じようず に お‐はなし なさる さう です ね。

11.—どう して さう いふ こと が あります もの です か。わたく し の はなし は じつ に まづう ございます。

12.—あなた の はつをん は たいさう‐よう ございます。

13.—もし すこし で も よければ それ は みな だんな‐さん の お‐かげ です。

14.—たく で は あなた の しんぼ は おどろく‐べき ほど だ と まうして をります。ソシテ あなた の お‐こし に なる の を たのしみ に して をります から, しゝう お‐いで くださいます の は まこと に けつこう で ございます。ちよつと ご‐めん くださいまし。これ から かつてもと の こと を みまはらねば なりません から。

15.—さて 「は」 の ことわざ に ついて いかゝ お‐かんがへ で ございます か。

10. *Mrs. M. (bowing)* :—My husband has often spoken of you. Are you not cold here? I will put some more charcoal on the fire. Please have some tea. Will you taste these cakes? I hear that you are beginning to speak Japanese beautifully.

11. *Mr. R* :—How can you say so? I am a very poor speaker.

12. *Mrs. M* :—Your pronunciation is excellent.

13. *Mr. R* :—If it is good at all, I am indebted for my improvement to your generous husband.

14. *Mrs. M* :—My husband says that you are making wonderful progress. He enjoys your visits. I am glad that you come to see him so often. Kindly excuse me now ; I must attend to some matters in the kitchen.

15. *Mr. M* :—Well, what do you think of our proverb for " *Ha ?* " I suppose that you had no desire to peep at the

おそらく あなた が タカチ さん の ぜつちやう
に おいで の とき に は はり の あな から
てん を のぞかう と いふ やう な かんがへ
は おこり は しなかつた でせう。

16.—さう です とも。あそこ に ゐて も どこ
に ゐて も その やう な かんがへ は おこり
は しません。わたくし は なに ごと に で
も ひろき くわんさつ を このみます。あの
ことわざ を いつた ひと は たぶん ごく
こゝろ の せまい ひと を しつて をつた の
でせう。あなた が この ことはざ を
あつせいか の ふがう だ と おつしやつた の
は ご=もつとも で ございます。この おほ
ぞら の やう な りつば な もの を じぶん
で みる こと が できる の に, はり の あな
を とをめがね に する と は. じつ に ばか
な にんげん で ありません か。

17.—だが, せけん に は さう する ひと
も ある の です。さう いふ ひと は しぶん
の ともだち や しごと や くに や その ほか
いろ〱 の ことがら を みる の に ちいさい
すきあな から のぞく の です。もちろん この
やう な ひとゝ は めさき の ちいさい とほり
に じんぶつ も ちいさう ございます。

18.—どうか もう すこし ゆる〱 お=はなし
を ねがひます。わたくし に は そんな に

sky through a needle's eye, when you were on the top of Takao-san.

16.—No, not there or any where else. I like a broad outlook for everything. The maker of that proverb must have known some people of very small minds. You well called it " the motto for bigots." What a fool man is, when he can see a splendid thing like the sky, to use the hole of needle as his telescope!

17.—But that is the way with some people. They see their friends, their business, their country, everything, only through little peep-holes. Of course, such persons are almost always as small in character, as they are in their eye-sight.

18.—Please speak more slowly. My ear is not quick enough for your words. I understand Mrs. Mikata much

はやく あなた の おーことば を きい−とる こと
が できません。 おくさま の はう が
あなた より は よほど きい−よう ございます。
なぜ <u>ニホン</u>ご を はなす の に つうれい
ふじん−がた の はう が をとこ の かた より
も じやうず な の で ございませう。

19.−たぶん ふじん の はう は ゆるく はなす
から でせう。 そこで わたくし の まうし
ませう と おもつて ある の は ほか で は
ありません。 いま は わが くに で は 「メイヂ」 の
じだい で ございまして, わが くに の
せんばい は いま から さん じふ ねん ほど
いぜん に, わが <u>ニホン</u> を せかい−ぢう どの
くに に も をとらぬ ほど に しんぽ−てき
に なつて ぶんめい に すゝめる くに に しやう
と いたしました が, こんにち と なる も
なほ むかし の ほうけん−せいど を くわいふく
したい と おもつて をる ひとゝ が ござり
ます。 かう いふ ひとゝ こそ, いはゆる はり
の あな から てん を のぞく れんぢう で
ございませう。

20.−その とほり です。 わたくし は しんじつ
<u>ニホン</u> の だい しやうり を のぞみます。

21.−もと より まだ なす べき しごと が
ひじやう に たくさん ござります が, しかし
われゝ は たへず しんぽ しつゝ ある こくみん

better than I do you.　Why is it that the ladies as a rule speak your language better than you men ?

19.—They have more leisure, I suppose.　I mean this. This is the era of Meiji for Japan.　Our country's leaders determined thirty years ago, to make Japan as progressive and as enlightened as any nation in the world.　But there are some people who even to-day wish that our ancient feudalism could be restored.　They are of the kind who look at the sky, through the eye of a needle.

20.—That is so !　I sincerely wish a grand triumph for New Japan.

21.—Of course, there is an immense work to do yet, But I think that as a nation we are moving steadily forward.　Do you understand me ?

だ と おもひます。 わたくし の まうしました
こと は お-わかり に なりました か。

22.—ハイ あきらか に わかつた と おもひます。
しかし この うへ この お-はなし を つけ
ましたら まるで あなた の かうしやく に
なつて しまいませう。 わたくし は あなた に
ことば を そへて それ を くわいわ に する
こと が できません。

23.—それ で は この だい は もう やめ
に いたしませう。 この ことわざ の いみ は
いま まで の お-はなし で じふぶん あきらか
に なつた と おもひます。これ から 「に」 の
ことわざ に どう いふ をしへ が ある か
しらべて みやう じや ありません か。

───────

だい し
に ふ ま
にんげん わづか ごじふ ねん。

1. ロビンソンーし:—この ことわざ は にんげん
の いのち の みじかい こと を しらせ やう と
いふ の でせう。 しかし なぜ かしこい ひと
は ごじふ ねん と いつた の でせう か。
わが アメリカ の さかしい ひと は これ より
は ゆるやか です。

22.—Yes, I think I do, clearly. But, if we are going to talk much more over this subject, I am sure that it will have to become a lecture on your part. I am not able to contribute enough to the talk to make it a conversation.

23.—Well then, let us drop our text. This proverb is plain enough, I imagine, with what we have already said. Now let us see what " *Ni* " has to teach us.

IV.   PROVERB FOR (に) *NI.*

Man's life is but fifty years.

1. *Mr. R:*—I suppose this is to remind us of the shortness of human life. But why did the wise man say fifty years ? Our wise men were more generous.

2.—どう して です か。

3.—わが くに で は 「ひと の よ は
ろくじふ ねん と また じふ ねん」 すなはち
しちじふ ねん だ と まうします。 しかし
ニホン じん は たん-めい で あります か。

4.—わたくし は さう で なからう と
おもひます。 わが くに の とうけいか の
あらはす ところ に よれば すくなく とも
きんだい に おいて は ながいき を した
ところ の ひと は おびたゝしう ございます。
もつとも むかし は いま ほど へいきん の
じゆみやう が ながく なかつた でせう が,
これ とて も たしか に はかられる こと で
ありません。 つまり どちら の ことわざ に
いつて ある こと も, にんげん の いのち は
みじかい もの で ある と いふ こと だけ
だらう と おもひます。

5.—たぶん この ことわざ の いみ は ひと
は ごじふ に なつた のち は すつかり じぶん
の かげふ を やめて らく-いんきよ に なれ
と いふ こと でせう。 これ は むかし
ニホン の ふうしう で ありません でした
か。

6.—ご-じようだん を おつしやいます。 で-
す が, あなた の おつしやる こと は たいへん
よく ことば の けいこ に なります。 この

2. *Mr. M.*—How is that?

3.—We say that " the days of our years are three score years and ten," that is, seventy years.   Are the Japanese a short lived people?

4.—I think not.   Our statistics show a great many centenarians living, at least in modern times.   In ancient times, perhaps the average of life was not so long.   But then, this is not a question of exact measure.   Both proverbs, I suppose, are meant only to remind men that life is short.

5.—Possibly it means that after fifty years a man should give up all his work, and become " an honorably retired one."   This was a national custom once, was it not?

6.—You are joking.   But then, what you say is good practice in language.   I do not see that we can argue much over this proverb.

ことわざ に ついて は あまり ぎろん が
できますまい。

7.―ぎろん を すれば わたくし の はう が
きつと まけ です。わたくし に は あなた の
ことば の ぐんぜい を ふせぐ こと が
できません。 しかし ぶつけうと ら が
じゆみやう の みじかい こと を なげく の
は どう いふ わけ でせう。 ぶつけうと は
この よ の せいくわつ を のがれる こと を
よろこばねば ならん はづ で ありません か。
せいくわつ は かれら に とりて は ばん-
あく ちう の もつとも おほひなる もの で
ある の です。

8.―です が, ニホン の にんげん は ことごく
ぶつけう-しんと で は ありません。それ に
また アメリカ の かたく が ほんたう の
きりすとけうと で ない と どう-やう に, ニホン
の にんげん も また ほんたう の ぶつけうと
で ございません。

9.―どう して そう です か。

10.―されば で ございます。おのれ を
すて、ひと の ため に なれ と いふ
キリスト の ほんたう の をしへ と, アメリカ
じん の じぶん を あいして かち を あらさふ
ことごと は はんたい して をります。それ に

7.—If we tried to, I am sure I should be defeated. I could not resist your army of words. But I do not see why a Buddhistic people should lament over the shortness of life. A Buddhist ought to be glad at the prospect of getting out of existence. Existence is the greatest of all evils.

8.—But all Japanese are not Buddhists. Then, again, Japanese are no more real Buddhists, than you Americans are real Christians.

9.—What do you mean?

10.—I mean that Christ's great doctrines of self-denial and sacrifice are opposed to your American self-love and struggle for success. The Japanese are fond of life, and they are a very happy people.

ニホン の にんげん は せいくわつ を たのしんで をりまして, また たいへん に ゆくわい な じんみん です。

11.—たぶん あなた の お-かんがへ は たゞしい の で ございませう。 しかし ご-しようち の とほり あなた の はう には ご-つがふ の よい こと が ございます。 わたくし は はなす こと さへ できた なら この こと に ついて いひたい と おもつて ゐる こと が たくさん ございます。 あなた は つぎ の ちゑ の きんドル すなはち 「ほ」 の ことわざ に ついて は いかに お-かんがへ です か。

———

だい ご
ほ は ね

ほまれ あらん より そしり なかれ。

1. ミカター-し:—この きんげん の しんり に ついて は べつ に ぎろん も ありますまい。

2. ロビンソン-し:—さう です か。 あなた は ほまれ が ある より そしり の ない はう が よい と お-かんがへ です か。 わたくし ども は すべて じぶん の よい こと が せかい に しられて をれば よい と おもふ じや ありません か。

11.—Possibly, you are right. But you know you have the advantage of me. If I could only talk, I would tell you much that I think about this question. What do you make of the next piece of your coined wisdom, the " *Ho* " proverb?

––––––

V. · PROVERB FOR (⌶) *HO*.

No blame is better than praise.

1. *Mr. M:*—There is no question about the truth of this saying.

2. *Mr. R:*—Is it so? Do you believe that absence of blame is better than praise of a man? We all like to know that the good in us is recognized.

3.—それ は そう です が, この よ-の-なか の ひと は あやまち を のみ さがして ゐる の です から, だれ も そしる もの が ない と いふ こと ほど りつば な ほまれ は ありません。 もしも ひと が 「あの をとこ に は いつてん の ひなん も ない」 と いつた なら それ こそ いはれる だけ の ほめ-ことば を いつた の です。

4.—そう いふ いみ で この ことわざ を お-とり なさる の なら それ で よう ございます が, しかし もし これ は よい ひと だ と お-かんがへ なさつたら なぜ その とほり に おつしやらない の です。

5.—ほめる こと と いふ もの は へつらひ と なり やすひ もの で ございます。 それ に ひと は ほまれ に あがく やう に なつて は はなはだ いけません。 ほまれ は だん々 に ひと を かうまん に いたします。 ひと は たい その こと が ぎむ で ある ため に ぎむ を つくす の で なければ なりません。

6.—わたくし は それ を しようにん いたし-ます。 しかし あなた の けんかい は つうれい の よわい にんげん に とりて は たかー-すぎ-ます。 もし とく に たいする むくひ が ない やう に なる とき に は よ-の-なか の ぜんじ

3.—Yes, but this is a fault-finding world. What better praise can you have than the fact that no one blames you? If one can say, " I find no fault in him," the most that can be said in praise of a man, is said.

4.—If you put that meaning into the proverb, you are right. But, if you think a man is a good man, why not say so?

5.—Praise too easily becomes flattery. Then, again, a man should not be hungry for praise. Praise tends to make one vain. Every one should do his duty for the sake of the duty only.

6.—I admit that. But you are taking rather high ground for weak human nature. If there were no rewards for virtue, there would be very little goodness in the world.

と いふ もの は ひじよう に すくなく なつて
しまいませう。

7.—さう か も しれません。しかし わたくし
は この ことわざ を つくつた ひと は
にんげん は かく ある べき もの だ と
いふ がわ から さう いつた の だらう と
おもひます。 その ひと は にんげん の
じつさい の ありさま を しつて ゐた の で-
せう が, だうとく-じよう ごく たかい ちい
に にんげん を あげ やう と して ゐた の
でせう。

8.—ぜん を われ〱 が よぢのぼる べき
ぜつちやう だ と すれば わたくし は この
ことわざ に ついて かれ これ まうしません。
しかし よわい にんげん の せいしつ を ためす
もの と する に は ひどい ことわざ です。
とにかく あなた は むるい な せんせい です。
それ に また たくみ な せつけうか です。
あなた は けつして つぎ の ことわざ に
あらはして ある ひなん を うけらるゝ こと
は ありますまい。

———

7.—You are probably right. But I suppose that the maker of this proverb meant to speak rather of men as they should be. He knew men as they are. He was trying to lift them to the highest moral level.

8.—If we think of goodness as a height to climb, I shall not question the wisdom of the proverb. But it is a hard test of weak human nature. You are an excellent teacher. You are a skillful preacher, too. Evidently you are not guilty of the fault that is shown up in our next proverb.

だい ろく
へ 屋

へた の なが だんぎ。

1. ミカター し：―あなた は まへ の しよう の いましめ を こわして をーしまい なさつた が，うちーあけて まうせば ほめらるゝ こと と いふ もの は うれしい もの です よ。ソコデ かんたん は とんち の ごくい で あります が，それ と とも に また ちゑ の ごくい で ございます。

2. ロビンソン し：―この ことわざ で わたくし は アメリカ で いうめい なる せつけうか の はかせ ライマン、ビーチャー の はなし を をもひーだしました。 ある あさ の こと です が，ビーチャー は ひじやう に ながい えんぜつ を しまして，こと に その えんぜつ の し やう が たいへん に さうくしく ありました が，あと で ひとり の まご が ビーチャー に むかひまして 「をーぢいちやん は なんで けさ あんな に どなつた の」 と いひ ました。 すると ビーチャー が こたへて いひ ます のに 「ぼう や。をーぢいちやん は なに も はなす こと の ない とき に は いつ も あんな に どなる の よ」 と。いかい です。ビーチャー

VI.   PROVERB FOR (⌣) *HE.*

An awkward priest for long sermons.

1.   *Mr. M:*—You are breaking our last commandment.
Yet, I confess, praise is pleasant.   Brevity is the soul of
wisdom, as well as of wit.

2.   *Mr. R:*—This proverb reminds me of a story told of
a famous preacher in America, Dr. Lyman Beecher.   One
morning he preached an unusually long sermon.   He was
very noisy, too, in preaching.   One of his grandchildren
said to him afterwards.   " Grandpa why did you ' holler '
(shout) so loud this morning ? "   " My dear," he answered
" when I have nothing to say, I always " holler."   You see,
he had not prepared his sermon as usual.

に は いつも の やう に えんぜつ の したく
が できて ゐなかつた の です。

3.—おもしろい はなし です ね。 しかし この
くに に は ビーチャーし の なかま は すく
なく ありません。 ニホン の えんぜつか や
ぼうさん など は たびゞ ビーチャー と よく-
にた こと を いたします。 この つぎ に
どう いふ こと を いはう か と かんがへて
ゐる じかん を ふさぐ ため に, はなし の
あひだ へ ことば や じくご など を おほく
つかひます。 もし かう いふ ひとゞ が いつた
こと を その とほり に ひつき しましたら
それこそ じつ に きめう な ぶんしやう が
できませう。 わたくし は ときゞ この へいがい
は ニホン いつばん で ある か と おもひ
ます。 わが くに の えんぜつ は まるで
ことば を ふきだした もの で ございます。
こうかい の えんぜつ など で ほんとう の
しさう と いつたら たいてい かいめん の なか
に ある みづ と おなじ でせう。 かいめん
は ひと-にぎり あつて も みづ は ひと-さじ
しか ありません。

4.—それ は あなたがた ばかり で は あり
ません。 どこ の くに へ いつて も みな
その とほり です。 どの くに の ことば で
も みじかい えんぜつ を こしらへる に は

3.—That is a good story.   It might have plenty of companions, however, in this country.   Japanese orators and our priests are often very like Dr. Beecher.   They use many words and phrases when speaking, just to fill up the time while they are thinking over what they shall say next.   If what many of them say were written down as it is spoken, it would make ridiculous reading.   Sometimes, I think that this fault is almost a national vice.   Our speeches are fairly puffed out with words.   The real thought in most public addresses, is like the water in a sponge,—a spoonful of water and a handful of sponge.

4.—You have no monopoly in this matter.   Every other people in the world keeps you company.   It takes a great deal of time to prepare a short speech in any language. The man who talks the most, as a rule, says the least.

じかん　が　おほく　かゝります。　たいてい
たくさん　しやべる　もの　に　かぎつて　すこし
しか　はなして　をりません。

———

だい　しち

と　と　空

とんで　ひ　に　いる　なつ　の　むし。

1. ミカター し：—あなた　は　あなた　と　わたくし
と　が　はじめて　あつた　とき　を　おぼえて
いらつしやいます　か。

2. ロビソソン し：—ハイ, よく　おぼえて　ゐます。
ちやうど　さんねん　まへ　で　カウヅ　と　ユモト
と　の　あひだ　の　てつだう-ばしや　の　なか　で-
した。　あの　ひ　は　これ　まで　に　ない　ひじやう
に　あつい　ひ　で　ありました　が, あなた　は
わたくし　に　はなし　を　して　くださつて　それ
に　また　あふぎ　を　かして　くださいました。
あの　とき　の　こと　は　たひく　おもひ-いだし-
ます。

3.—なぜ　いま　わたくし　が　あの　とき　の　こと
を　おもひ-だしました　か　お-わかり　に　なり-
ます　か。

4.—わかりません。　なに　か　ことわざ　に

VII.　PROVERB FOR (と) *TO*.

Summer insects fly into the fire.

1. *Mr. M :*—Do you remember the first time we met?

2. *Mr. R :*—Yes, very well.　It was in a tram car between Kōzu and Yumoto, three years ago.　That was one of the hottest days I ever felt.　You were kind enough to speak to me, and to offer me a fan.　I often remember that.

3.—Why, do you suppose, I recall that time now?

4.—I do not know.　Has it anything to do with our

くわんけい で も ある の です か。ハ丶ア
ナルホド、あなた は <u>ミヤノシタ</u> の かうちう の
こと を お-かんがへ なさつてる の です ね。

5.―「<u>ナラヤ</u>」ホテル で はじめて しよくじ を
した とき の こと は ようい に わすれられ-
ません。あなた は これ まで おたがひ に
あの へや の なか で みた やう に かうちう
の すまん の むれ が むづく うじく と
はい-まはつて ゐる の を ご-らん なさつた
こと が あります か。あの とき あなた が
かうちう の さら を けぢよ に さしだして
それ は なつ は かうちう の そつぶ を すか
ない と おつしやつた とき に は わたくし は
ほんとう に ふき-だそう と いたしました。

6.―あの をんな に は わたくし の しやれ
が わかりません でした。しかし あの とき
の ご-ちそう は くるしかつた じや ありません
か。へや は とても あつくて まど は しめ-
られず。サレバトテ かうちう の おしよせて
くる ありさま は まるで 「だんぐわん う ひ」
と いふ べき やう でした。

7.―たいてい やぶん に なる と むし が
わかり の はう へ とんで-くる の は どう
いふ わけ でせう。<u>ニユー、ヨルク</u> に をり
ました じぶん わたくし は いちど <u>スタツトン、</u>
<u>アイランド</u> へ ゆきまして、ともだち の うち

proverb? Oh, yes! you are thinking about the Miyanoshita beetles.

5.—I shall not soon forget our first dinner at the Naraya Hotel. Did you ever see such a swarm of buzzing, tumbling, crawling things as we had in that room? You amused me very much, when you handed back your plate of soup to the servant, and told her, you did not like beetle soup in summer.

6.—She did not understand my joke. But, was not that dinner a torture? The room was too hot to keep the windows closed. The attack of the beetles was almost like a shower of bullets.

7.—I do not understand why insects almost always fly straight for a light at night. When I was in New York, I went to Staten Island and spent a night at the house of a friend. The mosquitoes there were a terror. All the windows in my room were guarded by wire-screens. I slept comfortably. The next morning I got up early and

で ひと-ばん どうりう した こと が あります
が, あすこ の か と いつたら じつ に
ひどい もの です よ。 わたくし の へや の
まど は すつかり かな-あみ で はつて
ありまして, その ばん は こころよく ねむり
に つきました が, よく-あさ は はやく をきて
さんぽ に でかけます と, とぐち で
めしつかひ-の-もの が すせん の しんだ むし
を はき-あつめて やま に して をりまして,
げんくわん の らんぷ の した の ゆか
いちめん は むし で うづまつて をりました。
これ は よ-どほし そこ に らんぷ が ついて
をりました の で, いろ〱 の しゆるゐ の か
や やぶか や はひ や ひひる が なんぜん
と なく, ばからしく も ちいさ な からだ を
あかし に ぶつつけて しんで-しまつた の
です。

8.—あなた は いま むし の こと を
「ばからしい」 と おつしやいました が, わたくし
は たいいま の ことわざ は あらゆる
ことわざ の うち で いちばん こしらへ-
やすい もの だつたらう と おもひます。
ごく むかし から して にんげん は なつむし
を ばか だ と おもつて ゐた に ちがひ
ありません。 わたくし は スピリオル と いふ
みずうみ の そば で かじりび の わき に

went out for a walk.　At the door-way of the house I saw
a servant sweeping up into a pile thousands of dead insects.　They covered the floor under the porch-lamp.　The
lamp had been burning all night.　Mosquitoes, gnats,
flies, and moths of various kinds,—thousands of them,—
had flung their foolish little bodies against that light, and
been killed.

8.—You have just called the insects "foolish."　The
present proverb must have been one of the easiest of all
to make.　From the most ancient times, the miserable
little summer creatures must have seemed to men like
little fools.　Near Lake Superior, I have been beside a
camp-fire into which insects poured at night almost like a
stream.

みた こと が あります が, その かいりび
の なか へ よる に なつて むし の とびこむ
こと は まるで たき の やう でした。

9.—さう でした か。 なるほど みちーをーとくー
ひと が この こと を じんせい に もちゆる
の に むり は ありません。 にんげん は まい
むし と くらべて すこし も りこう で ない
こと が ございます。 なに か じぶん を
たのします こと を みれば すぐ その はう
へ とんでーゆき, その こと に ふけつて その
み を ほろぼして しまいます。 きんせん めいよ
じやうよく など は みな この おそるべき ひ
で ある と いつて よう ございませう。 ひと
は これら の もの の ため に しば〱 その
み を ほろぼします。 よのなか は かんがへ
の ない ばか で いつぱい で ありまして,
とき に は やけど を した ばつかり で
ひつこむ もの も あります が, たぶん は
ほのほ の なか へ とびこんで しんで
しまひます。

10.—それ では まづ わたくしども に とつて
は この いましめ が じぶん のみ の うへ に
あたら ない やう に ちうい する ほか
しかた が ありません。 (とけい を ながめて。)
しかし わたくし は たいへん に ちやうざ
を いたしました。 もう かーら なければ

9.—Really! Of course it is perfectly natural for a moralist to apply this fact to human life. Very often, men are not a bit wiser than the moths. They see something that fascinates them. They dash straight at it. They plunge into it. They are ruined. Money, fame, passion may all be fires that work ruin. They often do destroy men. Life is full of thoughtless fools. Sometimes they are only singed. They manage to crawl away. More often, their flight into the flame is their death.

.

10.—There is nothing for us to do then, I judge, but to take care that this moral does not apply to ourselves. *(Looking at his watch.)* But I am taking altogether too much of your time. I think I must be going now. I have no doubt you are very busy.

なりません。 ひじやう に お-いそがしう ございましたらう に。

11.—そんな に お-いそぎ なさら-なくつて も いゝ じや ございません か。 まだ じふ-いち-じ に なりません。 いま すこし みち を まなぶ の に じうぶん じかん が ございます。 コーット。 つぎ の もんく は どう いふ の でした か しらん。 サゥく ちり が やま に なる はなし でした ね。

12.—まこと に ありがたう ございます が けふ は もう かへつた はう が よい と おもひます。 かさねて お-さしつかへ の ない とき に うかゞひませう。

13.—ほんたう に お-かへり なさらなければ なりませぬ なら・お-とゞめ まうしません。 この つぎ に は いつ この ことわざ の はなし を いたしませう か。 あした ひるすぎ から てんき が よかつたら アカバチ の かわつぶち を ご-いつしよ に さんぽ しやう じや ありません か。 シブヤ へん の はなぞの で きく の けんぶつ も でき-ませう。 あすこ に は だいぶん めづらしい の が ある さう です。 ソシテ みちく お-はなし も いたされます。 わたくし の はう から お-たく へ うかゞう こと に いたし-ませう。

11.—Please do not hurry away. It is not yet eleven o'clock. There is plenty of time for a little more moralizing. Let me see! How does our next text read? Oh, yes! It is about dust becoming a mountain.

12.—You are very kind; but I think I would better not stay any longer to-day. I shall come again, at your convenience.

13.—I will not keep you, if you really must go. When shall we take up the proverbs again? If the weather is pleasant to-morrow afternoon, will you not join me in a walk out along the Akabane Creek? We can take a look at some chrysanthemums in a garden near Shibuya. I am told that there are some rare flowers there. And we can have a talk on the way. I shall meet you at your house.

14.—しようち いたしました。 しかし ひるすぎ は じかん が みじかう ございます から, にーじーはん ごろ に でかける と いふ こと に したら いかい で ございませう。

15.—よろしう ございます。 てんき が よかつたら その じぶん までに ようい を いたしませう。

だい はち

ち

ちり つもつて やま と なる。

1. ミカター し:—こなた では フジーさん の けしき が たいへん きれい で ございます ね。

2. ロビンソン し:—トウキヤウ で こゝ ほど よく みゆる ところ は なからう と おーもひーます。 わたくし は ちつと で も みえる とき には まいにち フジーさん を ながめます が, あさ はやく など は まこと に みごと です。 この ごろ の やう に はれわたつた あきーぞら で あさひ の でる じぶん しらゆき で おほはれて ある いたゝき と いつたら ひとつ の みもの です よ。 やま いちめん が うへ の はう は あかみーがゝつて しろく した の はう は むらさきーがゝつて あをく

14.—Very good! As the afternoons are rather short, suppose we start at about half past two.

15.—All right! If the weather is pleasant I shall be on hand at that time.

VIII. PROVERB FOR (ち) *CHI.*

Piled up dust becomes a mountain.

1. *Mr. M:*—What a beautiful view of Mt. Fuji you have here!

2. *Mr. R:*—There is no other place in Tōkyō with a better view, I think. I see Fuji every day, when it is visible at all. In the early morning it is glorious. During this clear autumn weather, at sunrise the snow-covered top is a splendor. The whole mountain pink-white above and purple-blue below, is magnificent beyond description. I send it my greetings every morning.

その　けつこう-さ　は　ことば　に　つくされ-
ません。わたくし　は　まい-あさ　フジ-さん　に
あいさつ　を　いたします。

3.—あなた　は　あの　やま　を　おがんで
いらつしやる　の　か　も　しれません。

4.—わたくし　の　みる　ところ　から　しうけう
を　こしらへる　の　は　ざうさ　ありません。
せけん　に　は　わたくし　の　フジ-さん　を
おがむ　の　より　も　はるか　に　れつとう　の
しうけう　が　ございます。

5.—あなた　は　あの　やま　へ　お-のぼり
なさつた　こと　が　あります　か。

6.—わたくし　は　この-ごろ　で　は　やま　へ
のぼる　こと　が　できません。しかし　わたくし
が　フジ-さん　より　にせん-じやく　たかい
バイクス、ピーク　と　いふ　やま　へ　のぼつた
とき　の　やう　に　てつだう　で　フジ-さん　へ
のぼられる　やう　に　なつたら　のぼつて　み-
ませう。

7.—ゑんぱう　から　ご-らん　なさつた　の　と
おなじ　で　ございませう。お-のぼり　なさる
だけ　の　ねうち　は　なからう　と　おもひます。
あそこ　で　は　なに　も　みる　もの　が
ございません。たい　やけいし　や　ほこり　や
いは　ばかり　です。それ　に　みえる　だけ　の

3.—It may be, you worship it.

4.—I could easily make a religion out of my view. There are worse kinds of religion than my Fuji worship would be.

5.—Have you ever been up the mountain ?

6.—I can't climb mountains now-a-days. When I can go up Fuji as I went up Pike's Peak, two thousand feet higher, on a railway, I shall go.

7.—Just as well to see it from a distance. I don't think it would pay you to make the climb. There is nothing to see there but lava-dust and rocks. The landscape below is all flattened, that is, when you can see it at all. I would rather see Fuji from a place like O-Tome-tōge, than see O-Tome-tōge from the top of Fuji.

けいしよく は のこらず ひらつたく みえます
わたくし は フジーさん の いだゞき から
オトメーたうげ の やう な ところ を ながめる
より, オトメーたうげ から フジーさん を みる
はう が よい と おもひます。

8.—あの やう に ひとりーだち に なつて
ゐる と は ふしぎ な やま です ね。
おほむかし の ニホソーじん が あの やま に
ついて いろゝ たくさん な いひつたへ を
のこした の は あやしむ に たりません。
わたくし が はじめて ニホソ の こと に
ついて しりました の は やま の づ を
あふぎ いつぱい に ゑがいた もの でした。
ヨーロッパ また は アメリカ で ニホソ の
こと を すこし で も しつて ゐる もの は
かならず この たかい フジーさん を しつて
をります。あの やま は いちーや の うち に
できた さう です ね。

9.—さう いふ はなし です。フジーさん が
とびだした とき に ビワコ の ある ところ
が ひつこんだ さう です。かみさま は
ニホソ に とつて そんとく の ない やう に
なさつた の でせう。そろゝ でかけた はう
が よい じや ありません か。

10.—さう です ね。もう さんじ で
ございます。わたくし は どうか して この

8.—A wonderful mountain it is, standing so alone! It is not strange that the ancient Japanese made so much of it in their traditions. The first thing I had of Japan was a fan covered with a picture of the mountain. In Europe and in America every one who knows of Japan at all, knows of this "Peerless Mountain." It was made in one night, was n't it?

9.—So, the story goes. When Fuji came up, the land where Lake Biwa is went down. The gods made an even thing of it for the country,—Don't you think we would better be going?

10.—Yes, it is almost three o'clock. I wish I could talk this terrible language of yours.

むつかしい あなた の をークに の ことば を
はなされる やう に なりたう ございます。

11.—ナニ ごーしんぱい なさいます な。あなた
の ちしき の すゝみました のに は をどろき
いります よ。ほん の さんねん-ほど まへ
はじめて をーめ に かゝりました とき に は
えいご のみ で をーはなし を いたし ました
が, いま で は あなた の <u>ニホソ-ご</u> を をー
つかひ なさる の は <u>ニホソ-じん</u> の とほり
で ございます。

12.—そう で ございます か。それ で は
わたくし は けうし の かんばん を あげて,
せいと は あなた の ところ へ をくつて
ほせう を して いたゝく こと に いたし
ませう か しらん。うら-もん から でゝ いき-
ませう。その はう が かはつぶち へ ちか-みち
です。

———

だい く

り 里

りか に かんむり を たゞさず。

1. ミカター-し :—わたくし が どく すきます
の は かう いふ さんぽ です。わたくし は

11.—Don't worry! You surprise me by the knowledge of it you have gained. Only three years ago, when we first met, we spoke altogether in English. Now, you talk Japanese like a Japanese.

12.—Is that so? I think I shall set myself up as a teacher, and send pupils to you as my endorser. Let us go out by the back gate. It is the short way to the creek.

IX. PROVERB FOR (♮) *RI.*

Adjust not your cap under a plum tree.

1. *Mr. M :*—This is one of my favorite outings. I enjoy the country more than the city.

しちう より おなか の はう を ゆくわい に
おもひます。

2. <u>ロビンソン</u>―し：―わたくし も その とほり
です。 わたくし は たび〱 この みち へ
で〵きます が, てつだう の むかう の でんぢ
は こと に よい と おもひます。 <u>ニホン</u> の
おなか は たいへん に じゆう で ございます
ね。 わたくし は とき〱 はたけ の なか を
なん―じかん も あるき―まはる こと が あります
が, いち―にん も わたくし を とがめる もの
が ありません。 わたくし も また ちつとも
ひやくしやう の じやま に ならない と
おもはれます。 わたくし の くに など で は
たいへん な ちがひ で ございます。 どこ へ
ゆきまして も かき が たつて をりまして,
や〵 とも すれば らうぜきもの だ と いはれ―
ます。

3.―わが くに の おなか に は さう いふ
こと が ありません から さんぼ を いたします
に は ごく ゆくわい です。 しかし わが くに
に も らうぜき を きんずる はふりつ や
しふくわん が ございます。

4.―むろん そう でせう。 しかし あなた の
お―くに の はたけ は ひじよう に ちいさう
ご―ざいまして, それ に しはう に みち が おほう

2. *Mr. R :*—So do I. I often come out over this road.
I like especially the fields beyond the railway. There is
so much freedom in the country in Japan. I sometimes
wander for hours among the fields. No one ever disturbs
me there. And I never seem to trouble the farmers. It
is very different at home. Everywhere fences are put up
there, and one is always in danger of being a trespasser.

3.—Yes, our open country makes rambling in it very
pleasant. But we, also, have laws and customs against
trespass.

4.—No doubt. But your fields, are very small. The
paths in every direction are many. One must deliberately
try to go out of his way, to be a trespasser.

ごーざいます から わざ〳〵 みち の そと へ
でなければ らうぜきもの に なる こと は
ありません。

5.—ふしぎ に も つぎ の ことわざ は
あなた が ゆくわい だ と おつしやる わが
くに の ゐなか の ありさま から おーとつた
の で ございます。わが くに では はだけ
に かき を して ございません。そして
くだもの の なる き を まゝ あきち に
うゑて ございます。そこ で むかし の ひと
は, ひと は あくじ に によつた こと を も
さけねば ならぬ と いふ こと を をしへ
やう と して, たくみ に も「うりーばたけ
を とほる とき に は うつむいて わらじ を
むすぶ な」と いふ ことわざ を つくつた の・
です。

6.—きもの の たもと へ そつと うり を
いれる こと が できる と おもつた の でー
せう か。

7.—そう です。それ から また「りーか に
かんむり を たゝさず」と いつて をります。
かう いふ ところ で かんむり を たゝして
をる うち に は, すもゝ の ひとつ や
ふたつ は すぐ て の うち に はいります。

8.—それ も また かしこい をしへ です

5.—Our next text,—curiously enough—grew out of this feature of the country which is so pleasant to you. Our fields are unfenced, and often our fruit trees stand out in the open. The wise wit of the ancients, when they wanted it to show that a man ought to avoid even the appearance of evil, produced the saying, " Don't stoop to tie your sandal when walking by a melon patch."

6.—He might slip a melon into his *kimono* sleeve ; did they think that?

7.—Yes! So, also, they said, " Don't fasten your cap under a plum tree!" A plum or two, you see, could easily get into a man's fingers while he was adjusting his hat at such a place.

8.—A wise saying it is, too. Few men, however, are

ね。 しかし よく き を つけて それ を おこなはう と する ひと は すくない でせう。

———

だい じふ

ぬ 男

ぬすびど を みて なは を なふ。

1. ロビンソン-し:—しかし マア にんげん は たにん が うたがはしき こと を する の を みた とて それ で うたがひ を おこす もの とも きまつて をりません。 よ-ねん いぜん に わたくし は あの やま の うへ の たふ の ある しろい いへ に すんで をりました。 わたくし は ぐるり の ひとぐ を みな しんじて をりまして, ぬすびど なんぞ が うち へ はいらう と は おもひ も よらん こと でした。 しかし なに ごと が おこりました か ご-しようち の とほり です。

2.—その のち とけい の たより は ちつとも ありません でした か。

3.—ちつとも ありません。 もう なに も なからう と おもひます。 しかし あの ばん に なる まへ に わたくし に ようじん を させる の には よほど つよい せうこ で も なければ いけ-なかつた でせう。

careful enough about applying it to themselves.

———

X PROVERB FOR (ぬ) *NU*.

He makes a rope having seen the thief.

1. *Mr. R :*—But after all, everybody is not suspicious, even when he sees others doing suspicious things.   Four years ago I lived in that white house on the hill,—that house with the tower.   I had confidence in every one about me.   As for robbery, I never imagined that a thief would think of entering my house.   You know what happened.

2. *Mr. M :*—Did you ever hear anything of your watch?

3.—No! and I suppose I never shall hear of it.   Yet, before that night, it would have taken the strongest kind of proof to set me on my guard.   I did not suspect that any one in Japan would care to trouble me.   But my confidence is gone now.   Locks and bars are on my doors and windows.   And a revolver lies at my bed-side.

わたくし は ニホン に わたくし を こまらす
やう な ひと が あらう と は おもひません
でした。けれども いま では もう しんよう
が うせました から, と と まど と には
じゃう や くわんぬき を つけまして ねどこ
の そば に は ピストル を そなへて
おきます。

4.—ニホン も ほか の くに の とほり で
ありまして, ニホン-じん の うち に も
わるもの は たくさん ございます。たしか
あの とし は こめ の ね が たい〜ん たかう
ございまして, トゥキヤウ に まい-にち なん-じふ
と いふ たうなん が ありました。あなた も
やはり その ため に ふかう に お-あい
なさつた の で ございます。どの くらい
な ぐ-そん で ありました か。

5.—みんな で しひやくごしふ ゑん ばかり の
しな でした。しかし この-つぎ に あゝ いふ
どろほう を しやう と する もの は あまり
まうから ない だらう と おもひます。……
この かは の どて-ぶしん は たいそう はやく
できました ね。にかねん たつ うち に こゝら
〜ん は ひじやう に かはつた じや ありません
か。

6.—そう です とも。やがて トゥキヤウ は

4.—The same things happen in Japan as elsewhere. There are plenty of rascals among our people. That year, I believe, rice was very high. There were burglaries by the score every day in Tōkyō. You were one of the unfortunates. How much did you lose ?

5.—Altogether about 450 *yen* worth. But it will be dear business for any one who tries that game again.— The improvement of the creek banks goes on very fast. How much this place has been changed in the last two years !

6.—Oh! in time Tōkyō will be all made over. How

のこらず　　たて-なほされる　　で　　でざいませう。
たいへん　に　あつたかい　じや　ありません・か。
そら-もやう　で　は　てんき　が　わるく　なり
さう　です　ね。　あそこ　が　ムメイ-さん　の
たく　です。　あの　かた　の　ひやうばん　は　ひと
ころ　せかい-ぢう　へ　ひろまつて　をりました　が,
あなた　も　ご-そんじ　です　か。

　7.—ハイ。　にど　ばかり　あひました。　お-
ちかづき　に　なりました　の　は　アメリカ　で
すねん　いぜん　です。　あの　かた　は　ニホン
から　ガッシウ-こく　へ　きた　はじめて　の
こうし　と　いつしよ　に　こられまして,　その
とき　は　まだ　こども　の　やう　でした。　それ
から　つい　きんねん　の　こと　でした　が
ふたゝび　あの　かた　に　あひまして,　あそこ　の
いへ　の　うしろ　に　ある　とやま　で　ゆくもい
な　はなし　を　いたしました。　もう　とし-つき
が　たつて　をりまして,　あの　かた　も　わたくし
を　おぼえて　いらつしやいませず,　わたくし　も
とちう　で　お-め　に　かゝつた　の　で　は
わからない　の　で　ありました。

　8.—むかう　の　はう　の　あの　おほき　な
まつ-の-き　の　した　の　ところ　に　わが　くに
で　ごく　いうめい　な　しやうくわん　が　すまつて
をられます　あの　かた　は　また　かうさいくわん
と　して　も　ひやうばん　の　ある　ひと　で

warm it is! The sky looks as though we might have bad weather. In that house Mr. Mumei lives. He had a world-wide reputation once. Do you know him?

7.—Yes, I have met him twice. In America, many years ago, I made his acquaintance. He was with the first embassy from Japan to the United States. He was a mere boy then. Not long ago we met again. I spent a pleasant hour with him on the hill there, back of the house. The years have changed us both considerably. He did not remember me. I should not have known him, had we met on the street.

8.—Over there, under that big pine, lives one of our most famous generals. He is celebrated too, as a diplomatic officer. He was active in bringing about the revisions of Japan's treaties with the Western nations.

ありまして，せいやう－かくこく と ニホン との ぜうやく－かいせい を しとげる の に うんどう せられました かた で ございます。

9.—このごろ は ニホン に とつて だいじ な とき で ございます。この くに の くわこ さんじふ－ねん の はなし を きけば まるで せうせつ の やう で ございます。わたくし は この くに の なりゆき を みる の を ひじやう な たのしみ に して をります。

10.—わが くに の せんばい の ちしき と じんみん の あいこくしん と に よつて わたくし ども は ぶじ に しんぼ して ゆく だらう と おもひます。

11.—だい－せいこう を うる が ため に は こくみん を あげて ひじやう に ほね を をら なければ なりますまい。いくた の きけん に あたる の じゆんび を も して をか なければ なりません。

12.—しかし まづ いま－まで の ところ で は，せいふ は よほど せんけん を いだいて をつた やう でした。

———

9.—These are great days for Japan. The story of this country, for the last thirty years, sounds like a romance. I am intensely interested in seeing how it is to go on.

10.—I trust in the wisdom of our leaders, and the loyalty of our people to carry us forward safely.

11.—Great success will be really the severest test of the power of the nation. Many dangers are to be prepared for.

12.—So far the government has apparently had much wise forethought.

だい じふ いち
る は

るいらん より も あやうし。

1. ロビンソン－し：－さう です。 わたくし も
さう おもひます。 しかし ときぐ ニホン の
しんぽ は はや－すぎ は しない か と お－
もはれます。 むろん わたくし は よげんじや で
ありません。 それ に また わたくし は
たいへん に ニホン の みかた を する はう
で ありまして, ひとへ に ニホン が しん－
じだい に おいて せいこう する の を
こひねがつて をります が, たい わたくし は
この くに で は いろぐ の しなもの を
その うへ へ その うへ へ と おそろしい
たかさ まで つみ－あげて ある と おもふ の
です。 ヨーロツパ で は ぶんめい の せい－
りよく や きかい を て に いれる の に
すひやく－ねん を ついやしました が この
くに で は いちどき に それ を じんみん の
なか へ つきこんだ の で ございます。 もし
じんみん が のこらず それ を とつて あんぜん
に つかふ こと が できましたら それこそ
じつ に おどろく－べき こと で ございませう。
たとへ なに か ひじやう の ひつばく の ある

XI.   PROVERB FOR (ろ) *RU.*

More hazardous even than a pile of eggs.

1. *Mr. R :*—Yes, I agree with you.   Yet, at times, it seems as though Japan's progress has been almost too rapid.   I am not a prophet, of course.   I am also so good a friend of Japan, that I wish only success for the empire in its new age.   But I see one thing piled upon another, to a dangerous height.   The forces and agencies of the civilization which it took Europe hundreds of years to secure, are here, all at once, thrust upon the people.   It will be a marvel if they can accept them all, and use them safely.   It would not be an inexplicable wonder, if under some great stress, the whole pile should tumble down.   I do not expect to see ruin.   Yet I am anxious about your future.

ため に やま が ぐづれて も それ は べつだん に わかり-にくい こと で も あり-ません。 わたくし は しつばい が あらう と は おもひません です が, たい あなた の おーくに の ぜんと を しんばい いたす の で ございます。

2. ミカターし:-わたくし は その やう な おそれ を いだきません。 わが くに の じんみん が あやふき こと を とりあつかふ てだて は おどろく-べき くらゐ です。 ナルホド「メイヂ」の こんにち は うごき-やすい やう に みえます が, しかし わたくし に は この やま が ひつくりかへつて えいゑん の はくわい に おはる もの だ と は おもふ こと が できません。

3.—それ は やり-やう しだい で どう と で も なりませう。 トニカク じいう を たもつ に は いつまで も ようじん が ひつよう です。 ついで に おーたづね まうします が, あなた は「イウテンヂ」へ おーいで なさつた こと が あります か。 たぶん この みち から ゆける の で ございませう。 わたくし は やけ ない まへ に いつて-みーなかつた の を ざんねん に おもひます。

4.—ほんたう に りつば な ところ で ありました。 あすこ に はえて-をつた すぎ-の-

2. *Mr M:*—I have no fear about it. Our people have the most surprising ways for getting along with dangerous things. The Meiji era may seem to be unstable. I don't think, however, that the pile will tumble and end in an everlasting smash.

3.—That all depends. Eternal vigilance is the price of any liberty. By the way,—have you ever been at Yūtenji? One can go to it by this road, I believe. I am sorry I did not visit it before it was burned. .

4.—It was an impressive place. The cryptomerias there were magnificent. The cemetery is surrounded and over-

き は まこと に みごと で ありました。
はかば の しはう は みな その すぎ-の-き
で おほはれて をりました。 がらん は しづか
なる ため に いつそう くわうだい で あり,
じない や みち や くわんぼく など は
あてやか で ありました。 わたくし は あすこ
へ たびく ゆきました。 <u>トウキヤウ</u> ぢか で
あれほど しん と した おくゆかしい ところ
は どこ に も ありません。

ふ.—どれ が その みち です か。 やけ-あと
で も まだ りつぱ で ありませう。

6.—もう むかし の りつぱさ は なからう
と おもひます。 こゝ から おーいで なさる に
は むかふ に ある ひだり の はう の はし
を おーわたり なさい。 それ から てつだう の
はし を つきぬけます と <u>ナカメグロ</u> の
むら へ でます。 むら の はずれ へ ゆきます
と, みち が ふたつ に なつて をりまして,
ひだり の はう の みち は <u>メグロ</u> の はら へ
ついいて-ゐます。 こだかい ところ を とつて
この はら へ でます と, すこし ひだり へ
よつて むかふ の はら に おほき な すぎ-
ばやし が みえます。 そこら-へん に は ほか に
その やう な はやし が あり ません。 その は-
やし の なか が 「イウテンジ」 で ございます。

shadowed by those majestic trees. The temple was grand in its solitude. The temple grounds, the walks, and shrubbery were lovely. I have often been there. There was no place near the city so solemn and restful.

5.—Which is the way? Its ruins may still be grand.

6.—I am afraid that the glory is gone. From here you must cross that bridge to the left. After going under the railway viaduct, you pass through the village of Naka Meguro. Near the end of the village street the road divides. The left hand road leads out towards the plain of Meguro. As you go over the hill into the plain, you will see a large grove of cryptomerias ahead, and a little to the left. There is no other group of trees like it out there. In that grove is Yūtenji.

だい じふ に

を 筬

をかめ はち もく。

1. ミカターし:―こゝ が うゑきや の にわ です。けふ は けんぶつにん が おほう ございませう。コレ, くるまや, みち を あけて くれ。だん が わるう ございます から, き を おーつけ なさいまし。

2. ロビンソンーし:―みごと な はな です ね。こゝら に かう いふ ところ が あらう と は おもひません でした。わたくし は いくーど も こゝ を とほりました が まつたく わうらい から かくれて ゐる もの です から つい なんだ か ぞんじません でした。

3.―まいねん にーど だけ は こゝ へ くる ねうち が ございます。はる は ぼたん が みごと で ありまして, あき は また きく が めう で ございます。これ を ごーらん なさい。この いつぽん の くき に はな が いくつ ある と おーかんがへ なさいます か。しひやくーりん から うへ ございます。これ ほど まで に はな を しあげる に は よほど じくれん が いりませう。

XII.   PROVERB FOR (を) *WO(O)*.

A bystander sees eight moves in the game.

1. *Mr. M :*—This is our florist's garden.   There must be a good many visitors to-day.   I say! *Kurumaya*, move out of the way.   Be careful!   The steps are bad.

2. *Mr. R :*—What splendid flowers!   I never suspected the existence of such a place as this, here.   I have passed it many times, and have not known what it is.   It is quite hidden from the road.

3.—Twice in the year it is well worth a visit.   In the spring, the peonies are superb.   In the autumn, the chrysanthemums are a wonder.   See that single stalk!   How many flowers do you think it bears?   More than four hundred.   It takes great skill to bring a plant to this high development.

4.—さう で せう ね。 いろ も また
たいてい ご-ざいます ナ。 ア, あの あを-ぎく
と いふ もの は こしら-へ-られ-ない もの
でせう か。 ごせん-ゑん だして あを-ぎく
を もとめた ひと が ある と いふ はなし
を きゝました が。

5.—その ごせんゑん を もらふ ひと は
なからう と おもひます。 あなた は こゝ
に あつめて ある なか で あを に によつた
いろ で も みる こと が できます か。

6.—わたくし は 「できぬ」 と いふ こと は
いはれ-ない もの だ と しんじて ゐます。
ソレ, あそこ の むれ の なか に あをみ-
がゝつた いろ が あります。 もし その かね
が もらはれる もの なら かうくわつ な やつ
なんぞ は あの いろ で かね を くれ と
いふ こと が できませう。

7.—どうも ばら や もみぢ の きれい な こと。
じつ に はでやか で ありません か。 'オヤ
ハヤシ-さん だ。「しばらく お-め に........。」
ハヤシ-さん, このかた は わたくし の
ともだち で アメリカ の ロビンソン-し で
ございます。

8. ハヤシ-し:—はじめて お-め に かゝります
わたくし は ハヤシ と まうします。 どうぞ
ご-こんい に お-ねがひ まうします。

4.—I should think it would.   Almost every color, too, is shown.   By the way, I wonder whether a blue chrysanthemum could be developed.   I have heard of a man who has offered 5,000 *yen*, gold, for a chrysanthemum of that color.

5.—He will keep his money, I think.   Do you see even a suggestion of blue in this collection ?

6.—I have learned not to say " impossible."   Yes,—there are tinges of blue in that group.   Some shrewd fellow may be yet entitled to ask for the money,—if it is to be had.

7.—What exquisite roses, too !   And those maples !   Are they not gorgeous ?   Ah, here is Mr. Hayashi. * * * It is some time since I have seen you.   Mr. Hayashi, this is my friend, Mr. Robinson, of America.

8. *Mr. H:*—The first time I have been honored with meeting you.   My name is Hayashi.   I beg your kind acquaintance.

9. ロビンソン-し:―わたくし は ロビンソン と まうします。どうぞ ご-こうさい を ねがひます。

10. ミカター-し:―よい じこう で は あり ません か。ことし は うゑきや の ていれ が よう ご-ざいます から, じぶん み に きた だけ の こと が ご-ざいます。

11. ハヤシ-し:―しばらく こしかけ よう じや ありません か。ねえさん お-ちや を もつて きて お-くれ。

    *   *   *   *   *

12. ミカター-し:―すつかり さむく なつて き- ました ね。たいやう も まつたく ぼつしました。 ロビンソン-さん, そろ〱 かへらねば ならぬ じや ありません か。ハヤシ-さん, あなた の おつしやつた こと に は まつたく どうい いたします。が, なほ その こと を かんがへ- て みませう。どうぞ ご-かない-さま へ よろしく。

13.―やま を こへて かへりませう, ごらん- なさい, みかづき が で ゐます。くも が きれい じや ありません か。あなた は ハヤシ さん は じつさい あなた を たすけて びやう- ゐん を たて やう と して をられる と お-かんがへ です か。

Mr. R :—My name is Robinson. I hope that you will honor me with your friendship.

10. *Mr. M :*—Charming weather, is n't it ? The gardener has made his place well worth a visit this year.

11. *Mr. H :*—Let us sit down for a moment. *Nesan,* bring some tea.

* * * * *

12. *Mr. M :*—It is getting to be quite chilly. The sun has almost set. Mr. Robinson, is it not about time for us to go ? * * * I quite agree with what you say, Mr. Hayashi. I shall think over the matter. Please remember me to your family.

13. *Mr. R :*—Let us walk back over the hill. See ! there is the new moon. How exquisite the clouds are ! By the way,—do you think Mr. Hayashi really wishes to join you in building the hospital ?

14.―なぜ です。

15.―わたくし に は あの かた は ハツメイ‐
はくし の じけふ に あまり ねつしん で
ない やう に みえる の です。 あなた が
しんじて ゐらつしやる ほど しんせつ で は
なからう と おもふ の です。

16.―ない か も しれません。 しかし あの
かた の たすけ は べつだん に たいせつ で
も ありません。 あの かた が たすけられ‐
ませう が, たすけられますまい が わたくし
に は あまり くわんけい が ございません。

　　　*　　　*　　　*　　　*　　　*

17. ロビンソン‐し:―はいつて あつたまつて
いらつしやいません か。

18. ミカタ‐し:―ありがたう ございます が,
しつれい いたします。 けふ の さんぽ は
ひじやう に おもしろう ございました。 ちから
に また やつて‐み‐やう じや ありません か。

19.―ちよいと おー‐まち なさつて ください。
これ が せんじつ おー‐はなし いたしました ほん
で ございます。

20.―ありがたう ございます。 けつこう な
ばん です ね。 おー‐やすみ なさいまし。

21. ロビンソン‐し:―(いりくち に て めしつかい に

14.—What do you mean?

15.—It seemed to me that he has precious little interest in Dr. Hatsumei's work.   I don't think he was anything like us cordial as you seemed to believe.

16.—Perhaps he was not.   But then his help is of no special importance.   It is a matter of indifference to me whether he takes hold or does not.

*   *   *   *   *

17. *Mr. R :*—Will you not come in and warm yourself?

18. *Mr. M :*—No, thanks !   I have had a most entertaining walk.   We shall try it again some time.

19.—Please wait a moment.   Here is the book I spoke of the other day.

20.—Many thanks.   Beautiful night !   Good night !

21.—*Mr. R :*—(*To servant at the door*).   Did any one call while I was away ?

むかひ、るす ちう に だれ も たづねて-き は
しなかつた か。

22―ハイ、 としよつた を-かた が を-いで
なさいまして、 てがみ を のこして いらつしやい-
ました。 あした の ばん まで は 「ティコク」
ほてる に を-いで なさいます さう です。
あんないじや を つれて いらつしやいまして、
あした よ-ぎしや で カウベ へ を-たち なさる
ご-やうす です。

―――

だい じふ さん

わ を 己

わざはひ も さいはひ の はし と なる。

(ミカタ-し の い へ にて。)

1. ミカタ-し:―どう して この やう な
あらし に を-でかけ なさいました か。

2. ロビンソン-し:―しうじつ とぢ-こもつて ゐ-
ます の で たいくつ いたしました が、
「クラブ」 は けふ の やう な てんき には
あまり とほう ございます の で、 こなた へ
あがつて しばらく を-はなし を しやう と
をもひました の です。

3.―それ は よく いらつしやいました。 コレ、

22.—Yes, sir.   An old gentleman left this letter for you.
He will be at the Imperial Hotel until to-morrow evening.
He had a guide with him.   He is going to Kōbe by the
night train to-morrow.

—

XIII.   PROVERB FOR (ㅎ) **WA.**

Even adversity becomes a bridge to pros-
perity.

(At Mr. Mikata's house.)

1. *Mr. M :*—What brings you out in this storm ?

2. *Mr. R :*—I got tired of staying in the house all day.
The Club is too far away for this weather.   I concluded to
come over and see you for a little while.

3.—You are always welcome.   *O Yone !*   Come here !
Make a fire in the foreign room.

お−ヨ子, せいやうま へ ひ を こしらへて
お−くれ。

4.—どうぞ その やう に お−かまひ ください−
ます な。

5.—イーエ, ちつと も お−かまひ まうし−
ません。けふ は たいへん くらくつて さむう
ございます の で, じぶん で も あすこ へ
ゆかう と おもつて ゐた の です。サァ
にかい へ あがりませう。

6.—あなた は たいてい こゝ に いらつ−
しやいます でせう ね。こゝ から シナガワ−
わん の けしき を みれば たいがい の
きまらない しあん も きまつて しまふ で−
せう。それ に また けつこう な ご−ぶんこ
を お−もち で ございます ね。

7.—この へや を こしらへました とき
に は べんきやう−しつ に しやう と おもつて
ゐた の です。ご−しようち の とほり こゝ
は わたくし が このーまへ エイコク から かへり−
ました すぐ あと に こしらへた の で ございー
ます。しかし おひく に した の こま の
はう が よく なつて まありまして, らいきやく
に あふ に も あすこ の はう が つがう
が よい の です。マァ お−かけ なさいまし。
ひざら の あいた ひ の そば に ゐる の は
こゝろもち の いゝ もの じや ありません か。

4.—Don't go to that trouble, please.

5.—It is no trouble.   Indeed, the day is so dark and cold that I thought of going there, myself.   Let us go up stairs.

6.—I should think you would spend a good deal of your time here.   This view of the Shinagawa bay would settle the question for me.   And then, you have this fine library.

7.—I intended to make this my work-room, when I built it.   I built the house, you know, just after my last trip to England.   But gradually I got to liking the little room down stairs.   It suits most of my visitors better. Sit down.   An open-grate fire is good company, isn't it ?

8.—ゆくわい で ございます ね。わたくし も けふ は たく で さん-がしよ に たきつけて をきました。 この やう に あらし が あつて くらい ばん に は ひ を も〜たゝします と へや の なか が ひじやう に やうき に なつて まゐります。どうも かぜ の ふきます こと。あめ は おそろしい おと を させ〜ます ね。しかし わたくし は けふ は あらし が あらう が なからう が あまり とんちやく いたしません。

9.—なぜ です か。

10.—じつ は さくばん よい たより が あつた の です。わたくし は その たより を はつかねん も まつて をりました。

11.—それ は お〜めでたう ございます。どう いふ こと を お〜きゝ なさいました か。

12.—かれこれ はつかねん ほど まへ の こと で ありました が ばうせき の あたらしい きかい を せいざう する くわいしや が たちまして そこ へ わたくし は ありがね を たいてい いれた の で ございます。さう し〜ます まへ に は できる だけ の さうだん を した の で あります が, にかねん たゝぬ うち に その くわい-しや は つぶれて しまいました。そこ で その たてもの

8.—Delightful! I have three of them going to-day. On a stormy, dark day like this, a blazing fire does much to cheer up a room. How the wind blows! The rain has a fierce sound. But, do you know, I don't much care to-day whether it storms or not?

9.—Why?

10.—I received good news last night. I have been waiting eight years for it.

11.—I congratulate you. What have you heard?

12.—About eight years ago, I invested nearly all the money I owned in a company organized to manufacture a new machine for cotton mills. I took the best advice I could get. Within two years the company failed. Its building and machines were turned over to me. They had been pledged as security for my investment. But I could do nothing with them for a long time. I could not sell them. At last, I managed to exchange them for some real estate. Then the real-estate market collapsed. For five years that property has been nothing but a burden on me. It has made a steady drain on my income. Last

と きかい と は わたくし の て へ わたり-
ました。 これ は わたくし の あづけきん
の ていたう に なつて をつた から で ご-
ざいます。 しかし わたくし は ひさしく それ
を どう する こと も できません でした。
うる こと も できなかつた の です。 さい-
ご に それ を ぢめん と ひき-かへる こと
に いたしました が, ひきついひて ぢめん の
ばいかひ が ふくはつばつ に なりました の
で, ご-かねん の あひだ この ぢめん は
おもに と なります ばつかり で, たえず
わたくし の しうにふ を へらして のみ をり-
ました。 ところ が さくばん の こと です が
しらせ が ありまして, これら の とち の
いつかしよ が うれた と いふ こと を
いつて まゐりました。 しく-かいせい の ため
に さうば が ついて きた の で ございます。
それ で わたくし の たいま の みこみ で
は, そん だ と おもつて ゐた ぶん を
のこらず とりかへして まだ その ほか に
よほど よけい な たか が あらう と おもふ の
です。

13.—それ は おーしあはせ で ございました。
しかし ときに さう いふ こと が ある もの
で ございます。 まづ なに ごと も まつて
ゐる かた へ まはつて まゐります。

night I heard that one of those pieces of land had been
sold. A new city improvement has brought the property
into the market. The prospect now is that I shall get
back all I thought lost, and much more.

13.—You are fortunate. But it often happens so.
Everything comes to him who waits.

14.—それ は なぐさめ に は なります が、ふしあはせ に よりて えられる しあはせ は うれしく ありません。 その かんがへ は けんぜん で は ありませう が、わたくし は ふしあはせ を かけはし と せない で しあはせ を えたい と おもひます。

———

だい じふ し

か ら う

かしら かくして を を かくさず。

1. ミカター し：—らんぷ を ともしませう か。 くらく なつて きた やう で ございます。 ひ が ひじやう に みじかく なりました の で、ごい に なる と もう よる で ございます ね。

2. ロビンソン し：—あなた さへ おーさしつかへ なければ わたくし は たきび の あかり の そば で はなしたう ございます。 ニホン に は まこと に よい せきたん が ございます ね。

3.—ハイ、ごく きた の はう と みなみ の はう と に たくさん でる ところ が ございます。 もうーすこし くべませう。

14.—That is comforting. Yet, prosperity through misfortune does not fascinate me. The idea may be a tonic.
I prefer prosperity, without having misfortune a bridge
to it.

XIV.   PROVERB FOR (カ>) *KA.*

Though the head be hidden the tail is seen.

1. *Mr. M :*—Shall I have the lamp lighted ?　It is growing dark.　The days are so short that it is almost night at
five o'clock.

2. *Mr. R :*—If you don't care, I would rather talk by the
fire-light.　You have excellent coal in Japan.

3. Yes, in the far north and in the south there are
immense coal deposits.　I will put some more coal on the
fire.

4.—じつ に ゆくわい な ほのほ です ね。
ところ が アノ けだもの が あたま を
かくす こと に ついて の ことわざ で ご-
ざいます が, あの ことわざ は けだもの の
うち に ある いつしゆ の きめう な
しふくわん から とつた の で ございます。
わたくし の くに で も あれ と おんなじい
ことわざ が ございまして, こども の とき
わたくし は だてう が まい すな の なか へ
あたま を かくす と いふ はなし を よみ-
ました。だてう は それ で じぶん の からだ
が のこらず かくれた と おもつて ゐる
らしい です。

5.—たしか わが くに の やま に ゐる
とり の うち に も その とほり ばか な
の が ある と おもひます。です が, この
ことわざ は よい いましめ と なる で は
ありません か。ひと は もし じぶん を
かくさう と おもつた なら ひと の め に
つき さう な こと は のこらず かくす やう
に しなければ なりません。たとへば どろぼう
に はいつて ゆか の うへ に なふだ を
おとして いく やう で は いけません。

6.—さう です。それ から また さくねん の
ふゆ わたくし が きゝました ある わかいもの
が した やう な こと を して も いけ-

4.—What a cheerful blaze! —— This proverb about animals hiding their heads is drawn from a queer habit among animals. We have the same thing in our popular sayings. When I was a child, I read that the ostrich often hides his head in the sand. He seems to think he is all hidden when he does that.

5.—I am told that one of our mountain birds is just as stupid. If a man wishes to hide he must be careful to cover up everything that would expose him. For example, don't rob a man's house, and leave your visiting card on the floor.

6.—Yes, and don't do what I knew a foolish young fellow do last winter. He wrote a scurrilous anonymous letter to a friend of mine, whose secretary was familiar with his handwriting.

ません。その にん は わたくし の ともだち
の ところ へ いやしき とくめい の てがみ
を おくつた の です が ともだち の しよき
は その にん の しゆせき を しつて ゐました
の です。

7.—わたくし は この ことわざ より も
すぐれた いましめ を しつて をります。それ
は じぶん を かくさねば ならぬ やう に なる
こと を すこし も しない の です。
たいてい かくす ひと は なに か あばかれる
やう な こと を のこして をく もの です。

だい じふ ご

よ ミ

よめ が しうとめ に なる。

1. ロビンソンし：—これ から しうとめ の
ことわざ に うつりませう。この ことわざ は
ぜうだん で ありませう か いましめ で
ありませう か。

7.—I know a better moral even than that.   Don't do at all
what would make you try to hide yourself.   The hiding
man almost always leaves something exposed, that betrays
him.

———

XV.   PROVERB FOR (ऱ) *YO.*

A bride will become a mother-in-law.

1. *Mr. R:*—Now let us take up the mother-in-law proverb.   Is this a joke, or is it a warning?

2. *Mr. M:*—Both, I suppose.   Let us call it a warning to
grandmothers.   I see in it, too, a warning to all who are
in authority.   The subject may become a ruler some time.

ひと も をさめる ひと に なる こと が
あります から。

3.—ニホン の ふじん の ちゐ は わたくし
の くに など と は すつかり ちがつて ゐ-
ます。

4.—それ は さう で ございます。 しかし
としつき の たつ に したがつて また よほど
の へんくわ が をこつて をります。 いぜん は
よめ と いへば をつと の りやうしん の
こゝろ-まかせ の もの で ありまして, よめ-
いり と いふ こと は つまり ふじん が
うまれた うち から よめいり を した うち
へ ひきわたさるゝ こと で ありました。

5.—いま で は よほど ちがつて をります
か。

6.—ハイ。 わたくし の しつて ゐます うち
で ずいぶん そこ の うち の むすめ が
よめいり を した のち まで も いぜん どほり
かぞく と なつて をる ところ が ございます。

7.—それ で も やはり しうとめ は よめ
に たいして よほど の ちから を もつて
をります か。

8.—むろん さう です。 それ が わが くに
の しふくわん の いちぶゝん で ある の
です。 その くわんけい に へんくわ が をこ-

3.—The position of woman is quite different in Japan from what it is with us.

4.—So it is. Time is making great changes, however. In the old days, a young wife became entirely subject to the will of her husband's parents. In fact, in ancient times marriage transferred a woman wholly from her own family to that of the man she married.

5.—Is it much different now?

6.—Yes. I have friends whose daughters are about as much members of their own families after marriage as they were before.

7.—But still, a mother-in-law has great power over her son's wife?

8.—Undoubtedly. That is part of our custom. Any change in that relation would be exceedingly slow in coming.

つて くる まで に は よほど の とき が
かゝりませう。

9.—それ から この ことわざ を もう ひとー
つ ほか の いみ に とる こと が できー
ませう。 すなはち もし じぶん の まご を
しんせつ に あつかつて もらいたい なら,
じぶん も また その よめ を しんせつ に
あつかはなけれゞ なりません。

10.—さう いふ いみ で ある か も しれー
ません、 わが くに の しふくわん は あなた
の おーくに から みる と ちがつて をります
が, それ が ため, わが くに の ふじん は
ごーしようち の とほり ふゆくわい で は ありー
ません。 いつたい しふくわん は どの やう で
ありませう が, しふくわん の おこなはるゝ
はうばふ さへ よければ それ で よい の
です。

──────

だい じふ ろく
た さ ゐ

たま みがゝざれば ひかり なし。

1. <u>ロビンソンーじ</u>:—まこと に ゐどいろ の いゝ
おーへや です コト。 そうして けつこう な ごー
ぶんこ を おーもち です ね。 ちかごろ おー

9.—The proverb yet holds good, then? If a woman wishes to have her grandchildren kindly treated, she should treat her daughter-in-law kindly.

10.—That is probably what it means. Our customs are different from yours. But our family life, you know, does not make our women unhappy. It is not the custom, but the way in which the custom is used, that is important.

———

XVI. PROVERB FOR (花) *TA*.

A jewel unpolished will not glitter.

1. *Mr. R:*—What a cozy place this is! You have an excellent library. Have you bought many new books lately?

もとめ の あたらしい ほん が たくさん ございませう。

2. ミカ゛ターし:──お゛─はづかしう　ございます　が、ございません。それ で も ぐわいこく から か゛──へりました じぶん に は いろ〱 の かんが゛へ も あつた の です。わたくし は わかい とき に は えいこくし が すき で ありまして、(ちよいと ごめん くださいまし、ひ を つけます から。) こゝ に ヒューム と マコウレー と グリーン と が ございます。これ は エイコク の ろんぶん─か の ぜんしふ で ございます。それ から えいこく の し で いちばん よい シエキスピヤ、ワーズワース、テニスン も ございます。ブラウニツグ の しゝふ は これ で ございます。

3.──いつ あがりまして も この お゛──へや は よう ございます ね。わたくし の みた ニホン の いへ で この お゛──へや ほど ヨーロッパ ふう な の は ございません。かう いふ ほんや、ゑや、ざう の ある ため、よほど じやう──ひん な お゛もむき が ございます。なぜ あなた は もつと この お゛──へや を お゛──つかひ なさらない の です。

4.──じつ は、さいしよ の かんが゛へ の やう に やつて ゆきます の は なか〱 ほね が

2. *Mr. M:*—I am ashamed to confess I have not. I brought good resolutions with me when I came home from abroad. I became intensely interested in English history when I was a young man. Excuse me! I will light the lamp. Here, you see, I have Hume, Macaulay and Green. Here is a full set of the British Essayists. I have even the best English poetry,—Shakespere, Wordsworth, Tennyson ; and here is a volume of Browning.

3.—I have always liked this room. It is more like a home room than any I have seen in other Japanese houses. These books and pictures, and these busts give it quite a scholarly air. Why don't you use it more ?

4.—To tell the truth, it was too much up-hill work to keep on as I started. I am sometimes sorry that I have failed. But the fact is, many things have kept me from

をれます の で, ときぐ ざんねん に おもふ
こと も あります が, どう も いろぐ な こと
が あつて おもふ やう に なりませず, だんぐ
かじ に ばかり ひきこまれる やう に なつて
ゆく の で ございます。 もつとも イキリス や
あなた の おーくに の こと は けつして わー
すれ は いたしません これ は あなた だつて も
さう で ございませう。

5.—それ は さう でせう。 しかし わたくし
は この おーへや の つかはれず に ある の
を みます と いつ も なぜ あなた は もつと
これ を やく に たつ やう に なさらない か
と おもひます。 それ に あなた は だんぐ
えいご を おーわすれ なさる やう です よ。
わたくし が はじめて おーめ に かゝりました
じぶん に は あなた の えいご は まこと
に りうちやう で, たいてい かどだつ こと も
ありません でした が, この ごろ で は めつー
た に あなた と えいご の おーはなし が できー
ぬ やう に なりました。

6.—おつしやる とほり です。 どうも わたくし
は しつてーゐた こと を だんぐ わすれて
まゐります。 わたくし が しよさい を つかはー
ない の も まつたく わけ の ある こと で
ございます。 ナルホド えいご で はなす こと
も むつかしく なつた に ちがい ありません

doing as I thought I should do.   I gradually became engrossed with home affairs.   My memories of England and of your country, of course, I shall never lose.   It would be the same with you, should our places be changed, I think.

5.—That might be.   But I often wonder, when I see this unused room, why you do not make it serve you better. And, do you know?   I think you are gradually losing your command of the English language.   When I first met you, you spoke English fluently, and with almost no accent. Now, I can scarcely ever get you to talk with me in English.

6.—You are right.   I believe I am fast forgetting what I knew.   There are good reasons why I do not use my library much.   It is true that even talking English is getting to be difficult.   Yet, you know I have very little inducement to keep up the old studies.   Japan and Europe are far apart in more ways than one.

が, しかし ご－ぞんじ の とほり <u>ニホン</u> と
<u>ヨーロッパ</u> と は いろ／＼ の こと が ちがつて
をります から, わたくし が もと の けいこ を
つ＼ける ひつねう は まこと に すくない の
で ございます。

7.―なるほど ご－もつとも です。 それ に
わたくし も あまり あなた の お－てつだひ
に なりません でした。 どう です あなた は
わたくし と いつしよ に えいしよ を お－よみ
なさいません か。 よろしく ば, ときぐ ご－いつ－
しよ に <u>グリーン</u> の れきし を よみませう。

8.―ハイ。 ドウカ さう ねがひたい もの と
おもひます。

─────

だい じふ しち

れ き

れい すぐれば しつれい と なる。

1. <u>ロビンソン</u>－し:―あらし は やまない で かー
へつて ひどく なつて まゐります。 あなた は
<u>エマースン</u> を お－よみ なさつた こと が ありー
ます か。 わたくし は こん－や の やう な
ばん に は きつと あの <u>エマースン</u> の
「あらし の よは の しづけき にぎはい」 と
いふ し を おもひ－だします。 わたくし は

7.—I understand. And I am not doing much to help you along. How would you like to join me in some English reading? I will read Green with you, turn and turn about, if you wish.

8.—Well, possibly I may take up with your offer.

———

XVII   PROVERB FOR (ﬅ) *RE*.

Too much politeness becomes rudeness.

1. *Mr. R :*—The storm does not let up. Indeed, it grows worse. You have read Emerson, haven't you? I never pass an evening like this, without thinking of his " tumultuous privacy of storm." That line always struck me as expressing perfectly the comfort of a fire-side, with a storm raging around the house. How the rain dashes against the window!

この く は いへ の そと に あらし が
ある とき に ゐろり の そば で たのしん-
で ゐる ありさま を まこと に よく あらは-
して ある と おもつて かんしん いたします。
ヤア ドウモ あめ が ひどく まど を うち-
ます ね。

2. ミカターし:―まど を しめませう。 ソレ。
これ で よう ございませう。 あなた は ごはん
を たべて いらつしやいません か。 その はう
が よう ございます。 モウ めし-どき で ご-
ざいます。 (て を うつ と おー<u>ヨ子</u> いで-き-
たる)。 ごはん は いゝ か ～。

3.―ハイ たゞいま。

4.―<u>ロビンソン</u>-さん が ごはん を おーあがり
なさる から。

5.―よろしう ございます。 たゞいま すぐ でき-
ます。 こゝ で めしあがります か。

6.―イヤ, した に いたしませう。

7.―ヨロシイ, したく が できたらば すぐ に
おーしらせ。

　　　*　　　*　　　*　　　*　　　*

8.―どうぞ そこ へ おーかけ なさい。 こゝ
は にかい から みる と よほど さむう ご-
ざいます。 もーひとつ の ひばち を もつて

2. *Mr. M :*—I will close the blinds. There! This is better. You will stay to dinner won't you? That is right! It is about time now for dinner. (*Clapping his hands. O Yone San appears.*) Is dinner ready?

3. *O Yone :*—Very soon, sir.

4. *Mr. M :*—Mr. Robinson will take dinner with me,

5. *O Yone :*—All right sir. Dinner will be ready in a few minutes. Shall I serve it here, sir.

6. *Mr. R :*—(*interposing*) Oh no! let us have it down stairs.

7. *Mr. M :*—Very good! Call us as soon as things are ready.

*   *   *   *   *

8. *Mr. M :*—Please sit there. It is much colder here, than up stairs. Bring another *hibachi*. Don't you want to put on your overcoat?

おいで。　あなた　は　ぐわいたう　を　おーめし
なさいません　か。

9.—イーエ　ちつと　も　さむく　ありません。

（ミカターふじん　つぎ　の　ま　より　おーヨ子　に
「けつとう　を　もつて　おーいで」　と　いふ。けつ
とう　きたりければ,　ふじん　は　これ　を
ロビンソン　の　すーあし　に　まきつけ,　わらひ
ながら,　「わたくしーども　は　この　うへ　に
のつて　あし　を　あたゝめます」　と　いふ。
ロビンソン　は　じたい　を　せし　が,　つひ
に　これ　を　うけ,)　いろ／＼　ごーめんだう　を
かけて　おそれーいります。

10.—かんーざけ　を　すこし　おーあがり　なさい
まし。　それ　で　へや　の　さむさ　が　とれ
ませう。

11.—しかし　へや　は　ちつと　も　さむく　あり
ません。　どうか　そんな　に　かまつて　くだ
さいます　な。　コレ　ハ　シタリ,　わたくし　の
あし　が　あなた　に　ふれました。　まこと　に
そさう　を　いたしました。

12.—イーエ,　わたくし　こそ　しつれい　を
いたしました。　マア／＼。　この　オムレツ　は　おー
あがり　なさられませう。　「てんぷら」　の　はう
は　いかゝ　で　ございます。

13.—ありがたう。　あなた　は　いつ　も　ごー

9.—No indeed! I am perfectly comfortable. (*Mrs. Mikata from an adjoining room says to O Yone, " Fetch me the brown rug." The rug is brought,—she wraps it about Mr. Robinson's shoeless feet, saying with a laugh, " We keep our feet warm by sitting on them." Mr. Robinson protests, but accepts, and adds.*) I am very rude to trouble you so.

10.—*Mr. M :*—Let me give you some hot *saké.* It will take the chill off the room.

11.—But the room is not chilly, I assure you. Please do not trouble yourself any more on my account. There! I have pushed my foot against you. I am very awkward.

12.—No! it was I who was rude. Don't move. Here is an omelet that you may like. And some fried fish.

13.—Thank you! You are always very kind. When I

しんせつ で ございます。 しかし わたくし が
じぶん の あし で あなた を つき, あなた
が いま の やう に おーたへ なさつた の
で, わたくし は フト わが アメリカ の
なんぶ の くに で, ある ぶたふしつ の なか
で おこつた こと, イヤ おこつた と まうす
こと を おもひだしました。 もちろん これ は
あなた の おーたへ を ひひやう いたす の
で ありません。 あなた の おーくに の れいぎ
は まつたく よろしう ございます が。 はなし
は かやう です。 ある ひと が たにん の
そば を とほつて その-ひと の あし を ふんだ
の です。 そこ で,「これ は しつれい」と いひ-
ます と, むとふ で も 「これ は しつれい
わたくし が ろさう を いたしました の で」
と いひました。「どう いたしまして わたくし
の はう が わるい の です」と まうします
と 「イヤ わたくし の あし が あなた の
とほり-みち に あつた の です」と いひ-
ました。「イヤ わたくし の め が ある べき
ところ に なかつた の です」と いひます と,
むかふ で は たち-あがりまして,「どう あつて
も わたくし の あし が あなた の とほり-
みち に あつた の です」と こたへました。
する と, こなた は するどき こゑ で いひます
に は 「あなた は わたくし を ぶちよく する
おーかんがへ です か」「ソレハ わたくし…の

pushed you with my foot, and you answered as you did. I could not help thinking of what took place,—or is said to have taken place,—in a ball-room in one of our Southern States. Of course, I make no criticism of your answer to me. Your country's polite forms are perfect. But the story goes ;—A man in passing another, trod upon the other's foot. "I beg your pardon, sir." "I beg *your* pardon," returned the other, "it was my awkwardness." "Not at all," said the first, "I was to blame." The other replied, "I assure you, sir, my foot was in your way." "I beg your pardon," retorted the first, "my eyes were not where they ought to be." "I say," broke out the second man rising, "I was in your way." "Do you mean to insult me, sir?" returned the first with a nettled tone. "I don't care whether you take my apology as an insult or not," added the second. "Well then, sir, here is my card, and I refer you to Major Bang." The result was a duel the next afternoon. One of the gentlemen received a bullet in his leg. Personal honor was satisfied.

———

いひわけ を ぶちよく と なさる と も なさら
ぬ と も あなた の ご-かつて です」「それ で
は よろしう ございます。 わたくし の めいし
を さしあげます。 そして バン-せうさ を
しめい いたします」 と いひました。 すなはち
この あらそひ の けつくわ は けつとう と
なりまして よくじつ の ごい に なり, ひとり
の しんし は あし に だん-ぐわん を うけ-
て, はじめて その-み の いちぶん を たて-
ました。

————

だい じふ はち

ろ そ つ

そで-うつし に もの を やる。

1.—みたり は いま の はなし にて ほ-
ほい に きよう に いり, やがて ゆふはん も
すみ, くわし や くだもの など を たべ,
ミカ,タ-ふじん は こと に あはせて むかし
の いさましき うた を うたひし が, つぎ に
しやみせん を とり-いだして こひ と ふく-
しう と の うた を うたひたり。 うた の
はなし は いつしゆ の ひげき にて, まつ-
たく むじつ なる はなよめ のみ に ほ-
こりたる ことがら なり。 ある わかき むすめ
ありて としよれる かね-もち の あきうど に

XVIII. PROVERB FOR (そ) *SO.*

Gives by passing it through the sleeve.

1.—The three friends had a good laugh over the story. At the close of the dinner, cakes, sweetmeats and fruit were enjoyed. Mrs. Mikata sang an ancient heroic song, accompanying herself with the *koto.* Then she took down her *samisen,* and sang a story of love and revenge. It was of a tragedy which was brought about in all innocence on the part of a bride. A young girl had been married to a rich old merchant. He was unloveable, and was excessively jealous. He suspected that his bride was enamoured of a young man who lived in a neighboring house. One day he saw her, as he thought, pass something through the hedge to some one in his neighbor's garden. He became angry and moody. He watched his wife continually. His suspicion fed upon trifles until he became mad with jeal-

よめいり せし に, この あきうど は なさけ-
ごゝろ の なき うへ に ねたみ-ぶかく して,
じぶん の つま は となり の うち の せう-
ねん に けさう せり と うたがひし が,
ある ひ の こと, つま が いけがき の あひだ
より となり の には に をる ひと に なに
か わたせり と おもひ-こみ, ふんぐ と して
いきどほりて たへず つま の そぶり に き
を つけし が, これ より は わづか の こと
まで も うたがひ の たね と なりて, しつと
の ほむら に むね を なやまし, しだい に
つま に つらく あたり, つひ に は あきら-
か に みさを を やぶりたり と て, つま の
つみ を せむる に およびし が, つま は
なに ごと を も しらず と いひて, あながち に
また いひ-とかん と も せざりき。 つぎ の
よ, つま は には に いでし が, あきうど は
これ を みて, いかり に たへず, しらは を
とつて あと を つけたり。 しかる に つま の
すがた の みあたらざる より, あかり を も-
ちて せんさく しい に, つま は すでに
しいて ありけり。 こ は あきうど の むはふ-
なる うたがひ の いけにへ と なりて, みづ-
から その み を ころせる なりけり。

2. ロビンソン-し:—どうも ありがたう ござい-
ました。 シカシ マア かなしい うた です ね。

ousy.   He gradually became cruel to her.   He finally accused her of unfaithfulness.   She denied everything, but would explain nothing.   The next night she went out into the garden.   He followed her infuriated, with sword unsheathed.   She was not to be seen.   With lantern then he sought her.   He found her at last.   She was dead ; killed by her own hand ; the victim of his insane suspicion.

2. *Mr. R :*—Thank you for the song.   But what a tragic story !

3. <u>ミカター</u>し:―ごーしようち の とほり わが くーに で は いゝ うた は たいてい かなしう ございまして, おも に ぎり, あいじやう, なんーぎ, し など の こと を うたつて ございます。

4.―たが きげき の うた は すこし も ありません か。

5.―たくさん あります が きゝーぐるしい もの ばかり で, こゝ で は おーきゝ に いれられーません。 この こと に ついて は よほど かいりやう が ひつえう で ございます。

6.―ヤァ もう くじ です。 かへらねば なりーません。 めしつかひーのーものーども は わたくし が どこ に をる か しらない の で ございます。 こんーや は ことし の うち で いちばん ひどい あらし です ね。 これ で は おほーみづ の ある の も むり で は ありません。

7.―ぜひ おーかへり なさらなければ なりません なら この うへ おーとめ まうしますまい。 ちやうーちん を おーもち なさいまし。

8.―ありがたう。 こんーや は ひとつ おーかり まうしませう。

3. *Mr. M:*—Most of our best music as you know is sad. It tells chiefly of heroism, or of love, and suffering, and death.

4.—But have you no comic songs?

5.—Plenty of them.   They are not, as a rule however, fit for polite ears.   You do not hear them in our homes. There is much need for improvement in that direction.

6.—Ah! it is nine o'clock.   I ought to return.   The servants do not know where I am.   This is one of the severest storms of the year.   I should not be surprised to hear of floods.

7.—If you *must* go, we shall not ask you to stay longer. Let me get you a lantern.

8.—Many thanks!   I will take one to-night.

だい じ ふ く
つ り ほ

つの を なほす とて うし を ころす。

1.—(ミカターし ロビンソンーし の いへ にて と を たゝき ながら,)はいつて も よろしう ございます か。

2.—オヤ,あなた で ございます か。どうも めしつかひーのーものーども が き が きゝません で。

3.—かね を うちました が だれ も でゝ こられません でした。そと では たいへん あつたか で ございます。あなた は ひ を たいて なに を なさいます か。もはや なつ に なつた やう です よ。

4.—わたくし の おき ない さき から たいて あつた の です。この へや は あさ の うち は いつ も さむう ございます。しかし,あなた は あるいて おーいで なさつた の です から,こゝ は あつーすぎる か も しれません。ニホン ふう の へや に まゐりませう。なるーほど これ は あつたか です。わたくし は くに の しんぶんし に おくる てがみ を かいて をりまして,けふ ぢう に それ を

XIX. PROVERB FOR (つ) *TSU*.

Intending to mend the horn, he kills the ox.

1.—(*In Mr. Robinson's house. Mr. Mikata knocking at a door. He says,*) May I come in?

2. *Mr. R :*—Oh! is that you? How stupid the servants are!

3.—I rang the bell, but no one came. It is very warm outside. What are you doing with a fire? Summer seems to have come back.

4.—The fire was made before I got up. This room is always chilly in the morning. It is too warm for you, perhaps. You have been walking. We will go into the Japanese room. Why, it *is* warm! I have been writing a letter for a home-paper, and I wanted to get it done to-day. So I have been keeping close to my desk.

しあげ よう と おもひました の で, つくゑ に
ばかり かゝつて をつた の です。

5.—それ ならば おーいそぎ に およびます—
まい。 きせん は あした で なくて は つきー
ません から。 わたくし は いま とーちう で
ゆうびんきよく へ よりました が, ゆうびんもつ
の しめきり は あした の ばん の しちーじ
と いふ くわうこく が でゝゐました。 しかし
おじやま を いたして は なりません。

6.—イヽエ, おーかへり なさいます—な。 あなた
と おーはなし いたしたう ございます。 ひさー
しく おめ に かゝりません でした。

7.—それ で は また ことわざ の はなし.
に いたしませう。 コート。「つ」 まで すんだ
はづ です ね。

8.—さう です。 には へ でゝ いらつしやいー
まし。 けさ の フジサン を おーめ に かけたう
ございました。 なん と も いはれぬ ほど,
きれい な いろ で, よほど ちかくて そうして
たいへん に たかい やう に みえました。
ズット ちかい やま の うへ に も ゆき が
みえます。 これ は この あひだ の あらし の
ため で ございます。 しばらく こゝ に すわー
らう じや ありません か。 けふ は ほんたう
に あつたか な ひ で ございます。 ソコデ

5.—There is no hurry. The steamer will not be here until to-morrow. In coming over I stepped into the post-office. A notice there says, that the mail will not close until to-morrow evening at seven. But I must not interrupt you.

6.—Don't go please! I want to talk with you. I have not seen you for several days.

7.—Shall it be the proverbs again? Let me think. We have read as far as " *Tsu,*" I believe.

8.—Yes. Come out into the garden. I wish you could have seen Mt. Fuji this morning. Its color was indescribably beautiful. It seemed so near and unusually lofty. The nearer mountains, too, have snow on them. That is part of the work of the storm the other day. Let us sit here for a while. Really, the sun is hot!—Well, what have you to say of our " *Tsu*" proverb?

「つ」 の ことわざ に ついて の おーかんがへ
は いかゞ で ございます か。

9.—それ は はうにん する を よし とす
と いふ こと だらう と おもひます。 あなた
は くわんぜん の ゑ と いふ こと の
はなし を おーきい なさいました か。 わたくし
は いちーど さう いふ を かゝう と おー
もつた ひと の はなし を きゝました。 ところ
が, その ゑ は どう して も できない の
です, きれい な ゑ は たくさん かきました
が それ を なほさう と する ので いつ も
それ を わるく して しまいました。 しかし
この りくつ を しる べき ひつえう の ある
ひと は まこと に すくない よう です。 よに
は じぶん の しごと を くわんぜん に しやう
と する ため に, いつ も しくじる ひと も
あります が, さう いふ ひと は おほく は
ありません。 つぎ の だい に うつりませう。

だい にじふ

ね 孫 を

ねずみ とる ねこ は つめ を かくす。

1. ロビンソンシーし:—これ は かうくわつ の
を しへ だ と はんじます。 て の うち に

9.—It means that we should let well enough alone, I suppose. Did you ever hear of "the perfect picture?" I read a story once, of an artist who resolved to paint such a picture. The picture never appeared. He made many lovely paintings, but in trying to improve them he invariably did them harm. However, there are very few of us who need the lesson of this wisdom. Some people always overdo in trying to perfect their work. But there are not many of that kind. Let us take up the next text.

XX. PROVERB FOR (11) *NE*.

The rat-catching cat hides her claws.

1. *Mr. R :*—This is a lesson in cunning, I judge. Don't

いれぬ　まへ　に　は　ぶき　を　しめすな　と
いふ　いみ　でせう。

2.　ミカタ-し:―さう　です　が，あらはし　かた　は
あまり　よくない　やう　です。　どんな　ねずみ
で　も　ねこ　を　みれば　すぐ　に　にげませう
から，ねこ　に　とつて　つめ　を　かくす　ひつ-
えう　は　ありますまい。　それ　より　は　ねづみ
を　とる　ねこ　は　あな　の　そば　に　かくれる
と　いうた　はう　が　よく　わかる　でせう。

3.―いつたい　　ニホン-じん　は　じぶん　の
ほんたう　の　かんがへ　を　かくす　こと　が
たくみ　な　やう　です。　わたくし　は　いつ　か
ひと　の　いふ　の　を　きゝました　に，この
くに　で　は　たにん　を　がい　しやう　と　おもふ
とき　に　す-ねん　かん　その　ふくしう　を
とらへる　もの　が　ある　さう　です。　その-ひと
の　しつて-ゐた　ふたり　の　をとこ　は　であつた
とき　に　は　ごく　なか　の　よい　ともだち　の
やう　でした　が，ある　ひ　その　ひとり　が　おほい
なる　ふかう　に　あひました　が，だん／＼　しら-
べて　みます　と，うら　で　そんがい　を　あた-
へた　の　は，ともだち　の　やう　に　して-ゐた
ひと　だつた　と，わかつた　さう　です。

4.―さやう。　それ　は　ぞんじて　をります。
ふくしう　は　むかし　わが　くに　で　は　めいよ-
はふ　で　あつた　の　です。　しかし　ふくしう

show your weapons until you are sure of your victim. Isn't that the meaning?

2. *Mr. M:*—Yes, but it does not seem to be very well put. Any rat will run at the mere sight of a cat. There is no need for the cat to hide her claws. The idea would be better put in this way ;—A rat-catching cat will hide near the rat-hole.

3.—It seems to me that the Japanese are especially skilful in hiding their real purposes. I once heard a man say, that a person in this country who has determined to injure another, will hold his revenge for years. He knew of two men who when they met, seemed to be of the warmest kind of friends. But one day a great misfortune happened to one of these men. It was learned at last that the apparent friend was back of the wrong done.

4.—Yes! I know. Revenge is part of our old code of honor. But you will admit, that, if revenge be a law, then of course any means to make revenge successful goes

が すで に はふりつ に なつて ゐた とき に
は, したがつて これ を たつする しゆだん
は いか やう で あつて も, むろん はふりつ
に とはれなかつた わけ でせう。 しかし
わたくし は むかし の はふりつ を べんご
する の で は ありません。 あなた も
<u>イタリヤ</u> の <u>イヤゴ</u> を べんご なさらん で-
せう。 <u>イヤゴ</u> は しいう にこく して ゐました
が, じつ は ひどい わるもの で あつた
さう です。

5.—むろん わたくし は べんご しません。
うらぎり は こんにち の よ に もちふる
ところ が ありません。 もし よ の ひと が
てき と ならなければ ならん なら, よろしく
おほやけ に てき と なる べし です。 ぜひ
と も けんくわ を せねば ならん なら,
すくなく と も りつぱ に けんくわ を すべし
です。 つぎ の かな の ことわざ は なん
です か。

——

だい にじふ いち

な ふ 郡

なきづら を はち が さす。

1. <u>ミカター</u>し:—これ は たい さいなん が
くる とき は ひとつ で すまない と いふ

under the shadow of the law. I do not defend the old
code. You would not defend the Italian Iago, I know.
He smiled, and smiled, and yet he was a villain.

5.—Of course not! Treachery, however, has no allowable
place any longer. If men must be enemies, let them be
enemies to the face. Let them fight out their quarrels
honestly at least, if they will quarrel. What is the proverb you have for the next syllable?

XXI. PROVERB FOR (ᚾ) *NA.*

Bees sting a weeping face.

1. *Mr. M:*—Only a quaint, old saying, that tells of the
queer fact that misfortunes never come singly.

きめう な こと を，むかし の ひと が
をかし な ふう に いひあらはして おいた
の です。

2. <u>ロビンソンーし</u>：―<u>ニホン</u> の はち は ないて
ゐる ひと を さす やう な こと が ある の
です か。

3.―それ は どう だ か しれません。とにかく，
かしこい をしへ に は さう いつて ある の
です。しかし それ は まこと で ない に
しろ，その さして ある ことがら は ほんたう
では ありません か。

4.―じつ に さう です。せいくわつ の けい―
けん は いちどき に くる やう です。い丶
とき も あり わるい とき も あります。
わが くに で も，「あめ ふらず に，おほみづ
が くる」と まうします。しかし この こと―
わざ は かう いふ こと を・をしへ は しま―
せん か，どこ に ゐて も にこく して
をれば はち が よりつかない と。わたくし は
に―さん ねん まへ に ひじやう に よく
しあげた じむか と ちかづき に なりました
が，その ひと の はなします の に は
その ひと の こども で あつた とき に，
その はいおや は，どんな ばあひ で も
ちから を おとす なと をしへ，また よ に
いで丶 しごと を もとめ やう と する とき

2. *Mr. R:*—Is it true that Japanese bees will sting a man who is crying?

3.—How do I know? At any rate, that is what the " wise saw " said. But even if it is not true, the thing it aims at is true. Don't you find it so?

4.—Certainly! The experiences of life seem to come in groups, sometimes good and sometimes bad. We say in our country,—" It never rains but it pours." But the proverb teaches this lesson, does'nt it?—If one carries around a cheerful face the bees will let him alone. I knew a remarkably successful business man, a few years ago. He said, that when he was a boy, his mother told him to keep up a brave face under all circumstances. She urged him, when he started out to find work, never to complain if he did not find work at once. If he had to wait a long time, and even if he grew hungry waiting, she commanded him always to wear his best clothes, and never to tell of a hungry stomach. He succeeded because he always *seemed to* be successful, he said.

に, すぐ に それ が めつから なくつて も,
ふへい を いふ な, ひさしく またなければ
ならぬ やう な こと が あつて, まつて ゐる
うち に ひもじく なる こと が あつて も,
いつ も いちばん じやうとう の きもの を
つけて, けつして ひと に ひもじい と いふ
こと を いふ な, と いひつけた さう です。
その じむか の しあげた の は, いつ も
しあげた ふう を して ゐた から だ と,
いつて をりました。

5.—さやう〲。 おほく の ひと は おほかみ
と おなじ です。 びやうにん や けがにん の
ある とき に は これ を たすけ は し-
ないで, かへつて これ を くつて しまいます。
ふしあはせ な ひと や よわき ひと を
めぐむ の は ごく〱 ひらけた くに に のみ
おとなはる〱 こと です。

だい にじふ に

ら　ら　歴

らつくわ ねだ に かへらず。

1. ロビンソンーし:—ナント マア, めずらしく
けつこう な ひ では ありません か。 わた-
くし は どこ か やま の わき に ねころんで,

5.—Yes, many men are like wolves. They would soon-er kill their sick and wounded than help them. Kindness to those who are unfortunate and weak belongs to a high civilization.

———

XXII.   PROVERB FOR (5) *RA.*

A fallen flower returns not to its branch.

1. *Mr. R:*—What a rare day! It makes me want to lie off on a hill-side somewhere and simply enjoy the world.

たい よ の なか を たのしんで ゐたい やう
に おもひます。

2. ミカター し：—わたくし は はる より あき
の はう を すく の か ぞう か しりません
が, こんな やはらか な くうき ほど こゝろ-
もち の よい もの は じつ に ない と
おもひます。

3.—とを-か ほど まへ には, こゝ は まこ-
と に きれい で ありました。 ちやうど おほ-
かぜ の おこつた まへ の こと でした が,
たに の わき では き の いろ が じつ
に みごと で かき-の-き の わき に ある
き は, まるで まつか な ほのほ の やう で,
また あの いてう-の-き は きん の かた-
まり の やう で, には の うち は なに も
か も むらさき や とび-いろ や みどり の
は で おほはれて をりまして, ばら まで も
なつ が まだ すまない か の やう に はな
を もつて をりました。 が, たゞいま では
どう で ございませう。 ときはぎ より ほか の
き は みな は を なくなしました。 あらし が
みな おとして しまつた の です。 たゞ たい-
やう のみ が は の なき えだ の あひだ
から わたくし-ども の からだ を やいて ゐる
だけ です。

2. *Mr. M:*—I don't know whether I like autumn more than spring, or not. But certainly there could be nothing more delicious than this soft air.

3.—About ten days ago it was simply perfect here. That was just before the big storm. Across the valley the coloring of the trees was superb. That tree near the cryptomeria was fairly a blaze of scarlet. That *ichō* was a mass of gold. All around the garden, purple, brown and green foliage covered everything. Even the roses were blooming, as though summer had not passed. But now look at it! All the trees except the evergreens have lost their leaves. The storm tore them away. The sun fairly roasts us through the bare branches.

4.—ことし は ワウヂ へ お-いで に なり-ました か。もみぢ は たいへん に いゝ さう です。すくなく と も あらし の まへ に は よかつた と まうしました。

5.—ことし は まゐりません でした。この まへ の しう に は ニックワウ へ ゆかう と おもつて をりました。あめ が ふり さへ しなかつたら いつて みました の です。ちやうど じせつ の よい とき に お-いで に なります と チウゼンヂ まで の みち が まこと に みごと で ございます。きよねん は じふ-ぐわつ の すゑ に ミヤノシタ へ ゆきました が キガ まで の みち は しはう の けしき が じつ に あてやか で-した。しかし いま で は どこ の けしき も みな お-しまひ に なりました。わたくし は こゝら の このは を はき あつめて, すつかり それ を やひて しまひました。

6.—わたくし は もう そろ〱 まち へ ゆか-なければ なりません。ハヤシ-さん の やりかた は あなた の いぐわい な くらゐ です。わたくし-ども は ハツメイ はくし の ために しけんじやう を たて やう と いふ の です が, ハヤシ-さん は ろれ に ごひやく-ゑん きふ なさいました。

4.—Have you been at Ōji this year? The maples there are unusually rich. At least they were before the storm, a friend told me.

5.—I have not gone out there this year. But I intended to go to Nikkō last week. I should have gone, but for the rain. The road up to Chūzenji is glorious, if you take it just at the right time. Last year I was at Miyanoshita at the end of October. The walk to Kiga is bordered by gorgeous color. But the show is over everywhere, now. I have had the leaves here all swept up and burned.

6.—It is about time for me to go down town. Mr. Hayashi has done better than you thought he would. We are about to build an experimental hospital for Dr. Hatsumei. Mr. Hayashi has subscribed 500 *yen* towards it.

7.—なるほど、これ は けつこう です。わたー
くし も ねどこ いつきやく の だいきん を
きふ いたしませう。たくさん は できません が
すこし づゝ でも おーたすけ に なりませう。

8.—それ は まこと に ありがたう ぞんじー
ます。ちから に わたくし の たく へ れー
いで を れーまち まうします。はなし の だい
も はや はんぶん ばかり すみました ね。それ
で ちよつと れもひだしました が ことわざ は
どれ でも わたくしーども の きやうぐう に
まこと に よく あひます ね。

9.—その とほり です。「いろは」の うた は
だれ が こしらへた の か しりません が,
よほど かなしい うた で は ありません か。
わたくし は つい この あひだ チヤンバーレン
はくし の かきました 「ニホン の じぶつ」と
いふ ほん の なか に ある ほんやく を
よみました が, あなた は あの ほん を
ごーらん なさいました か。

10.—イヽエ。どう いふ ふう に ほんやく
して あります か。

11.—あの ひと は この うた は ぶつけう
の きやうもん に よつた もの で ある と
いつて をります。その かき やう は このごろ

7.—Indeed! Then I congratulate you. Let me pay for a bed in it. I can not do much, but every little will help.

8.—Thank you, sincerely. I shall expect to see you over at my house soon. Do you know we have talked through about half of our texts? And just now, as I think of it, all the proverbs we have had so far, suit the scene around us perfectly.

9.—So they do! Who invented the verse for *I-ro-ha?* Rather melancholy poetry, is it not? It was only the other day I read the rendering which Prof. Chamberlain gives of it in his book on "Things Japanese." Have you seen it?

10.—No! How does he give the verse?

11.—He says, it is of Buddhist origin, founded on one of the *Sutras.* He transcribes it according to modern pronunciation. As far as we have talked he renders the

の ゐん で ありまして, いま まで に はなした
ところ は かう いふ ふう です。

いろ は にほへど

ちりぬる を

わが よ たれ ぞ

つね ならん。

その ほんやく は 「いろ は あてやか なれ－
ど も はな は ちり されり, されば なん－ぴと
か よく この よ に ながらへん や」 と いふ
の です。

12.—たいさう よく できて ゐます ね。 いつ－
たい むかし の いみ を すつかり うつす の
は むつかしい こと です が, あの ひと の
は たいてい ちがひ は ない やう です。
しかし わたくし－ども は いちばん あと. の
かな を まだ よみません。 それ は 「む」 の
じ です が, あの ひと の は 「ん」 と
なつて をります。 しかし この ふたつ は
じつさい どういつ で ある の です。「む」 は
「ん」 の むかし の かたち です。 わたくし
は あなた の れ－ため に なる やう に 「む」
の ことわざ を ひとつ えらびました。 しかし
お－ため と まうして も, だうとく－じやう の
こと で なく, ちしき－じやう の こと で
ごさいます。 それ は ほか で も ありません。

initial syllabics of our proverbs in this manner ;—

> " *Iro wa nioedo,*
> *Chirinuru wo—*
> *Waga yo tare zo*
> *Tsune naran ?* "

His rendering runs ;—" Though their hues are gay, the blossoms flutter down, and so in this world of ours who may continue forever ? "

12.—Excellently done! It is difficult however to render the old idea perfectly. He comes very near it. But, the last syllable, we have not had yet. That is *Mu*. He makes it *N*. The two, however, are practically one and the same. *Mu* is the ancient form of *N*. I have selected a proverb in *Mu* for your benefit. I do not mean for your moral, but for your intellectual, good. This is it.

だい にじふ さん

む 竜

むり が とほれば だうり ひつこむ。

1. ロビンソンーし:—わたくし は この ぶん の いみ を じふぶん れうかい して ゐる と れもひます。この あひだ <u>シンバシ</u> の すてい—しよん で その ときあかし に なる こと を みました。ちやうど わたくし が <u>ヨコハマ</u> ゆき の きしや へ のらう と れもつて ゐます とき、わめき—ごゑ が きこゑました して、ふたり の をとこ が かとう の くるま から かけて でゝ きました。そして ふたり とも しきゐ—いし の うへ へ たをれました が、ひとり は たちまち からだ を ふりーはなしまして、とびーあがり さま あひて の かほ を ひどく けりーました。けられた はう は いき が たねました が それ で も けつた はう の ひと は やめません でして、らんばう にも じぶん の げた を ぬいで、いき の たねて をる ひと の あたま を たゝき だしました。この とき すていしよん の やくにん が その ひと を さゝへて けんくわ を やめ させません で した なら きつと あひて の ひと を ころしーて しまつた の でせう と れもひます。この

XXIII.   PROVERB FOR (ʦ) *MU.*

Reason shrinks back when passion goes by.

1. *Mr R :*—I understand the meaning of these words thoroughly, I think.   I saw an illustration of them at the Shimbashi station, a short time ago.   I was about to get into a train for Yokohama.   I heard angry cries.   Just then two men came tumbling out of a third-class carriage. Both fell upon the pavement.   One of the men suddenly released himself from the other's clinch.   He jumped up and kicked the other man full in the face.   The other was knocked senseless.   But this did not stop the one who kicked him.   He furiously tore off one of his own *geta*, (clogs) and began to hammer the senseless man on the head with it.   I think he would have killed the fellow, if some of the station guards had not grabbed him and put a stop to the fight.   He seemed to have gone crazy with fury. How it all ended, I do not know.   The train just then pulled out of the station.   The man had lost control of himself.

ひと は いかり の ため に き が ちがつて
ゐた やう でした。 それ から あと は どう
なりました か, きしや が すてゝしよん から
でました の で ぞんじません でした が, その
をとこ は じぶん を せい する ちから を
まつたく うしなつた の です。

2. ミカターし:— さやう。 だうり と かんじやう
と は ともなはない もの で ございます。
しかし もう れーいとま いたさねば なりません。
あなた の にはばん は たいへん よく うゑき
を ていれ いたしました ね。 つゝぢ の
きれい な こと。 いま に はな が たくさん,
さきませう。 うめ の らうぼく も また はな
を ださう と して をります。 あなた の
ところ の 「しやうちくばい」 の うち では
まつ—の—き が うめ と たけ の わり に
は れほきく なりました ね。

3.— ハイ, わたくし は ちいさい の と うゑー
かへ やう と れもつて をります。 わたくし の
きんぎよ は いかゝ で ございます か。

4.— きれゝ で ございます ね。 さやうなら。
ちかく に れーいで なさいまし。

5.— アゝ, いつさくじつ は けつこう な かき
を おくつて くださいまして, ありがたう ございー

2. *Mr. M :*—Yes, reason and passion will not go together. But I must return now. Your gardener has trimmed your shrubbery excellently. What fine camellias! You will have a mass of them in bloom before long. The old plum tree too seems to be getting ready to show what it can do. The pine in your *Shōchikubai* is becoming rather big for the bamboo and the plum.

3.—Yes, I am thinking of having a smaller one planted. How do you like my gold fish?

4.—They are beauties. Well, good bye! Come over soon.

5.—By the way, I almost forgot to thank you for the delicious persimmons you sent me the day before yesterday.

ました。れーれい を まうす の を わすれ やう
と して をりました。

6.—ナァニ, つまらない もの で。

———

だい にじふ し
う 宇

うり の たね に なすび は はえぬ。

1. (<u>ロビンソン-し</u> <u>ミカター-し</u> の いへ にて
めしつかひ に むかひ):—だんな は れーうち
です か。

2.—たつた いま れーでかけ で ございました。

3.—すぐ に れーかへり でせう か。

4.—いつて たづねて まゐりませう ....。
れくーさま の れつしやる に は, だんなーさま は
れつゝけ れーかへり なさいます から どうぞ
れーはいり なさいまし。

5.—それ で は れくーさま に よろしく いつて
ください。 わたくし は いちーにーじかん の
うち に かへつて きます から。................
イヤ チョット はいりませう。 まーもーなく れーかへり
でせう から。

6.—どうぞ こちら へ。

6. —Pray, don't mention it.

XXIV.   PROVERB FOR (5) *U.*

An egg-plant does not grow from a melon seed.

1. *(Mr. Robinson, to servant at Mr. Mikata's house.)*—Is your master at home ?

2. —He is absent just now.

3. —Will he be back soon ?

4. —I will go and inquire............Madame says, that master will return before long.   She invites you to come in.

5. —Please present my compliments to madame, and say that I shall come back in an hour or two.   Yet, wait a moment.   I will go in now.   I suppose your master will not be long gone.

6. —This way, please sir.

7. <u>ミカター</u>ふじん:―オヤ マア よく れーいで なさいました。 どうぞ れーかけ なさいまし。 やど は いち じかん ほど まへ に きやう－だい の やくしよ へ ゆきました が, いま に も かへつて くる だらう と れもひます。 ちかごろ は いかゞ で ございます か。

8.―きのふ は <u>ウヘノ</u> へ いつて いち－にち ほど あそんで きました。 びじゆつくわん は こと に れもしらう ございまして, <u>ヨーロツパ</u> ふう の ゑ を しばらく けんきう して きーました が, なかく よう ございます。 もつとも いろ は ちつと しつこい やう です が よほど のぞみ が ございます。 しかし なん です ね, <u>ニホン</u> りう の ひつばふ は どれ に でも みにて います ね。 すひやく ねん らい の えいきやう を <u>ニホン</u> の びじゆつ から とりさる に は よほど の とき が かゝりーませう。 <u>ヨーロツパ</u> と <u>ニホン</u> と の びじゆつ の ふう は すつかり ちがひます。

9.―やど で は わが くに の ある ぐわか の やりかた に さんせい いたしません。 あの ひと は たいがい の こと は ぐわいこく－ずき です が, この しん－くふう は このみません です。

10.―さやう。 わたくし など も <u>ニホン</u> の むかし の ふう を このみます。 わたくし の

7. *Mrs. Mikata:*—Ah! Mr. Robinson, you are very welcome. Pray, be seated. Mr. Mikata went to his brother's office about an hour ago. I am expecting his return at any moment. What have you been doing lately?

8.—I went to Ueno yesterday, and spent most of the day there. I was particularly interested in the Fine Art Exhibitions. The pictures in European style I studied for some time. They are much to be commended. It seems to me, however, that their coloring is rather heavy. They promise well. But,—do you know?—I think the hand of artistic Japan shows itself in almost all of them. It will be a long time before the influence of the centuries here can be removed from art. The styles of art in Europe and in Japan are quite unlike.

9.—Mr. Mikata does not approve the attempts which some of our painters are making. He is in favor of most things foreign,—but the new art he does not like.

10.—Well, for my part, I prefer in Japan the old style. I was charmed beyond telling, with some of the purely

みた ある じゆんすい の ニホン ふう の ゑ
には ひじやう に かんぷく いたしました。
なか には ニホン ふう と も ヨーロッパ ふう
と も つかない まぜあはせ の いや な ゑ も
ありました が, あすこ に かり あつめて ある
ゑ を みた とき に は わたくし は ほんたう
の びじつてき かんじやう を れこしました。
わたくし が みました タンイウ の いつゝ
むつ の けいしよく の ゑ ほど きれい な
もの は みた こと が ない と れもひます。
それ は ごく わづか な ほねをり で じん
りよく の をよぶ さいじやう の れもむき を
あらはして ございました。 たつた いちーど いぜん
キヤウト の 「ニシホングワンジ」 の ひろま で
ニホン の ゑ に かんしん した こと が
ございます。 そこ の ゑ は わが くに で
いふ ラフエール-ぜん の もの だけ で あり
ます が みな じゆんすい の ニホン ふう で
ございました。

　(ミカター し いり きたる)。

　11.—オヤ ロビンソン-さん よく れーいで で
ございました。 (ミカター ふじん は をつと の
かへりたる とき の ふつう の あひさつ
にて 「お-かへり」 と いひ, ミカター し は 「たー
いま」 と こたへて ロビンソン-し に はなし
を つゝけぬ)。

Japanese pictures that I saw. There were some half-and-half paintings that were abominable. I had a genuine art sensation, however, in the "Loan Collection." I do not think I ever saw anything finer in its way than the five or six Tanyū landscapes. There was perfection of effect in them with the smallest amount of effort. Only once before, in Kyōto, in the big hall of the Nishi Hongwanji, have I been so delighted over Japanese painting. The pictures there are almost what our people would call pre-Raphaelite. Yet, they are purely Japanese.

(Mr. Mikala enters.)

11.—Ah ! Mr. Robinson this is a pleasant surprise. *(Mrs. Mikala greets her husband with* " O kaeri " *the usual salutation at a return home to which he answers,* " Tadaima ! " *and continues, speaking to Mr. Robinson :)*—

12.—ひさしく お-まち で ございました か。

13.—ナニ ざんじ です。 おく-さま の お-
はなし で たいへん おもしろう ございました。
ちかごろ は いかゞ で ございます か。

―――――

だい にじう ご

ゐ井

ゐ の なか の かはづ だいかい を しらず。

1. ミヵター-し:—さくじつ お-はなし まうした と-
ほり せいふ は しようだく を あたへました。
らい-げつ は しけん-びやうゐん の ため に
じつけん-しつ を たて はじめます。 かね も
じふぶん に きふ に なりました。

2. ロビンソン-し:—それ は おもつた より
お-しあはせ で ございました。 よほど の はん-
たい が ある だらう と おもつて をりました
に。

3.—たゞ すこし めんどう で あつた の は,
びやうゐん の ゐち の こと で ありました。
わたくし-ども が きめました とち の きんじよ
の ひとゞ が いろゞ じやま を いたしました
の です。 しかし, いま では しんぱい する
に およばない と いふ こと が わかつた

12.—Have you been waiting long?

13.—Not long. Mrs. Mikata has been making the time pass very agreeably. How goes it with you?

XXV. PROVERB FOR (る) (*W*) *I*.

The frog in a well does not know the ocean.

1. *Mr. M:*—It is just as I told you yesterday. The Government has given its consent. We shall begin building the laboratory for the experimental hospital next month. Money enough for it has been subscribed.

2. *Mr. R:*—You are much more fortunate than I had expected. I supposed that you would have a great deal of opposition.

3.—The only serious trouble we have had has been over the location of the hospital. The people living near the lot of land we selected, have put all sorts of obstacles in our way. But I think they see now that there is no danger for them to be afraid of. At any rate, everything is settled. Soon after the New Year we shall begin to build.

だらう と おもひます。 とにかく ばんじ の
とりきめ が つきました から, しんねん に は
すぐ に たて はじめる つもり です。

4.―ぐち な ひと の まどひ ほど あつかひ
にくい もの は ありません。 わたくし が
こども の じぶん に いちど したてや へ
つかひ に ゆきました が, その みせ へ
はいる と にかい で ひどい さわぎ が ある
の で びつくり した こと が ありました。 あと
で きいて みます と あるじ が しよくにん
と たいきあい を して ゐた ので, その
おとり は もちぬし が とうじやう へ きかい
を いれた ところ が しよくにん―ら は この
きかい が くる と じぶん―ら の しごと が
すぐ に ひま に なる だらう と おもつて,
これ を うちこはした の で ございました。

5.―さう でした か。 ガツシウゴク に その
やう な こと が おこつた と は ぞんじ―
ません でした。

6.―ソリヤ モウ。 どこ に で も おこる
こと で ございます。 アメリカ で はじめて の
てつだう や はじめて の かりとみきかい や
はじめて の くつ の きかい や, その た あら―
ゆる はじめて の こと に ついて も ひじ―
やう に ばか な しわざ が ありました。 せけん

4.—Ignorant prejudice is one of the difficulties hardest of all to overcome.   Once, when I was a boy, I went on an errand to a tailor's shop.   When I got to the shop I was frightened by dreadful noises from up stairs.   I found out afterwards that the proprietor was having a fist-fight with some of his workmen.   They had broken into pieces a sewing machine, which he had put into his work-shop.   The men imagined that the machine would soon throw them all out of work.

5.—Is that so?   I did not know that such things ever happened in the United States.

6.—Oh! they happen everywhere.   The most absurd things are told about the first railways in America, about the first reaping machines, the first shoe-making machines, the first power printing presses ;—in fact, about the first everything that means progress and greater prosperity. There are so many men who can not see beyond their noses.

には めさき の みえぬ ひと が かやう に たくさん ある の です。

7.—さう です。ニホン でも くわと さん-じふ ねん の あひだ に この きんがん の れい と なる こと が たくさん こざいました。 しかし よ の ひと は じぶん-ら の ばか で あつた こと を すぐ に わすれて, いぜん こばんだ もの を もちひて をります。 あなた の お-ため に ねらびました ことわざ の なか に ともつて をる しんり は せけん の たくさん の ひとく に も あたる と おもひます。

8.—それ は なん です か。

———

だい にじふ ろく
の ゐ 代

のどもと すぐれば あつさ を わする。

1. ミカタ-し:—ひと くち のみこむ と すぐ に あつさ を わすれる と いふ こと を をしふる の です。

2. ロビンソン-し:—この ことわざ の うち に も いくぶん か よき しんり が ある に ちがひ ありません が, その おうよう は ほか の いゝ ことば ほど に ひろく は あり—

7.—Yes, we have had plenty of illustrations of that short-sightedness during the last thirty years in Japan, too. Yet, people soon forget how foolish they were, when they are enjoying the good things which they once tried to prevent. The truth that is shut up in one of the proverbs I selected for your benefit applies to multitudes of people.

8.—Which proverb is that ?

XXVI.   PROVERB FOR (の) *NO.*

If a thing be swallowed its heat is forgotten.

1. *Mr. M* :—The one that tells of how we forget the heat as soon as we have swallowed the mouthful.

2. *Mr. R :*—To a certain degree, doubtless that proverb tells a pleasant truth. But its application is not so broad as that of many others of the wise sayings. Only this morning I was compelled to accept an unpleasant ex-

ません。すぐ けさーがた の こと でした が,
わたくし は いや な こと を きかねば ならぬ
やう に なりまして, それ は いつ まで たつて
も わすれない と れもひます。

3.ーなに ごと が あつた の です。

4.ーこの とち の もの で いま で は に-
ねん の うへ も いろく わたくし が せわ
を して やつた ところ の せうねん が あり-
まして, その して やつた こと を まうし-
あげる ひつねう は ありません が, に-さん-が-
げつ まへ に すこし ばかり の かね を
かした こと が ありました。かし の つけこみ.
は あります が いり の つけこみ は ない
の です。ところ が けふ また その せうねん
が きまして たのみ を いひました から,
わたくし は その たのんだ ところ へ せわ
して やりました が, その かへりーしな に
なりて ぐうぜん わたくし は この はる かした
かね を かへした か どうだ か と たづね-
ました。わたくし は かね の こと は れも-
つて ゐない の で かへした と いつた とて
その こと を うたがふ わけ で も なく, たゞ
フット たづねて みやう と れもつた だけ で
あつた の でした が, いぐわい に も その
せうねん は つゝたちーあがつて, わたくし は
もう あなた と はなし は しません。あなた

perience which I shall not forget for a long time, I am
sure.

3.—What has happened?

4.—There is a young man in the city whom I have been
trying to help in many ways, for more than two years now,
I need not tell what I have done for him. Some months
ago, however, he borrowed a small sum of money from me.
I have a record of the loan, but I have no record of its
repayment. To-day he came to me with a new request for
help. I referred him to the place he needed. Just before
he went away I casually asked him whether he had ever
returned the money I gave him in the spring. I did not
care for the money. I should not have doubted his word
had he said he had repaid it. I merely wished to satisfy
an inquiry which then arose in my thoughts. To my
dismay the young fellow started up, and said, " I will talk
no more with you. You think I am a bad man. I will go.
You think I am a thief." What could I do? The boy
wholly misunderstood me. I tried to explain. But he
no longer could control himself.   He could not tell
whether or not he had "repaid the money." But, I
thought him "a bad man," he insisted. He went off,
distressed, as though I had accused him of dishonesty and
robbery. I like the young fellow. I am grieved deeply
that he should so misunderstand me. I have had to

は わたくし を あくにん だ と れもふ の
です。 わたくし は かへります。 あなた は
わたくし を ぬすびと だ と れもふ の です
と いひました。 どう したら い でせう。
まつたく わたくし を ごかい した の です。
わたくし は ときあかし を しやう と こゝろみ-
ました が せうねん は もう きゝいれません。
かね を かへした か かへさん か は いふ
こと が できない で, たゞ わたくし が むかふ
を あくにん だ と れもつた と のみ いひ-
はつて をりまして, なにか わたくし に ふせい
な こと を して もの を ぬすんだ と でも
いはれた か の やう に かなしんで をりました。
わたくし は その せうねん を きらひ は し-
ません。 その わたくし を ごかい した こと
は ふかく かなしみます。 けれども せうねん の
ひなん は のみこんで しまはなければ なり-
ません。 わたくし が わるく れもつて ゐる
と いふ うたがひ は とり やう が あり-
ません。 あなた の れ-はなし の ことわざ は
かう いふ ことがら に は あたりません
です。

———

swallow all his reproaches.   I do not see how I can remove his conviction that I suspect him of evil.   Your proverb does not hold good in a matter like this.

だい にじふ しち

れ お

れに の ねんぶつ。

1. ミカターし :―その わかい をとこ は しやう―
じき だ と れ―かんがへ です か。

2. ロビンソンーし :―べつ に うたがふ べき
りいう も ありません。 わたくし は あれ を
ぎぜんしや だ と いふ より は き が
よわい と いふ はう が てきたう だ と
をもひます。 あれ は めいよ を をもふ の
じやう が つよ―すぎる の で, ちよつと さわ―
つて も ちいみこむ やう な ふう で ある
の か も しれません。 あるひは わたくし に
たいする あいじやう が つよい の で, ほか
の ひと から は むきだし に あばかれて も
こらへる こと が できる の で も, わたくし
から は とひ を うける こと で さへ も
できぬ の か も しれません。 たい わたくし
が もつとも ふくわい に をもひます の は
さん―ねん の あひだ いろく せわ を して
やりました の に, むかふ の こいろ に
しんよう が をこつて ゐません で, わたくし が
いつた こと は ほか に いみ が ない と
いふ こと を をもふ やう に ならない と いふ

XXVII. PROVERB FOR (♭) O.

A devil's prayer.

1. *Mr. M:*—You think the young fellow sincere?

2. *Mr. R:*—I have no reason for doubting him. I should rather say that he is weak-minded than that he is a hypocrite. It is just possible, too, that his sense of personal honor is so tender that it shrinks even from a touch. It may be that his affection for me is so strong that he can not bear even a question from me, while he would endure downright accusations from others. What I feel most troubled about is, that all I have done for him for the last three years has not aroused in him a confidence that would prevent him from thinking that I meant more than I said. I despise hypocrisy. And I demand in my friendships a confidence that will assume my honesty and frankness throughout everything.

こと です。わたくし は わたくし と まじはる
ひと〻 が よく わたくし を しんじて，わたくし
が ばんじ に しやうじき で さつぱり と
して ゐる と おもつて もらひたう ございー
ます。

3.—その ごちうもん は よわい ひと-ごゝろ
に とつて は ちつと むり で ございます。
ひと は じぶん を もつて たにん を はんー
だん いたします。

4.—さう か も しれません。しかし しやうー
じき な ひと〻 に は なす べき こと が
いろ〻 あります が，めいはく な しようこ が
あつて うたがはなければ ならん やう に なりー
ます まで，じぶん の ともだち を しんずる
こと は その ひとつ だらう と おもひます。
わたくし は ひどい うたがひ を して まうけ
を とります より，しんよう を わたくし の
きしつ と して そん を うけたう ございー
ます。

5.—その お-ことば は まこと に ご-しんせつ
です が，よわたり の ため に なる をしへ
で は ありません。イヤ たいがい の ひと が
まもつて ゆく ところ の きそく で は ありー
ません。しんよう は けつこう な もの です
が，それ を かふ あたひ は すこし で ありー
ません。どの てん にて ちかづき や とも-

3.—You are rather exacting of weak human nature. Men judge others by themselves.

4.—That may be. But there are traits which all honest men should show. One of these traits is confidence in their friends until compelled by clear proof to doubt them. I would rather have faith as a permanent thing in my character, and suffer loss by having it, than a chronic suspicion by which I might gain much.

5.—That is generously spoken. But it is not worldly wisdom. I mean rather, it is not the rule by which most men work. Confidence is a treasure that costs much to get. At what point a man can trust neighbors or friends fully, is one of the hardest of all questions to answer.

だち を しんずる こと が できる か ど
いふ こと は, あらゆる もんだい の うち で
いちばん こたへ にくひ もんだい で ござい－
ます。

　6.—それ は その とほり です。 あなた の
はう に は さう いふ じいつ が たくさん
ございます。 これ は ひさしい いぜん に
わたくし の ときやう に おこつた こと です
が, ある ぎんかう の くわいけい に しんせつ
な じんばう の ある ひと が ありまして,
その つま が しんだ ため, さびしく くらして
をりました が, まもなく ぐわいこくじん が
ふたり この とち へ きました。 ひとり は
まさしく はいびやう の ため に なやんで
をり, いま ひとり は びやうにん の きやう－
だい で ありました。 そくさい な はう の ひと
は まもなく くわいけい と ちかづき に なりま－
して, ときどき ぎんかう へ おほき な あづけきん
を いたしました。 くわいけい の つま は
はいびやう で しにました ので しわいけい は
ふたり の ぐわいこくじん に たいして いうじ－
やう を もちました。 くわいけい と そくさ－
い な あきうど と の じやう は しだい に
しんみつ と なりまして, つひ に この をとこ
は くわいけい の うち へ しいう くる ひと
と なりました。 わたくし が こちら へ あがり－

6.— Yes, I know that. On your side is such a series of facts as these, which, long ago, took place in my native town. The cashier of one of our banks was a cordial, popular citizen. His wife died, leaving him desolate. Not long afterwards, two strangers came to the town. One of them was suffering, apparently, from consumption. The other was the invalid's brother. The well man had plenty of money. He soon became acquainted with the cashier, and at times placed large deposits of money in the bank. The cashier's wife had died of consumption. The cashier's sympathy, therefore, went out to the two strangers. An intimate friendship gradually sprang up between the cashier and the well brother. This brother at length became a frequent visitor at the cashier's house. He went freely to the house, as I come here. This intimate relationship grew stronger through a large part of the year. The stranger became a regular church-goer, too. He even took part in the most sacred act of Christians, the Lord's Supper. The cashier was a truly sincere religious man. Well! I must make a long story short. The stranger at length concluded that the climate of that place was "very good for his brother's health." He "decided to buy an estate near the town." All this was made known to his

ます やう に じいう に その うち へ いつ-
た の で ございます。 そして つきひ の たつ
と とも に たがひ の なか は ますく よく
なりました が ぐわいこくじん は また たねず
けうくわい に かよふ ひと と なり キリスト
しんじや の ごく しんせい な ばんさんしき に
も くとはりました。 くわいけい は ごく せ-
いじつ な しうけうか で ありまして。 イヤ
ながい はなし は つめなければ なりません が,
とにかく ぐわいこくじん は つひ に この とち
の きとう は その きやうだい の けんかう に
たいへん よい と いひました。 そして この
まち の きんぺん に とち を かはう と け-
つしん いたしまして, その こと を あたらしく
できた すべて の ともだち に しらせ ま-
した。 しかる に しやうぐわつ の ある ばん
に ごく おどろく べき こと が おこりました。
おほかぜ は ふき, ゆき あられ あめ も ふり
まち に ひと-どほり も なく, くわいけい は
ぎんかう の じぶん の へや で しごと を
して をりました。 この ぎんかう は くわいけい
の いへ の なか に ある の で ありまして,
じふ-じ じぶん の こと です が, との すい
が なります の で めしつかひ が かどぐち へ
ゆきます と びやうにん の きやうだい の
ブラウン-し が そこ に をりました。 ブジウン
は わたくし が こなた へ とほされます やう

many new found friends. But one night in December, a most startling thing happened. A wild wind was blowing. Snow, sleet and rain were falling. The streets were deserted. The cashier was working in his private office, in the bank. The bank was in a part of the cashier's house. The door bell rang. It was near ten o'clock. A servant went to the door. Mr. Brown, the invalid's brother, was there. He was admitted as freely as I would be admitted here. He went into the cashier's office. He said, that he had just received by express a package containing ten thousand dollars. He was afraid to keep it at the hotel. He had brought it to the bank for safe keeping. The cashier replied that he would take it for his friend, and, he added, that when the watchman came in at half past ten he would open the vault and put the package away. At the same time he opened a drawer in his desk to put the package into it. In doing that, what was his horror! A cloth was thrown over his head. He heard Brown's voice saying that he did not want to kill him, but that the vault must be opened then. The cashier struggled desperately with the hypocrite friend. The noise of the struggle was heard up stairs by the cashier's brother, and by the servants. The servants ran out shouting for help. The burglar hearing the alarm sprang away from his victim. By this time, men from the hotel next door had rushed into the back-yard of the bank. The burglar fled out by the back-door. He jumped from the door steps directly into the midst of a half-dozen men. He was

にじいう に とほされまして くわいけい の し
つ ～ ゆき, くゆいけい に むかひ, いまがた
つううん で いちまん どる の つゝみ を うけ
とつた が やどや に おく の は しんばい で
ある から ぎんかう ～ しまつて もらふ ため
に もつて きました と いひました。 する と
くわいけい は いうじん の もの として それ
を うけとらう, そして じふ-じ-はん に なつて
ばんにん が きた とき に きんと を ひらい
て つゝみ を しまひませう と いひ, つくゑ
の ひきだし を あけて, つゝみ を いれ やう と
しました が, この とき の おどろき は どん
な で ございましたらう。 じぶん の あたま は
きれ で つゝまれて ブラウン の こゑ で, こ
ろさう と は おもはん が, きんと を すぐ
に あけなければ ならない と いひました。
くわいけい は この いつはり の ともだち と
いつしようけんめい で くみあひました が その
おと が にかい の くわいけい の きやうだい と
めしつかひ と に きこえました の で, めし
つかひ は おほごゑ を あげて たすけ を
よびました。 どろぼう は よびごゑ を きく
と とも に あひて を すてゝ にげました
が, その じぶん に は となり の やどや の
ひとゝ が ぎんかう の うしろ-には ～ かけて
きて をりました の で, どろぼう が うしろ
の くち から にげ やう と して, だん を

caught. He was tried and convicted of his crime. He is now in the penitentiary. But the shock to the cashier's mind and body was so terrible that within a few years afterwards he died.

.

とびおります と, てうど そこ に ゐた
ご-ろく-にん の ひとゞ の まんなか へ おち-
ました。 そして すぐさま とらへられて ぎんみ
に あひ, つみ の せんこく を うけました。
ところ が くわいけい は こゝろ と からだ
と の おどろき が ひじやう に ひどかつた
の で, その に-さん-ねん たつ うち に
この よ を さりました。

7.—それ は マァ ひじやう な はなし です。
しかし その くわいけい は あなた の おつし-
やつた ひと を しんじる ひと で あり-すぎた
の で ございます。 ひと を しんじた ため
に そん を した の です。 あなた は ぎん-
かう の くわいけい だけ は ひと を しんよう
すべき ひと から とりのけなければ なり-
ますまい。

8.—もちろん とりのけ の ない きそく と
いふ もの は ありません。 わたくし は けつ-
して あくま の たのみ を しんぜ よ と
しゆちやう する もの で は ありません。

———

7.—That is an extraordinary story.   But the cashier was too much like the confiding man of whom you spoke. He trusted and lost.   I suppose you exclude bank cashiers from your list of believers in men ?

8.—Of course there is no rule without exceptions.   I am no advocate for trusting in praying devils.

だい にじふ はち

くく塁

くち に と は たてられぬ。

1. ミカターし:—あの わるくち を いふた かーねかり の こと も ひと を しんずる こと が できぬ しようと に なる でせう。 あなた が ひと を れーしんじ なさいます じやう も いま では よほど うすらいだ だらう と おもーひます。 あなた は かね を とられ しんせつ を むに せられ その うへ に また あなた の ともだち の うち で も うそつき の ため に だまされて をる ひと が ある で ありません か。

2. ロビンソンしーし:—さう です とも。 さう です とも。 しかし ミカターさん, はなし が たいへん はげしく なりました。 おくさま は もうーすこし おもしろい こと を おーきゝ なさーりたい でせう。

3. ミカターふじん:—ほか の ことわざ に ついて ひとつ ふたつ おーまなび なさつたら いかゝ で ございます。 どこいら へん まで おーまなび なさいました か。

XXVIII.   PROVERB FOR (く) *KU.*

A door can not be made for a man's mouth.

1. *Mr. M :*—The scandal monger, too, is another offset I would propose to general confidence in men.   I should think that your confidence would be somewhat weakened by this time.   You have been robbed.   You have misplaced your kindness.   And you know how fiendishly some of your friends have been treated by liars.

2. *Mr. R :*—I know ! I know ! But, see here ! Mr. Mikata, our talk is becoming too serious.   I am sure that Mrs. Mikata would rather hear of something pleasant.

3. *Mrs. M :*—Why do you gentlemen not take a lesson or two from some others of your proverbs ?   How far have you talked ?

4. ロビンソン―し：―く まで いつた と おもひ―ます が, なに を だい に なさいます か。

5.―つぎ の ことわざ も また あなた が いま いやがつて お―いで なさつた の より いゝ ふう に ひと の せいしつ を うつし―て ない の で とまります。 すなはち この むかし の をしへ は ひと の くち には と が つくられぬ と いふ の です。

6.―ところ が と は つくられます よ。 あなた は イソツプ の はなし を お―よみ なさつた こと が ございます か。 イソツプ の ふかい たくみ な はなし の うち に すくな―く も いつ―しゆ の ひらいた くち を よほど むまい ぐあひ に とざした こと が ございます。 で―しようち でせう が ぐわいこく へ いつて をつた ひと が くに へ かへつて き―て いろ〱 な ところ で した と いふ おほき な こと を たねず じまん して をりまして, たとへば をれ は ロ―デス に おいて は だれ も まね が できぬ ほど な ひじやう な とびこし を した, この こと を みて ゐた ひと は たくさん あつた, それ を ほしよう―する しようとにん も たくさん だ と いひます と, その はなし を きいた ひと が この をとこ に むかひ, さう か も しれません が, もし それ が ほんたう なら いま お―いで の

4. *Mr. R:*—I believe we have reached " *Ku.*" What have you to set up as the text for that?

5.— I am sorry our next proverb does not suggest any better trait of human nature than the one you are now trying to get rid of. This old bit of wisdom says, that " a door can not be built for a man's mouth."

6. Oh! yes, it can. Did you ever read "Aesop's Fables?" One of those ancient, witty stories tells of how at least one kind of an open mouth was most effectually closed. A man who had been in foreign countries, on his return home, you may remember, was always bragging of the big things he had done in different parts of the world. In Rhodes, for instance, he said, he had made such an extraordinary leap that no man could come near doing it. There were " plenty of people who saw him," he said. He had " many witnesses to prove it." " Possibly," said a man who heard him talk, " but if this be true, just think that where you are now is Rhodes. Show to us one of those big leaps." That man's mouth was shut up, at least about his big jumping powers.

ところ を かり に ローデス だ と みなして, さういふ おほき な とびこし を ひどつ やって みせて ください と いひました。 そこで おほき な とびこし を する ちから が ある と いふ こと だけ に ついて は, この をとこ の くち は とぢられて しまいました。

だい にじふ く

や 屋

やす-もの かひ の ぜに うしなひ。

1. ミカターし:―あなた は たいへん むまい いいまはし を なさつた が, いま-すこし けいこ の はう を いそがなければ なり-ません。 これ から 「や」 に うつりませう。 あなた の お-はなし の ばん は すみました から, こんど は わたくし が お-かはり を いたしませう。 びんぼふ だいとく と いふ こと を お-きい なさつた こと が ございます か。

2. ロビンソンーし:―ナニ びんぼふ だいとく です と。 だいとく が びんぼふ と は いま が はじめて で ございます。 どう して かね-の-かみ が びんぼふ に なつた の です か。

3.―わたくし の まうします だいとく は びん-ぼふ で あつた の です。 すくなく も その

XXIX.   PROVERB FOR (ゃ) *YA.*

He who buys cheap loses his money.

1. *Mr. M :*—A very good showing you have made for the other side of the argument.   But we ought to be getting on with our lessons a little faster.   Let us take up *"Ya."* You have just had your turn at story telling.   I should like a chance for myself.   Did you ever hear of "The Poor Daikoku ? "

2. *Mr. R :*—The poor Daikoku?   I never knew that a Daikoku could be poor.   How can the god of riches be poverty stricken ?

3. —Well, this Daikoku I speak of was poor.   At any rate an image of him was shabbily carved.   But, mean looking

だいこく の ざう が まづく ほつて あつた
の です。 しかし みかけ は まづく ありました
が, ある らうじん が すーねん の あひだ
ふかく それ を しんじん いたしまして, まい-
にち｛ ふく を あたへ よ と いつて いのつて
をりました が, どう した こと か ちつと も
りやく が ありません ので, さすが の らう-
じん も もう しんかう も しんばう も なく-
なして しまいまして, じふん の まご を よび-
まして, 「コレ コウキチ, この だいこく の
でき は まこと に まづくつて, ちつとーばかり
の かね も しあはせ も くれあーしない から,
あいつ を どこ か へ もつて いつて うつちやー
つて こい。」 と いひました。 コウキチ は
こゝろえて その ば を たちまして, だいこく
を とつて ぶちやり に ゆきました が, しば-
らく たつ と かへつて きまして, 「おらァ だい-
こく を ぶちやらう と する と よそ の
ひと が そば へ きて, よからう が わるからう
が おまへ の だいこく を かひたい と
いつた から, にじふーごーせん もらつて うつて
やつちまつた よ」 と いひました。 らうじん は
これ を きゝます と とびーあがりまして, 「ナンー
ダト あん な みつともない もの を。 びんばうー
だいこく め。 いま まで ながく をれ の うち
に ゐあがつて。 をれ の うち を でる と すぐ

as he was, an old man for many years trusted in him
deeply, and daily prayed to him for wealth and goodness.
But no answers came.   At last the old man lost faith and
patience for his god.   He called his grandson,—"Here,
Kokichi!   This god Daikoku is miserably made, and he
will not give even the smallest wealth or blessing to me.
Go and throw him away somewhere."   Kokichi started to
do as he was commanded.   He took Daikoku, and went out
to throw him away.   After a few minutes he came back.
"When I was about to throw Daikoku away," he explained,
"a man came along.   He said, that good or bad he would
like to buy my Daikoku.   I sold him, by good fortune, for
twenty-five sen."   As the old man heard this he raised
himself up, and exclaimed;—"What! that looking thing?
That poor Daikoku?   Until now he has lived in my house.
Just as soon as he gets out of it he hurts another man's
pocket."

に ひと の さいふ を やぶり やがつた」と
いひました。

4.―おもしろい らうじん です ね。そして うま―
い ひひやう です。なに しろ その うち に
おほい に しんり が ともつてる で は あり―
ません か。

―――

だい さんじふ

ま 酒

まがらねば よ に たゝれず

1. (ロビンソン―し の はなし の つゞき):―もう
かへらねば なりません。たゞいま どん が
なりました。

2. ミカタ―し:―マア おーまち なさいまし。もう
ひとつ ことわざ を やつて おーいで なさつたら
いかゞ です。さう する と 「いろは」うた の
く が また ひとつ をはります。つぎ の 「ま」
の じ の ことわざ は まがらねば よ に た―
ゝれぬ と いふ の で ございます。

3.--よろしい。その く を しまひませう。
ところ が まこと に よく この ことわざ に
あつて をる はなし が ございます。イソツプ
の ぢいさん が いひます の に ある か―

4.—What a comical old fellow! And yet a shrewd comment! A good deal of truth in it after all, isn't there?

XXX. PROVERB FOR (ま) *MA.*

No keeping up in the world without bending.

1. (*Mr. Robinson continues*) :—I must go back to my house now. The noon gun has just been fired.

2. *Mr. M* :—Don't go yet! Let us have one more proverb before you go. It will just finish out another verse of the *I-ro-ha* poem. "If you do not bend you can not stand up in the world"—is the maxim I have for " *Ma,*" our next syllable.

3.—Very good! Let us finish the verse. I know a story that suits this proverb exactly. Old Aesop said, "An oak that had been rooted up by the winds, was carried down the stream of a river. On the banks many reeds were growing. The oak wondered to see that things so slight

しは一の一き が ありまして, かぜ の ため に ひき－
ぬかれて かは一しも の はう へ ながれて ゆき－
ました。ところ が つゝみ の う へ を みます
と よし が たくさん はえて ゐます の で, かー
しは は こんな ほそい よわい もの で さへ
あらし に たゆる の に, じぶん は おほき
な つよい き で あり ながら ひきぬかれた
の は どう も ふしぎ で ある と うたがつて を一
ります と, あし は かしは に むかつて, ちつ－
と も ふしぎ で は ありません。あなた は あ一
らし と たゝかつた から それ で たふされて
しまつた の で わたくし一ら は ちよつと一した
かぜ に も まがる から たすかつた の だ
と いひました。

4.一なるほど りこう な あし です ね。しかし
いかなる ことがら に たいして も くつして
のみ をります より, とき に は たゝかつて
まける はう が よい こと も ございませう。

5.一りやうはう へ きかない の は つまらない
きそく です。もう かへります。いぐわい に
ちやうざ を いたしました。さやうなら。

and frail had stood the storm. He, a great, strong tree,
had been rooted up. 'Cease to wonder,' said the reed,
'you were overthrown by fighting against the storm. We
are saved by bending to the slightest breath that blows.'"

4.—Cunning reeds were they not? Yet, it seems to me
better sometimes to fight and be beaten, than to yield to
every passing thing.

5.—It is a poor rule that will not work both ways. Now
I must go. I have made an unconscionably long visit.
Good bye, for to-day.

だい　さんじふ　いち

けゝ

けを ふいて きず を もとめる。

（こゝ　は　シナガハ　の　すていしよん　なりc
ロビンソン－し　じんりきしや　にて　とやま　を　く－
だり　きたれり。　くるまや　は　かけはしれり。
ロビンソン－し　は「はやく〱　きしや　が　つき
さう　だ」と　さけび，ミカタ－し　は　すていしよん
の　いりくち　に　たちをれり。）

1.—ロビンソン－し：—どうも　お－またせ　まうし－
まして　あひ－すみません。（くるまや　に　むか－
ひ。）ろく－じ－さんじつ－ぷん　まで　に　シンバシ
へ　いつて　をつて　もらひたい。もし　その　と－
き　の　きしや　で　つかなかつたら　つく　まで
まつて－ゐて　お－くれ。（ミカタ－し　に　むかひ。）
きつぶ　を　お－かひ　なさいました　か。

2.　ミカタ－し：—かひました。サァ　やくにん　が
よんで　をります。

3.—（くるま　に　いりて，ロビンソン－し　は　ミカタ－
し　に　むかひ。）ちうとう－しつ　へ　のつた　の
で　ございます　か。

4.—ハイ。どちら　で　も　お－よろしからう　と

XXXI.　PROVERB FOR (ʧ) *KE.*

He blows away the hair only to find a wound.

(Railway station ai Shinagawa. Mr. Robinson comes down the hill in a jinrikisha ; the kurumaya running fast. " Hurry up ! Hurry up ! " cries Mr. Robinson, " The train is coming." Mr. Mikala standing at the station doorway.)

1. *Mr. Robinson :*—I am so sorry to have kept you waiting.　(*To the kurumaya*) Meet me at Shimbashi at six-thirty.　If I am not on that train, wait until I come.　(*To Mr. Mikala.*)　Have you bought the tickets?

2. *Mr. M :*—Yes.　Come !　The guard is calling.

3.—*(Entering the train, Mr. Robinson asks.)*　Are we going second class?

4.—Yes.　I thought it would be all the same to you.

おもひまして。ぐわいとくじん は めつた に この やう な はやい くるま に のられません。

5.—わたくし に は どちら で も いゝ の です。あなた は いつ も じやうとう へ お-の-りだ と おもひました が。

6.—ながい たび を します とき は さう です が, トウキヤウ と ヨコハマ との あひだ は ちうとう で らく で ございます。

7.—この くるま は たいへん に さむい です ね。わたくし は まち に こほり の ある の を みて きました。けふ は じふにぐわつ の じふ-よつか です。もう くるま の なか へ 「スチーム」を いれて も いゝ じぶん で ありま せん か。

8.—しかし この ごろ の ひ は すぐ に あつたか に なります。フヂサハ へ ゆく まで に きつと あつたか に なる だらう と お-もひます。フヂサハ へ は じふ-じ まへ に つかれる でせう。

9.—わたくし は もう いち-ねん の よ も エノシマ へ まゐりません。てんき は よく なり さう です ね。わん の ところ の もや が はや あかるく なりました。あの うみぎは の へん は むかし の じぶん の しほきば で ありません か。「トクガハ」-じだい に は

Foreigners hardly ever take this early train.

5.—It is a matter of indifference to me.   I thought you usually travelled first class.

6.—Only when I take long trips.   Between Tōkyō and Yokohama the second class carriages are comfortable enough.

7.—This carriage is very chilly.   There was ice in the streets, I noticed.   To-day is the fourteenth of December. It is time, I think, for having the heaters in the carriages.

8.—But the days soon grow warm.   We shall find it warm enough, I dare say, before we get to Fujisawa.   We shall reach there before ten o'clock.

9.—I have not been at Enoshima for more than a year. We shall have a perfect day.   The haze over the bay is already brighter.   Is not that the old Yedo execution ground,—over there by the sea?   In the Tokugawa days that was a ghastly place, I am told.   I wish I could have travelled over the Tōkaidō fifty years ago.

ぶつさう な ところ だつた さう です ね。
ごじふ-ねん ほど まへ に トウカイダウ を
あるいて みたい もの でした。

10.—しおきば の あつた じだい は もう なく-
なつて しまひました。あんな じだい の また
と こない の は ほんたう に けつこう です。
わたくし は あの とき の こと を おもふ
の は じつ に いや で ございます。こんにち
わが くに の ぐんたい が シナ や テウセン
で ほろぼさう と して ある ところ の もの
を おもひだして なりません。おそろしひ がう-
もん だ の, ざい-にん の くび を さらす
こと だ の, その ほか むかし の じだい に
おこなはれた いろ／＼ の ざんこく な けいばつ
は こんにち シナ で おこなはれて ある
もの と たい-へん よく にて をります から
わたくし は あの とき の こと を おもふ
の が いや で ならん の です。

11.—むかし の ざんこく は ちつと も ニホン
の ふめいよ に なりません。ヨーロツパ に も
ちかく まで は おなじ こと が あつた の
です。せいやう しよ-とく の まつりごと が
やはらいで きた の も いち-に-ひやく-ねん
まへ から です。ニホン が こんにち テウセン
や シナ の ため に つくせる こと は
ヨーロツパ や アメリカ が ニホン の ため

10.—The days of that execution ground are gone, never to come back. I am glad they are gone forever. I do not like to think of them. They remind me too much of what our army is now trying to destroy in Korea and in China. The horrible torture, the exposure of heads of criminals, all the cruelty of the old punishments, and so much else in the old times, were too much like what is now to be seen in China for me to want to remember them.

11.—The ancient cruelties are nothing against Japan now. It is not so very long since the same things were done in Europe. The Western nations were made humane in their legislation only within the last century or two. Japan is now doing for Korea and China the same good that Europe and America have done for Japan, and that, before that time, reformers did for Europe and America. Mankind is larger now than tribe or nation. All men ought to help one another, and ought to recognize one

に つくした こと で, その まへ に は かい-
かくからーら が ヨーロツパ や アメリカ の ため
に つくした こと です。じんるゐ は しゆぞく
や こくみん より は ひろい ことば で, ひと
は みな アジヤーじん で あらう が, ヨーロツパ-
じん で あらう が, アメリカーじん で あらう
が, あるひは その ほか の ところ の にん-
げん で あらう が, たがひ に あひ たすく
べく, また その たすけ を しようにん すべき
もの だ と おもひます。

12.—その とほり です。しかし ニホン は
さういふ ことがら に おいて は したがふ
より, みちびいて をつた なら よかつた と
おもひます。

13.—けれども こんにち で は ニホン が
みちびいて をります。その こと と それ から
どんな こくみん で も いちど は したがふた
と いふ こと を おもつて ごーらん なさい。
いま より ろくーせんーねん まへ の エヂプト の
じだい より こんにち まで の くてみん. は
みな その とほり です。

another's help, whether they are Asiatics, Europeans, Americans or human beings from anywhere.

12.—Very good. But I wish Japan had led in these matters rather than followed.

13.—But Japan is leading now. Remember that. And also remember that every nation that leads, once had to follow. This is true of nations from Egypt's time six thousand years ago until to-day.

だい　さんじふ　に

ふ　　　　旭

ふるき　を　たづねて　あたらしき　を　しる。

1. ミカター し:—わたくしども　が　いま　とほつ-て　ゐます　ところ　は　すーねん　いぜん　モルス-はくし　が　はつけん　いたしました　かひづか　で　ございます。　みちばた　に　ちらかつて　ゐる　かひ　を　ごらん　なさい。　むかし　は　この　つゝみ　が　はま　だつた　と　まうします。ミルン-はくし　の　せつ　に　よれば　この　きし　は　だん/\　に　あがつて　ゆく　さう　です。　こ-\ら　へん　が　うみぎは　で　あつた　じぶん　に　は　こゝ　に　ゐた　じんみん　が　はま　で　かひ　を　くつて　をりました。　そして　その　かひ　の　おほき　な　やま　を　こしらへまして，　その　なか　へ　たくさん　だうぐ．や　きかい　を　のこ-して　ゆきました。　さう　いふ　ふるい　もの　に　よつて　れきし　いぜん　の　ことがら　が　おほい　に　わかつて　くる　やう　に　なりました。　オホモリ　の　かひづか　の　しらべ　を　しゆつぱん　した　もの　が　ございます　から　おーあげ　まうしま-せう。

2. ロビンソン-し:—ありがたう……この　カハサキ

XXXII. PROVERB FOR (ふ) *FU*.

New things are learned by studying the old.

1. *Mr. M:*—We are now passing through the shell-heap which Prof. Morse discovered some years ago. See the shells scattered all along the road side. It is supposed that this bank was the sea-shore in past ages. Prof. Milne thinks that the coast is slowly rising. When the shore line was here, the old fellows who lived in this neighborhood used to eat shell-fish on the beach. They left big piles of shells, and also left many of their utensils and implements in the shell-heaps. Out of these old things a good deal of knowlege of the pre-historic times has come to light. I have some published discussions about this Ōmori shell-pile which I will give you.

2. *Mr. R:*—Thank you!................... Isn't this

の はし から みた フジーさん の けいしよく は
いゝ じや ありません か。 やま が ゆき
で まつしろ で ございます。 はた の あれて
ゐる こと。 しかし なつ は きれい です ね。
わたくし は はじめて トウキヤウ へ きました
とき の こと を わすれ は しません。 ちや-
うど あき の すゑ で ございました が, はた
に なんに も なくつて さびしう ございました
の で, わたくし は ツヒ こきやう を した-
ふ やう に なりました。 なつ の はじめ
は はた が ひじやう に きれい な の で,
はんたい で ふゆ に なる と どうも ひじやう
に きたなう ございます。.....モウ カナガハ へ
まゐりました。

3.—つきひ が たつ と ものごと が かはる
もの では ありません か。 わたくし が はじ-
めて カナガハ を みました の は やつつ の
とき で ございまして, ちゝ に つれだつて
ナゴヤ から エド へ ゆく みち で ございま-
した。 その じぶん に は がけ の きは の
みち が ひと で いつぱい で ありまして,
あらゆる のりもの だ の, かご だ の, くるま
だ の, うま だ の, それから また かち の
たびびと だ の が ゆきゝ を して をり-
ました。 わたくしども も その へん の ちやや
で いつぱく いたしました。 その じぶん に

Kawasaki bridge view of Fuji superb? The mountain is perfectly white now. How desolate the rice fields! They are beautiful in summer. I remember the first time I went to Tōkyō. It was in the late autumn. The dreariness of the empty rice-fields made me home-sick. They are just as extremely ugly in winter as they are extremely lovely in early summer.........Here we are at Kanagawa.

3.—How time changes things! When I first saw Kanagawa I was only eight years old. My father and I were on our way to Yedo from Nagoya. The road there, along the bluff, was crowded. All sorts of *norimono, kago*, carts, horses and post-travelers, were going and coming. We spent the night in a tea-house over there. Yokohama then was almost nothing. Now Yokohama is everything, and this miserable place is almost nothing.

は ヨコハマ は つまらん もの で ありました
が, いま では ヨコハマ は りつば な もの
と なりまして, こゝ の はう が かはいさう
に つまらん もの に なりました。

* * * * *

4.—おーれき なさいません か。 フジサハ へ
きました。 ほん の じふーでーふん だけ おくー
れた の です。 ホドガヤ で とまつた とき に
は たいへん またねば ならん と おもひました
が。 このごろ の きしや は ひじやう に ふきー
そく です。 じかんへう は いくさ で もつて
むちやーくちや に なりました。

―――――

だい さんじふ さん

こ あ

こどば おほければ しな すくなし。

1. ミカターし:—あなた は くるま を きめて
ください ません か。 わたくし は ちよつと ちー
やや へ よりたう ございます から。

2. ロビンソンーし:—(くるまや に むかひ,) オイ
くるま が にーだい いる の だ。 エノシマ へ
いつて そこ で しよくじ を しまつて それ
から こゝ の きしや の まに あふ やう

*　　　*　　　*　　　*　　　*

4. *Mr. R.*—Wake up! We are at Fujisawa. We are only fifteen minutes late. I thought that when we stopped at Hodogaya we were in for a long wait. Trains are very irregular these days. They war upsets the whole time table.

XXXIII. PROVERB FOR ( ) *KO.*

Many words, little matter.

1. *Mr. M* :—You get the *kuruma,* please. I wish to step over to the tea-house for a moment.

2. *Mr. R :*—(*To a kurumaya.*) Here! I want two *jinrikisha.* We wish to go to Enoshima, to take tiffin there, and afterwards to go on to Kamakura for the five o'clock train. How much will you take us for?

に カマクラ へ いく の だ が, いくら で
やる か。

3.—ヘイ〱。 いつてう に ふたり いります か。

4.—イヤ ひとり で たくさん だ。

5.—どうも みち が たいへん わるう ございー
まして。

6.—さう いふ こと は どう で も いゝ。
いくら で いく の か。

7.—どうして も いちにち かゝります。 エノシマ
の あんない は いります か。

8.—イヤ をれ が いつた こと の ほか は
なんに も いらない。 なぜ をれ の とふた
こと に へんじ を しない か。

9.—ヘイ〱。 しかし カマクラ まで いきます
と とまらなければ なりません。 ゆふがた まで
に もどれます と よほど ちがふ の で ご
ざいます が, どーじ で は くらう ございます。

10.—しやべつて ばかり をつて は しかた が
ない。 いくら いる か いへば いゝんだ。

11.—ヘイ〱。 それ で は はちじつーせん で
まゐりませう。

12.—はちじつーせん だ と。 とほう も ない。
ぐわいこくじん だ から むちやくちや な ね

3.—Yes sir! Do you want two men for each *jinrikisha?*

4.—No! One will do.

5.—The road is very bad, sir.

6.—Nonsense! How much will you go for?

7.—It will take all day. Do you want a guide for Enoshima?

8.—No! I want nothing except what I am asking for. Why don't you answer my question?

9.—Well, sir, if I go on to Kamakura, I shall have to stay there all night. If I could get back home before evening, it would make a difference. But it is dark at five o'clock, sir.

10.—Don't stand there chattering like that, but tell me how much your fare is?

11.—Yes sir! I shall have to ask you eighty *sen.*

12.—Eighty *sen?* Ridiculous! I suppose, because I am a foreigner you think you can put on fancy prices. That

が いへる と おもつてる ナ。 ソリヤ いけない。
エノシマ まで にじつ-せん, それ から エノシマ
から カマクラ まで にじふご-せん やらう。

13.—ソリヤ あなた あんまり やすう ございま-
す。 ろくじふ-ごせん で まゐりませう。 そ-
れ が ほんとう の ね で ございます。

14.—だめ だ と いふ に。 しじふご-せん で
いく なら のつて ゆかう が, それ で ゆか-
なければ ばか に される より は あるいて
いく よ。

15.—どうか もう-すこし やつて くださいま-
し。

16.—これ だけ の みち に しじふご-せん な-
ら たくさん だ。 ソレニ カマクラ で とまらう
が こゝ で とまらう が おまへ の はう に
ちがひ は ありや しない。 しかし いやだ け-
れど ごじつ-せん やる と しやう。 それ で い-
かね なら, カタセ から カマクラ まで さうお-
う な ね で やとふ の は ざうさ ありや し-
ない。 いつしよ に おーいでる の は この おー-
かた だ。

17.—よろしう ございます。 すぐ に くるま を
もつて まゐりませう。

———

won't do at all. I will **pay** you twenty *sen* to Enoshima, and then I will give you twenty-five *sen* from there to Kamakura.

13.—Oh! sir, that is too cheap. I will go for sixty-five *sen*. That is the real price.

14.—Rubbish, I tell you! If you will go for forty-five *sen* I will take you. If you won't go for that, I will rather walk than be imposed upon.

15.—Please give a little more, sir.

16.—Forty-five *sen* is plenty for the trip, It makes no difference to you, I know, whether you sleep in **Kamakura** or here. Yet, while I do not like to give it, I will say **fifty** *sen* for the trip. If you won't take that, it is easy enough to get men from **Katase** to Kamakura for a decent price. **Here is the gentleman who is going with me.**

17.—All right, sir. I shall have the *jinrikisha* here in a moment.

だい さんじふ し

に え

にみ の うち に やいば を ふくむ。

1. ミカターし：—あなた は いま こ を ごらん
なさつた ばかり で, ろつぴやく-ねん ほど ま-
へ に この へん が <u>ニホン</u> の うち で
じんこう の ごく おほかつた ところ だつた と
は おもはれますまい が, につさい この へん は
わが くに で いちばん かんじん な ところ
で あつた の です。

2. ロビンソンーし：—うんめい と いふ もの は
としつき の たつ うち に たいへん に かはつて
くる もの で ございます。 あの <u>ニホン</u> の
<u>ルーテル</u> と いはれた <u>ニチレン</u> が ふしぎ を
あらはした の は この, へん で ありません
か。

3.—さう です。 この みち を もう-すこし ゆき-
ます と お-てら が たつて ゐます。 そこ で
<u>ニチレン</u> の てき が <u>ニチレン</u> を ころさう と
した の です。 あなた は その はなし を ご-
ぞんじ です か。

4.—ハイ, せんだつて <u>ウヘノ</u> の びじゆつくわん
で そこ の ところ の ゑ を みました が,

XXXIV.　PROVERB FOR (ゑ) *E.*

Conceals a sword within a smile.

1. *Mr. M :*—You would not imagine, to look at it now, that six hundred years ago this neighborhood was one of the most populous parts of the empire.　It certainly was the most important place in Japan.

2. *Mr. R :*—Fortunes change much in time.　And was it not near here that Nichiren, who is called the Luther of Japan, had some of his wonderful experiences?

3.—Yes!　Not far ahead on this road, is a temple built upon the spot where the enemies of the reformer tried to have him put out of the way.　You remember the story?

4.—Yes, I saw a good picture of the scene at the Ueno Art Exhibition not long ago.　It was capitally done.　The

たいへん　よく　できて　をりまして，　しおきにん
は　ニチレン　の　くび　に　かたな　が　たゝない
の　で　おどろいて　をり，　ニチレン　の　かほ
に　は　きれい　な　ひかり　が　かゝつて　ゐま
した。　が，　どう　も　ぶつけう　と　きりすとけう
と　の　ゑ　は　たいへん　よく　にて　ゐる　の　が
おほう　ございます　ね。

5.—ニチレン　は　ご一しようち　の　とほり　か一
ひづか　の　ありました　オホモリ　の　そば
の　イケガミ　で　しにました。

6.—わたくし　は　じふぐわつ　の　たいさい　に
イケガミ　へ　いつて　みました　が，　あすこ　の
もり　ほど　きれい　な　の　は　みた　こと　が　ご一
ざいません。　あれ　は　「イウテンジ」　の　もり　に
ひつてき　しませう　か。

7.—あれ　より　も　おほきう　ございます　が，
あれ　ほど　りつば　で　は　ありません。

8.—わたくし　は　さく一ねん　フジサン　の　にし
の　はう　の　やま　に　ある　ニチレン　の　れい一
じやう　の　ミノブサン　へ　ゆきました　が，　こゝ
は　ご一しようち　の　とほり　ニチレン　の　らうね
ん　の　とき　の　すみ一か　で，　その　へきち　まで
きゝ　に　いつた　おほぜい　の　でし　を　をしへた
ところ　です。　いま　で　も　たいへん　かけは一
なれた　ところ　です　が，　たくさん　ある　たてもの

executioner was amazed at finding his sword powerless on the saint's neck. A lovely light irradiated Nichiren's face. How much alike many Buddhist and Christian symbols are!

5.—Nichiren died, you know, at Ikegami, not far from Ōmori, where we saw the shell-heap.

6.—I have been at the great October festival at Ikegami. The grove is one of the finest I ever saw. Does it equal the one at Yūtenji?

7.—It is larger, but not so impressive.

8.—Last year I was at Minobu, the Nichiren sanctuary among the mountains west of Mt. Fuji. Nichiren, you know, lived there in his later life, and taught the crowds of disciples who went into the wilderness to hear him. It is a far-off place even now, but among the many buildings there, there is one, the "Temple of the True Bones," which is worth seeing. That is the richest and finest single room by far, of all I have yet seen in Japan. I was astonished at its wealth and beauty.

の うち に ほんどう と いふ の が あり
まして, いっぺん いって みる だけ の ねうち
が ございます。 ひとつ の へや です が
わたくし が ニホン で みました うち で は
いち-ばん はでやか で きれい で ありまして,
わたくし は その かねめ の ある の と
うつくしい の と に びっくり いたしました。

(カタセ の ちゃ-や。)

9.—(ちゃ-や をんな) いらっしゃい。 おーやすみ
なさい。

10.—ありがたう。 かへり に は ちよっと
よって も いゝ が, いま は じかん が
ない から。 イヤ あんない は いらない。
こゝ で まって ゐ な。 サア ロビンソン-
さん, まゐりませう。 もう じふ-いち-じ です。

11.—すなやま の はう へ のぼりませう。
どうも けふ の みづ の きれい な こと。 しほ は
も たいへん に たかい やう です ね。 オホシマ
が ちかく みえる こと。 ふんくわざん も
けふ は たいそう な けむり を だして をり-
ます な。

* * * * *

12.—ふたり は いし-おほき むら の ほん-
みち を のぼり ゆけり。 みち-すがら みち-ばた
の すゝじふ の みせ より 「いらっしゃい」
「おーよんなさい」 とう の ことば を うけ-

(Tea house at Katase.)

9.—*(Waitress)*, **Please come in.**

10. *Mr. M :*—We have not time now. Thank you! We may stop for a moment on our return. No! we do not need any guide. Wait here for us. Come, Mr. Robinson, let us go. It is almost eleven o'clock.

11. *Mr. R :*—Rather hard climbing over this sand-pile! Ah! how lovely the water is to-day! The tide is very high. How near, Ōshima seems. The volcano is having a big smoke to-day.

*   *   *   *   *

12.—(The friends climb up the narrow, stony, main street of the village. They are greeted all the way by cries of " Welcome! " " Please look! " and the like, from the scores of shops that border the road. They keep on up the hill. They pass along the western face of the

たり。 なほ のぼり ゆき, がけ にて かこまれ-
たる みさき の にし-がは を すぎて,「ベンテン」
の いはや に いたりし が, これ まで いく
たび も みし こと なれば いはや の なか
へ は いらざりき。 この へん に は また
おほく の こども ありて, かれら に ねだりて
すゐちう に ぜに を なげ-いれ しめ その
わづか のり の ため に, じふ-ぐわつ にて
も すゐちう に とびいる もの ありし が,
それら の ため に も おほく の かね を
つひやさゞりき。 この ひ ふたり は たゞ
くうき と うみ と を たのしまん ため たが-
ひ に きゝ-なれし ところ に きたりし のみ
なり。 かくて しばらく の あひだ いは の
うへ に こし を かけ, うちよする なみ を
ながめし のち, がけ の いたゞき に よぢのぼり
まんなか の みち より ひがし の がけ へ
もどりし が, しよくじ を なさん が ため に
「キンキロウ」 に たちよりたり。

13.—こゝ の けいしよく は わたくし が
みた うち で は じやうとう の ぶるゐ です。
もつとも アタミ へ ゆく みち に は この
けいしよく に も おとらぬ ほど の ところ
が ありまして, アタミ の 「ウオミ」 の はう
が こゝ より も すこし ばかり きれい か
も しれません。 きよねん の はる は あそこ

cliff-bound promontory as far as the "Benten Cave." They do not go into the cave, however. They have seen it several times in former years. They do not waste much money on the boys who pester them to throw pennies into the water, and who dive, even in December, for such small gains. The friends have come out for the day to a place familiar to both, just for the pleasure of the air and the sea. After sitting on the rocks for a while, and enjoying the dash of the waves, they climb to the top of the cliff. They go back by the central path to the east bluff, as far as the Kinkirō where they stop for tiffin.)

13. *Mr. R:*—This is one of the best views I know of. On the road to Atami there are spots which almost equal it. The Uo-mi at Atami is perhaps somewhat finer. Last year in the spring I spent several hours up on that balcony. I am always charmed with this exquisite combination of coast and sea.

の にかい で に-さん-じかん あそんだ こと
が あります が, うみ と きし と の うまひ
ぐあい に ついて ゐる ところ は いつ
みて も よう ございます。

14.—オヤ〱, みづ が この がけ の ねき へ
はひ-あがる こと。 どうも いけない。 よほど
いんけん な ふう だ。 いま は ねこ の
やう に ごろ〱 いつて をります が, あした
は とら の やう に はげしく なる でせう。

15.—あなた は うみ が お-きらひ だ と
みえます ね。 それ で は ふね も お-きらひ
でせう。 わたくし は いま で は ふね に
ゑふ こと は ありません。 いつ で も きしや
より は ふね の はう を えらびます。

16.—ご-ちさう が きました。 さけ は なに
に しませう。 きりん-ビール に しやう じや
ありません か。

17.—さう しませう。 ねへ-さん おほき な
こつぶ を もつて きて お-くれ。 わたくし は
この アメリカ-れうり の たまご を たべ-
ませう。 この やき-ざかな は たいへん うまい。
これ は ニホン-れうり の うち で わたくし
の ごく すき な もの です。

18.—この ほか に なに が ご-すき です
か。

14. *Mr. M:*—Look! how the water crawls up to the base of this cliff. I do not like it ; it seems so treacherous. It is purring like a cat ; to-morrow it may be as fierce as a tiger.

15.—Evidently you are no friend of the sea. But I believe you are not a good sailor. Now, I am never seasick. I would rather take a voyage, than a railway trip at any time.

16.—Here comes the tiffin. What shall we drink ? Let us have some Kirin Beer.

17.—All right. *Nesan,* bring me a large cup. I shall eat my eggs in Yankee style. * * * The baked fish is delicious. This is one of the Japanese dishes I thoroughly enjoy.

18.—What else do you like ?

19.—「チヤツ゛ンームシ」「ウナギーメシ」「ミソーシル」「トリーナベ」それ から「タマゴヤキ」の うち に も すき な の が ございます。かう いふ もの は みな ご-そんじ でせう。マア あなた の ご-ぜん の なか の もの に して も わたくし の きらひ な もの は まこと に すくなう ございます。

20.—この ゑび の しる は よほど よう ございます。あなた は だいこん-づけ が ご-すき な やう です ね。

21.—すき な の も ございます。わたくし に は こめ は いつ も たんぱく-すぎまして だい-こん-づけ を たべます と こめ の あぢ が つく の です。ぐわいこくじん の くち は あなたがた の しよくじ より も つよい あぢ に なれて をります。……… こ丶 の ねへ-さん は ぐわいこくじん の ほしがる もの を しつて ゐる と みえて, わたくし の たまご に は しほ を そへて きて くれました。ビール を もう いつぱん とりませう。……… これ から「じぶん の やど で しぶん を なぐさめ」ながら, はまき を ひとつ すひませう。あなた も ひとつ いかゞ です。

22.—ありがたう。けふ は ひとつ すひませう。いつも は かみまき の はう を すふ の です

19.—*Chawan-mushi, unagi-meshi, miso-shiru, tori-nabe,* some kinds of *tamago-yaki,*—you know what they are. There are very few things on your table, for example, that I do not like.

20.—This prawn soup is excellent. You like pickled *daikon,* I see.

21.—Some kinds are palatable. It gives some taste to the rice, which I usually find rather insipid. The foreigner's palate is used to stronger flavors than your ordinary food has. ⁎ ⁎ The waitress has brought some salt for my eggs. She seems to know what a foreigner would ask for. Let us have another bottle of beer. ⁎ ⁎ ⁎ Now for a cigar while I "take mine ease in mine inn." Will you not have one, too?

22.—Thank you! I will take one to-day. Usually I prefer cigarettes. But, being at Enoshima I shall celebrate.

が, けふ は <u>エノシマ</u> へ きた の です から,
お-いはひ に ひとつ やりませう。

———

だい さんじふ ご

て　　て

て の うら を かへす。

1. <u>ミカター</u>し：―もう に-じ です が, でかけた
はう が よう ございません か。

2. <u>ロビンソン</u>し：―こゝ で も もう じうぶん
に ゆくわい です。<u>カマクラ</u> へ は けふ は
いつて も いかなくつて も よろしい の です。
わたくし は もう すこし こゝ に をつて
もと の みち で かへらう と おもひます。

3.―です が もう いち-じ-かん も たつ うち
に は お-こゝろ が かはつて まゐりませう
よ。いま の うち は かぜ の こゝろもち も
よう ございます が, <u>フヂサハ</u> へ お-かへり
なさらなければ ならぬ じぶん に なります
と, でかけて をれば よかつた と お-おもひ
なさる に さうい ありません。サア, <u>カマクラ</u>
へ まゐりませう。

4.―さう です ね。どちら で も よろしう
ございます。

XXXV. PROVERB FOR (て) *TE.*

Reversing the hand's palm.

1. *Mr. M:*—It is two o'clock now.   Don't you think we would better be going?

2. *Mr. R:*—I am perfectly comfortable where I am.   I don't care whether we go on to Kamakura to-day or not. I would just as soon stay here, and go back as we came.

3.—I think you would change your mind in another hour.   The air is delightful now.   But before it would be time for you to start back to Fujisawa, you would be glad to be on the move.   Come! let us go on to Kamakura.

4.—It is just as you say.   I am agreeable to anything.

5.—それ で は これ から でかける と いたしませう。 けふ は ちよつと だいぶつ を みて-ゆきたい と おもひます。 オイ, ねへ-さん, かんぢやう して を-くれ。 わたくし の はう で はらひます。.........いくら。 いち-ゑん-しじつ-せん。 よろしい。

6.—(ちや-や をんな。) を-つり で ございます。

7. ミカタ-し:—すこし だ が, この しじつ-せん は こゝ の うち の を-ちや-だい だ。 この にじつ-せん は おまへ に あげ やう。

8.—(ちや-や をんな。) どうも ありがたう ございます。 また どうか いらつして ください-まし。

*　　　*　　　*　　　*　　　*

9. ロビンソン-し:—きれい な みち です ね。 ちつと かぜ が ふいて きました。 すこし あゆみませう。 イツ の やま は すゐしやう の やう に きれい です ね。 ハコネ の やま を ごらん なさい。 フジサン に くも が かゝ-つて をり ます よ。

10.—かう あつたか で はれて ゐて は あし-た の てんき は むつかし さう です ね。 どよう まで さんぽ を のばさなくつて まこと に よう ございました。 かぜ が とうなん から ふいて きました。.........こゝ は

5.—If that is so, let us start now. I should like to have time for just one look at "Daibutsu" this afternoon. *Nesan,* bring the account, please. I will be paymaster. * * * How much? One *yen* forty *sen?* All right! * * *

6.—*(Waitress).* Here, sir, is your change.

7.—*Mr. M :*—Take forty *sen* as a small bit of tea-money for the house. Here are twenty *sen* for yourself.

8.—*(Waitress).* Grateful thanks, sir! Please come again.

*   *   *   *   *   *   *   *   *

9. *Mr. R :*—Beautiful road this! It is growing a little windy. Let us walk a while. The Izu mountains are crystal clear. See the Hakone hills! Fuji is putting on a cloud-cap.

10.—The day is too warm and bright for good weather to-morrow, I am afraid. It is just as well, I think, that we did not put off our outing until Saturday. The wind is coming in from the south-east. * * * *. Here is where the messenger from Kamakura, sent to reprieve Nichiren, met the messenger from the execution grounds

カマクラ から ニチレン を ゆるし に きた
つかひ が, しおき-ば から ニチレン を すく-
ふた ふしぎ の あつた こと を やくにん に
しらせ に ゆかう と して をつた つかひ に
であつた ところ です。 ご-しようち でせう
が ニチレン が カタセ の そば で ふしぎ の
ため に たすかつた とき に, やくにん は
ゆめ の うち に ニチレン を ころす なと
いましめられた の です。 ふたり の つかひ が
こゝ で で-あつた の で, こゝ の とがは
が なだかく なりました。 さか の うへ から
は くるま に のりませう。

      *   *   *   *   *

11. ロビンソン-し:—こんな あれはてた すなつ-
ばら を みて, もと こゝ に ひやくまん-にん
も すまつて ゐた まち が あつた と は どう
して もゝはれませう。 マァ その はんぶん の
ひと が をつた に して も もうーすこし
おほくの あとかた が のこつて をり さう な
もの です ね。

12.—わが くに の たてもの は むかし の
ローマ の と ちがひまして, ニホン の まち
の あとかた は ひと が ゐなく なる と
すつかり きえて しまひます。 だが, こゝ に
だいぶつ が ございます。 まち の はう は
せんさう や, くわじ や, おほみづ や, ぢしん

who was going to tell the Regent of the miracle which had taken place in Nichiren's behalf. You remember that at the same time that Nichiren's life was saved by the miracle near Katase, the Regent was warned in a dream not to kill him. The meeting of the two messengers has made this little stream famous. Let us ride from the top of the hill.

*   *   *   *   *

11. *Mr. R:*—Who would think, to look at it, that this barren sand-waste ever had a city of a million people on it ! Well, even a half-million ought to have left more traces behind them than can be found here.

12.—Our buildings are not like those in ancient Rome. All signs of a Japanese town soon disappear after it is deserted. But here is the Great Buddha. This has stood all the war, fire, flood and earthquake which blotted out the city.

の ため に ほろびて しまひました が, この
だいぶつ だけ は その まゝ で あつた の
です。

13.—わたくし は この りつば な ぶつけう
の ざう を みる の に あく こと は あり-
ません。りつば と いふ の も てきとう な
ことば で ありません。その ほか に なに か
まだ おもむき が ごさいます。 えいご ならば
マァ "rapt sublimity," と か, "sublime calm,"
と か " perfect withdrawal from this world," と か
"divine absorption," と か いひたい ところ
です。 ニホン に も てうど これ に あたる
やう な ことば が ある で こざいませう。

14.—イヽエ わたくし に は どう したら
あなた の おもつて お-いで なさる こと を
あらはす こと が できる か わかりません。
たぶん ぼうさん の うち に は きとう の
なか に ちやうど その やう な ことば の
ある の を しつて ゐる ひと が ある
だらう と おもひます が, わたくし は ぶつけう
の ぎしき の こと は いつさい しりません。

15.—どう の ぐるり に お-てら が あつた
じぶん に は, ざう の おもむき が いつそう
りつば だつた に ちがひ ありません。

16.—わたくし は いま ほど に りつば で

13.—I never get tired of looking at this majestic symbol of Buddhism. Majestic is not just the word I ought to use. It is something other than majestic. In English I should say perhaps, "rapt sublimity," or "sublime calm," or "perfect withdrawal from this world," or "divine absorption." Perhaps you have just the word for it in Japanese.

14.—No ! I do not know how I would convey what you want to express. But perhaps some of the priests would say it for you exactly in their prayers. I am not familiar with the Buddhist rituals.

15.—The effect of this image must have been grand when the temple stood around the statue.

16.—I don't think it could have been nearly as impressive

は　なかつたらう　と　おもひます。　ナラ　の　「だ
いぶつ」　で　もつて　おーわかり　に　なりませう
が,　あすこ　の　ざう　は　やね　や　どへい　の
ため　に　おしつぶされて,　りつば　な　こと　は
さておき,　まじめ　な　おもむき　も　ない　では
ありません　か。

*　　　*　　　*　　　*　　　*

かぜ　が　ちつと　さむく　なつて　きました。
「ステーション」　へ　ゆきませう。

17.—「キンキロウ」　で　ひ　の　あたつてる　じぶ
ん　に　おつしやつた　おーことば　は　かはる　だ
らう　と　おもつて　をりました。　おつしやる　と
ほり　いそぐ　はう　が　よう　ございませう。　もう
よーじーはん　です。

18.—あすこ　の　うみ　から　「ハチマングウ」
まで　の　まつーのーき　の　はえた　むかし　の　わう
くわん　は　たいへん　ものさびしい　ふぜい　です。
いつたい　カマクラ　は　あまり　ゆくわい　な　と
ころ　では　ありません。

*　　　*　　　*　　　*　　　*

19.—(シナガハ　にて　くるま　に　のりこみ　な
がら)　わたくし　の　しよさい　に　たいて　ある
ひ　を　みる　と　よほど　こいろもち　が　いい
だらう　と　おもひます。　かぜ　が　ひじやう　に

as it is now.   You know how it is with the "Daibutsu" at Nara.   The statue there is so cramped by the roof and walls that the effect is anything but impressive, or even serious.

*   *   *   *   *

The wind is growing rather cold.   Let us go on to the station.

17.—I thought you would change the mood you had in the sunshine up at Kinkirō.   Yes, we would better be hurrying on.   It is after half-past four.

18.—That old pine avenue from the sea to Hachiman's temple looks quite mournful.   Kamakura is not a very cheerful place.

*   *   *   *   *

19.—*Mr. R:—(Getting into his kuruma at Shinagawa.)* My library fire will be a welcome sight.   The air is very raw and chilly.   Good night! My compliments to Mrs. Mikata.

しめつて つめたう ございます。 さやうなら。 ど-
うぞ おくさま へ よろしく。

———

だい さんじふ ろく

あ ゆ

あたま ゆらん より こゝろ を それ

（しやうぐわつ の はじめ, ミカター し の いへ
にて）

1. ミカター し:— あけまして おーめでたう ございー
ます。

2. ロビンソン し:— あなた に 「さいはひ なる
しんねん を。」 そうして 「いくど も その とほり
で あります やう に。」 わたくし は ニホン
ふう の しゆくし で あなたの おーいはひ に
おーこたへ まうす はづ です が あなた に
「さいはひ なる しんねん を」と まうす はう が
いひーやす.くつて しぜん である の で ございます。

3. — ありがたう。 やすみ ちう は いかゞ おー
くらし で こざいました か。

4. — わたくし は さくしう アタミ へ いつて
をりました。 あなた も どちら へ か おーでかけ
で ございました か。

XXXVI.   PROVERB FOR (あ) *A*.

Cleanse the heart rather than shave the head.

(Mr. Mikata's house.   Early in January.)

1. *Mr. M :*—My congratulations at the opening of the New-Year!

2. *Mr. R :*—A " Happy New Year!" to you, and "Many Returns!" of the same.   I suppose I ought to give you the Japanese salutation in answer to your greeting, but it comes easier and is more natural for me to wish you a "Happy New Year!"

3.—Thank you!   How are you spending your holidays?

4.—I have been away for the week past at Atami.   Have you been off too?

5.—イヱ, わたくし は しやくわい の ぜん-
りやう なる いちにん と して, ぎむ を つく-
して をりました。 あの かど の なか に は
わたくし に きた きやく の めいし が ござ-
います。 ソシテ わたくし は ちき の もの に
わたくし が その ひとく を わすれて をらぬ
と いふ こと を おもはする ため に しち-
う を たて よこ に あるきました。

6.—わたくし の るす の あひだ に も た-
くさん の めいし が わたくし の うち に おー
いて ありました。 わたくし は あす から いち-
りやう-にち かゝつて, すにん の ともだち に
その しんせつ を しようち して ゐる と いふ
こと を しらせ やう と おもひます。 あなた は
<u>シバ</u> の こうゑん の そば に たい〜ん りつば
な たて の あがつて ゐる の を みて
いらつしやいました か。 どの くらゐ おほきい
か ぞんじません が, あの へん に あがつて
うなつて ゐる ほか の より は おどろく ほど
おほきい やう で ございました。

7.—イヤ わたくし に は き が つきません
でした。

8.—わたくし は たこあげ が たい〜ん すき
で ございます。 しんねん の あそび の うち
で わたくし は たこあげ と はねつき を いー
ちばん ゆくわい に おもひます。 さくじつ の

5.—No! I have been doing my duty as a good member of society. In that basket are some hundreds of visiting cards which have been left for me. I have been going the length and breadth of the city, reminding my acquaintances that I have not forgotten them.

6.—I found quite a number of cards at my house, which had been left while I was away. I shall take the next day or two to show my few friends that I appreciate their kindness. Have you seen the splendid kite that is flying down near Shiba Park? I do not know how big it is, but it is so much larger than any of the others which are soaring and humming there, that I was surprised.

7.—No! I have not noticed it.

8.—I like the kite-flying exceedingly. That and the battledore playing I enjoy more than any other of the New Year amusements. As I came from the station yesterday afternoon, the streets were full of girls

でゝ 「ステーション」 から でゝ きます とき
は, まち の とほり が はね を ついて ゐる
むすめ で いつぱい で ございまして, こども
の じやま に ならぬ やう に する の は
わたくし の くるまや に とつて よほど こんなん
な こと で ございました。 わたくし が みわたす
かぎり, せまい とほり は はねつき で ぴか〳〵
して をりました。 こども が あたらしい きもの
や おび を つけて ゐた の は じつ に
あいらしう みえました。

9.—わが くに の しん-ねん は じつ に
せかい で もつとも たのしい しゆくじつ の
ひとつ で ございます。

10.—さく-ばん わたくし が 「ロクメイクワン」
で しよくじ を しまつて たく へ かへります
みち で, しよく の てら を かけまはる とこ-
ろ の かんちう の ぎやうじや すなはち かん-
まゐり を ひじやう に たくさん みました。
こん-ねん は かん-まゐり が よほど おほい
やう です ね。

11.—さやう。 しかし どういふ わけ か しりー
ません。 この ふうしふ は きん-ねん は あまり
おこなはれない やう です が, わたくし の
ちひさい とき に は いま より も よほど
りうかう して をりました。 その じぶん に は

swinging battledores.   It was really difficult for my *kurumaya* to keep from hurting some of the children.   As far as I could see down the narrow street, it was all twinkling and flashing from the driven battledores and shuttlecocks.   What a lovely sight the children make in their new *kimono* and *obi* !

9.—Our.New Year is really one of the happiest festivals in the world.

10.—Last night I took dinner at the Rokumeikwan. On the way homeward I saw an unusual number of the mid-winter devotees, the *kan-mairi*, on their run from temple to temple.   There are very many of those runners out this year.

11.—Yes ! I do not know why. The custom has not been followed much in recent years.   When I was a child it was much more in vogue than it is now.   Then the men ran almost naked, dashing tubs of cold water over their bodies every here and there. Water for the purpose would be set out for them by the pious town

かん-まわり を する ひとゞ は ほとんど まる-
はだか で, はうゞ で をけ の ひや-みづ を
ひき-かぶり ながら かけ-あるいて をりました。
そうして その みづ は てうない の ねつしん
な しんじゃ が したく を して をく の
です。 げん に わたくし も しつて をります
が かん-ちう とほりつめる やう な てんき
に まる いつ-か-げつ の あひだ まいばんゞ
その とほり に いたします ひとゞ が あり-
ました。

12.─わたくし の おもひます に ニホン に
は しうけう の ぎやう-じや が むしろ ざん-
こく に からだ を とりあつかふ ところ が
ずゐぶん ある やう です。 いつぞや たい-へん
さむい ひ の こと でした が, メグロ の
「フドウィン」 の 「ドッコ」 の たき の した
に, わかい-もの が たつて ゐる の を み-
ました。 いつたい かやう な くぎやう に ほん-
たう の しうけうしん が たくさん ともなつて
ゐる でせう か。

13.─わたくし は そんじません。 しかし かう-
いふ ぎやう を すれば, たとへ せいしん の
うへ に は ない に しろ, からだ の うへ
に は たくさん りやく が ある と おもはれ-
て をる の です。

14.─それ で は かん-まわり は ないぶ の

people. I have known them to do it in freezing weather, and every night for a whole month.

12.—I believe there are a good many places in Japan where religious devotees subject their bodies to rather severe treatment. Once on a very cold day, I saw a young fellow standing under the *Tokko-no-taki* at the Fudō-in in Meguro. Is there much real religious feeling along with the torture?

13.—I do not know. I think, however, that there is a great deal of benefit supposed to come from the act,—if not for the soul, at least for the body.

14.—A *kan-mairi* is not necessarily, then, an "outward

めぐみ が そと に あらはれた しるし と も
かぎらない と おもひます。

15.ーさやう。さう と も かぎりますまい。けれ
ども かういふ くぎやう を する ひと が
たいてい ねつしん に こりかたまつて ゐる
こと は うたがひ ありません。

────

だい さんじふ しち

さ を ほ

さる も き から おつる。

1. ロビソソンーし:ーすこし さんぽ を したら
いかい です。

2. ミカターし:ーどこら へん へ おーいで なさー
います か。

3.ーわたくし の ところ の やとひーにん が
けさ けしやうーかいみ を こはした の です。
その にん は いつも は たいへん き を
つける はう で ありまして, これ まで は
なに を こはした こと も ない やう で でー
ざいました。わたくし の ともだち の うち に
は いつ も さら や がらす の きぶつ の
こはれた の に こいと を いふ ひと が
あります が, わたくし は その てん に は

sign of inward grace," I suppose.

15.—Not necessarily! Yet, I have no doubt that many of these ascetics are dead in earnest.

XXXVII. PROVERB FOR ( ) *SA.*

Even monkeys fall from trees.

1. *Mr. R:*—Don't you want to take a short walk?

2. *Mr. M:*—Where do you propose to go?

3.—One of my servants broke my shaving glass this morning. He is usually very careful. I don't know when he has broken anything before. Some of my friends are always complaining of smashed dishes and glassware. I have been exceptionally fortunate. I am going down to the *kwankōba* to buy a new mirror.

ひじやう に しあはせ で あつた の です。
それ で いま あたらしい かゆみ を かひ に
くわんこうば へ ゆかう と おもふ の です。

4.—わたくし は けさ から まだ そと へ
でません。さく-ばん は たいへん つかれました
から, すこし さんぽ を したら よく なる
だらう と おもひます。

(ふたり は そと へ いづ。)

5.—あなた の ところ の いりくち の
かざり は よほど りつぱ な ふう に なつて
をります ね。わたくし の ところ の の は
ひじやう に そまつ です。あした は おほ-
さうじ が はじまつて 主な-もの が みな かた-
づく だらう と おもひます。

6.—サヤウ, いつ主うかん の あそび も もう
すみました。「ベンテン」どう を おりて <u>マルヤマ</u>
を とほらう じや ありません か。「ソウシヤウジ」
の じない で さんぽ が できませう。わたくし
は まち の はう より は もり の なか
の とみち を このみます。

7.—「コウヱウクワン」 は ひる みる と なん
の ふぜい も ありません。こ丶 は ちかごろ
は ひじやう に はんじやう いたします ね。
に-さん-にち まへ に <u>タカラ</u>-さん が ぐわい-
こくじん を よんで ひらかれた えんくわい など

4.—I have not been out to-day yet. Last night I was very tired. But, I suppose a short walk would do me good. (*The friends go out.*)

5. *Mr. R:*—Your doorway decorations are on rather a grand scale. Mine are very modest. To-morrow I suppose, a general clearing away begins, and everything will settle down into its usual order.

6.—Yes, the week's play is over. * * * Let us go down by the Benten temple and over Maruyama. We can walk through the Zōjōji grounds. I like the by-way through the grove better than the street.

7.—The Kōyō-kwan looks quite dull by day-light. It has been unusually lively of late. The banquet given there a few days ago by Mr. Takara to some foreign friends, I hear, was one of the most entertaining ever known in the history of the house. A number of the best actors from the Kabukiza were there, Kikugoro and others. I am

は 「コウェゥクヮン」 たちはじまり いらい いち-
ばん おもしろい もの だつた と まうします。
「カブキザ」 から いゝ やくしや が たくさん
きまして, キクゴラウ なんぞ も きた さう
で ございます。 げいしや の うち に やり に
つかれて けが を した もの が あつた さう
です が, だいした こと は なかつた の で-
せう。 きやく は みんな で ごじふ-にん から
うへ だつた さう です。

8.—いけ も ちかごろ は さびしい ふぜい
です。 オヤ いけ の なか の とほり は よほど
あつい の だ。 こゝ は はる と なつ に なる
と こゝら へん で いちばん おもしろい ところ
じや ありません か。 こゝ に さく さくら の
みごと な こと と いひ, それ から ふじ と
いひ, それ から はちす と いひ, それ から
もみぢ と いひ, しー-ぐわつ から じうー-いちー-ぐわつ
まで の あひだ は この ちいさい 「ベンテン」
だう が ひじやう に ひと の こゝろ を
ひきよせます。 あそこ に ふじだな の した
に あゝ いふ こしかけ を おいた の は
よほど の かいりやう じや ありません か。

9.—わたくし は たびゝ こゝ へ まゐります。
わたくし は また やま の ぐるり に ある
こみち を このみます。 たいへん に きれい
で うつくしう ございます。 トウキヤウ に ここ

told that, one of the *geisha* was hurt by an accidental thrust of a spear, but I think not very badly.   There were more than fifty guests in all.

8.—The pond is desolate looking now.   Why, the ice on it is quite thick !   In spring and summer it is the most charming spot in this part of the city, isn't it?   How exquisite the cherry blossoms are here !   And then the wistaria ! And then the lotus !   And then the maple leaves !   From April to November, this little Benten temple is exceedingly attractive.   It is a great improvement, putting those seats over there under the wistaria trellis.

9.—I often come here.   I like the walks around the hill, too.   They are so quiet and lovely.   It is a grand thing for Tōkyō to have in it, two such noble parks as this and Ueno.

と ウヘノ の やう な じやうひん な こう-
ゑん が ふたつ まで も ある の は さかん
な こと です。

10.—むかふ に イノ、チウケイ の せきひ が
ございます。あの ひと は ニホン で ちづ を
こしらへる じゆつ を はじめた ひと です。
いち-に-ふん かん こしかけ やう じや あり-
ません か。こゝ から わん が よほど よく
みえます。

———

だい さんじふ はち

き き

きん-げん み、 に さかふ。

1.—ロビンソン-し:— ちやうど いゝ をり です
から, アノ きんげん みゝ に さかふ と いふ
ことわざ の ときあかし に なる と をつ-
しやつた, イタクラ、ダイゼン の はなし を きか-
せて くださいません か。むかふ の はう で
からす が ひどい さわぎ を して をります。
わたくし は からす の こゑ が ひと の
みゝ に さかふ はう が きんげん が みゝ
に さかふ より も ひどい と おもひます。

2. ミカタ-し:—それ は かう いふ はなし
です。「むかし キヤウト の 「ショシダイ」 すな-

10.—There is Inō Chūkei's monument. He was the founder of the art of map-making in Japan. Let us sit down for a moment or two. Here is a good view of the bay.

XXXVIII. PROVERB FOR (き) *KI*.

Wise sayings are disagreeable.

1. *Mr. R:*—This is a good opportunity for telling me the story of Itakura Daijen, which, you said, would explain to me our proverb about wise sayings that are unpleasant to a man's ears. The crows are making a hideous noise up there. I should think they would annoy one's hearing more than any golden saying could.

2. *Mr. M:*—The story is this. "A *shoshidai*, or governor, of ancient Kyōto, called Itakura Daijen, was known as

はち ちじ に <u>イタクラ、ダイゼン</u> と いふ ひと
が ありまして, けんしや だ と いふ ひやう-
ばん で ありました。 その ころ おなじ まち
に すむ ふたり の ひと が ありまして,
じめん の さかひ の こと に ついて けんくわ
を いたしまして, いつち の できない ところ
から ふたり とも そしよう を いたしました。
が, ひとり の をとこ は その あひだ に
ないく で <u>ダイゼン</u> こう の ところ へ
たづねて ゆきました。 <u>ソレハ</u> その じぶん は
まだ なつ の はじめ で ありましたので
その をとこ は <u>ダイゼン</u> こう へ じぶん の
はだけ に できた はつもの ＼ しんうり を
おくらう と した の です。 そこ で その
をとこ は <u>ダイゼン</u> こう の くりや へ めづ-
らしい うり を たくさん とゞけまして,
じぶん は かう して ちじ を て に いれた
から かつ に ちがひない と しんじて をり-
ました。 したがつて しんばい を も せず たの-
しんで をりました が, やがて にちげん に
なります と, やくしよ の はう から ふたり
の とち を あらそへる もの に でゝ こい
と いふ せうくわん が きまして, みんな が
あつまつた とき に かう いふ めう な こと
が おこつた の です。 すなはち その とき に
<u>ダイゼン</u> こう は おほぜい の どく くらゐ
の たかい やくにん の まへ で, うり を

a wise man. In his time there were two fellow townsmen
who had a quarrel over the boundary line of their lands.
They made a suit at law out of their disagreement. One
of the men, meanwhile, went secretly to Lord Itakura's
house. The season was still at the beginning of summer.
He wished to make a present to Lord Itakura of some
early melons, the first fruits of his field. He delivered
many rare ones at Lord Itakura's kitchen. He was confident that, in this way he would win the governor over to
his side, and thus gain a victory. He was consequently
happy and unconcerned. In due time the government sum-
moned the two disputants about the land to appear.
When all had assembled, this extraordinary thing occurred.
Lord Itakura, in the presence of many officers of the
highest rank, turning to the man who had brought the
melons to him, said in a clear, loud voice, 'Many thanks
for the delicious melons you gave me the other day. As
to the land business, it will be well for you to let your
neighbor have at once the boundary in question.' The
man who had secretly taken the melons to Lord Itakura's
house grew very red in the face. He obeyed with fear.
He yielded the land to his neighbor. Then, all the people in court went back to their homes." That is the story.
Our children read it. Don't you think that the man who
attempted to bribe the governor was rather annoyed by
what he heard?

もつて きた をとこ に むかつて はつきり と
した おほき な こゑ で 「この あひだ は
うまい うり を おくつて くれて まこと に
ありがたい。 さて, また, とち の こと に
ついて は, もんちやく に なつて をる さかひ
を, すぐさま となり の をとこ に わたし
たら よからう。」 と いひました。 ダイゼン
こう の ところ へ ないく で うり を もつて
ゆきました をとこ は まつか に なつて
かしこまりまして, となり の をとこ に とち
を わたしました の で, やくしよ の ひと
も みな うち へ かへりました。』 はなし と
まうします の は かう いふ の で ございます。
わが くに の こどもら も この はなし を
よみます が, あなた は ちじ に まひなひ
を やらう と した をとこ は あゝ いふ
こと を きいた とき に こまつた と おも-
はれません か。

3.—おもひます と も, きんげん も さう いふ
ふう に なる と いや な こと を する やう
です。 すこし ゆかう じや ありません か。 も-
う ひる です。

3.—I should say so.   Put in that way I suppose a golden saying can do disagreeable work.   Well, let us go on. It is almost noon.

だい　さんじう　く

ゆ　も

ゆだん　たい　てき。

1. ミカターし：—こゝら　の　じめん　が　かいりよう　されやう　と　しとる　の　は　たいへん　けつこう　です。　この　やま　の　した　の　みち　だの　あの　あたらしい　みぞ　なぞ　は　よほど　よく　なりました。　いちじ　は　この　もり　を　くさーだーらけ　に　して　すてゝ　おく　の　か　と　おもつて　をりました　が。

2. ロビンソンーし：—わたくし　が　はじめて　ニホン　へ　きました　とき　から　みる　と　とうゑん　の　ぜんたい　の　けしき　は　よほど　よく　なりましーた。　ぢめん　も　よく　ていれ　が　できて　みち　も　きれい　に　なつて　をります。　にじふーねん　いぜん　に　は　じない　が　かう　いふ　こと　に　ならう　と　は　おもひ　も　よらぬ　こと　で　ありーましたらう。　その　じぶん　こゝ　に　あつた　けつーこう　な　たてもの　は　みたい　もの　で　ありまーした。

3. —わたくし　は　よく　おぼえて　をります。　その　とき　の　くわじ　は，やつた　こと　は　ひどう　ございます　が，じつ　に　りつぱ　で　ございました。　あすこ　の　おほき　な　あかもん　は　たいてい　もと

XXXIX.   PROVERB FOR (ゆ) *YU.*

Negligence is a great enemy.

1. *Mr. M:*—I am glad to see that something is being done to improve these grounds.   This walk down the hill, and these new waterways are a great change for the better. I thought at one time that the grove would be left to run to weeds and ruin.

1. *Mr. R:*—The whole park looks better than it did when I first came to Japan.   The grounds are better cared for. The walks are kept clean.   There must have been rather a hopeless , outlook for the temple grounds twenty years ago.   I should like to see the splendid building that stood here then.

3.—I remember it.   The fire was a grand sight, bad as its work was.   The big red gate there remains pretty much unchanged.   But it has been shamefully neglected, along with the rest of the buildings here.   Better times, however, are coming for both the buildings and grounds.   So many

の とほり です が, ほか の こゝ に ある
たてもの と おなじく すつかり うつちやつて
ありました。 しかし だんゝ たてもの も じめん
も いゝ じせつ に むかつて まゐります。
こゝ に はうむつて ある 「ショウグン」 の かー
ず は よほど おほう ございます から,「ゐしん」
の せんさう の ため に うつちやつて あつた
こと を その まゝ に しとく の は とくー
ぢよく の ひとつ です。 せいふ は しうけう の
ほじよ は まつたく たつ に しろ, こゝ の
「トクガハ、シヤウグン」 の やしろ だけ は ほ-
ぞん しなければ なりません。

4.—わたくし は この ふるい りつぱ な かね
は やがて よく しまつ を される だらう と
おもひます。 この かね は わたくし の みた
かね の うち で いちばん はでやか で, いちー
ばん ね が ふかう ございます。 たびゝ あさ
の よーじ じぶん に その おと を きゝます
が, その とき の くうき は まるで その
ふかい おんがく と いつしよ に うごく やう
で ございます。

5.—この やう に おほき な からかね の
とうろう が いくーれつ と なく ある の を
みます と, むかし の 「シヤウグン」 の けん-
りよく の つよかつた こと が じつ に よく
わかります。 こゝ の とうろう の かず は

of the Shōguns are buried here, that it would be a national disgrace, if the neglect which arose out of the war of the Restoration were allowed to continue. Even though the government may withdraw its support wholly from religion, these shrines of the Tokugawa Shōguns ought to be preserved.

4.—I hope that this grand old bell will soon be well housed. It has one of the richest tones, and it has the deepest tone, I ever heard. Often, in the morning at four o'clock, I hear it. The air then seems actually to throb with its profound music.

5.—These rows upon rows of great bronze lanterns impress me deeply with the power of the old Shōgunate. There are two hundred and twelve of them, they say. And how many of these big stone lanterns there are, I do not know. All are presents from daimyōs in memory of their lords, the Shōguns, of the middle of the last century.

みな で ひやく-じう-に ある さう です が,
あそこ の おほき な いしどうらう は どれだ-
け ある か しれません。これ は みな この
まへ の せいき の なかごろ じぶん に「ダイ-
ミャウ」 だち が「シャゥグン」へ の きねん
に けんじやう した の です。

————

だい 志じふ

め 免

めくら へび に おぢず。

（ふたり は ニテンモン を いでい ほん-
みち に うつりし が, ミカタ-し は ひとり
の つうかうにん を みとめて ロビンソン-し
に むかひ。)

1. ミカタ-し:—いま とほつて いつた をとこ
は ごく ふかう な めに あつた もの です。
あなた の おつしやつた やう に ひと を
しんじ すごして なんぎ に あつた の で
は なく, だれ で も あいて に する ひと
を うたがつた はう です が, たい とき に
よつて ひと を みる こと が できず, また
とき に よつて ひと を みやう と しない
をとこ で あつた の で, この あひだ の

XL. PROVERB FOR (め) *ME.*

A blind man is not afraid of a snake.

(The two friends pass through the Ni-ten-mon on to the public road.   Mr. Mikata recognizes a man who is passing.   He then speaks to Mr. Robinson.)

1. *Mr. M :—*There is a man who has just gone through a most unfortunate experience. He is not one of your victims of misplaced confidence. He is ready enough to suspect the men he deals with. But he is a man who sometimes can not see, and who sometimes will not see. His last experience came out of both these troubles.

こと など も この ふたつ の ふつがう から
おとつた の です。

2. ロビンソンシーし：—それ は どう した こと
です か。

3.—あの をとこ には じぶん の こ が
ありません でして，しち-ねん ほど まへ に
わかい をとこ を やうし に して，じふん の
むすめ の をつと に しました が，こんいん
ご さん-ねん ほど にて むすめ は しに-
ました。わかい をとこ は むすめ の いき-
てる じふん から で さへ ばくちとき で
ありまして，いま とほつて いつた をとこ が
しやうばい を やめて いんきよ を して
やうし を かはり に たて やう と した
とき など は しんるゐ が いぞん を いひ，
やうし の あくじ を ちいちや に つげました
が，どう いふ もの でした か あの をとこ
は ちつと も その と の わるい こと を
まこと と おもはず，かへつて しんるゐ が
わるい たくみ を もつて をる と うたがつ-
て をりました。が，たうとう やうし が ひど-
い わる-もの で ばくち とき の うへ に
どろばう で ある と いふ こと を さとつて
かなしむ やう に なりました。しかし これ と
いふ の も じぶん が わるい ので，よ に
は ひと を みる こと が できぬ もの ほど

2. *Mr. R :*—How was that?

3.—He has no children of his own. About seven years ago he adopted a young fellow. He made him the husband of his daughter. The daughter died about three years after the marriage. The young fellow had become a gambler, even while his wife was alive. That man who just passed proposed to retire from his business (become *inkyo*), and to put his adopted son in charge of it. His own family relatives objected. The son was even accused of his vices to the father. But, somehow, the father would believe nothing wrong of the boy. He rather suspected his relatives of interested motives. In the end he found out to his sorrow that the boy was a rascal,—a gambler and a thief. But he has himself to blame. There are none so blind as those who will not see. *(Entering the Kwankōba.)* Not many people are out buying to-day.

はなはだしい めくら は ありません。（くわん-
とうば に いりながら） けふ は かひ-もの
に でかけて をる ひと は すくない やう
です ね。

4.—おほく の きやく に とつて は しん-
ねん の のち が はや すぎる じや あり-
ません か。わたくし が じふにぐわつ に
こゝ へ きました とき など は ぐんじゆ の
なか を とほられぬ ほど の ひとごみ で
ありました。

* * * * *

5.—おほき に あふ やう な かいみ が
ありました か。

6.—これ が いち-ばん いゝ やう です。
わたくし は ニホン の しやうにん が みな
その しなもの に しやう-ふだ を つけて
くれゝば いゝ と おもひます。しなもの に
ついてる ねだん より いち-もん も ちがはぬ
と いふ こと が わかる と, きつと おび-
たゞしい きやく が ついて まゐりませう。

———

4.—I suppose it is too soon after the New Year for many buyers. I was here in December. It was so crowded then that one could scarcely move along the passages.

*   *   *   *   *

5. *Mr. M :*—Have you found a glass to suit you.

6.—I think this one will do very well. I wish that all the Japanese merchants would adopt fixed-prices for their goods. The knowledge that here there is no change whatever from the figures marked on the articles brings hosts of purchasers.

だい 志じふ いち
みゝ

みめ より こゝろ。

1. ロビンソン－し：－まち の はう から もどり－ませう。あたらしい はし を ちよいと みたう ございます から。しく－かいせい も だん〴〵 はか－どつて まゐります。わたくし は <u>トウキヤウ</u> を かいせい しやう と いふ くはだて の こと を おもふ たびごと に，いつ も かんじます。ひやく－にじふ－ねん かゝつて できる くはだて を さいよう し，とうじ の ため に におく－しせん－まん－ゑん，すなはち いちねん に に－ひやく－まん－ゑん あて つひやさるゝ さう です ね。

2. <u>ミカター</u>－し：－さう です。すつかり この まち を つくり－かへて，りつば な おほみち だ の，よい すゐだう だ の，それ から こうゑん だ の，でんきとう だ の の ある まち に する つもり でせう。じつ に おほき な かんがへ です。しかし これ も 「メイヂ」 の あひだ に おこつた ほか の こと と ちがい は しませ－ん。

3.－<u>ニホン</u> の ひと が たいへん てをくれ に なつた こと を とりかへさう と される

XLI. PROVERB FOR (み) *MI.*

The heart rather than the face.

1. *Mr. R :*—Let us go back by the street. I wish to take a look at the new bridge. The city improvements are going forward steadily. I never think of the plans made for the transformation of Tōkyō without wonder. Plans for one hundred and twenty years work, I am told, have been drafted. Two hundred and forty millions of *yen* are to be expended on the work, that is, two millions each year.

2. *Mr. M :*—Yes, I believe it is proposed to make the city over so that it shall be a city of splendid avenues, good drainage, parks and lighting. Truly, a big idea! But it is just like everything else that has sprung up during Meiji.

3.—I am not surprised at the determination of your people to make up for long-lost time. I sometimes ask, however,

のは もつとも だ と をもひます が、ニホン じんの ほんたうの しんぱ は さう いふ ぐわいぶ の りえき に とものふ か しらん と をもひます。

4.—その こと は いくたび も をーはなし まうした こと です が わたくし の しんずる ところ は これ まで も まうしーあげました とほり、あなた の おほい に たつとばれる ところ の もの も うつちやられる こと は なからう と いふ の です。あなた は わたーくしーども が てつがく や しうけう に ふねーつしん な こと を をーとがめ なさいます が、こんにち わたくし を ねつしん に しやう と いふ こと は のぞみ がたい こと で でーざいます。われ〱 は まづ われ〱 の いへ を をさめなければ なりません。われ〱 の けーつしん の をこつた の は しうけう の はう で ありません。アメリカ や ヨーロツパ だけ で いふて も しうけう の うら には しやーうばい が ございます。われ〱 が うけいーじやう に よわき こと は せかい かくとく と の かうさい の じやま に なりました から、われ〱 は まづ うけいーじやう の じやくてん を のぞかなければ なりません。われ〱 が じーいう に なり、つよく なれば、ほか の ことーがら は ざうさ が ない と をもひます。

whether the real progress of the people will keep pace with
these outside gains.

4.—We have talked that matter over many a time. I
believe, as I have often said, that the things you put so
much value on will not be neglected. You complain that
we take no deep interest in philosophy, or in religion.
You really can't expect us to do so, under the circumstances. We must put our home in order, first. Our revolution was not started in the interests of religion. Trade
was at the back of it, so far as America and Europe were
concerned. Our physical weakness has been in our way
in all our intercourse with the Powers among nations. We
must get rid of our physical inferiority first. The other
things will more easily come when we are free and strong.

5.—わたくし は じふん に あなた の お‐
こゝろ を くみとつて をります から, この う‐
へ あなた に たいして ぎろん は しません
が, とにかく わたくし も わたくし の ほんい
を まもります。 およそ <u>ニホン</u> で も また
は いかなる せかい の じんみん で も えらく‐
なり じいう に なる の に は たましひ に
のみ よる と いふ こと は まちがひ の ない
こと です。

———

だい 志じふ に

し 志

志ゆ ふ まじはれば あかく なる。

1. <u>ミカター</u>し:—あなた は いま とほつて‐いつた
ばしや の なか の 志んし を ご‐ぞんじ で‐
す か。

2. <u>ロビンソン</u>‐し:—き が つきません でした
が, どなた でした か。

3.—<u>イセイ</u>‐さん です が, むろん ご‐ぞんじ
でせう。 あの ひと が わが くに の せいねん
と ちうねん の ひと に およぼした せい
りよく は, <u>トウキヤウ</u> に をる どの ひと より
も よけい です。

4.—ハイ, むろん わたくし は ひやうばん を

5.—I sympathize with you too much to argue long against you. But, after all, I go back to my regular position. It is true of the Japanese, and of every people in the world, that by "the soul only they shall be great and free."

XLII. PROVERB FOR (ㄴ) *SHI.*

He who handles vermilion is stained red.

1. *Mr. M:*—Do you know that gentleman who was in the carriage just driven by?

2. *Mr. R:*—I did not notice. Who was it?

3.—That was Mr. Isei. You know of him, of course. He has had more of the young and middle-aged men of the country under his influence than any other man in Tōkyō.

4.—Yes, of course I have heard of him. If there were

きゝました。 もし ニホン に この やう な
ひと が せん-にん も, イヤ, ひやく-にん も あ-
つた なら, すくなく と も この くに の
つぎ の じだい の こと に ついて は いつ-
とき の しんばい も いりません。 あの ひと
は こゝろ と いひ, おとなひ と いひ, からだ
と いひ, をとこ の てほん です。 もし も
ひと が たにん と まじはつた ため に かは-
る こと が できる なら, ニホン に は おも
に イセイ-さん から 玄ぶん の いゝ ところ
を もらつた ひと は なん-ぜん-にん ゐる
か 志れません。

     *   *   *   *   *

5.—ちよつと お-より なさいません か。 ちやう-
ど めしどき です から。 いかゞ です。

6.—ありがたう ございます が, この つぎ に
いたしませう。 たく に したく も できて を-
ります し, それ に あし も ぬれて をり-
ます から。 志も が とけた ので みち が
たいへん わるう ございます。 くつ を ぬいで,
くつたび を かへなければ なりません。 ど-
うぞ おくさま に よろしく おつしやつて く-
ださいまし。

7.—あぢ の いゝ しなみかん が あります
から, ひるから せう〱 お-とゞけ まうしませ-
う。

a thousand such as he in Japan, or even a hundred, no one need have an hour's solicitude for the country for at least three generations to come.   He is a model man himself, mentally, morally and physically. So far as men can be shaped by contact with others, there are thousands of men in Japan who owe most of what is best in them to Mr. Isei.

*   *   *   *   *

5.—Come in for a few moments!   It is just tiffin time. Come in !

6.—Thank you!   Not to-day.   My tiffin is awaiting me. Besides, my feet are wet.   The roads are very muddy from the melted frost.   I must get off my shoes and make a change of socks.   My best regards to Mrs. Mikata.

7.—I have some delicious Chinese oranges.   I shall send you some this afternoon.

8.—いつ も どうも ありがたう ございます。

だい 志じふ さん

ゑ

ゑば は にくい もの に あたへ よ。

（ミカターし の いへ にて。）

1. <u>ミカタ</u> し:—この へや は あなた の たいーへん でーすき な へや で ございます。 あなた の でーちうこく に したがひました が, こゝ は いゝ やう です。 てんき は どう です か。

2. <u>ロビンソン</u> し:—ゆき は やん で, そら は だんく きれい に はれて くる やう です。 くも の なか から つき が でーたり はいつーたり してる の が みえまして, よる の けしき は まる で せんにん の くに の やう で ございます。 わたくし は いま つき の ひかり が ゆき や, き を てらす の を みーやう と おもつて でゝ きました が, こなた の おーには は まる で せんにん の やしき の やう に なりました。

3.—それ は にはかーばれ で ございます。 いちーじーかん ほど まへ に は ゆき が ひどーく ふつて をりました。

8.—You are always doing me favors.

———

XLIII. PROVERB FOR (ゑ) *E* (*WE*).

Give food even to detestable things.

(At Mr. Mikata's house.)

1. *Mr. M :*—You find me, you see, in the room you enjoy so much. I am taking your advice, and I like it, too. How is the weather ?

2. *M. R :*—It has stopped snowing. It is clearing off beautifully. You should see the moon sailing in and out among the clouds. The night is like fairy-land. I came over just for the sake of seeing the moon-light upon the snow and the trees. Your garden is transformed into a wizard's palace.

3.—It is a sudden clear off. An hour ago the snow was falling heavily.

4.—さう でした。 わたくし も こんや は やすまう と して をりました が, さきがた らうか へ でました とき に, には が ひる の やう に あかるくて, くさむら も き も かき も いけがき も やね も すつかり ゆき で もつて おほはれて, つき の ひかり を うけて きらくくして をりました。 が, あした あさ はやく ひ が でゝ きます と, この きれい な もの が みんな なくなる で あらう と おもひました ゆゑ, この ふしぎ な せかい を みのがす の が いや で, でゝきた の で ございます。 こゝ へ きて おーうち の には を ごらん なさいません か。

*   *   *   *   *

5.—ヤァ, ドウモ, なに も か も かはつた こと。

6.—ゆき が ふつた ため, き が みな それぐ の せいしつ を あらはした で ありません か。 まつ も かき も すぎ も もみ も かへで も ざくろ も やなぎ も あらゆる くさばな も みんな たいへん に ちがつた で ありー ません か。 それ に あの むめ の はな は ゆき で おほはれてる ため に きのふ の ありさま から みる と きめう な ちがひ で ありません か。 なに も か も じつ に めう です ね。

4.—So it was! I had settled down for the evening. But I went out into my corridor a few minutes ago. My garden was almost as bright as day. All the bushes and trees, the fence, the hedge and the roofs, were covered with snow, and were glistening in the moon-light. I know that to-morrow the sun will spoil all the beauty early in the morning. I did not want to miss seeing the magic world that the snow has made, so I came out. I have had an entrancing walk. Come, look at your own garden. * * *

*   *   *   *   *

5.—Marvellous! How it is all changed!

6.—Do you see how the snow brings out the individual character of each tree? The pine, the cryptomeria, the fir, the pomegranate, the maple, the willow, all the shrubs, how distinct they are! And what a queer contrast those plum blossoms make with what they were yesterday, being covered with snow. Oh! how exquisite it all is!

7.—ふゆ に なつて から これ が ほんたう
の はつゆき です。

8.—わたくし は もう ふゆ が すんだ と
おもつて をりまして, ツヒ いつさくじつ の
こと でした が, カメ井ド へ ぐはりよう-ばい
を み に ゆきました。けふ は カハサキ の
そば の カマダ の ばい-ゑん へ ゆかう と
おもつて をりました が, わたくし は カメ井ド
の より カマダ の はう が いゝ と おもひ-
ます。

9.—はいらう じや ありません か。あさ に
なつて も いち-じ-かん や にー-じ-かん は
この ふしぎ な とち に をる こと が でき-
ませう から, わたくし は はやく おきて みる
こと に いたします。ひ の そば へ よつて
おー-あたん なさい。わたくし は いま まで むかし
の ゐ を よんで をりました が, あなた は
ニホン の ゐ を ごー-ぞんじ です か。

10.—ほん の すこし です, みほん だ と
いつて ひとつ ふたつ ほつく と たんか と
を くれた ひと が ありました が, よほど
つくり-かた の むづかしい ゐ の やう で
ございます。ほつく や たんか など に ぢうぶん
の いみ を いれる に は, よほど ことば の
じくれん が なければ なりますまい。

7.—This is the first real snow-fall we have had this winter.

8.—I thought that the winter was over. Only the day before yesterday I was at Kameido to see the old dragon plum-trees.—*(Gwaryōbai)*. I intended to go to-day to the Kamada garden near Kawasaki. I think I prefer it to the garden at Kameido.

9.—Let us go in. For an hour or two in the morning we shall be in wonder-land. I shall get up early to look at it. Draw your chair to the fire and be comfortable. I have just been reading some old poems. Do you know Japanese poetry?

10.—Very little. A friend once gave me a few specimens of it, the *hokku* and the *tanka*. It must be rather a difficult kind of verse making. To get complete sense and expression into the *hokku*, or even into the *tanka*, must require a great deal of word-skill.

11.—よい いみ を いれる に は その
とほり です。

12.—マア どう でせう。 たつた ご しち
ご の ゐん の さん-く で, し が ひとつ
でき, ご しち ご しち しち の ゐん の
ご-く で も ひとつ の し が できる の
です。 じつ に おどろきいる くみたて じや
ありません か。 <u>イギリス</u> の たんし など は
ひじやう に まづい です。

13.—しかし わが くに の ぶんがくか の
うち に は かう いふ ぶんしやう を よほど
よく やつた ひと が ございます。 むかし の
きふじん は たいてい この こと に おほく
の じかん を つひやしました。 わたくし は
だいいま まで ある くわうどう の かゝれた
たんか を よんで をりました が。 かう いふ
の です。

しんだらば
  やく な うめる な
の に すてて
  やせたる いぬ の
  はら を こやせ よ。

わたくし が しんだ さき に, わたくし を やく な
わたくし を うめる な。 の に わたくし を すてい
やせた いぬ の すき-はら な こやせ よ。

11.—Yes ! To get *good* sense into them does.

12.—Just think ! Three lines of only five, seven, and five syllables for one complete poem ; and five lines of five, seven, five, seven, and seven syllables, for another kind of complete poem. Such writing would drive me wild. The English sonnet is bad enough.

13.—But some of our writers have been very successful with this kind of writing. Many of the ladies in the ancient days devoted a good deal of time to the art. I have just been reading a *tanka* written by an empress. Here it is :—

" *Shindaraba,*
        Yakuna, umeruna,
    No ni sutete,
        Yasetaru inu no
        Hara wo koyase yo."

(When I die, burn me not, bury me not. Into the wilderness cast me, that the starving dogs may fill their empty stomachs.)

14.—じやうず に できて をります が, きめう な ねがひ です ね。

15.—ところ が きめう で ない の です。かう いふ なさけ-ごゝろ は むかし の わが くに の ぶんがく, こと に ぶつけう が じやうとう しやくわい に をこなはれて をつた じぶん に は たびゝ ありました。あの くわう-ごう は ひ や むし の ため に からだ を なくして しまふ より, かはいさう な けだもの を たすけた はう が よほど とく だ と をもはれた の です。もう ひとつ たんか が ございます。かたち は あまり よく ありー ません が, いみ の をもしろい ところ から ちよつと よみませう。わたくし は この うた と やま の うへ の をしへ に ある こと と あまり ちがはない か と をもひます。

> にくまれて
>   にくみ かへす な
> にくまれろ,
>   にくみ にくまれ
>   はてし なければ。

  にくまるゝ さ も にくみ に にくみ を かへす な。にくみ を うけ よ。もし にくみ に にくみ を かへさば にくみ は はてざらん。

16.—ようにん と いふ こと の よき をしへ です。しかし わたくし は やま の

14.—Skilfully done! But what a strange wish!

15.—Oh no! Such humane feeling often appeared in our ancient literature, especially when Buddhism had the upper classes under its influence. The empress considered her body put to a much higher use in saving even a miserable outcast beast, than in feeding either fire or worms. Here is another *tanka*. It is not perfect in form, but I want to read it for the sentiment it expresses. I can not see much difference between this and some parts of the "Sermon on the Mount."

> " *Nikumarete*
>   *Nikumi kaesu na.*
> *Nikumarero.*
>   *Nikumi nikumare*
>   *Hateshi nakereba.*"

(If you are hated hate, for hate do not return. Receive the hatred. If you give hatred for hate, hating has no end.)

16.—An admirable lesson in tolerance! But I am sure that the "Sermon on the Mount" goes farther and higher

うへ の をしへ の はう が これ より も
いつさう ひろくて かうしやう だ と おもひ-
ます。こゝ に をしへて ある きしつ は しのぶ
と いふ こと だけ で, ゆるす と いふ こと
で ありません。けれども エス は しのぶ
こと を をしへし のみならず, ゆるす こと
を も をしへ。ゆるす こと を をしへし のみ-
ならず, にくむ ところ の もの を も あい-
せ よ, いぢわるく わるくち を いふて くる-
しめる ところ の もの を も あいせ よ と
をしへました。

———

だい ゐじふ し

ひ

ひと の よ を わたる は まろきばし の
ごとし。

1. ミカタ―し:―あなた の ご―せつ は ご-
もつとも の やう で ございます。 しかし
キリスト の きそく は せいじやだち に あた-
へた の で, よわたり を する こと に あた-
へた の で ない やう で ございます。もつとも
むかし の やう な けんくわ―ずき な きしやう
を おこして は なりますまい。この たんか は
いかゝ です。

than this. The disposition taught here is mere endurance. It is not forgiveness. Jesus taught not only endurance, but forgiveness, too ; and not only forgiveness, but love to them that hate, and love even to those who spitefully abuse and persecute.

———

XLIV. PROVERB FOR (ひ) *HI.*

Man's journey through this world is like crossing a round-bridge.

1. *Mr. M :*—I suppose you are right. But Christ's law seems given for saints, not for men of the every-day world. However, we shall not take up our old bone of contention. What do you think of this *tanka*?

ふじ の やま
　のぼりて みれば
なに も なし。
　よき も あしき も
　わが こころ かな。

フジ-さん に のぼりて せかい を みる に。み ふ。
なに も なし。されば よき も また あしき も ただ わが
おもひ に ある のみ なり。

2. ロビンソン-し：—わたくし の てつがく に
する に は ちつと ふかう ございます。イヤ
かうしやうー すぎる と まうした はう が
いい か も しれません。この し を つくつた
ひと は なに を おもつて ゐた の で ござい-
ませう。いつ か あなた が わたくし へ の
おはなし に, フジ の やま の うへ から
みる と せかい が みな ひらつたく なつて
やま も たに も のはら の やう に みえる
と おつしやつた の を おぼえて をります
が, この たんか を かいた ひと も, じぶん
の もつて をつた てつがく から みる と, よ
の なか の ぜん あく が なくなる と
おもつて ゐた の でせう か。あるひは
また ぶつけう の をしへ を をしへ やう と
おもつて, いのち と いふ もの は みな
まよい で ある と か, また は ゑんばう の
やま の うへ に ふしぎ な もの が ある
と おもつて ゐて, しまい に なんに も ない

" *Fuji no yama*
Noborite mireba
Nani mo nashi.
Yoki mo ashiki mo
Waga kokoro kana."

(When I ascend Mount Fuji and thence view the world,
see! there is nothing. So, good and also evil are only
in my feeling.)

2. *Mr. R :*—That is rather deep for my philosophy, or, I
should say, too high for it. What did the poet mean? I
remember, you told me once that from the top of Mount
Fuji all the world is flattened out so, that hills and valleys
look like a plain. Did the writer of this *tanka* mean,
that from the heights of such philosophy as his, the good
and evil of the world disappear? Or, did he mean to teach
a lesson of Buddhism, that all life is an illusion? Or, that
life is like the dream of him who puts wonderful things on
far off summits, only to find that they are not there
when he scales the heights?

と いふ こと を さとつた ひと の ゆめ の
やうだ と いつた の でせう か。

3.—それ は どうだ か わたくし に は わ-
かりません。わたくし は たい し を よみます
から, あなた は ご-つがふ の い、やう に
お-はんじ なさいまし。

4.—その お-ことば で あなた に お-たづね
まうしたい と おもつて いた こと を お-
もひだしました。この あひだ カメ井ド へ ゆき-
ました とき に ふじ の には の ある お-
てら へ ちよつと よりまして, そこ に ある
はんゑんけい の はし を わたつて きました。
が, いぜん わたくし は ミヤジマ の じない
で も おなじ はし の おほきい の を わた-
つた こと が あり, その ほか はうぐ で
おんなじい はし の おほきい の を いろ〳〵
みた こと が ありました の で, さきがた
これ から まだ お-はなし しなければ ならぬ
ことわざ の こと に なりました とき, あなた
は ひ の じ に ひと の いのち は まるき-
ばし の ごとし と いふ の を お-えらび に
なりました が, わたくし は カメ井ド の はし
に はひあがる の に も, ミヤジマ の はし
に はひあがる の に も, よほど ほね が をれ-
ました から, あなた に お-たづね まうしたい
の は, ひ の こと-わざ を つくつた ひと

3.—I do not know. I read the poem, and you can make it fit your own divinations.

4.—That brings to mind something I wanted to ask you. When I was at Kameido the other day, I stopped in for a moment at the temple where the wistaria garden is. I went over the semi-circular bridge there. I have been over a much larger bridge of the same kind in the temple grounds of Miyajima. I have seen several bridges like these in different parts of the country. Now, a short time ago, in going over the proverbs which we have yet to talk about, you gave one for *"Hi"* which says something about human life being like crossing a round-bridge. I had hard work scrambling over both the Kameido and the Miyajima bridges. I wanted to ask you, whether the maker of the *"Hi"* proverb was not a man who had had a pretty hard life of it. I thought that perhaps he was a priest who had to go every day over one of these round-bridges, on the way to his temple.

は, づゐぶん つらい せいくわつ を ゐくつた
ひと で なかつた か と いふ の です。
わたくし の かんがへる ところ で は この
ひと は ばうず で あつて, まいにちく てら
へ ゆく みち で, こんな まるきばし を
とほらねば ならなかつた ところ の ひと
だつたらう と ゐもふ の です。

5.—あなた は どうも わたくしども の こと
に ついて むとんぢやく で こまります。 あ
いふ はし は なるほど こはい に は ちがひ
ありません が, はだし で ゆけば わたる の
に ざうさ は ありません。 志かし わたくし は
この ことわざ を つくつた ひと が をしへ
やう と ゐもつて ゐた の は, いのち が
くう だ と いふ こと で, へいめん から せい-
ねん の ちやうじやう に いたつて また へい-
めん に くだつて くる, うまれて から しぬる
まで の せいくわつ の きよくせん を いつた
の だ と ゐもひます。

* * * * *

6.—もう ゐ-いとま いたしませう。 わたくし
は これ から <u>シバ</u> の とうえん へ よつて
まゐります。 あなた も ゐ-いで に なつて
あそこ の き だの ゆき だの を ご-らん
なされば いゝ と ゐもひます が, かう いふ

5.—I am afraid you will never be serious over some of
our things. Those bridges are a terror, I know. But go
at them barefooted, and they will be easy enough to pass.
The proverb-maker, I suppose, had in mind another lesson,
—on life's vanity,—the curve of life from birth to death, up
from the level to the summit of manhood and down to the
level again.

*   *   *   *   *

6.—I must say good night, now. I shall walk over to
Shiba Park. I should like to have you go with me and see
the trees and the snow there. But I do not think I could
get you away from this snug-harbor.

らく な ところ から あなた を つれだす
わけ に は ゆきますまい。

7.—ありがたう ございます が, こんや は
ゆきますまい。

8.—ことし は かう いふ きくわい は また
と ありますまい。 つき は まんげつ で
あり, かぜ は なし。 わたくし の ところ の
うめ を じつ に おーめ に かけたう ご一
ざいます。 おほき な あかい はな が えだ に
いつぱい で, どう して こぼく が あの やう
に はでやか に さいた か わからぬ やう
です。 どうぞ おーをり なさいます な。 そと の
はう で は もう なに に も か に も,
ゆき が さんーずん も つもつて をりませう。
あした の みち は じつ に ひどい でせう。
わたくし は こんーや は はらーいつぱい けしき
を みて まゐります。 さやう なら。

———

だい 志じふ ご

も と

もえくひ に は ひ が つき やすい。

1:—しぐわつ なかごろ ミカターし ちん の うち
にて てがみ を よみ をれり。 この てー

7.—Thank you, I won't go out to night.

8.—I know I shall not have such a chance again this year. The moon is at the full. There is no wind. Oh! you should see the old plum-tree at my house. Its branches are crammed with big, red blossoms. You would not imagine that the old ruin could bloom out in such vigorous gorgeousness. Please do not come down stairs! Outside, there must be at least three inches of snow over everything. To morrow, the slush will be fearful. I shall take my fill of the beauty to-night. Good bye!

XLV.   PROVERB FOR (♮) *MO.*

A charred stick easily takes fire.

1. *(Mr. Mikala is seated in his garden house in mid-April*

がみ は ロビンソン-し より おくれる もの
にて, ところづけ は アタミ なり。その もんく
しも の ごとし。

2:—あなた は わたくし を これ まで より
も はなはだしい やつきもの だ と おもはれます
に さうゐ ありますまい が, わたくし は ことし
は さくら の じゆんれい を して みたくて
たまりません でした。かう まうしあげまして
おーわかり に なりませう か。ごーしようち の
とほり, この てん に ある やう な うるはー
しい けしき が じうぶん に みられます まー
へ に, あめ かぜ など ゝ いふ あくしん
が これ を ほろぼす こと が, おほう ございー
ます。ところ が, ことし は ながい さむい
しめつぱい ふゆ の ありました あと で
はる に なります と すつかり こゝろ よく
そら も せいく と して をりまして, こんー
にち まで も はる の けしき は その まゝ
で, なくなり さう に は ありません。とをーか
ほど まへ に わたくし は ウヘノ へ ゆきまー
した が, はくぶつくわん の ところ まで みー
ちーばた に ある おほき な き の つぼみ が
やさしく さいて かゝやいて をる の を みまー
した ので, にわか に ニホン で いちばん
よい さくら の めいしよ へ いつて みたい
こゝろ に なり, よくじつ だれ に も いとまー

reading a letter.   The letter is from Mr. Robinson, and is dated at Atami.   It says :—)

2.—" I know you will think me more of a run-away enthusiast than ever.   I could not resist the temptation to make a cherry-blossom pilgrimage this year.   Do you know what I mean by that?   Every year,—this you know,—for about a fortnight Japan becomes Paradise.   Often the powers of evil,—wind and rain,—destroy the celestial beauty before it can be seen in perfection.   But this year, after a long, cold, wet winter, spring, with all generous warmth and with cloudless skies, came, and, so far, has remained without seeming to wish to leave us.   Ten days ago I was over at Ueno.   The sight of the tender, flushing buds of the big trees on the avenue up to the museum, made me long to see for once some of Japan's most famous cherry-flower places.   The next day, without saying good bye to any one, I left by an early train for the west.   I can never forget the exquisite charm of the day's trip.   All along the road, the trees, as our Whittier said, were " growing misty green with leafing buds."   In every village and in almost every farm-yard, plum-blossoms still were there, bidding welcome to the new cherry-blossoms.   This year the winter

ごひ を しない で にし の はう へ いち-
ばん-ぎしや で たちました。 が, じつ に その
ひ の たのしみ と いふ もの は わすれる
こと は できません。 みちばた の き は みな
ホ井ッチヤ の いつた やう に,「は の ある
つぼみ で うす-あをく なつて」 をりまして'
ど の はら に も たいがい の はたけ に
も まだ うめ が ありまして, あたらしい さ-
くら の はな に あいさつ を して をりまし-
た。 ことし は ふゆ の すみ やう が おそ-
くつて, はる の き やう が はやかつた の
で, うめ と さくら の はな を いつしよ に
した, にじう の たのしみ が ございます。 わ-
たくし は はじめて の ばん は ナゴヤ に
たうちやくし その よくじつ は ヒコネ まで
ゆきまして, もと, 井イ、カモンノカミ の すまひ
で あつた はたごや に とまりました。 井イ、カモ-
ンノカミ は いま の よ に なつて から,
ニホン で はじめて の しんぼてき の さいし-
やう でした。 この はたごや は きれい な
いへ で ひろく おもむき の ある うつくしい
には も ありました。 が, わたくし の いつた
の は さくら の じせつ に は はや-すぎて
をりました。 この とち は よほど たかくて,
さらされて ゐます の で, むら の まち の うち
に は ゆき が みえました。 よくじつ の ひ-
る-まへ に は, キヤウト へ ゆきました。 が,

stayed so long, and spring came so fast, that we are having
a double feast of plum and cherry-flowers together. The
first night I reached Nagoya. The next day I went as far
as Hikone. I stayed over the night at a hotel that was
once the residence of the Ii-Kamon-no-Kami, the first progressive Prime Minister of Japan under the present order
of things. A lovely house and a spacious, tasteful, charming garden. But I was too soon for the cherries. The
place is so high and exposed that I found even snow in
the streets of the village. Before noon of the next day I
was at Kyōto. I had reached there just in time. The
next morning I rode out to Arashi-yama, and had several
hours of enjoyment. The effect of the hundreds of trees
standing out in full blossom from the dark ever-green
back-ground of the mountain-side, is exquisite. But the
sparkling river mirroring the base of the mountain ; the
gaily decorated boats on the water ; the long lines of pic-nic
booths built up on the river-bank opposite Arashi-yama ;
and the care-free, merry crowds of sight seers in their best
clothes, make one feel as though the world were made
only for one to be happy in. The next day I was off for
Yoshino. I got there an hour before sun-down. Until
night came, I revelled in the luxury of color which day by
day is now growing richer over that long, up-hill avenue.

わたくし は ちやうど よい じせつ に ゆき-
ました の で, よくあさ くるま で アラシヤマ
へ いつて いくじかん も たのしんで きました。
あの さんぷく の くろみがゝつた ときはぎ
の あひだ から, すひやつ-ぽん の き が まん-
かい に なつて ならんでる ありさま は まこ-
と に みごと でした。 それ に また やま
の ふもと の はう を ぴかゝ と ながれて
ゆく かは や はでやか に かざつて ある かは
の なか の ふね や, アラシヤマ の むかふ-
ぎし に たつて をる かり-ぢやや の ぎようれつ
や, また は はれぎ を きて しんぱい も なく
にぎやか に して をる けんぶつ の ぐんじゆ
など を みた とき は, よ の なか と いふ
もの は まる で たのしむ ため に できて をゝ-
る もの の やう に おもはれました。 その よく-
じつ は ヨシノ の はう へ しゆつたつ して,
ひ の くれる いちじかん ほど まへ に そこ
へ つきまして, よる に なる まで きれい な
はな の いろ を みて たのしんで をりましー
た。 はな の いろ は ちやうど あの ながい
さか の とほり-みち いちめん に, ひにくゝ
きれい に なつて ゆく さいちう で ありましー
た。 こゝ で みた こと は かへつた とき に
みな お-はなし まうしませう。 よくじつ は
また その ち を たちまして, ふつか かゝー
つて やま-ごえ に イセ の ヤマダ へ つきー

I shall tell you all about what I saw there, when I get back. The next day I started again, and in two days more had made my way across the hills to Yamada in Ise.   I saw the sights of that Mecca of loyal Japanese.   I got back to the railway at Tsu the next day, and came on straight to this place, where I am basking in a sunshine almost like that of summer.   The glory of the big grove of plum-trees here is not all gone yet.   I am going up to see it this afternoon.   I may be an enthusiast, but I am having a good time."

ました。こ〻 は ちうぎ な ニホン－じん の
メツカ と も いふ べき ところ で ありまし－
て，わたくし は こ〻 の けしき を けんぶつ
して よくじつ は きしや で ツ へ かへり，
それ から すぐ に この ち へ きまして，
なつ の やう に おもはれる につこう に
ひあたり を して をります。この ち に ある
おほき な うめ の き の はやし は，まだ
その りつば な けしき を なくなして をり－
ません。けふ は でい から，それ を み に
ゆく つもり です。わたくし は どう も や－
つきもの か も しれません が，この ごろ は
じつ に おもしろい こと で ございます。

- - -

だい 志じふ ろく

世 勢

せんどう おほく して ふね やま へ のぼる。

（ロビンソン－し の 志よさい。）

1. ミカター－し：－ア、 お－かへり なさいました か。
お－てがみ を どう も ありがたう ございました。
たいへん よく きうか を お－つかひ の やう
でした ね。 いつ お－かへり で ありました
か。

anretto dezaimasuta

XLVI.   PROVERB FOR (ﬞ) *SE.*

Too many sailors put the ship ashore.

(Mr. Robinson's study.)

1. *Mr. M:*—So you are back? Many thanks for your
letter.   You seem to be making excellent use of your
vacation.   When did you return?

2. ロビンソン－し：－さく－ばん　です。　ろく－じ
じぶん　に　かへる　つもり　でした　が，　はち－
じ　じぶん　まで　きしや　が　「ステーション」　へ
つきません　でした。　この　ごろ　の　てつだう
は　ちつと　も　といのつて　をりません。　わたくし
は　やくにん　の　はう　で　その　せきにん　を
わかち－すぎる　の　で　ないか　と　おもひます。
すぐれた　やくにん　が　いち－にん　だけ　をつた
なら，　この　こんざつ　は　きつと　をさまる　に
ちがひ　ありません。　ご－しようち　の　とほり，
さく－ねん，　こゝ　と　<u>カウベ</u>　と　の　あひだ　の
じかん－へう　が　せう　かはりました　とき　など
も，　ちつと　ばかり　きまり　が　つく　まで　に
は，　ひと－つき　の　よ　も　かゝり，　に－しう－
かん　ほど　と　いふ　もの　は　まるきり
くわうこく　どほり　に　やつて　ゆかう　と　は
しません　でした。

3.－まつたく　その　とほり　でした。　わたくし
も　こゝ　と　<u>オホサカ</u>　と　の　とちう　で　とめ－
られました。　が，　なん　どき　に　きしや　が　くる
と　も，　ゆく　と　も，　いつかう　に　しれない
の　で，　じやうきやく　は　たゞ　「ステーション」
の　そば　に　とゞまつて，　どう　か　なる　の　を
まつて　をる　だけ　でした。

4.－わたくし　は　いつたい　かう　いふ　こと　の
おこる　の　は　あらゆる　じむ　を　ひきすべる

2. *Mr. R :*—Last night. I expected to be at home at about six o'clock, but the train did not reach the station until nearly eight. The railways do not seem to be at all well managed now. I am afraid that the administration is dividing responsibility too much. One first-class manager could bring order out of this chaos, I am sure. Last year, you remember, when the time tables between here and Kyōto were somewhat changed, it was more than a month before anything like regularity was restored. There was about a fortnight when no attempt was made to keep to the published schedules.

3.—Yes, I recollect. I was caught on the road between here and Ōsaka. There was no telling when trains would come or go. The passengers simply stayed about the stations, and waited until something was done.

4.—I suppose that most of the trouble has come from dismissing capable heads of departments, and leaving the

ちから が ある ところ の かしら を おひだ-
して, あまる ほど の した-やくにん の
すき な とほり に しごと を させる から
だ と おもひます。 てつだう の はう で も,
また ふね の はう で も, じうぶん に
ちから が あり, また せきにん が ある
かしら を いち-にん もちゆる の は, いくら
できて も たくさん の した-やくにん を
もちゆる より は はるか に まし です。

5.—とにかく, あなた が お-かへり なさい-
まして, うれしう ございます。 これ から しば-
らく は お-うち に いらつしやいませう。

6.—ところ が, わられない の です。 もし
わるい てんき の ため に さまたげられ さへ
しなければ, わたくし は しまひ まで さくら
の はな を みる つもり です。 ムカウジマ へ
は ゆかう と は おもひません が コガネ井
と ホリノウチ と へ は ゆく つもり です。
わたくし は ホリノウチ は さくら の めい-
しよ の うち で, いちばん いい ところ だ
と おもひます。 あそこ の はな は たいてい
みな おほき な やへ-ざくら です。 さく の
も また いちばん をはり です。 てんき の
いい ひ に あそこ へ いつて もと の
「ハチマン」 の ぢない を とほつて 井ノカシラ
へ ゆき ます の は, トウキヤウ へん で

service at the mercy of too many under-officers. For a railway, as well as for a ship, one thoroughly competent and responsible head is far better than a dozen, even though skilful, sub-managers.

5.—At any rate I am glad to see you back. I suppose you will rest awhile now at home.

6.—Indeed not! I shall see the cherry-flowers through to the end, unless bad weather stops me. I am not going to Mukōjima. There is too much of a crowd there, on too narrow a road, for real pleasure. But I am going to Koganei and to Hori-no-uchi. Hori-no-uchi is to me one of the most enjoyable of all the cherry-places. The flowers there are nearly all the big, double-blossomed *yae-zakura.* They come last. The ride out there, and to I-no-kashira through the old Hachiman temple grounds in good weather is one of the most attractive, to my liking, of all around Tōkyō.

の わたくし の いちばん すき な あそび で
ございます。

———

だい 志じふ 志ち
す そ

すみかき の なか から めいけん が でる。

1. ミカター し:―せんすゐ の ふた を おーとり
なさいました ね。 うを は よほど なくなり―
ました か。

2. ロビンソン―し:―さん びき だけ は ふゆ の
うち に しんだ やう です が, まだ せん―
すゐ に は ひやく から う へ をります。
たいへん に しあはせ で ございました。 ふた
は キャウト へ ゆく ま へ に とらせた の
です。

3. ―ひじやう に おもしろい たび で ございー
ましたらう。 ちつと も わるい てんき に
おーあひ で ありません でした か。

4. ―イセ の くに を とほつて をります
とき, すこし ばかり あめ に あひました。 が,
もう ヨシノ の はな を みた あと で ありー
まして, あめ も あらし と いふ ほど に
ひどく なり は 志ません でした。   .

XLVII. PROVERB FOR (ず) *SU.*

Famous swords are sometimes made from fire-scrapers.

1. *Mr. M :*—I see you have taken the cover off your pond. Did you lose many fish ?

2. *Mr. R :*—No ! Three, I think, died during the winter. There are more than two hundred in the pond. I have been quite fortunate. I had the cover taken off before I went to Kyōto.

3.—You must have had a wonderful trip. No bad weather at all ?

4.—Only a slight shower when I was crossing the Ise country. But I had seen the Yoshino flowers then. The rain did not amount to a storm.

＊   ＊   ＊   ＊   ＊

5.—けふ は ちつと い〻 お-はなし を もつて あがりました。 志つけんじやう が 志-あがりまして, ハツメイ-はくし は ごぐわつ の はじめ から 志ごと を はじめ やう と して をられます。

6.—ソンナニ はやく なりました か〻 よほど きびん に お-やり なさいました ね。

7.—ハイ, はじめる 志ぶん に は すこし いはひ を する つもり です が, あなた も どうか お-いで なさつて くださいません か。 ごぐわつ やうか の に-じ から 「サンエンテイ」 で いたします つがふ です。

8.—まゐつて も よければ まこと に けつこう です。 こ〻ろ から わたくし は お-いはひ まうします。

9.—その つぎ に まうしあげましたい の は, ハヤシ さん は ごく ねつしん な さんせい-じや に なられまして, ご-じぶん の きふきん を に-ばい に されました うへ, あの かた の ちから の およぶ だけ は, ハツメイ-はくし の じげう の ため に せいふ の ほじよ を え やう と して をられます。

10.—それ は ます〱 けつこう です。 わたくし

*   *   *   *   *

5.—I came over with a bit of good news for you. The hospital laboratory is finished. Dr. Hatsumei expects to begin work there early in May.

6.—So soon? You have been enterprising.

7.—Yes! We shall have a little celebration at the opening. Will you come? It will be on the 8th of May at two o'clock, at the *San yen-tei.*

8.—I shall be much pleased to be there. I congratutate you with all my heart.

9.—Then I wish to say too, that Mr. Hayashi has become one of our most earnest supporters. He has doubled his subscription and is determined, as far as he can bring it about, to get government assistance for Dr. Hatsumei's work.

10.—Better and better! I give in. I misjudged Mr. Hayashi entirely.

は ほんたう に <u>ハヤシ</u> さん を ごかい して をつた の です。

11.—こんにち あがりました の は, もう ひとつ の こと が あります の で。<u>コウバフダイシ</u> の 「いろは」 うた を ぉ-め に かけたい と ぉもふ の です が, あなた は ご-ぞんじ です か。

12.—イーエ, みた こと が ございません。

13.—さう です か。 たぶん あなた も ぉぼえて ゐらつしやいませう が, さくねん の ふゆ あなた の ぉ-はなし の けいこ の ため に きめました ことわざ の へう は たいてい ぉ-しまい に なりまして, いま で は のこ-らず の ことわざ を いろ〳 の かたち に して, いろ〳 の ばあひ に あてはめて しまひ-ました が, これ は よほど あなた の ぉ-やく に たつた と ぉもひます。 かない は あなた の ぉ-はなし は <u>モウ</u> たい〳〵 らく に でき-て, まつたく <u>ニホン</u> じん の とほり だ と まうして をります。 とにかく, わたくし-ども は いち〳 「いろは」 を しらべて たいてい できる だけ ひと-とほり の かたち を とらせ-ました。 もつとも, まだ 「ん」 の じ が のこ-つて をつて, これ に あたる ことばざ は こしらへて ありません。 が, 「ん」 で は どんな ぶんしやう を も はじめる こと が できん

11.—Another thing brought me over to-day. I want to show you Kōbō Daishi's *I-ro-ha* hymn. Do you know it ?

12.—I never saw it.

13.—Well! Perhaps you have remembered that we are now finishing the list of the proverbs I laid out last fall for your practice-talk. We have had the proverbs in use in all shapes, and under all sorts of circumstances. They have been of great service to you. I can easily see that. Mrs. Mikata says, that you speak now with great ease, and altogether like a Japanese. In one way or another, we have had every one of the *I-ro-ha* before us, and turned them around in almost every ordinary form the syllables can take. There remains the " *N* " character to be sure, for which I did not propose any proverb. But " *N* " can not begin any sentence. We can use it, however, in a way that will not be much out of place. We can put it on to the end of a sentence. I have a proverb for "*N*" used in that place. With that proverb we can appropriately close our *I-ro-ha* talks.

の です。 しかし あまり むり で ない やう
に つかふ こと も できませう。 すなはち
ぶんしやう の をはり に おかれます。 ちう
いふ ふう に した 「ん」 の じ に ひとつ
の ことわざ が あります が, この ことわざ
で 「いろは」 の はなし を しまつたら てうど
よからう と おもひます。

14.—どう いふ ふう です か。

———

だい 志じふ はち

ん

いち じ せん きん。

1. ミカター し:—かしとき をしへ に したがへば,
わたくし-ども の はなし に つかつて をつた
もんじ は みな せんきん の あたひ が ある
と いふ の です。

2. ロビンソン し:—けつこう。 ソレデハ わたく-
し-ども は ひじやう な かねもち です ね。
しかし マア じようだん は やめまして, わた-
くし は じつ に せんきん で も つくなふ
こと が できぬ ほど の ごーしんせつ を
うけました。

... ... zhitsu ni senkin de ... ... tsukunafu
... ... koto ... ...
uke mashta.

14.—How ?

———

XLVIII.   PROVERB FOR (人) *N.*

One letter is worth a thousand dollars.

1. *Mr. M :*—By accepting the wise saying that every one of the letters we have been using for our talks is worth a thousand pieces of gold.

2. *Mr. R :*—Well done ! How rich we are ! But, all joking aside, I am exceedingly indebted to you for a thousand kindnesses ! I never could repay them even with a thousand pieces of gold.

3. イ、エ　どう　いたしまして。「いろは」は　もう　すみました　が,「いろは」の　はなし　を　させました　いうじやう　は　まだ　すみません。それ　は　なほ　すーねん　の　あひだ　つゞく　だらう　と　おもひます。

4.―それ　では,　あなた　は　いま　まで　まなんで　をりました　もじ　で　できてる　志　の　うち　で　をはり　の　しーく　に　ある　えんせいーてき　の　はんだん　に　いつち　は　なさいますーまい。

5.―どう　いふ　の　です　か。

6.―さいしよ　の　しーく　は,　さくねん　の　じーふいちぐわつ　わたくし　の　ところ　の　には　で　よみました　が,　あなた　は　おぼえて　おーいで　です　か。

7.―おぼえて　ゐます　と　も。おつしやつた　とほり　に　おぼえて　ゐます。

いろ　は　にほへど
ちりぬる　を
わが　よ　たれ　ぞ
つね　ならむ。

8.―それ　から　さき　の　「いろは」　の　く　は　チヤンバレンーし　に　したがへば　かう　いふ　ふう　です。

3.—Pray don't mention that! We have gotten through with the *I-ro-ha,* but we have not gotten through with the friendship which has carried us in our talks over the letters. That is to go on, I trust, for many years yet.

4.—You do not, then, accept the pessimistic judgment which makes up the last four lines of the poem that is formed by the characters we have been studying.

5.—How is that?

6.—I repeated the first four lines in my garden last November ; do you recollect?

7.—Oh! yes. As you read them :—

> *Iro wa nioedo,*
> *Chirinuru wo—*
> > *Waga yo tare zo*
> > *Tsune naran?*

8.—Then, we have had the rest of the *I-ro-ha* in this shape :—

うゐ の おく やま
けふ こえて
あさき ゆめ みし
ゑひ も せず。

チヤンバレン-し は され を やく しまして、
「けふ じんせい の やまぢ を こえし も、
たい つか の ま の ゆめ を みし のみ
にて、ゑひ は せざりき。」と いひました。

9.—イヤ、わたくし は さう いふ しさう を
とり は しません。わたくし は じんせい を
すて やう と は おもひません。こと に じ-
んせい に かぞく や、ともだち など が あれ-
ば なほさら の こと です。それ に わたくし-
ども の「いろは」を まなんだ の も じんせ-
い を きらふ ため で なく して、これ を
すいて、もちゆる ため です。モウ、おーいとま
いたさねば なりません。これ は コウバフダイシ
の うた だ と いふ の です か、コフバウ-
ダイシ は これ を みた こと で さへ も
ある か おほい に うたがはしひ の です。し-
かし、て は いて です。うた の なか
の く は みな「いろは」じゆん に はじめて
ございます。あなた は かな だけ で できた
し の いみ を おきらひ なさる と どうやう
に、この うた の いみ を も おーきらひ な-
さる か も しれません が、この うた の

"*Ui no oku-yama*
  Kyō koete,
    Asaki yume mishi,
    Ei mo sezu :—

which is, being interpreted, Professor Chamberlain says;—
"Having to-day crossed the mountain-fastness of existence, I have seen but a fleeting dream, with which I am
not intoxicated."

9.—No! I will let that sentiment go. Life, especially
with home and friends in it, I am not willing to give up.
We have learned the *I-ro-ha,* I say, not to hate life,
but to like it and to use it. I must go now. Here is Kōbō
Daishi's hymn. It is very doubtful if Kōbō Daishi ever
saw it. But it is a good piece of writing. Each line in it
begins in succession with the *I-ro-ha.* You may not
like the sentiment of it any more than you do that of the
verses made out of the syllabics only. But, as I say, it is
a good piece of composition, and you may like to keep it as
memento of our *I-ro-ha* talks.

ぶんしやう は, いゝ ぶん だ と おもひます
から,「いろは」の はなし を した きねん に
ほぞん なさつたら いかゝ です。

10.—ソレデハ けふ は お-わかれ まうします。
はな-み を お-しまひ なさつたら, すぐ に ま-
た お-いで なさいまして わたくし かた の
には で お-あそび なさいまし。さやうなら。

———

10.—Good bye, for to-day.   As soon as you get through with your flower-seeing come over and rest yourself in my garden.   Good morning !

———

いろは わさん。

まへ の しやう の はなし ありし より すー
じつ の のち なる が, ミカター-し の もと
へ ゆうじん ロビンソン-し より いつ-つう の
てがみ とゞきたり。 てがみ の うち に しも
の ごとき ぶん ありたり。

『せんじつ あなた より きふ-とふ ちう の
ゆくわい なる おーはなし の きねん に ちやう-
だい いたしました 「いろは わさん」 は ひじ-
やう に おもしろう ございました。 あなた が
コウベフ-だいし は この うた を みた こと
で さへ も ある か しらん と おつしやつた
の は ごーもつとも で ございます。 わたくし
の しよき は ごーしようち の とほり ニホン
の ぶんがく に は くらからぬ はう で ありー
ます が, この うた は クワイハン と いふ
ある ばうさん の かゝれた もの だ と いひー
ました。それ から この うた の ひやうだい
に は 「のり の はつ-ね」 と ある さう です。
クワイハン は コウベフ-だいし が ほどけ の
みち を ニホン の ひと に をしふる ため
に 「いろは」 を つくりし ごとく, じぶん も
コウベフ-だいし の きねん の ため に だいし
の つくられました 「いろは」 の もじ を とり,
それ を じぶん の うた の く-ごと の

I-RO-HA HYMN.

A few days after the last conversation took place, Mr. Mikata received from his friend Robinson a letter which, in part, read as follows :—

"I have been exceedingly interested in the *I-ro-ha* hymn which you gave me the other day as a memento of our pleasant talks during the past winter. But you are more than right in your doubt as to whether Kōbō Daishi ever saw it. My secretary, who is, as you know, familiar with Japanese literature, tells me that this hymn was written by a certain Buddhist priest named Kwai Han. I am told also that the book-title of the hymn is *Nori no Hatsu-Ne* or 'First Note of the Law.' Kwai Han, it is said, wrote,—as Kōbō Daishi composed the *I-ro-ha* that he might clearly teach the essential law of Buddha to the Japanese people, he would, himself, in honor of his spiritual ancestor, Kōbō, take these same *I-ro-ha* characters and make them the crowns of the separate lines of his own hymn, and thus advance Kōbō's pious object.— I have been amusing myself with making, from my secretary's literal translation of the poem, a metrical paraphrase of the lines—line for line. I enclose a copy of my verse to you in exchange for the original hymn you so kindly gave me. I hope that you will keep my offering, as I shall keep your gift, in memory of our winter's pleasures."

かしら-じ に して, だいし の きぐわん を
とげ やう と した の だ さう で ございー
ます。 わたくし は なぐさみ がてら しよき
の とゝのへました この うた の ちよくやく
にて ゑいーやく の ゐ を つくりました。 べつし
うつし は せんじつ ちやうだい いたしました
もと の うた の おーれい に けんじやう
いたします。 わたくし は あなた の くだされー
もの を ほぞん して おきます から あなた
も この しな を きふーとふ の たのしみ の
きねん に ほぞん して おーおき なさる やう
に ねがひます。

のり の はつーね。

いたづらごと に ひ を かさね、

ろくしゆ るてん の たね を まき、

はかなく この よ を すごす なり。

にんげん しやう を うけし より、

ほどけ に なる は いま なる ぞ、

へんじ も たのめ しんず べし。

とかく この よ は ゆめ の よ の、

ちり に まじはる うき み なり。

りんき はらだち にくて ぐち、

Nori no Hatsu-Ne.

In spending my days chasing things that are trifles;

In sowing the seed of the six-fold migration ;

I pass through the world with my life-purpose baffled.

Since gaining a birth among those that are human,

Just now I have learned that I may become godlike,

So now I seek Buddha's help, trusting the promise.

This world, after all,—it is only a dream-world ;

And we, after all, are vain selves with dust mingled.

Our jealousies, angers and scoffing reproaches,

ぬらくら かざる あく ごう も、
るいせき つひ に やま と なり、
をのれ と をつる さんづ がは、
わが なす わざ の むくひ なり。
かならず たにん を うらむ まじ。
よ に ながらへて いなづま の、
たゝ いつしやう は ゆめ の よ ぞ、
れんり と ちぎる つま や こ も、
それ も しばし の なさけ なり。
つくゞ おもへ わが こゝろ、
ねんゞ うき よ に ほだされて、
なむ と たのみし こと も なし、
らいせ の こと は ばじ の かぜ、
むじやう の あらし いつ の こと、
うそ ばし いふ と うたがふて、
いま の いま まで ひ を くらし、
のぞみ は すべて のち の ため、
おもへば わが み が うらまし や。
くろう の うち に うれしき は、
やみ じ を てらす み-ほとけ の、

All evils we do, though disguised by our cunning,

At last become massed like the bulk of a mountain,

And we are cast down to " The River of Three Paths; "—

A fitting reward for our self-prompted actions,

Whose ills each must bear, never blaming another.

Live I a long life,—'tis like flashing of lightning.

Live I but one life,—lo ! 'tis lived in a dream-world.

Grow I into one life with wife and with children,

The love of such one life abides but a moment.

Think how to the depths has my heart been affected !

Engrossed by my bonds to a world that is fleeting,

Naught led me to pray,—" *Namu Amida Buddha ;* "

As wind to a horse-ear were things of the future ;

Reminded of death's blast, I answered, " When comes it?"

The preacher I trusted not ; thought he spoke falsely ;

And so has my time sped to this very moment.

Desire I thought was for good that would follow ;—

Oh ! how I lament as I think of what has been.

But yet in this troubled life comes consolation :—

Adorable Buddha enlightens the dark way ;

まつせ の しゆじやう を あはれみて、

けやく に めぐる をん じひ は、

ふち に も やま に も ひし がたし。

こうだい む〜ん の ご−けどう に、

えんじ あふ み ぞ ありがたき。

てんじやう てんげ を ゆびさして、

あまねく しゆじやう を さとし ける。

さながら ゆいほう うけし み は。

きえ ぶつ ぼう そう の さん ぼう を、

ゆめ に も となへ たてまつれ。

めい ご は こゝろ の はな なれば、

みだ も らせつ も あらはるゝ、

しんく こらし ねんず べし。

ゐう り さんづ の せいぐわん は、

ひとへ に まんだら いつ けん を、

もとめし ゑにし の くどく なり。

せめて くせう の とく あれば、

すぐ に じやうど に いりぬ べし。

——◦→≻◦≺←◦——

Has pity on all those who live in these last days ;

To all gives compassion and blessed redemption,

Whose depth or whose height passes ocean or mountain.

To Buddha's salvation so bountiful, boundless,

Thanksgiving forever ;—to me it is given.

Up pointing towards heaven, down pointing 'neath heaven,

The Buddha sheds light upon all who are living.

Now, knowing the Law as the Law has been given,

The blest triple treasure,—Rite, Priesthood and Buddha,—

I lift up my song, though I sing in a dream-world.

If sorrow and knowing are both the mind's flowering ;

If demon or Buddha with each is attendant ;

Then let all my faith upon knowing be centered.

Up-striving, away from " The River of Three Paths,"

A glance at the Fulness Divine of all Goodness

Will gladden my eyes,—the reward of my striving.

Recite then the Prayer ;—for by its mere virtue

Your pathway will enter the " Land of the Holy."

NOTES ON THE CONVERSATIONS.

CONVERSATION FIRST.

だい さん,—"Third," see paragraph 283, page 180.   しやう, "Chapter," pronounced *shō*, see paragraph 50, 1.

For どし read どうし,—adverb indicating association or companionship, as here, "Friends together speaking."

"Proverb,"—を,—accusative sign, see paragraphs 106, and 247. きいて, gerund form of the verb きく, "hear," see 163; see also 97, "Proverb 1." and 98, *b.* じふ,—*jifu* pronounced *jŭ,* see 50, 1.

"Place etc."—literally, "Here as for (it) is Tōkyō's Mr. Mikata's house. Mr. Mikata, being in south-fronting room, before (a) flower-garden is doing (a) writing thing." In this description, given in written rather than in colloquial style, し is substituted for さん, (295,) the ordinary term for "Mr." なり = colloquial だ, or です, which are contractions of the verb ある, or でざる, "to be," combined with the particle で, which emphasizes merely the "being" when compounded with these verbs. せる = colloquial してゐる, a combination of the gerund form of する, (197), and the verb ゐる "be." It expresses being in action. にて = the colloquial で (250). なし = ねて "doing." をれり = colloquial ゐる = "be," "is."

SPECIAL EXPLICATION.—It is advisable for the student before entering upon a study of the "Conversations" to familiarize himself with a few special facts concerning the important verbs ある and ゐる, just spoken of, together with ねる another much used equivalent of the English "to be."

a. ある. Simple positive existence, or possession, is indicated by the verb ある, see 273, 274. ある consequently has ordinarily the meaning "there is," or "(I) have." For its peculiar forms in inflection, see 167. But a negative conjugation for ある does not exist in speech, excepting the negative probable present, あるまい, see 187. Instead, the adjective form ない meaning "not existing," is used in its various inflections for the conjugation of ない, see "Inflection of the Adjective,—Negative Forms," 219, where ない is inflected with あたらしく and ふるく.

b. ある becomes polite when its Main Stem あり is used with ます, for which, see 197. ある becomes yet more polite when, from あります, it becomes でざります, usually in speech でざいます. No real change of meaning takes place with these changes made for the sake of courtesy. あります and ございます have proper negative conjugations.

c. When the particle で is prefixed to ある or ござる and their various forms of inflection, the meaning of the combined result is that simply of "being." The notion of "possession" disappears. で is another form for the gerundial particle にて, "being." で ある or で ござる expresses merely "being." But, as usually spoken, で ある, で あらう etc., are abbreviated into だ, だらう (darō), だつた (datta), etc., and で あります, で ございませう, で ございました etc., become です, でせう, でした etc. see "Examples" in 241 and 243, for the use of some of these forms; see also 192.

d. There are other verbs much used in polite intercourse terminating with ある, such as いらつしやる, "being in a place" = "dwell," "come," "go;" くださる "being in descent" = "condescend," "give from above;" なさる, "causing to be" = "deign to do" = "please do;" おつしやる, "being under instruction" = "please to communicate to another" = "deign to say." These verbs, like ござる, when, for increased courtesy's sake they are combined with ます, are as a rule written いらつしやいます, くださいます, なさいます, おつしやいます and thus throughout their inflection forms. The imperatives in simple form of these verbs are by usage いらつしやい, ください, なさい, and sometimes おつしやい. In more courteous form their imperatives are those regularly formed with ます, e.g. いらつしやいまし, なさいまし, etc. Yet other changes in the inflection of these verbs take place, Most noticeable among these is the elision of the a in the terminal ある in several other inflection forms than those already noted, e.g. the gerund of いらつしやる is not いらつしやつて but いらして, of なさる is not なさつて but なして etc., etc.

e. ゐる. "State" or "condition of being" finds expression in the verb ゐる, which, chiefly as an auxiliary to other verbs in their gerundial form, gives a continuative force to such verbs. This association of ゐる with other verbs is very like in effect the association of the English verb "to be" with participial forms of other verbs, such as "is writing," "is sleeping," "am studying." ゐる frequently coalesces with the gerund forms by merging its i sound into the final sound of the gerund, e.g. して ゐる "is doing" may become してる; ねて ゐる, "is sleeping," ねてる. ゐる is conjugated in simple form according to the second conjugation, It appears in polite form with ます, as ゐます, etc., etc.

f. れる. There is but little, if any, difference in ordinary usage between れる and ゐる. Both the words indicate "state" or "condition of being." れる may at one time have referred by preference to living or moving beings. The inflection of れる is made according to the first conjugation. Its polite form is れります.

In the First Conversation the student will find nearly all the specifications of these verbs, here given, amply illustrated.

REMARK 1.

NOTE. In these notes the *figures* in the middles of the pages refer to the separate remarks of the speakers in the "Conversations." The side *letters a, b, c.* etc. refer to the successive sentences in the "remarks." The *numbers within the text* of the notes refer to the paragraphs of the book, unless otherwise specified.

a. いりきたり, = colloquial はいつて きて, = "coming entering." はいつて, gerund of はいる, "enter," 167. きて gerund of くる, "come," 197. あいさつ を して. literally "doing greeting" = "bows." むかひ.—Main Stem of むかふ, (168). "to stand with the face towards." The Japanese phrasing, in somewhat literal form is,—"Mr. Robinson, coming into this place, makes salutation, and fronting Mr. Mikata" (says). See 96.

b. れ-はやう ございます, etc., 309.

c. れ-じやま etc., "Will there not be honorable obstruction?" That is, "If I come in shall I not interrupt you?" The honorific れ is used, not because the interruption is worthy of honor, but because everything connected with an honored person spoken to, should be spoken of with respect, 295. For the polite inflection of a verb with ます, see 189. See 218, for the form はやう, or the adjective forms preceding ござる. See 240, for this use of は. See 100, for meaning of か as used here. ありますまい is polite probable present negative form of the verb ある, "be," with ます, "be." See 189—191.

2.

a. イーエ, 233. すこし も, 309.

b. れ-かけなさいまし, 193, *e.* かけ.—Main Stem of かける, second conjugation; see 145. The phrase is an abbreviation from こし を かける, "to place the loins," = "to sit."

c. れ-まち まうして ゐた さころ です. まち,—Main Stem of まつ (166) "wait." まうして,—gerund of verb まうす "speak," much used with other verbs as an auxiliary to show respect in address. ゐた,— certain past of ゐる "be." さころ, literally "place," and has the force here of the phrase, "just the time when." The sentence is equivalent to " I have just been awaiting you."

3.

a. **ありがたう ございます,**—193. 218.

b. **はなはだ,** etc., " Very rude being is (it), but in this way (I) sit." **が** "but," 267. An apology for an awkward manner in taking his place upon the matting in a Japanese room. **はなはだ,** 227.

4.

a. **どうぞ,** etc. " Please at (your) honorable convenience (sit down)." **ご,**—a polite prefix, 295. The sentence is incomplete, like many sentences heard in Japanese conversation. Here the words "sit down," are not spoken, but understood,—102.

b. **いす は** etc. "As for a chair how is (it)?" **は** pronounced *wa,* see 42. For **は** as used here, 240.

c. **いす の はう,** etc. " The chair's side, cushion than, easy is." **はう,**—" side," is much used in talk to specify persons, things, places. Here it specifies a chair as being much more comfortable for sitting on than a floor-cushion. **より,** gives comparative value to **らく,** see 211. See for construction, 96, *Exception.*

5.

a. **イーエ との やう に,** etc,—literally, " In this manner shoving out my feet even, if it is well, this way, on the contrary, is a convenience for me." **やう に,** 229. **も,** 270. **よろし-ければ** conditional present verbal form of the adjective **よろし,** "good," 219. **かつて,** gerundial adverb, 231.

6.

a. **さあこと,** mark of repetition of the syllable, 74. **さあ,**—exclamation urging compliance with the request, 280. Another example of incomplete speech = " There! At ease!" (place yourself), 102.

b. **さ,** 275. **の,** sign of possessive case, 106 and 245. **なか,** here, "intimacy" of friendship. " In our intimacy, ceremony enters not."

c. **コレ,** an exclamation sometimes used in calling a servant; but even here an abrupt direct imperative is replaced by the politer form **もって た-いで,** " which in usage, but not literally, means " bring!" 299.

d. **ちまつ な,** etc., literally, "Coarsely made tobacco, but deign to partake." The Japanese are in the habit of depreciating, but merely as a form, their gifts to others, however excellent the things may be. **ちまつ な,** 221. **が,** 267, **めし-あがり,** 297.

7.

a. いかにも, etc., literally, "Indeed, a splendid garden it is, isn't it?" けつとう pronounced *kekkō*, 55 and 43. ね, 221. ね, 280.

b. こなた, etc. lit. "As for here (this side) because (から) entirely cold wind protected from is, although (が) this morning outside really cold wind blowing is, this room as for perfectly warm being is." まつたく, (228) from まつたき, "whole." さむい, (215) from さむ, "cold," から, 269. じつに, "really," 229. さむい かぜ が, see for this が, 239. をります が, see for this が, 267. あつたか, pron. *attaka*, is a Tōkyō abbreviation of あたたか, "warm."

8.

a. かんちう, etc.,—lit.—"The midst of the cold season even, the sun's shining time during, (に) the *shōji* all being left open, (here) one can live," 97. でも, (277) a phrase conjunction meaning "even," "although." に, 253. ひ の さき に, "in the time of the sun's shining." をられます potential present form of をる to "live," or "be,"—200 and 203.

b. につちう に, etc. 253. も,—270. いりません polite negative present form of いる "want," "need."

c. ほさんど, etc., here literally, "Very much, by the sun I can be shone upon, in degree." ほさんど ——— くらゐ, expressive of the great measure of the sun's shining. てり-つけられる present potential of てり-つける "shine upon."

d. いつぶく "a sip;" for *fuku* see 281; for change of ふく to ぶく see 122, SPECIAL NOTE. ね あがり なさいまし,—polite substitute for the direct imperative, 193, *e.*

9.

a. ありがたう,—102.

b. さき に, etc., somewhat literally,—"Now, (さき に) recently (この あひだ) the proposed (ね-はなし いたして をきました, speech-doing-put) conversations (くわいわ) although (が) to-day (けふ は) wishing to begin, (はじめたう ございます), you (あなた は) as yet (まだ) concerning that (それ に ついて) any good thought (なに か よい ね がんがへ が) has not been? (ございません でした か)." Or "Now, although wishing to begin to-day our recently proposed conversations, have you as yet any good plan concerning them?" Study this sentence in connection with the paragraphs 96, 97, 100 and 101. さき に,— "at the time" = "now," = "well!" この あひだ,—"this while," = "recently," = "the other day." ね-はなし いたして をきました

くわいわ,—"speech doing put conversation" = "conversation put into speech," = "conversations we spoke of." The student has already probably noticed the redundancy of verbal forms peculiar to Japanese speech ;—as here, the apparently superfluous use of をきました. The sense intended is complete without it. Explanatory of the use of this verbal form here, and of much else of the kind appearing in these "Conversations," we quote a note from Prof. Chamberlain's "Handbook." He says,—"The Japanese have a great fondness for rounding off their sentences by one of the equivalents for "to be," or by *kuru*, *oku*, *shimau*, or *yaru*. The plain verb, without one or other of these auxiliaries, is apt to sound bald.—Where an English idiom for the most part simply states the occurrence of an action, Japanese idiom delights in describing more particularly the manner of the action's occurrence with reference to the subsidiary ideas of "coming," "finishing," etc. which the auxiliaries express. For instance, an English maid-servant, speaking of a piece of dirty linen, will say, 'I will have it washed, Sir.' Her Japanese sister would say "*Arawashite okimashō*,—lit.," 'Having caused (some one) to wash (it, I) will put (it),' "that is to say," 'I will have it washed *and there it will be*.' The simple verb merely states the dry fact. The addition of the auxiliary makes the action seem to pass vividly before you. The sentence becomes life-like and picturesque." けふ pronounced *kyō* (44). はじめたう polite desiderative form of はじめる, "begin," 193. ついて gerund of つく "cleave to," "belong." について, 256. なに か, 131. また, 227. ございません でした, 192.

c. と—しようち etc. somewhat literally, "As you know, as for words, already (I am) tolerably acquainted, and (し) hearing (きく とき) also as for the most part (I) understand, but (が) when (き) it becomes (なる) to (に) speaking (はなす とき) really (じつ に) (I am) troubled (とまります). と—しようち の とほり,—lit., "way of honorable assent" = "as you know." もう an abbreviation of もはや = "already." も,—274. For use of とき as here きく とき, and はなす とき, see 112. じつ に, 229.

d. それ ゆゑ, etc. lit. "Therefore, by some means, your manner of person, that drill (I) wish to do." それ ゆゑ, "upon that" = "therefore." どうか, a compound of the interrogative か, and the adverb どう, "how?" is equivalent to the questioning, "how shall it be done?" and the answering, "somehow or other." と, is a conjunction particle indicating that which has been thought by the speaker,—see 275, *b.* See also 99.

10.

a. しかし, etc. lit., "But only for the sake of (ため のみ に) speaking, (はなし を する), as for the thing called speaking, (はなし を する さ いふ の は) rather tedious thing (it) is." さ いふ の see 128, 130; but also note that the particle の here stands as an equivalent for とさ "thing," or "act." The expression さ いふ is one of the commonest idioms of Japanese speech. It is used to distinguish, or to specify definitely, something named; as につぽん さ いふ くに, "The country called Japan," = "Japan." はる さ いふ をんな, "The woman called Haru," = "Haru." ふで さ いふ もの, "The thing named writing-brush," = "pen."

b. わたくし は etc.,—rather freely,—"As for me, (if) somehow you, my country's words, freely way of using, acquire, good, that I think." ね-つかい なさる, = "use;" the verbal form つかひ is made polite by the addition of なさる. Mr. Imbrie in his "Hand-book of Japanese Etymology" says, "when the person addressed or referred to is the agent in the action, the verb assumes the stem" (Main Stem) "form (excepting those verbs made up of a noun and *suru* in which the *suru* becomes *nasaru*) and is followed by *nasaru* or *ni naru.*" Here it is the main stem of つかふ with なさる. なれば, conditional present of なる, "be," "become."

c. もし それ が etc., "If that you had done, your in Japan living fact, even now than, a great deal interesting become may be." もし, here an adverbial form meaning "if," "perchance," "in case that," etc. でき たら, certain past conditional of できる, "do," "be able." すまひ. Main Stem of the verb すまふ, used substantively, = "period of living," = life, 147. いま より, 265, with 211. ごさいませう probable present, or future, of polite verb ござる "be;" itself in polite form with ます.

d. どういふ, etc, "In what manner, if chosen is good, that, in various ways thinking (I) have looked, but." どう いふ, = "what?" はうはふ, is another spelling of はふはふ pronounced *hōhō*, "method," "mode of doing." よれば, present conditional present of よる, "select" or "choose." か gives an interrogative form to the preceding clause. いろく sign of repetition, 74; plural form for いろ, 104. *c.* さ, a subordinating conjunction, indicating that which had just been said, 275, *b.* かんがへて みました, "thinking have looked," = "have thought and tried." When みる is combined with a gerund it has the meaning of "trying," "seeking." The Japanese sentence is carried forward to the next sentence in the English text by the particle が "but," or "however."

e. あなた が etc. This sentence can hardly be reproduced intelligibly with any nearer approach to literalness than is given in its equivalent on the opposite page. よんだり, かいたり, are alternative forms (137) of よむ and かく "read," and "write," and should be rendered " reading and writing." For euphonic changes of よむ, see 165; of かく see 163. する とき = " to do." When とき is added to the present of a verb it gives the verb somewhat the character of the "infinitive" in English. を-ならひ なさつた とき の とざわざ, "learned-time proverbs," = "proverbs of the time when you learned the *Hiragana*," etc. はなし を して は いかが でせう, "speech making as for, how is (it)?" = "how would you like to talk," etc?

11.

a. あなた は etc., "As for you, because to me service doing condescending, physician that same is, anything in your way of command, (I) shall do." せわ して くださる, "service doing condescending," = "condescending to do service." を-いしや さま さ をねじ です = "physician that same is," = "the same as being a physician to me." を-さしづ どほり に, "by way of command;" *dōri* for *tōri*, see 122, SPECIAL NOTE; pronounced *tōri*, see 45. せわ, "help," して from する (196) "do;" therefore せわ して "assisting," "befriending." くださる, "condescend;" abbreviation of old potential form of くだす *i.e.* くだされる, "to let down," now used as polite expression for "condescension," "receiving as from a superior," 297. See also, "SPECIAL EXPLICATION," p. 533, *d.* を-いしや さま a double honorific for いしや, "physician," 295. あなた の "your," 124.

b. あなた の etc. "Your thought, that named thing as for, what named thing is (it)?" or "What is your plan?" Notice the repetition of の as さ いふ の, and どう いふ の. See Remark 10, *a.*

12.

a. さう です ね.—" like it is!" = "so it is" = " well!" or " why!" as a meditative opening of the sentence. さう contraction of さやう, and this of あの やう, "like that."

b. これら の, etc. "These proverbs' interior, what kind of meaning is, seeking way of looking, is it not?" これら, plurality for これ by adding ら, 104, *b.* and 123. とざわざ の うち, "proverbs' interior," = "in the proverbs. For possessive form, see 106 and 245. どう いふ,

"what called," = "what kind of." さがして み-やう, "way of looking" = "finding out;" compare Remark 10, *d*. み-やう "mode of looking for anything" = "to find out." じや, contraction of the associated postpositions で and は; は serving to give emphasis to で.

c. ことわざ は, etc , "As for a proverb being (で ありまして) turned into things like dollars, being current in the world, riches of people it becomes, (that become thing is)." ドル "dollar," = generic name for "coin" among the Japanese. で ありまして, = "being," has here conjunctive force like が "but," in the same position. Again observe the use of の as equivalent to "thing." For と again see 275, *b*.

d. これら の, etc. "These proverbs, Japan's old precious things a portion are." ふるき "old," see 219.

e. これ が etc. "This, those proverbs are." が, 239.

f. わたくし は, etc. "I, *I-ro-ha* order in, arranging have put." For use of auxiliary れきました "have put," see Remark 9, sentence *b*.

g. これ は, etc. "'This, conversations' themes for making, how will it) be?" に して は, 256.

13.

a. よう ございませう, "Good probably will be!" = "All right!"

b. しかし, etc. "But you, interpreter doing condescending, if it be not becomes not." = "It will not do if you do not kindly become interpreter." In Japanese speech the notion of necessity to do something is conveyed by the use of a double negative, as here, なければ なりません, "if it is not won't do," = "the thing won't do if you are not (interpreter)," = "you must be the interpreter." なければ, present conditional of なかる, (なく and ある) "not is," = "is not."

14.

a. あなた の, etc., "As for your part, by you, sufficiently you can do." で, "by," 250.

b. さて, etc. "So then, hereupon the い proverb is." さて, a word often used either at resuming a conversation or commencing a new subject.

c. わたくし は, etc., "Sometimes, (とき どき) this proverb, really your affair well touches, that I think." ときどき, 74, and 104. *c.* と れるひます, "that I think," = "I think that," of English speech.

d. もちろん, etc. Of course, that (the proverb) "ten hearing one knows" "that (so) made if it were, even a little with you connection is not," = English equivalent on opposite page.

15.

a. ご-あいさつ, etc. "Honorable salutation thankful wish is." = "Thanks for the compliment!" と honorific.

b. との のち, etc. "Hereafter, at praising wishing to receive time, banquet for I will arise."

c. です が, etc. "It is, but, (the) in America called Ireland-man's riddle, that like thing if it were, need is not." Or, "Yes, but I do not need anything like what is called in America an Irishman's puzzle." です が pronounced *desu nga*; ordinarily the *u* in *desŭ* is silent; see 5, *b.* For なぞ a better word would probably be あてつけ, "allusion," "insinuation."

17.

a. あし で もつて, etc. "By foot, me, house's outside to, kicking cast out, (in order that) that house's master, (with) me as guest, not pleased, that thing to let me know, that fact is." で もつて much used as emphatic compound postposition = "by means of." ヘ 246. とのまぬ, "not pleased with," certain present negative of とのむ, "like," "pleased with," 187. For さ いふ, あ いふ, かう いふ, = "that," and "this," as demonstrative pronominal forms, see 128. しらせ, causative form of しる = "know," 206.

18.

a. あなた の, etc. "Your speaking way, as for, this proverb in strange relation usage (use thing) is." The first use of の is as sign of genitive, 215; the second and third uses of の are as equivalents for "fact," or "thing," here used after verbal forms; but see also 261.

b. だ が, etc. "But you with that different thing said by reason of, this proverb's meaning clear became," or, "But by reason of your saying a different thing with it, the meaning of this proverb became clear." だ が, more familiar form of です が, = "It is so, but," Remark 15, *c.* ちがつた, certain past of ちがふ, "differ," 168. おつしやつた, certain past of polite verb おつしやる, "speak," 167. ため に "for the sake of," = "on account of." あきらか に, adverbial form of "clear," 229.

c. しろい もの, etc. "Because (から) also white thing black thing at the side of put, that more white visible way is" の そば に, "beside," 255. なほ, "still more." しろく adverbial form, しろい simple adjective form of しろき, "white." みゆる = みへる, potential form of みる, 205.

19

あて はまりませう, probable present of あて はなる, "apply to," = "true of." いかが でせう, = "How may it be?"

20.

a. とくみん さ して, "Nationally, (as a nation), if seen, fool being (we are) not." さ して "that doing" gives an adverbial quality to the word to which it is annexed. みれば, conditional present of みる, "see." われ〱 = "we," 104 c. では, here は gives force to the postposition で. ありません, negative present of ある, = "be."

b. いち ぶ, etc., "Only (ばかり) one part heard being, conclusion guess at, rather acute (we) are." ばかり "only," 227. さつする, "guess at," pronounced sassuru, 55.

c. わが くに で, = "Our country's." とく りうから する = "most popular." なぞ で できて をります, "made of enigmas;" this phrase does not render well the words, "suggestive fancies" given in the English text.

d. をれ に また, = "Now again." ぎろん の はじめ を "argument's beginning," = "beginning of an argument," with accusative sign を. ただち に, "immediately." うの けつろん, = "that argument's conclusion." とんで ゆく, "flying go." とんで from とぶ, "fly," 165. さ いふ ひなん, "that censure." たび〱 からむります, "often receive." たび〱 230. から むります, polite reference to Japan's critics. "We are often blamed," as politely expressed in Japanese, is "We often receive from our superiors this censure."

21.

a. あなた の を-くに の ひと, "Your honorable country's people," is Japanese polite periphrasis for "your people." よほど = "for the most part," = "very."

b. わたくし の うち の めし つかひ の ものら, "My house's call and message bear things," is considered a rather refined form of expression for the simple English "my servants." Note the plural sign ら with もの, 104, b. たさへば, = "for example." でも, = "even." うまつ なる, = "badly." めいづる とさ, "commands," to inferiors. しようち いたします, "consenting do" = "respectfully listen to."

c. しば しば, "often," 230. をどろく とさ, "astonish thing," = "astonishment," 112. ござります, polite certain present of the polite verb ござる, "be." Hitherto this verb has appeared in these conversations as ございます, which is the usual form for ござる when compounded with ます; the r being then dropped. The same peculiarity is true of the verbs いらつしやる, "go," "come," "be," くださる, "condescend;" なさる "deign to do," and れつしやる, "deign to say." See SPECIAL EXPLICATION, p. 533.

d. うれ とう, "that," with emphatic particle, = "Indeed!" いはう pronounced *irō* = future of いふ. いはう さ れもつて ゐる とさ を, = "that which I thought to say." きかぬ うち に, = "before hearing." うち に with negative of a verb, = "before." れもつてる = れもつて ゐる, see SPECIAL EXPLICATION, p. 533, *e*. しようち した, = "acknowledgment has done," = "have understood." さを pronounced *tō*, "ten."

<h2 style="text-align:center">22.</h2>

a. うの さほり です, "That way is," = "Yes, that is so."

b. わたくし も, etc. "I also, we Japanese people too quick understanding carried to excess, that think." はや がてん, "quick understanding," see 119. とすぎる, "do exceed" = "carry to excess." すぎる, expresses "excess" for an action or thing.

c. われく, etc. "Our minds are quick of perception, (びんせふ) but, on account of that mental quickness some times not known thing even knowing is, that (we) think." しつて ゐる, illustration of a common combination of a gerund with the auxiliary ゐる, or れる, "be," forming compound progressive or continuous tenses corresponding to such English expressions as "I am giving," "I was doing etc." "Sometimes we think that we are knowing even not known things." See page 533, *e*.

d. もつさも, etc., "Properly, there are times, four if hearing we should know six, convenient would be." つがふ の よい, "good of condition," = "convenient," 224.

e. また, etc., "Again, hearing seven and even know three (things) is a splendid thing, but, one (thing) hearing ten know, that thinking, when (さき に) that scarcely heard one thing even was not known, really a not convenient thing (it) will be." れもつて ゐた;—ゐた is certain past of ゐる. しらなかつた, certain past negative of しる, "know." なら, conditional present of なる. ふつがふ, pronounced *futsugō,* = "inconvenient;" ふ, negative prefix.

f. さうして みれば, etc. "Thus, this proverb clever men praising, rightly good thing is, but everybody at once, this his own thing is, that thinking is not good." さうして みれば, "so doing if seen," =

"thus." たれ で る, 131. たれ polite form for だれ. だ, "is," contraction of で and ある, p. 533, c.

23.

a. b. ちやうざ, etc. "Long-sitting-doing, excuse is not." まうしわけ, same as *ii-wake*, "excuse," or "explanation." まうし, polite prefix for verbs instead of いひ.

c. しつれい な こざ, etc. "Rude manner of speech is it, but, your wisdom-concerning-instruction myself for the sake of, becomes your word-concerning-instruction, not an inferior thing." み, "body," or "self." れざる, "to be inferior in excellence."

d. うれ では, etc. "That being, honorable leave say," = "Well then, I must go." Polite idiom used in taking one's departure from another.

24.

a. いま まだ, etc., "As yet plenty of space of time is, but though that, if honorable returning is, again to-morrow (I) await, (you)."

b. ゆふかた, etc. "Evening six o'clock time at, coming thing is (it) not able?" れ-いで なさる こざ, polite expression for "coming." れ-いで なさる, is an honorific phrase verb constantly in use meaning not only "to come," but, according to its context, also "to go," "to dwell in," and "to be."

c. ど-いつしよ に, etc. "Together, evening meal we will eat." いつしよ に, 255. ばん めし, "evening boiled-rice," = "supper." たべませう, probable present or future of たべる, "eat."

25.

a. ありがたう, etc., here very polite use of ござる.

b. れ-ところざし, etc. "Your intention deeply admire (or appreciate)." The use of the honorific れ or ご is, as a rule, a good substitute for "the second person," grammatically speaking, in the impersonal Japanese language, 295. ふかく, adverbial form of the adjective ふかい, 219. しやうくわん いたします, polite form of しやうくわん する, "admire," "praise."

c. さやうなら, the usual equivalent for the English, "farewell!" or "good bye!" lit., "If that be so," leaving certain words to be understood, as, probably, "we shall meet again";—the Japanese "*auf wiedersehen*," or "*au revoir*."

26.

a. b. コレ, etc. "The honorable visitor honorable returning is." Here the honorifics are used *of* the person not *to* him. The servant must put up the with superior だ (*de aru*) instead of the polite で ございます which would be used in an address to the guest.

c. ぼうし さ, etc., "Hat and outside things being." さ, "and," 275.

d. ね き を, etc., "Mind deign to apply," = "Be attentive!" = "Take care of yourself!" ね-つけ なさいまし, polite imperative form of つける "apply," 193, *e.*

CONVERSATION SECOND.

REMARK 1.

a. こんばん は,—"As for this evening," (it is "cool," "warm," "pleasant," etc.,) 102; a salutation, = "Good evening."

b. ひじやう に,—"exceedingly," 229. ぐづ〱, (ぐづ ぐづ) して, "lazy," 232. つひ, etc., "alas, slow became."

2.

a. まだ etc., "Yet so much late is not."

b. やう〱, contraction of やうやく, = "hardly," "scarcely," 74. じつ-ぷん, pronounced *jippun*, 55.

c. わるい, "bad," here = "ill."

3.

a. びやうき, pronoun *byōki.* が, = "but." さくばん, "last evening." さけ, = "rice-wine." のみすぎました,—certain past of のみ-すぎる, "to over-drink." やくに たいん の, "to duty does not stand up one,"= "is not useful," = "not to be depended upon." やく, "duty." たい-ん の, for たいぬ の, "not stand up one." たいぬ, is negative present of たつ, 187.

b. めしつかひ に, = "As a servant." のんだくれて とまります, = "drinking, I am troubled." *i.e.* "he being fatigued by drinking, it troubles me." のんだ くれて, gerund of compound verb, のんだ くれ-る, "exhausted by drinking." とまります, polite from of とまる, a verb used to express one's sense of "annoyance," "perplexity," "trouble."

4.

a. くるま ひき, "*kuruma* pullers," from くるま and ひき, 121. のうちに, "among," 255. あり うち の こと, "customary thing."

b. あれら, "those persons"="their;" not a polite form of expression; 123 and 104. しごと, "work." なか なか, = "more really than one would suppose." ほねが れれます, "bone is broken;" idiom for "hard worked." から, "because." つひ, expression showing "regret," "disappointment," and the like. くせ が つく, "habit sticks to," = "to form a habit."

c. わたくし の うち の, "my house's" = "my own." も, "also." どうも, しかた が ない,—"Even, how doing side is not," = "Really! there is no other way." = "Can't be helped." どうも, 280. しかた, etc., a phrase constantly heard in Japan telling of "helplessnes," or "inevitable submission." と いつて, etc., 275, *b.,* "that saying is," = "that he says."

d. どうぞ とちら へ, etc., "Please, hither mending or adjusting, deign to do," = "Please take your seat there." へ, 261. なほり, from なほる, "be mended," "translated," "cured," etc., 187.

e. ごらん うけ の さほり,—"See, reception's way," = "See, how I receive you." ほんの, abbreviation for ほんさ の, "real." かない の ひざ, = "person of the home," = "member of family." どうやら, "same way."

f. "Japan cookery's different (things), anything is not; = "Nothing other than Japanese food." なに も ございません, 131.

5.

a. わたくし の ため に, "For my sake." ゆふ-とぜん の れしたく, "supper's preparation." かへて くださらぬ はう, "altering do not cordescend side," = "do not change." かへつて, etc., "on the contrary thankfulness is." かへて gerund of かへる, "change," or "alter." かへつて, adverb, "on the contrary," from かへる, "return."

b. けつこう, much used in conversation for the English "fine," "delicious," "splendid," etc.

6.

a. と じいう に, "without constraint," "freely."

b. か, here as interrogation between ビール and さけ. か indicates an alternative. めしあがり ます か, polite form of request concerning one's eating or drinking, 297.

7.

a. いたゞきません, present negative of いたゞく, "put on the head," = "to receive respectfully;" is a polite verb in use for もらふ "receive."

b. ゝれより, = "rather than that," indicates here, preference.

8.

a. もう, "more." なに も, "anything;"—here, with negative verb = "nothing," 131.

b. こゝ に ある もの, "at here being things," = "these things." さげて, from さげる, "lower down," = "to carry away;" gerundial form.

c. いかに, interrogative adverb, "what?" as, here, "what thought?" = "what do you think?"

9.

a. せかい ちう, "the whole world." おこる こと, "arise thing," = "that which happens." てき-ひやう, "fit comment."

b. と-しようち, etc., here = "It is acknowledged." たくみ なる こと;—たくみ, "skill," combined with なる, "become,"=たくみ な こと, = skilful. しんり, "truth." For しやうと, read しようと, "proof."

c. で, here "at" or "in;" so, "children of schools in America." とく よい, "extremely good," = "the best." をしへ の いちぶ, "part of lessons," = "some lessons." まつたく, "wholly." この ことわざ の うち に, "within this proverb."

d. For the use of や here, see 276. また は, is equivalent here to "and also." が as adversative conjunction, "but." れきし, "history," "chronicles." しつて をります, = "knowing is," = "knows;" from しる "know," with auxiliary をる "be." ひさ-びさ plural of ひさ = "men," 104, *c.* いづれ も, "who even," = "every one." もろん に は まけました, "argument in yielded," = "was defeated." まけ- ました polite form of まけた, 188. じつさい の, "really." かち を とりました, "the victory took,"= "were victorious."

10.

a. うの さほり です, "That way is," = "It is that," = "Yes!"

b. かり に, = "for the time being." よ の, "of the world," = "world's." かいかくしや, "reform persons," = "reformers." This しや as used in compound words, = "thing," or "man;" as がく-しや, "learning-man" or "scholar," etc. ふとう, "fitting to," "appropriate to."

c. これ から, "after this," = "now." と いつて よからう と おもひます, "that saying (it) will be well, that I think," = I think it will be well to say that (the IIa proverb is appropriate to bigots, etc.).

d. げじよ, "servant girl." いりきたる, compound verb, from いる, "enter," and きたる, "come."

e. f. あの れ-かた の, "that honorable side of," = "the gentleman's." めい し, = "a visiting card." めい, used in compound words to convey special honor, as "celebrated," "illustrious," etc.; shows great respect on the part of the servant.

g. こちら へ, = "Hither honorable guiding say," = "Ask the gentleman, etc. な, a contraction of なされ, = an affirmative imperative, with the main stem of the verb.

h. きのどく, lit., "poison of spirit," is the common expression of "sorrow for," or "sympathy with," others. と い まで, "until here," = "at this place." れかなければ なりません, "if not put aside will not do" = "must stop," Conv. 1, 13, *b.*

i. "Really now from Kyōto a friend having come," etc. たいせつ な, "important." さるだち が ひとり, 104, *a.*

j. ねがわれませう, = "may I ask," from ねがふ "to ask." The negative stem of ねがふ is ねがわ, 169. From the negative stem is formed the passive or potential form ねがわれる, (200) whose polite form is ねがわれます, of which the future as ねがわれませう, = "may I ask, or "expect," or, in this connection, with か = "can you come?"

11.

a. いつでも, "when whatever, = "at any time," or "always."

b. "For (で) my pleasure." (れ-じやま, etc.,) "obstruction doing becomes not," = "must not become an inconvenience."

c. いつ も, "always." うけて, "receiving." たいてい なん じ とろ, "about what hour time?" ひま, "leisure."

12.

a. すぐ のち, = "immediately after." なら, contraction of ならば, = "if." いち ばん よい = "best," 213.

b. れ-いで なれば, = "if you come." いたされませう, potential future of いたす, "can be done." じうぶん, "fully."

13.

a. れくさま from れく, "back part of the house," with the honorific suffix さま, = "lady of the house;" it having been customary for a lady in ancient Japan to stay in rooms remote from the front of a house. よろしく, "well," = "compliments;" the words "please say," = "present," or "give," being understood, 102.

b. どうぞ とれ にて, "Please with this," *i.e.* "Please stop here."

c. **げんくわん**, etc., "As far as the porch it is unrest," = " I shall be very much disturbed if you go with me to the door." The phrase is a polite protest.

14.

a. **いや**, etc., "No, there is no reason at all for being disturbed."

b. **それ に**, "besides." **むかへ に でます から**, "because to meeting go out," = "because I go to meet." **でます**, from **でる**, "go out."

c. **てうちん**, pron. *chōchin*, etc., "Lantern honorable possession is?" = " Have you a lantern?"

15.

a. **みち**, etc., "Way well knowing is," = " I know the path well."

b. **お-やすみ なさい**, "Honorable rest deign to do," = "Good night!"

CONVERSATION THIRD.

The accusative sign **を** should be inserted in the "Proverb" before **のぞく**.

REMARK 1.

a. **しばらく**, etc., a customary form of apology,—"For some time honorable negligence have done." **しばらく**, "some time," long or short. **ご-ぶさた**, "remissness," from **さた**, "communication," **ぶ**, negative prefix, and **ご**, honorific prefix for the sake of the person addressed.

b. **ごらん に なりました か**, = " Have you seen?" **ごらん**, "august look," used only in polite address to another, 297.

2.

a. **ハイ**, exclamatory acknowledgment. It may mean "Yes!" or "I hear you," 233 and 280.

b. **ぜんくわい**, = "complete restoration to health." **だらう**, a familiar verb form from **で** and **あらう**;--**あらう** being the probable present of **ある**, "be." The two words here = I suppose," or "I hope." **いったい**, literally, "one person," but used here adverbially, = "really";—thus, "Really what having deigned to do thing is it?" = "What happened?"

3.

a. **かぜ を**, etc., "Wind having drawn, cruel affair met," = "Having caught cold I had a severe experience."

b. せんだつて, etc., "Recently here to came (time), the day after affair it is."

c. d. うして, "and." あるいて あがりました の で, "walking went up thing, by means of." ひじやう に あつく なつて きました, "exceedingly hot became," (becoming came). あせ を かく, "perspire." たいさう, = "freely."

e. ところ が, = "So then." てら, "temple." さき に, "in time" = "when." ふいて ゐまして = "was blowing," see 98. *b*; see also p. 543, 22, *c*. しばらく の あひだ, "period of short time," = "a little while." きうそく いた して をります さ, "rest doing, that being," = "to rest." In the sentence, つひ ぞく〻 さ さむく なつて をりました, the words ぞく〻 さ さむく, express the chill and cold feeling of "catching cold;" なつて をりました, "becoming came." = "became."

4.

a. ぶようじん, from ようじん, "caution," or "prudence," and ぶ, negative prefix. ね, 280.

b. もち で なかつた, "possession being without," = "not having." もち from もつ, "to hold" or "possess." なかつた "was not," or "had not;" certain past of なかる, (なく and ある), "is not," or "have not." See 219, negative verbal forms of adjective. Also above, Conversation 1. "SPECIAL EXPLICATION," p. 532, *a.*

5.

a. もつて, etc., "As for having it was, but," etc. ふもさ の はう, "mountain foot's side," = "at the foot of the mountain." はう, "side." Conversation 1. Remark 4, sentence *c.*

b. れいて きた, "placing came," = "put," or "left." — れいて gerund of れく, "to put," 163.

6.

a. とのころ, "lately." あき の ひより, "fine fall-days." けんのん "danger."

b. たにま, "valley-spaces." いたゞき, is used here literally as "the top of the head," or "summit" of the mountains. The figurative use of いたゞく, when one "receives respectfully" from another has been noticed. See also 297, for note of its figurative use.

7.

a. れうく なつて から, = "After becoming late." "*Kara* only has the sense of "after," when suffixed to the gerund in *te*, and in a few special locutions, as, *itte kara,* "after going," *mimashite kara,* "after seeing," *kore kara* "after this," *sore kara* "after that." The past *itta kara* means "*because* he has gone," etc.,—Chamberlain's "Hand book," paragraph 100. ひのくれがた,—"sun's going down side at,"= "towards sunset." だんだん, "gradually."

b. だいぶん, "large part," "considerable," = "quite." たうとう, "in the end," or "as the result." いつしうかん ばかり, "one week only," = "about a week." ひつこんで ありました, "withdrawing have been," = "confined." たくに, "to the house." ひつこんで, 165.

8.

a. もう, abbreviation of もはや, "already." すつかり によろしい, "clearly good," = "all right."

b. ミカタ ふじん;—ふじん, is "a noble's wife;"—here, "Mikata lady," = "Mrs. Mikata."

9.

a. とんにち は, "As for the day, etc.," = ordinary salutation for "Good day."

b. c. ひさつき あまり, etc., "More than a month honorable eyes have not hung upon has been, but to-day after a long time it is," (that I see you.) These sentences contain the form of salutation common when friends in Japan meet socially, = "For some time I have been very rude to you." "It is a long while since I have hung upon your honorable eyes" *i.e.* "been seen by you."

10.

a. におじぎ, = a salute made by bowing. なして gerund of なす, "cause to be," = "make."

b. たく, "a house," but here used humbly to indicate the master of the house, *i.e.* the speaker's "husband." にうはさ, "talk about another," = "what my husband has said of you."

c. d. e. f. にはなし なさる さう です. In this clause the phrase "I hear that," of the English equivalent on the opposite page is rendered by the suffix さう, = "looks like," "it is said that." With さう and a verbal phrase such as, にはなし なさる, an idiomatic expression conveying what is "said to be," or "is probably true," is made in Japanese. にじようづ に, "cleverly," "skilfully."

11.

a. どう して, "How (is it possible)?" さう いふ こと, = "such a thing." あります もの, "is thing," = "is."

b. Read, **わたくし** not **わたく し**. **じつ に**, "really." **まづら**, "unpleasant to hear," or "taste."

13.

a. **すこし で も**, etc. "If even a little, it is good," etc. **だんなさん の**, "the master's, = "husband's." **お−かげ**, "shade," "power," "help."

14.

a. **おどろく べき ほど**, = "must be astonished at quantity," = so great (a progress) that it is wonderful." **べき**, see below, Rem. 21, *a.* a suffix which gives an adjectival quality to verbs and the meaning of "can," "should," or "possibility," and "necessity." Notice the polite **まうして おります**, as an equivalent for "says."

b. **お−こし に なる の を**, = "honorable crossing over become things," = "your visits." **たのしみ に して**, = "causing pleasure." **から**, "on account of this." **しぢう**, etc., = "always coming." **まこと に けつこう**, etc., "Really it is splendid!"

c. d. **かつてもと**, "convenience department," = "kitchen." **みまわらねば なりません**, = "must go around overlooking;" from **みまわる**, "oversee," "superintend."

15.

a. b. **おそらく**, contraction of **おそらく は** = "I am afraid that," "I suppose." **せつちやう**, pronounced *zetchō*, = "mountain summit." **さ いふ やう な かんがへ**, "that kind of thought." **しなかつた**, 197.

16.

a. **さう です と も**, = "That is even so."

b. **あうと に いて も**, etc. "Being there or being any where, that kind of thought does not arise." For **も** repeated in a negative sentence, see 272.

c. **なに こと に で も**, "in everything." **とのみます**, from **とのむ**, "to enjoy."

d. **いつた ひと**, "said person," = "person who said," or "made (that proverb)." **とく ところ の せまい ひと**, = "persons of very small heart." **しつて おつた**, = "knew," from **しる**, and **おる**; here with **でせう**, the verb-phrase = "probably knew."

e. **と もつとも**, "honorably right," *i.e.* "You were right (in calling it, etc.)"

f. **おほぞら**, "the sky," 115. **りつば**, "magnificent." **じぶん で**, "by himself," = "by means of his own sight." **みる こと が できる**,

= "can see." ざをめがね, "far eye glass," = "telescope." ばか な にん-
げん, "foolish man," = "fool." ありません か, "is he not?"

17.

a. だが せけん, etc., "Yes, but, in the world, so doing people also
there are." だが, 277.

b. さう いふ ひ̀と, "that kind of people." や, 276. ̀その ̀ほか
"besides these," "moreover." いろ〱 の こ̀とから, "all kinds of circumstances." すき あな, = "peep-holes," 120.

c. この やう な, "this kind of," = "such." じんぶつ ̀も, "character
also."

18.

a. た̀-はだ̀し を ねがいます, "(more slowly) honorable speaking I
request."

b. わたくし に は, = "for me." ̀そんな に はやく, = "so quickly."
き̀い̀-̀とる こ̀と, = "hearing seize fact," = "understanding." でき-
ません, "can not."

c. "Why (なぜ) the ladies' way (ふじん がた の はう が), common for speaking (はなす の に つうれい), the Japanese language
(ニホン-ご の), than men's (を̀とこ の かた より), clever one (じやうず
な の), may be? (で ございませう)."

19.

a. "Because (から) probably (たぶん) the ladies (ふじん の はう)
speak without hurry," (ゆる〱 はなす). This rendering is not a good

equivalent for "they have more leisure," given in the English text
on the opposite page.

b. ̀うこ で, etc., "There, my probable saying that thinking is,
besides, is not," = "Well, what I am thinking I may say is nothing
but this," = "I mean this."

c. じだい,—"age," "era." わが くに の せんばい, "our country's
leaders of the past." いま から——いぜん に, "from now about thirty
years ago." いぜん に, "previously." わが ニホン, "Our Japan."
どの くに に ̀も を̀とらぬ ほど に, "whatever country it may be, to
that degree not inferior." ̀んぽ-てき に なつて ぶんめいにすゝめる
くに に しやう と いたしました が, "capable of progress becoming,
enlightenment in advancing, national disposition that did, but."
こんにち さ ̀なる, etc., "To day even still the old feudal system, wish
to restore (くわいふく したい), that thinking persons there are.

Here, the thoughts expressed in four sentences of the English text are involved by the Japanese speaker in only one sentence. This is a peculiarity with which the student early in his study should become familiar. "One of the most essential characteristics of the Japanese language," says Professor Chamberlain, "is the extreme degree to which it pushes the synthetic tendency in the structure of sentences. Japanese always tries to incorporate the whole of a statement, however complex it may be and however numerous its parts, within the limits of a single sentence, whose members are all mutually interdependent. In fact the normal Japanese sentence is a paragraph, or (so to say) an organism." See 96, 97, 98.

d. かう いふ ひさ〴〵とち, "such people;" とち is a particle, placing especial emphasis upon the word or phrase it follows. いはゆる, "as aforesaid," an exceptional verbal form of いふ, and = "the so-called," "the abovementioned." のぞく れんちら, "exercise themselves in peeping."

20.

a. b. ゑんじつ, (に understood), = "sincerely." だいしやうり, "great victory."

21.

a. もさ より, "From the beginning,"="Of course!" なすべきしとさ, etc., "Must be done work extraordinarily enough yet is, but." Mr. W. G. Aston says of べき, "It is used in many different shades of meaning such as to express probability, possibility, moral obligation, necessity, futurity etc., and may be rendered according to circumstances by "probably," "may," "ought," "must," "should," "will" etc." たへず, "unceasing," negative gerund of たへる, "to end," "fail." しんぽ, "progress." しつゝ, a combination of し, main stem of する, "do," and つゝ, a verbal suffix showing *simultaneity* of time of action, = "at the same time with," or "that;" here, "I think that as a nation at the same time we are unceasing (ly) doing progress."

22.

a. b. しかし とのうへ, = "But beyond this." れ はなし をつけ- ましたら, "if we had continued the talk." まる で, = "wholly." あなた の あうしやく に, "in your exposition." なつて しまいませう, "becoming will end," = "will become." Here the auxiliary verbal form from しまう "to finish," expresses the complete transformation of Mr. Mikata's talk into a lecture, not the ending of the talk. The

verb しまう, merely aids the expression of the idea involved in なつて.
うへて, from うへる, "to add," as a smaller thing to a greater.

22.

a. やめ に いたしませう, a much less abrupt form of speech than
the English "Let us stop!" = "Let us make an end."

b. c. しらべて みやう, "knowing see," = "look for." じや ありま-
せん か, an idiomatic expression by which the Japanese avoid the
English imperative "Let us." It ends the sentence with a request
instead of a command.

CONVERSATION FOURTH.
REMARK 1.

a. みじかい とさ = "shortness," 111. しらせ やう, "so as to
cause to know," = "to let us know," 206. やう, indicates "manner,"
"mode," "in order to." さ いふ の, here の, as observed before,
appears as one of the most common idioms of Japanese speech: it is
an equivalent for とさ or もの, "fact," or "thing." In speech this の
often loses its vowel sound and becomes a mere interposed *n* between
the words adjoining.

b. しかし, "nevertheless," "but." しかし concedes the previous
statement, but adds an elucidating statement or inquiry. かしこい
ひさ, "a wise man." わが <u>アメリカ</u> の, "Our American" (wise man).
The historical error of confusing the Hebrew Psalmist who is referred
to in the English text with the "American wise man" spoken of in
the Japanese text does not harm the verbal form of these Japanese
words. わが holds in it the notion of "own," as "my," "his," or
"our own."

3.

a. ひさ の よ, "generation of man," = "days of our years." さ
また, "and also." すなはち, here "consequently," "that is to say."
さ まうします, "that say," = "say;" 275 *b.*, from polite verb まうす.

4.

a. さう で なからう, "'Will not be so,' that I think."

b. さうけいか の あらはす さところ に よれば, "According to our
country's physicians' reports." に よれば, "according to." すくなく
とも, "although few," = "not extensive." なが いき, = "long-life
ones," = "centenarians." した さところ の ひさ, = した ひさ, "did persons," = "the long-lived people" spoken of. The words さところ の,

are here superfluous ; but, as Prof. Chamberlain says of these words, they are often used by the upper classes in relative phrases as a sort of substitute for the relative pronouns " who," " which," and " that." They " add nothing to the sense and only encumber the construction." **たびたびしう,** " many."

c. **もつさ-も,** " however." **いまほど,** " present amount." **へいきんの じゆみやう,** " average of life." **なかつた でせう,** " was probably not." **これさて も,** = " even if this," = " however this may be." **たしかに,** etc., " Exactly to be measured thing is not," = " something not to be measured absolutely."

d. **つまり,** " After all." **どちら の――とさ も,** = " also the things spoken of in either proverb." **だけ,** here, " only." **だらう,** gives the force of " supposition " to the remark.

a. **すつかり,** " wholly," " without reserve." **のち,** " after " (he has become fifty). **かげふ,** pronounced *kugyō,* " business." **らく-いんきよ,** = one who has retired from business to enjoy leisure in old age.

b. **ふうしう,** " habit," " propensity."

6.

a. **ご-じようだん,** etc. Very polite form of reply.

b. **あまり,** " exceedingly," " too much ;" it becomes " not much," " not very," when used with a negative verb, as here.

7.

a. **ぎろん を すれば,** " If we did discussion," = " if we argued." **わたくし の はう,** " my side," = " I."

b. **ふせぐ とさ,** " resist fact," = " resistance," 111.

c. **ぶつけうさら,** = " Buddhist persons." **ら** plural sign, which, in printing here, should have been joined to the word **ぶつけうさ. なげく の は どう いふ わけ でせう,** " lamentation as for, what reason may there be?" **この よ の せいくわつ,** " living of this world," = " this life." **のがれる とさ,** = " escape." **よろこばねば ならぬ はづ,** " ought to be glad." **よろこばる,** " to be glad," said of others. **はづ** a word indicating " obligation," or " duty." It is much used as an auxiliary in speech to show what " ought," or " should " be done.

d. **かれら に さりて,** " with regard to these." **ばん-あく ちう の,** " among all evils." **もつさも えらひなる もの,** " greatest thing." **もつさも** here used as superlative sign.

8.

a. **ぶつけう しんさ,** " Buddhist believers."

b. われ に また, = "then again." ない "(are) not." どう-やう に, "in the same way." どう-やう should be printed as one word. The sentence reads, somewhat literally;—"Then again, in the same way that the American people are not real Christians, Japanese people again also real Buddhists are not."

10.

a. されば = さ あれば, "if it be so," = "well then." われの れ を, etc., "self casting away." ひと の ため に なれ, "for man's sake to live." ほんたう の をしへ, "real doctrine." じぶん を あいして, "loving self." かち を あらさう とす, = "struggle for victory." はんたい して, = "contrary," "opposing."

b. たのしんで をりまして, = "enjoy."

11.

a. ただしい, = "right," "correct." The "probability," or "possibility," expressed in the sentence lies in both たぶん, the first, and ございませう the last, words.

b. ご-しやうち の とほり, = "as you know." ご-つかふ の よい, = "know well how to use the language," = "have the advantage."

c. さへ できた なら, = "if there were ability (to talk)." このこと に ついて, "concerning this matter." いひたい, "wish to say." れもつて ゐる, "am thinking."

d. ちゑ の きんドル, "wisdom's gold dollar," = "coined wisdom." すなはち, etc., "that is to say, in relation to the *Ilo* proverb what honorable thought is there?" or "have you?"

CONVERSATION FIFTH.

REMARK 1.

a. きんげん, "golden saying," = "maxim." べつ に, "separately." ぎろん も ありますまい, "argument also will probably not be."

2.

a. b. ほまれ が ある, "praise is," = "having praise." そしり の ない はう, "not being of praise side," = "absence of praise." れ-かんがへ です か, "honorable opinion is it?" = "do you believe?"

c. わたくし ども, = "we," 123. すべて, = "all;" from すべる "to unite in a whole." せかい に しられて をれば, = "if to the world known is," 201; p. 533, *e.*

3.

a. **よ の なか の ひと,** "the world's within's people," = "the human world." **よ の なか —— です から,** = "Because this world's people are seeking only **(のみ)** fault." **だれ も —— ありません,** "Whoever blame has not, the thing in proportion to, there is no splendid praise."

b. **もし も,** "In case that." **いつてん の ひなん,"** one spot's fault," here with **ない,** = "no fault." **さ いつた なら,** "that if it be said." **いはれる だけ の ほめ ことば,** = "as much praise as possible." **ほめ ことば,** "praise-words," 120. **いはれる,** passive, or potential of **いふ,** "say," = "can be said," 199, and 203.

4.

a. **れ-とり なさる の なら,** = "If you take (this proverb with that meaning)." **それ で よう が,** "it is right, but." **その とほり,** "in that way," = "so," as in "why not say so?"

5.

a. **なり やすひ もの,** "becomes easily thing," "easily becomes,"

b. **それ に,—いけません,** "Then, again, a man engaging in a struggling after praise, really it won't go."

c. **だん〳〵 に,** "gradually." **かうまん,** "haughtiness."

d. **ぎむ,** "duty." **つくす,** "to do the utmost." **なければ なりません,** expresses the "obligation" intended by the speaker, = "should."

6.

a. **しようにん いたします,** = "to do acknowledgment," = "admit."

b. **けんかい,** "opinion." **つうれい の よわい にんげん に とりて,** "With regard to common weak humanity." **たか すぎます,** "too high."

c. **とく に たいする,** "fronting virtue," = "for virtue." **むくひ が ない やう に なる とき に,** = "no time of reward." **ぜんじ,** "good-deeds." **ひじよう に すくなく,** = "extremely few."

7.

a. **さう か も しれません,** An idiom indicating "probability." Literally "Is it so? even can not be known," (but it probably is so).

b. **ことわざ を つくつた ひと,** "man who made the proverb." **かく ある べき もの,** = "as should be," literally, "must be manner." **がわ から,** "from the side of." **がわ** for **かわ,** "side-row." **さう いつた だらう,** "so probably said." **じつさい の ありさま,** "actual condition." ありさま, from main stem of ある "be," and さま "form," or "condition." ゑつてゐたのでせうが, = "probably knew, but." だうさく-じやう, = "morally," from だうさく, "morality" and じよう "above," *i.e.* "morally high." ちゐ に, "to the grade," or "level."

8.

a. よち のぼる べき せつちやう, "a summit that must be scrambled up to." かれ とれ まうしません, "that or this, say not," = "I shall not say anything one way or another about it."

b. ためす もの, "trying thing," = "test." ひどい とざわざ, "severe proverb."

c. さにかく, "at any rate." むるい な, "unequalled." せつけう-か, pronounced *sekkyō-ka*, "preacher." This か is an affix of "occupation," *e.g.* はなし-か, "story teller."

d. けつして, "never" 231. つぎ のとざわざ に, "in the next proverb." あらはして ある ひなん, "visible fault," = "fault shown up." うけらるゝ とさ は ありますまい, "to be the subject of is probably not," = "are not guilty (of the fault)."

Nori no Hatsu-ne, (pp. 526–531).

い *line.* ひ を かさね, literally "to pile up the days," *i.e.* to spend or waste the time for any purpose.

ろ " るてん, literally, "flowing and rolling: transmigration of the soul into angel, man, brute, etc., according to the merits of its deeds."

は " はかなく, "without success," "evanescent."

ほ " The writer of this hymn belonged to a Buddhist sect which believes it possible for all mankind to attain to perfect Buddhahood. ほさけ, or "Buddhas, are men, who have toiled upward through successive stages of existence to the calm of perfect holiness."

ち " うきみ. うき, "floating," "drifting." み, "body," "concrete self." うきみ, is "uncertain" or "changeable life," = "vain selves."

を " さんづがは, "River of Three Paths"; a river flowing in the underworld according to the Buddhist mythology, over which the souls of the dead go; at which a road divides into three paths leading respectively to the worlds of "Demons," of "Brutes," and of the "Hungry Ones."

れ *line.* **れんり**, "union by growing together." Two branches of a tree becoming one branch are thought of as a symbol of happiness. The Japanese refer to it as a figure of the dearest human relation, that of husband and wife.

な „ **なむ** refers to the sacred phrase "NAMU AMIDA BUDDHA," peculiar to some of the Buddhist sects, *e.g.* Jōdo and Shinshiu. The believers in AMIDA BUDDHA, gain salvation simply by their faith in AMIDA. "Salvation" is "the attainment of Nirvana, which means eternal happiness." "From the time of putting faith in the saving power of Buddha, we do not need any power of self-help, but need only keep his mercy in heart and invoke his name."

ら „ Unheeded advice is likened to the blowing of the east-wind into a horse's ears.

む „ **むじやう の あらし** or **かぜ**, "not-constant" wind, = "Death wind." "He was carried away" by this wind, = "he is dead."

い (ゐ) *line.* **いま の いま まで**, "till now of now," "till the present of the present," = "at this very moment." This line properly should commence with **ゐ** not **い**, but the writer of the hymn apparently had not at command a fit word beginning with **ゐ**.

て *line.* When the Buddha was born he sank from his mother's side upon a blue lotus-flower, and, says the legend, from his body radiated a brilliant light that illuminated the universe. Soon afterwards the child descended from the lotus, pointed with his right hand to heaven, with his left to the earth, and exclaimed with the voice of a lion ;—"I alone of all beings in heaven above and under the heavens am worthy of honor."

さ „ **さんぼう**, the *Sambō*, are the three precious things of Buddhism, namely, the Buddhist ritual and body of doctrine, or the "Law"; the priesthood, or the "Church," and salvation into Nirvana, or "Buddhahood."

せ „ The Jōdo Buddhists believe that salvation is merited by one's simply repeating the invocation to Amida, "NAMU AMIDA BUDDHA," "I adore thee, Eternal Buddha."

GENERAL INDEX.

ERRATA.

PAGE 18, *line* 4, *for* "Tokyo," *read* "Tŏkyŏ," also on pages 28, 167, 169, 170, 173.

,, 25, ,, 12, ,, "syllable," *read* "syllables."

,, 57, ,, 18, ,, "*shu*," *read* "*shū*."

,, 59, ,, 12, ,, "syblable," *read* "syllable."

,, ,, ,, 17, ,, "タテタレヌ," *read* "タテラレヌ."

,, 64, ,, 3, "the," is omitted at end of of line.

,, 67, ,, 3, ,, "designates," *read* "designate."

,, 71, ,, 10, supply a comma after "*part.*"

,, 76, ,, 16, ,, "トフ," *read* "トヲ."

,, 85, ,, 8, ,, "coalesent," *read* "coalescent."

,, 98, ,, 3, omit both commas.

,, 100, ,, 17, ,, "かげ," *read* "かぜ."

,, 101, ,, 2, ,, "orignally," *read* "originally."

,, 115, ,, 20, ,, "lose," *read* "lost."

,, 116, ,, 19, ,, "Disiderative," *read* "Desiderative."

,, 118, ,, 8, put a comma instead of period after "Stem."

,, 125, ,, 11, ,, "ひつとん," *read* "ひつとんで."

,, 134, ,, 1, ,, "does," *read* "did."

,, ,, ,, *last line*, ,, "rom," *read* "from."

,, 151, ,, 8, ,, "220," *read* "200."

,, 153, ,, 11, ,, "syllablis," *read* "syllables."

,, 162, ,, 16, ,, "verb," *read* "verbs."

,, 165, ,, 16, before "ガ," *insert* "this."

,, 166, ,, 8, ,, "disagreable," *read* "disagreeable."

,, 169, ,, 21, ,, "Omori," *read* "Ŏmori."

,, 174, ,, 18, ,, "houses," *read* "house."

,, 175, ,, *last line*, supply "ゆ," before "へ."

,, 198, ,, 10, ,, "three," *read* "two."

PAGE 208, *line* 2, *for* "とし," *read* "とらし."

,, 225, ,, 11, insert "of," before "reformers."

,, 228, ,, 6, after "てん," insert "を."

,, 257, ,, 1, ,, "SENENTH," *read* "SEVENTH."

,, 270, ,, 20, ,, "り あ," *read* "りあ."

,, 276, ,, 5, ,, "み て," ,, "みて."

,, 334, ,, 3, ,, "さ て," ,, "さて."

,, 413, ,, 4, ,, "They," ,, "The."

,, 439, ,, 12, ,, "Shinagawa," *read* "Shimbashi."

,, 519,
,, 521, } ,, 1, ,, "(す) SU," *read* "(ん) N."

THE END.

明治廿九年五月十三日印刷

仝　年仝　月十六日發行

版權所有

定價金五圓

著作者

東京市芝區三田二丁目二番地寓房

米國人

クレイ、マツコーレイ

發行兼印刷者

東京市芝區三田四圖町廿六番地

神田佐一郎

印刷所

東京市牛込區市ケ谷加賀町一丁目

十二番地

株式會社　秀英舍第一工塲